The Interpersonal Dynamics of Emotion

Emotions are an elemental part of life – they imbue our existence with meaning and purpose, and influence how we engage with the world around us. But we do not just feel our own emotions; we typically express them in the presence of other people. How do our emotional expressions affect others? Moving beyond the traditional intrapersonal perspective, this is the first book dedicated to exploring the pervasive interpersonal dynamics of emotions. Integrating existing theory and research, Van Kleef develops the Emotions as Social Information (EASI) theory, a ground-breaking comprehensive framework that explains how emotional expressions influence observers across all domains of life, from close relationships to group settings, conflict and negotiation, customer service, and leader-follower relations. His deeply social perspective sheds new light on the fundamental question of why we have emotions in the first place – the social influence emotions engender may very well constitute their raison d'être.

GERBEN A. VAN KLEEF is Professor of Social Psychology at the University of Amsterdam. He obtained his PhD from the University of Amsterdam in 2004 and has held visiting appointments at UC Berkeley and Columbia University. He received numerous awards for his scholarship, including the best dissertation award of the International Association for Conflict Management, the early career award of the European Association of Social Psychology, and the most influential paper award of the Academy of Management. He is currently Chair of the Social Psychology department of the University of Amsterdam and Associate Editor of *Social Psychological and Personality Science*.

STUDIES IN EMOTION AND SOCIAL INTERACTION
Second Series

Series Editors

Keith Oatley
University of Toronto

Antony S. R. Manstead
Cardiff University

(Continued after Index)

The Interpersonal Dynamics of Emotion

Toward an Integrative Theory of Emotions as Social Information

Gerben A. van Kleef

CAMBRIDGE
UNIVERSITY PRESS

CAMBRIDGE
UNIVERSITY PRESS

University Printing House, Cambridge CB2 8BS, United Kingdom

One Liberty Plaza, 20th Floor, New York, NY 10006, USA

477 Williamstown Road, Port Melbourne, VIC 3207, Australia

314-321, 3rd Floor, Plot 3, Splendor Forum, Jasola District Centre, New Delhi-110025, India

79 Anson Road, #06-04/06, Singapore 079906

Cambridge University Press is part of the University of Cambridge.

It furthers the University's mission by disseminating knowledge in the pursuit of education, learning and research at the highest international levels of excellence.

www.cambridge.org
Information on this title: www.cambridge.org/9781107686649

© Gerben A. van Kleef 2016

First published 2016
First paperback edition 2018

A catalogue record for this publication is available from the British Library

Library of Congress Cataloging in Publication data
Kleef, Gerben A. van, author.
The interpersonal dynamics of emotion : toward an integrative theory
of emotions as social information / Gerben A. van Kleef.
Cambridge, United Kingdom : Cambridge University Press, 2016. |
Studies in emotion and social interaction
LCCN 2015048602 | ISBN 9781107048249 (hardback)
LCSH: Emotions – Social aspects. | Emotions – Sociological aspects. |
Interpersonal relations.
LCC BF531 .K54 2016 | DDC 152.4–dc23
LC record available at http://lccn.loc.gov/2015048602

ISBN 978-1-107-04824-9 Hardback
ISBN 978-1-107-68664-9 Paperback

To my parents, with love and gratitude

Contents

Figures

Tables

Preface

The social nature of emotions has interested me ever since I took a course on emotions by Nico Frijda at the University of Amsterdam, in 1997. In the years to come, my fascination with this topic would be nurtured by close collaborations with fellow emotion researchers such as Tony Manstead, Dacher Keltner, Agneta Fischer, and Stéphane Côté, as well as by the writings of numerous other inspiring scholars whose work is featured in the pages of this book.

At the time when I took Frijda's classes, scholarly awareness of the social effects of emotions was clearly on the rise, but empirical research was scarce. Now, almost two decades later, there is a burgeoning literature on the social functions and consequences of emotional displays. Researchers have begun to examine how emotional expressions shape close relationships, influence group processes, regulate the negotiation of social conflict, affect consumer behavior and customer service encounters, and contribute to (or undermine) effective leadership. Although research is quickly accumulating, the literature is scattered, and no single volume exists that brings together the important theoretical and empirical advances that have been made over the past years.

Now that a substantial body of research on the social effects of emotions has been amassed, the time seems right for a comprehensive review and theoretical integration of this literature. What have we learned from more than twenty years of research? Do we see recurring patterns in the social effects of emotions across social, clinical, developmental, and organizational domains of inquiry? Where are the inconsistencies in the empirical record? Can we start building an integrative theory of the social effects of emotions? Which important questions remain unaddressed? And where should we go from here?

This book presents my attempt at addressing these questions. Being the first volume dedicated specifically to the relatively young research field of the social effects of emotions, it should be seen as a beginning rather than an end point. My intention is to provide a theoretical framework that can be used to interpret and integrate previous findings and to guide future research. I hope this book will be instrumental in spurring new research that will bring us closer to a full understanding of the social nature of emotions.

In addition, it is my hope that this book will prove useful as a teaching resource. During ten years of lecturing on the social effects of emotions, I have been frequently alerted by both undergraduate and graduate students that there is a need for a book that offers a comprehensive treatment of this rapidly growing field of research. I have therefore tried to make this text accessible to students as well. If this book turned out to be half as stimulating to a new generation of emotion researchers as my personal heroes have been to me, I would be very satisfied indeed.

Gerben van Kleef

Acknowledgments

The ideas and research presented in this book reflect the collective efforts of a large group of scholars. Several of them have contributed directly to my own work through various collaborations. I thank Hajo Adam, Adi Amit, Bruce Barry, Bianca Beersma, Arik Cheshin, Stéphane Côté, Frederic Damen, Carsten de Dreu, Xia Fang, Agneta Fischer, Allison Gabriel, Adam Galinsky, Fieke Harinck, Skyler Hawk, Marc Heerdink, Ivona Hideg, Astrid Homan, Dacher Keltner, Lukas Koning, Gert-Jan Lelieveld, Tony Manstead, Christina Moran, Liat Netzer, Bernard Nijstad, Chris Oveis, Lisanne Pauw, Katerina Petkanopoulou, Davide Pietroni, Jeffrey Sanchez-Burks, Disa Sauter, Marwan Sinaceur, Eftychia Stamkou, Wolfgang Steinel, Maya Tamir, Ilja van Beest, Helma van den Berg, Ilmo van der Löwe, Joop van der Pligt, Eric van Dijk, Evert-Jan van Doorn, Daan van Knippenberg, Paul van Lange, Victoria Visser, Lu Wang, and Barbara Wisse for the pleasant collaborations and inspiring discussions. In addition, I am indebted to the countless scholars with whom I have had the pleasure of interacting during conferences and other meetings. Their work, much of which is covered in this book, has greatly influenced my thinking.

At this point I would also like to acknowledge the financial support I have been offered by the Netherlands Organisation for Scientific Research. The various research grants I have been privileged to receive have catalyzed my research on the interpersonal dynamics of emotion and have allowed me to create favorable conditions for writing this volume.

I am grateful to my colleagues at the University of Amsterdam for contributing to a stimulating intellectual environment, and to Columbia University for hosting me during part of the time when I was working on this book.

Finally, I would like to extend a warm thank-you to Tony Manstead for the honorable invitation to contribute a volume to this series, which is so close to my heart, and for providing valuable comments on a previous draft of the manuscript.

CHAPTER 1

Emotion

An interpersonal perspective

> Emotion accomplishes very little in the social world unless it is communicated.
>
> Planalp (1999, p. 138)

Emotions are a defining feature of the human condition – they shape our social relationships and imbue our lives with meaning and purpose. Few would disagree that our emotions influence how we perceive the world, how we think about it, and how we engage with it. What may be less obvious, however, is that our emotions can have far-reaching effects on the thinking and actions of *others*, and, logically, that the emotions of others influence our own cognition and behavior. This book is about these social effects of emotions.

Questions about the nature and meaning of emotions date back to at least the old Greek philosophers (e.g., Plato, Aristotle), and these very questions later propelled the conception of psychology as a scientific field of inquiry (see James, 1884). What are emotions? Why did they evolve? Are emotions functional or dysfunctional? Do our emotions cloud our rationality and misguide our behavior, as suggested by philosophers like Descartes and Kant, or are they the fuel that gets us going and steers us toward great achievement, as proposed by thinkers such as Hume and Nietzsche? Do emotions disrupt evenhanded social interactions or are they the cornerstone of well-adjusted relationships?

Inspired by Darwin's (1872) seminal book *The expression of the emotions in man and animals*, scholars have increasingly embraced the notion that emotions are functional in that they help the individual to adapt to an ever-changing environment. Classic theorizing and research have emphasized the individual-level functionality of emotions (Frijda, 1986; Lazarus, 1991; Oatley & Jenkins, 1992). Emotions are believed to regulate bodily adaptations to environmental changes (Farb, Chapman, & Anderson, 2013). This involves regulation of the autonomic nervous system, endocrine system, and immune system. It has been demonstrated, for example, that anger leads to enhanced distribution of blood to the hands, whereas fear involves reduced blood flow to the periphery (Levenson, 1992). These patterns can be interpreted as adaptive responses to challenges involved in fighting an enemy versus escaping one with minimal loss of blood (Keltner, Haidt, & Shiota, 2006).

I do not dispute this individual-level functionality of emotions. At the same time, however, it is clear that the individual perspective alone cannot account for the full breadth of emotional phenomena. After all, if emotions were only functional at the individual level, why would they show on our faces? Why would they become audible in our voices and visible in our bodily postures? And why would so many people feel the urge to communicate their emotional experiences to others (Rimé, Philippot, Boca, & Mesquita, 1992)? As a result of these various expressive tendencies, our emotions often do not remain confined to our individual minds and bodies.

Whoever first coined the term "emotion" was surely aware of this. Before the term was introduced, thinkers commonly used the word "passions" to refer to emotional phenomena. The word "passion" is derived from the Greek πάσχω, which means "to suffer" and thus emphasizes individual experience. The word "emotion" is derived from the Latin *emovere*, which means "to move out." The very meaning of the term suggests that emotions are about bringing out, and making known to observers, the internal state of the individual, thus emphasizing the social nature of the phenomenon. As we will see, there is considerable debate in the literature as to whether emotional expressions reflect internal feeling states and/or (deliberate) communications (see, e.g., Parkinson, 2005). This controversy notwithstanding, the active *moving* that is implied in the word "emotion" better captures the essence of the phenomenon than the passive *undergoing* that is implied in the archaic "passions." Emotions actively set things in motion. They move ourselves and they move others.

Although emotions can of course be privately experienced, more often than not they are expressed in one way or another – whether verbally or nonverbally, mildly or intensely, knowingly or unknowingly, deliberately or inadvertently (Ekman & O'Sullivan, 1991; Manstead, Wagner, & MacDonald, 1984; Scherer, Feldstein, Bond, & Rosenthal, 1985). The very fact that emotions tend to be expressed means that they will often be observed by others, who may in turn respond to the expressions. Put differently, our hardwired tendency to express our emotions implies that emotions may have *social* functions and consequences in addition to their more commonly studied and widely accepted intrapersonal effects.

Indeed, emotional expressions have been proposed to contribute to the effective regulation of social interaction. According to this perspective, emotions may have evolved in part because they help us address social-relational concerns (Fischer & Manstead, in press; Oatley & Johnson-Laird, 1987). Some have argued, for instance, that emotions help to solve problems of commitment and cooperation, which are central to human ultrasociality (Frank, 1988; Keltner et al., 2006). Emotional expressions carry information about one's (desired) relationship with another person. For example, love and compassion signal psychological attachment and commitment to a relationship (Ellis & Malamuth, 2004; Gonzaga, Keltner, Londahl, & Smith, 2001; Hazan & Shaver, 1987). Embarrassment and shame appease dominant individuals and signal submissiveness (Keltner & Buswell, 1997; Semin & Manstead, 1982). Pride protects the social status of accomplished individuals (Tiedens, Ellsworth, & Mesquita, 2000). Anger motivates punishment of individuals who violate norms of reciprocity and cooperation (Lerner, Goldberg, & Tetlock, 1998), and its expression helps to identify and rectify social problems (Averill, 1982; Fischer & Roseman, 2007). Guilt motivates reparation after wrongdoing (Trivers, 1971) and signals interpersonal concern (Baumeister, Stillwell, & Heatherton, 1994). In other words, emotions may be thought of as modes of engagement with the social environment (Parkinson, Fischer, & Manstead, 2005). This view highlights the potential social functionality of emotions as instruments that help individuals find adaptive ways of relating to one another.

Scholarly attention to the interpersonal consequences and possible social functionality of emotional expressions has increased steeply over the past two decades (see, e.g., Côté & Hideg, 2011; Elfenbein, 2007; Fischer & Manstead, in press; Frijda & Mesquita, 1994; Hareli & Rafaeli, 2008; Keltner & Haidt, 1999; Niedenthal & Brauer, 2012; Parkinson, 1996; Parrott, 2001; Tiedens & Leach, 2004; Van Kleef, 2009). Despite this growing interest, however, a comprehensive theory of the social effects of emotions is lacking. Moreover, at present no single source exists that brings together the recent empirical efforts and advances in the study of the social effects of emotions. With this book I aim to change this state of affairs by outlining a broad theoretical framework for understanding the social effects of emotions and guiding future research in this area and by reviewing and integrating the important discoveries that have been made over the past years. Before moving on, however, it is important to briefly consider some definitional issues.

Definitional issues

When William James published his famous article titled "What Is an Emotion?" in 1884, he implied that the answer is not obvious. Indeed, a century later, Fehr and Russell (1984) observed that "everyone knows what an emotion is, until asked to give a definition. Then, it seems, no one knows" (p. 464). The question of what constitutes an emotion has occupied philosophers, psychologists, and other social scientists for ages, and it continues to do so. Countless definitions of emotion have been advanced, attesting to the difficulty of formulating one that is satisfactory to all who are interested in the phenomenon. Nevertheless, there is considerable consensus with regard to a number of key elements of emotion.

Many theorists believe that emotions arise as a result of an individual's conscious or unconscious evaluation or *appraisal* of some event as positively or negatively relevant to a particular concern or goal (Frijda, 1986; Lazarus, 1991; Ortony, Clore, & Collins, 1988), although the exact role of appraisals in the emotion process remains a topic of considerable debate. Furthermore, there is substantial agreement that emotions involve specific patterns of phenomenological experience (Scherer & Tannenbaum, 1986), physiological reactions (Levenson, Ekman, & Friesen, 1990), and expressions (Ekman, 1993). Finally, emotions tend to be accompanied by a sense of action readiness (Frijda, 1986), in that they prepare the body and the mind for behavioral responses aimed at dealing with the circumstances that caused the emotion.

Various terms have been used to refer to emotional phenomena. The most commonly used terms are "affect," "mood," and "emotion." Affect is the most general concept, referring to a subjective feeling state that can range from diffuse moods such as cheerfulness or depression to specific and acute emotions such as happiness or anger (Frijda, 1994). The word "affect" is also used to refer to relatively stable individual dispositions (i.e., trait positive and negative affectivity; Watson, Clark, & Tellegen, 1988). Emotions and moods are generally seen as subtypes of affect. They are differentiated by the degree to which they are directed toward a specific stimulus – be it a person, an object, or an event (Frijda, 1994). As Parrott (2001) puts it, "emotions are about, or directed toward, something in the world ... In contrast, moods lack this quality of object directedness; a person in an irritable mood is not necessarily angry about anything in particular – he or she is just generally grumpy" (p. 3). Emotions are also typically more differentiated and of shorter duration, whereas moods tend to be more enduring and pervasive, if generally of lower intensity (Frijda, 1994). Finally, in contrast to diffuse moods, discrete emotions are associated with distinct subjective experiences (Scherer, Wallbott, & Summerfield, 1986), physiological reactions (Levenson et al., 1990), expressions (Ekman, 1993), and action tendencies (Roseman, Wiest, & Swartz, 1994).

In this book I will use these terms accordingly. I use the word "emotion" to refer to valenced responses to relevant events that are accompanied by specific patterns of experience, physiological changes, expressions, and/or behavioral tendencies, and that are associated with an identifiable cause or object. I reserve the term "mood" for more diffuse and undifferentiated feeling states that are not connected to a particular antecedent event or object. I use the word "affect" as an umbrella term to denote both discrete emotions and diffuse mood states and valenced evaluations of objects or people, such as likes and dislikes and related sentiments (Frijda, 1994).

An interpersonal approach to emotion

Traditionally, theorizing and research on emotion have been concerned first and foremost with the antecedents and individual-level consequences of emotions. Consider the case of anger. In the past fifty years or so, emotion scholars have made a lot of progress in mapping the types of situations and events that may trigger anger. For instance, appraisal theorists have argued and shown that anger may arise when a person feels that his or her goals are being frustrated and someone else is to blame (e.g., Frijda, 1986; Kuppens, Van Mechelen, Smits, & De Boeck, 2003; Roseman, 1984; Scherer, Schorr, & Johnstone, 2001; Smith, Haynes, Lazarus, & Pope, 1993). Along similar lines, research in the area of organizational behavior has revealed that perceptions of injustice are a prominent precursor to anger in the workplace (Barclay, Skarlicki, & Pugh, 2005).

In addition, a large body of research has been dedicated to investigating how an individual's experience of anger shapes his or her own cognition and behavior. Studies have shown, for instance, that feelings of anger undermine trust (Dunn & Schweitzer, 2005) and interpersonal concern (Allred, Mallozzi, Matsui, & Raia, 1997) and enhance the tendency to blame others for negative events (Lerner & Tiedens, 2006; Quigley & Tedeschi, 1996). Furthermore, anger has been associated with feelings of hostility and a desire for revenge and retaliation (Allred, 1999; Baron, Neuman, & Geddes, 1999; Skarlicki & Folger, 1997). Behavioral findings mirror these effects, with feelings of anger undermining cooperation and increasing competition (Forgas, 1998; Knapp & Clark, 1991; Pillutla & Murnighan, 1996) and sparking aggressive behavior (Averill, 1982).

As is clear from the example of anger, the classic approach to emotion has contributed greatly to scientific understanding of the antecedents and individual-level consequences of emotions. More recently, this traditional focus has been complemented by theorizing and research on the interpersonal effects of emotions – the topic of this book. Moving beyond the question of where our emotions come from and how they influence our own thinking and behavior, the interpersonal perspective raises the complementary question of how one person's emotional expressions influence the feelings, thoughts, and actions of other individuals.

This interpersonal perspective opens up a host of exciting new research questions that have only recently begun to receive systematic scholarly attention. For instance, when and how do individuals use the emotional displays of others to make sense of the world around them? Do people deliberately use their emotions to influence others, and if so, which emotions are effective under which circumstances? How do emotional expressions shape the quality of close relationships? When and how do emotional displays contribute to the coordination of behavior in groups? How do emotional expressions influence conflict resolution versus escalation? Does the impact of persuasive messages depend on the emotional displays of the source? What are the consequences of emotional communications for consumer behavior and the quality of customer service? How does a leader's emotional style influence his or her effectiveness? And how do teachers' emotional expressions influence the performance of their students? These and many other questions pertaining to the interpersonal dynamics of emotions are addressed in this book.

Goals and overview of the book

My goal with this book is threefold. First, I intend to develop an integrative theoretical framework to enhance understanding of the mechanisms and contingencies that govern the social effects of emotions. Second, I set out to provide a comprehensive overview of extant research on the social effects of emotions across domains of life. Third, I aim to identify gaps in our knowledge and provide an agenda for future research.

These three objectives are addressed in the three parts of this book. The first part of the book (Chapters 2–4) outlines a broad theoretical framework that informs understanding of the social effects of emotions and that may serve as a guide for future research: Emotions as Social Information (EASI) theory. In Chapter 2 I develop the general idea that a primary function of emotions is to disambiguate social situations by providing relevant information to other individuals in the social environment. I will discuss theorizing on the evolution and social functions of emotions, research on social referencing in humans and emotional understanding in nonhuman primates, claims regarding the universality of emotional expressions, and evidence for the deliberate targeting of emotional expressions to other individuals and for the modulation of emotional expressivity by the presence of others. I then review illustrative research on the role of emotional expressions as cues to social predispositions. The chapter closes with a brief discussion of psychological disorders and physical conditions that compromise social interaction by disrupting the social-communicative functions of emotions.

Chapter 3 addresses the two processes of emotional influence that are featured in EASI theory, namely affective reactions and inferential processes. The section on affective reactions describes how the emotional expressions of one person may elicit reciprocal or complementary emotional reactions in one or more others and how emotional expressions shape interpersonal liking. The section on inferential processes addresses the ways in which individuals may extract relevant (social) information from the emotional expressions of others. Downstream consequences of both processes are also discussed.

In Chapter 4 I propose two classes of moderators that determine the relative predictive strength of affective reactions and inferential processes in shaping observers' responses to others' emotional expressions. The first factor is the information-processing depth of the observer. Drawing on classic dual-process models of information processing, I review personality characteristics and environmental influences that shape an individual's information-processing motivation and ability. The second factor concerns social-contextual influences that shape the perceived appropriateness of emotional expressions. This section addresses characteristics of the situation, the emotional expression, the expresser, and the observer that influence the perceived (in)appropriateness of emotional expressions.

The second part of the book (Chapters 5–9) presents a comprehensive review of empirical research on the social effects of emotions. This review is organized according to the five broad domains of research in which the social effects of emotions have so far been investigated most extensively, namely close relationships, group life, conflict and negotiation, customer service and consumer behavior, and leadership. In each of the chapters, the empirical record will be discussed in relation to the theoretical ideas outlined in the preceding chapters.

Chapter 5 is concerned with the interpersonal effects of emotions in close relationships. The guiding question in this chapter is how the emotional expressions of one person (e.g., a friend or relationship partner) shape relationships by influencing the emotions, cognitions, attitudes, and/or behavior of a social partner. The chapter begins with a discussion of theoretical perspectives and empirical research on the functionality of emotional expressivity in close relationships and related work on the effects of emotional intelligence on relationship success. I then move on to consider the role of emotional convergence in interpersonal relationships, after which I summarize research on the social consequences of four main classes of emotional expressions that are associated with affiliation (e.g., happiness), supplication (e.g., sadness), dominance (e.g., anger), and appeasement (e.g., guilt).

Chapter 6 addresses the social effects of emotions in groups. The chapter starts with a brief discussion of theorizing on the social functionality of emotions in groups. Against that background, I will discuss classic work on various types of affective processes in groups, including emotional contagion, affective convergence, and affective divergence, which will be followed by a review of research on the consequences of group-level affective states such as group affective tone and affective diversity for group functioning. I will then proceed to review more recent work on inferential processes that may be triggered by emotional expressions in groups and their downstream consequences for group processes and outcomes. The chapter ends with some emerging conclusions regarding the contingencies that govern the social effects of emotions in groups.

In Chapter 7 I review research on the interpersonal effects of emotions in conflict and negotiation. The key question here is how emotional expressions influence cooperation versus competition in situations of mixed-motive interdependence. I review research on the influence of emotional expressions in the context of a variety of conflict management settings, such as negotiation, dispute resolution, and coalition formation. These studies indicate that emotional expressions shape conflict behavior and the resolution versus escalation of conflicts by instigating affective reactions as well as inferential processes in observers, depending on observers' information-processing tendencies and on the perceived appropriateness of the emotional expressions. I also discuss emerging research on the role of emotional intelligence in conflict and negotiation.

Chapter 8 then reviews the literature on the social effects of emotions in the context of customer service and consumer behavior. The first part of the chapter reviews research on the effects of service providers' emotional displays on the emotions, product attitudes, purchase intentions, and actual behavior of consumers. In this context I will also discuss work on emotional labor and the perceived authenticity and appropriateness of service providers' emotional displays. Reversing the focus, the second part of the chapter addresses research on the effects of customers' emotional expressions on service employees' emotions, job satisfaction, well-being, cognitions, and performance. In the third part of the chapter I then move on to review studies on the effects of emotional expressions on the effectiveness of persuasive communications. The fourth part is devoted to emerging research on interpersonal emotion regulation in customer service. The final part of the chapter addresses the role of emotional intelligence in the service industry.

Chapter 9 is concerned with the role of emotions in leader–follower relations. The central question in this chapter is how the emotional expressions of a leader influence the emotions, cognitions, attitudes, and behaviors of followers, and what the consequences are for leadership effectiveness. Research in this area has documented that leaders' emotional expressions may influence follower behavior and leadership effectiveness by triggering affective reactions (e.g., emotional contagion, liking of the leader) as well as inferential processes (e.g., inferences regarding performance quality) in followers. I will discuss studies on the contingencies of these processes and their outcomes, many of which relate to followers' information processing or the perceived appropriateness of the leaders' emotional displays. In this area, too, emerging evidence points to a critical role of emotional intelligence in determining the social effects of emotions, and this research is also reviewed.

The third part of the book (Chapters 10 and 11) summarizes the current state of the art, highlights implications for theory and research, and discusses caveats and future directions. Chapter 10 offers a critical evaluation of the empirical support for EASI theory, discusses how EASI theory compares to other theoretical perspectives, and highlights some of the implications of the current analysis. Finally, Chapter 11 discusses limits to our current understanding and provides an agenda for future research.

PART I

Emotions as Social Information Theory

CHAPTER 2

Emotions as social information

> The face has the only skeletal muscles of the body that are used, not to move ourselves, but to move others.
>
> Smith and Scott (1997, p. 229)

One of the key challenges of social life is to figure out what other people are about: what they are thinking and feeling, what they expect or want from us, how they are likely to act, and so on. This is not a trivial task. In many situations, people have limited insight into each other's feelings, goals, needs, desires, and intentions. This lack of information poses a significant challenge to social interaction. If one does not know what goes on in other people's minds, it is difficult to relate to them, anticipate their behavior, and determine an appropriate course of action. Is the person across the street of good intent or should he be avoided? Will the bus driver remember to give me a sign when we have reached my stop? Is the animated group of friends at the party interested in expanding their company or do they prefer to be among themselves? Is the "independent" financial adviser trying to find the best solution for my situation or does he have ulterior motives?

Without insight into the feelings, intentions, and motives of other individuals, navigating social life is like walking through a misty city. We can make out the silhouettes of the people surrounding us, but we have no idea what they are up to. This creates challenging and potentially dangerous situations. If we do not know what other people expect from us and what they are after, it is virtually impossible to respond aptly when interacting with them. Therefore we are continuously (and often nonconsciously) on the lookout for cues that may tell us something about others' intentions. As part of this quest to make sense of ambiguous social situations we seize on subtle and indirect signals available in the situation, such as other people's emotional expressions (Manstead & Fischer, 2001; Van Kleef, De Dreu, & Manstead, 2010). Thus the intimidating expression of the man across the street tells me to stay away. The bus driver's friendly nod reassures me that she will let me know where to get off. The aloof looks of the people at the party inform me that they don't feel like chatting with a stranger. The financial adviser's phony smile warns me not to do business with him. Whenever individuals do not explicitly disclose their honest opinions and intentions, their emotional expressions are among the few leads to provide some insight into their internal worlds (DePaulo et al., 2003; Ekman, 2001; Ekman & Friesen, 1969). In other words, other people's emotional expressions are the flashlight that helps us find our way in the mist of social interaction.

But what does this flashlight look like, and how does it work? In this and the following two chapters I outline my attempt at a general framework for investigating and explaining how emotional expressions help us navigate the inherent challenges and ambiguities of social life: Emotions as Social Information (EASI) theory. EASI theory is rooted in the interpersonal approach to emotion that I discussed in the previous chapter. It seeks to elucidate how the emotional expressions of one person may influence the feelings, thoughts, and actions of others. As reflected in its name, a fundamental assumption underlying the theory is that emotional expressions convey social information that may be picked up on and interpreted by observers, who may thus be influenced by the emotional expressions. In Chapters 3 and 4 I will discuss how and when people use others' emotional expressions to make sense of (social) situations and to inform their behavior. But let us first take a step back to consider why we express our emotions in outwardly perceptible ways in the first place.

Emotional expressions as evolutionary adaptations

Humans are an ultrasocial species, accomplishing many tasks relevant to survival and reproduction (e.g., provision and distribution of resources, raising of offspring, protection against predators) in highly coordinated, close-proximity, face-to-face relationships and groups (Caporael, 1997). Group sizes increased over the course of evolution, possibly in response to increasing risk of attacks by predators in the open fields (Dunbar, 1992, 2004). A critical challenge in human adaptation thus has long been (and still is) to navigate the myriad relationships involved in group life (Baumeister & Leary, 1995; Fiske, 1991). According to the *social brain hypothesis*, humans and other primates evolved increasingly large brains to manage such complex social systems (Dunbar, 2009).

In the early stages of group life, our hominoid ancestors likely had to communicate and coordinate without formal language. Given that that the emotional systems of the human brain (e.g., the amygdala and other parts of the limbic system) evolved much earlier than the centers that are responsible for language and speech (which are located in the cortex; see MacLean, 1990), it stands to reason that emotional expressions and other nonverbal behaviors constituted the primary communication devices in preliterate times. In the absence of formal language, observable nonverbal behaviors – including facial, vocal, and postural expressions of emotion – provided useful clues to other people's motives and intentions (Fridlund, 1992), making such expressions especially vital for adaptive social responding, survival, and reproduction (Dunbar, 2004; Tooby & Cosmides, 1990). It seems reasonable to assume that emotional expressiveness and the ability to decode others' emotional expressions were assets that helped our ancestors in dealing with the complex social problems that were posed by the emergence of group life (Boone & Buck, 2003; Buck, 1984).

With later evolution came humans' unique mastery of language, which has added an additional layer of sophistication to emotional expression (Oatley, 2003). Rather than supplanting the critical functions of nonverbal expressions, language has provided humans with complementary ways of expressing their emotions and navigating increasingly complex social realities (Keltner, Haidt, & Shiota, 2006; Oatley, 2004). Although there are certainly situations in which it may be advantageous to hide one's emotions, the ability to express one's emotions to others in appropriate ways, whether nonverbally or verbally, still is key to well-adjusted social relations and general life success (Keltner & Kring, 1998). For instance, children who more effectively convey distress to their caregivers are more likely to be nurtured, and parents who are better attuned to their children's suffering are more likely to intervene when needed, thereby increasing the chances of their offspring's survival. Individuals who display anger at appropriate times and in the appropriate manner are more likely to scare off enemies and to defend their interests, just as challengers who are better attuned to signs of anger in their counterparts are more likely to avoid combat (Fridlund, 1994). People who express happiness in the right circumstances may develop better social networks, receive more social support, and lead more successful social lives (Lopes, Salovey, Côté, & Beers, 2005). In short, appropriate use of and responses to emotional expressions are vital to successful social adaptation, and these benefits derive in large part from the evolved social-signaling functions of emotional expressions.

It is important to acknowledge at this point that the fact that a certain characteristic has evolved to the present day does not prove in any way that it is (or once has been) functional (Buss, 1999). Moreover, any behavioral consequences of emotions that may have been adaptive once in a different ecology are not necessarily adaptive today. Although caution is therefore warranted when making claims pertaining to the evolutionary adaptiveness of current-day characteristics (see e.g., Fridlund, 1991a, for an in-depth discussion), several lines of research are consistent with the possibility that emotional expressions have evolved in part because of their critical role in coordinating social interaction, and that they have over evolutionary history become hardwired systems of communication. Babies as young as four months can already discriminate between facial expressions of emotions such as happiness and fear (Nelson, 1987). By fourteen months of age, human infants understand that others' emotional expressions are directed at particular objects (Repacholi, 1998), and by eighteen months they recognize that such emotional signals contain information about the expresser's desires vis-à-vis those objects (Repacholi & Gopnik, 1997). In other words, before children can communicate using language, they already know how to use others' emotional expressions as a source of information (Tronick, 1989).

Social referencing in human infants

The potential adaptive value of the informational function of emotional expressions is nicely illustrated by classic work on "social referencing" in infants (e.g., Klinnert, Campos, Sorce, Emde, & Svejda, 1983; Sorce, Emde, Campos, & Klinnert, 1985). When an infant is confronted with an ambiguous situation, it looks to the face of another person to search for emotional cues that may help interpret and evaluate the ambiguity. "If the observer can identify emotional expressions and can assume that the expressing person is reacting to relevant environmental circumstances," Sorce and colleagues reasoned, "then it seems quite likely that the attitude and/or behavior of that observing person will be influenced by noting the other's emotional expressions" (p. 196).

Classic studies on social referencing utilized a visual cliff paradigm to investigate this possibility. The visual cliff usually consists of a glass-covered table that is divided into two halves: a shallow side under which a patterned surface is placed immediately beneath the glass plate, and a deep side under which a similar surface is visible at some distance below the glass (Sorce et al., 1985). In a typical experiment, the depth of the visual cliff is calibrated so as to be perceived as somewhat frightening by the child. In combination with an attractive toy placed at the deep side of the cliff, this creates an ambiguous situation in which the baby is scared off by the visual cliff yet simultaneously motivated to crawl over the cliff to get to the toy.

The critical manipulation in classic studies such as these consists of a caregiver (often the mother of the child) being positioned at the deep side of the visual cliff and showing certain emotional expressions, for instance happiness in one condition and fear in another. In one of the studies reported by Sorce and colleagues (1985), none of the babies crossed the visual cliff when the mother looked fearful, whereas 74 percent of the babies crossed the cliff when she looked happy. Presumably the mother's emotional display signals that the environment is safe (happiness) or unsafe (fear), which informs the infant's behavior. Interestingly, this program of research has also revealed that a caregiver's emotional expressions are particularly influential in ambiguous situations, suggesting that individuals deliberately seek and use the information conveyed by others' emotional expressions to make sense of the situation (including other people in that situation) and to guide their behavior.

Later studies showed that human infants understand the referential content of others' emotional expressions and use this understanding to draw inferences about the expresser's preferences. In an illustrative study by Repacholi (1998), fourteen-month-old babies saw an adult open two boxes and show a facial display of happiness or disgust depending on the content of the boxes. The infants were subsequently more likely to select the box that had elicited a happy expression from the adult than the box that had elicited a disgusted expression. Other studies revealed that slightly older infants possess a nonegocentric understanding of the differences between their own desires and those of others. In one study, eighteen-month-olds viewed an adult's emotional responses to different food items and subsequently handed over to the adult that food item which had elicited a positive emotional reaction from the adult, even when their own preferences were different (Repacholi & Gopnik, 1997).

Emotional understanding in nonhuman primates

The presumed functionality of emotional expressions can also be observed in nonhuman primates that do not master formal language yet live in complex social constellations that create a need for behavioral coordination. Reflecting the often noted similarities between facial expressions of humans and nonhuman primates (e.g., Darwin, 1872; Redican, 1982), systematic observations indicate that various primate species possess the ability to express and recognize "basic" emotions such as fear, anger, joy, and disgust (Parr, Hopkins, & de Waal, 1998). Moreover, apes as well as certain types of monkeys are capable of using other individuals' emotional expressions to gain information about these individuals' desires and to anticipate their behavior (Buttelmann, Call, & Tomasello, 2009), which helps them coordinate their mutual actions and solve (social) problems (de Waal, 2009).

Early studies indicate, for instance, that rhesus monkeys use the emotional expressions of their conspecifics to inform their own behavior (Miller, Murphy, & Mirsky, 1959; Mirsky, Miller, & Murphy, 1958). In some of these studies, rhesus monkeys witnessing expressions of fear in another monkey that anticipated an electrical shock quickly learned to switch a lever that eliminated the shock. Apparently the monkeys used the emotional expression of the distressed individual to develop an understanding of what was happening and to determine what action was needed. The authors therefore concluded that emotional expressions play an important role in nonverbal communication among monkeys.

More recent work demonstrates just how sophisticated great apes' emotional understanding is. Buttelmann et al. (2009) adapted the above-mentioned paradigm by Repacholi (1998) to investigate whether and how chimpanzees, bonobos, gorillas, and orangutans use humans' emotional expressions to make inferences about the humans' desires and to determine their own course of action. In one experiment, Buttelmann and colleagues found that apes used the experimenter's expressions of happiness versus disgust to inform their choices in a decision task. In this study, the experimenter reacted emotionally upon viewing the contents of two boxes, which were unknown to the subjects. The apes were subsequently more likely to pick the box to which the experimenter had reacted with a happy expression than the box to which the experimenter had reacted with an expression of disgust.

In a follow-up experiment, Buttelmann and colleagues (2009) obtained evidence that this effect was not due merely to automatic processes (e.g., primitive emotional contagion; Hatfield, Cacioppo, & Rapson, 1994; see Chapter 3) or simple valence-based responding. This study was set up in such a way that successful performance required selecting the box that had elicited a negative emotional response from the experimenter. Apes in this experiment more often chose the container to which the experimenter had reacted negatively, presumably based on the inference that the experimenter had just eaten the content of the box to which he had reacted positively, meaning that the other box still contained food. These findings suggest that the apes inferred from the experimenter's emotional expressions how the experimenter felt about the contents of the various containers, which helped them decide which container to pick for themselves.

The relevance of such referential abilities for survival and reproduction is nicely illustrated by an example described by de Waal (2009). He witnessed a chimpanzee mother accidentally sitting down on top of her young, thereby risking smothering it to death. The mother did not hear the young's muffled cries of distress and only realized what she was doing when she saw the worried looks of a few other chimpanzees in the colony who had watched her as she sat down. Upon seeing the distress in the expressions of her fellow chimps she understood what was going on and saved her baby from suffocation. Examples such as these elucidate the importance of emotional expressions for communication and coordination, and although certainly not definitive evidence, they are consistent with the possibility that emotions have evolved at least in part because of the adaptive advantages that are afforded by their expression.

The universality of emotional expressions

Further suggestive evidence for the hypothesis that facial emotional expressions provided an evolutionary advantage comes from studies on the universality of emotional expressions. Guided by Darwin's (1872) assumption of the phylogenetic continuity of the emotion system, a considerable body of research has documented similarities between human and nonhuman emotional expressions (Redican, 1982). Many human facial expressions appear to be rooted in ancestral primate communicative displays (Parr, Waller, Vick, & Bard, 2007; van Hooff, 1972) that are believed to serve a critical role in sustaining cooperative societies (Parr, Waller, & Fugate, 2005). Furthermore, there is evidence for mutual recognition of emotional displays across species boundaries, as shown for instance in the aforementioned work by Buttelmann and colleagues (2009) on the referential effects of human emotional expressions on the behavior of nonhuman primates and in studies on the recognition of macaques' affective vocalizations by humans (Linnankoski, Laasko, & Leinonen, 1994). Studies such as these point to the possibility that the expression of emotion is universal and therefore presumably biologically evolved.

Another line of inquiry that is pertinent to this idea is research on cultural universals versus variations in the recognition of emotional expressions. Classic studies indicate that displays of basic emotions are well recognized across cultures that have had little or no exposure to one another (e.g., Ekman, 1972; Ekman et al., 1987; Izard, 1971), supporting the claim of universals in emotional expression and recognition. Other authors have advanced the opposing view that emotional expressions are shaped by cultural norms and socialization (e.g., Lutz & White, 1986; Wierzbicka, 1994). After decades of fierce debate (for reviews and meta-analyses, see Ekman, 1994; Elfenbein & Ambady, 2002a, 2002b; Mesquita & Frijda, 1992; Russell, 1994), a growing group of scholars nowadays take an intermediate position, suggesting that the facial expression and recognition of emotions is characterized by a combination of universals and cultural variations (e.g., Elfenbein & Ambady, 2003; Mesquita, Frijda, & Scherer, 1997; Scherer & Wallbott, 1994).

Although less extensively studied, the recognition and interpretation of vocal expressions of emotion appears to be characterized by a similar pattern (Sauter, Eisner, Ekman, & Scott, 2010; Scherer, Banse, & Wallbott, 2001). Scherer and colleagues examined the decoding accuracy of vocalizations of joy/happiness, anger, sadness, fear, and disgust across nine countries spanning three continents (Europe, North America, and Asia). They found that, in general, accuracy was substantially greater than chance and, more importantly, that patterns of confusion were very similar across countries and languages. The authors concluded from these findings that there is a considerable degree of universality in the recognition of vocal expressions of emotion. Sauter and colleagues compared European native English speakers with the Himba, a seminomadic group of pastoral people living in remote, culturally isolated villages in Namibia. They found that vocalizations of the basic emotions like anger, disgust, fear, joy, sadness, and surprise were recognized across cultural boundaries, whereas vocalizations of nonbasic emotions like achievement/triumph, relief, and sensual pleasure were recognized within but not across cultures.

In short, even if one can argue about the proportion of universals relative to cultural variations in emotion expression and recognition, it is clear that basic emotions such as joy/happiness, sadness, fear, anger, and disgust (see, e.g., Ekman, 1982; Izard, 1977) tend to be well recognized across cultural boundaries. Moreover, research has documented that differences between the basic emotions are substantially larger than differences between cultures in terms of patterns of subjective feelings (e.g., duration, intensity), physiological symptoms (e.g., arousal, temperature), and expressive tendencies (e.g., approach motivation, verbal, nonverbal, and paralinguistic expression) involved in each of the emotions (Scherer & Wallbott, 1994). Altogether, although perhaps not conclusive, the current body of evidence is consistent with the position that emotional expressions are to a considerable degree rooted in biological affordances, which points to the possibility that emotional expressions have evolved because of the adaptive advantages they provide – a key element of this adaptive benefit being the informational value of emotional expressions.

Proposition 1: Emotional expressions have evolved, at least in part, because of the informational value they represent to observers, which helps coordinate social interaction.

It is important to note that the possibility that emotions have evolved due to the adaptive functionality of their expression does not imply that each and every emotional expression is going to be functional in each and every situation. It takes only shallow introspection and cursory observation of everyday emotional dynamics to realize that both the experience and expression of emotions can have disadvantageous consequences. As is true for any evolutionary account, the position that emotional expressions have been selected for over the course of evolution rests on the assumption that emotional expressions afford a *general* advantage across situations; it does not assume or require that all expressions are always functional. Although it is often possible to develop some rationale as to the functionality of particular effects that seem maladaptive at first, doing so entails the risk of neglecting evidence of dysfunctional emotional episodes and constructing circular and unfalsifiable arguments (Parrott, 2001). Thus, even though I believe that our emotional system has evolved because it serves important social functions, I acknowledge that any particular instance of emotional expression can in principle have both beneficial and detrimental consequences. As will be discussed in detail in Chapter 4, the social functionality of emotional expressions hinges critically on the accuracy of the appraisals that gave rise to the emotions (Parkinson, 2001) as well as on the adequate regulation (Lopes et al., 2005; Parrott, 2001) and appropriate expression of the emotion in light of prevailing norms and expectations in a given social context (Fischer, Manstead, & Zaalberg, 2003; Shields, 2005; Van Kleef, 2010).

What do emotional expressions signal?

Another important question to consider is what exactly emotional expressions signal. This question, too, has ignited considerable debate (for a review, see Parkinson, 2005). At the heart of this debate is the question of whether facial expressions do in fact reflect internally felt emotions. According to the emotional readout hypothesis (Buck, 1980, 1985), facial expressions constitute external "readouts" of motivational and emotional processes that had social significance during the course of evolution. This view is grounded in the assumption that innate primary affects are associated with universal facial expressions (Darwin, 1872; Ekman & Oster, 1979; Izard, 1977; Tomkins, 1962, 1963), as discussed above. Buck (1985) suggested that the more the survival of a species hinged upon the effective coordination of behaviors among individuals (e.g., for procreation, care of young, or distribution of food), the more important it became that certain motivational-emotional states were externally visible, so that communication could occur.

According to this view, emotional expressions may have evolved because they facilitated behavioral coordination that was critical to survival (Andrew, 1963, 1965). For instance, nonverbal displays of dominance versus submissiveness enable the establishment of hierarchies without costly fights, infants' expressions of neediness and dependence encourage caregiving, and courtship displays facilitate the coordination of reproductive behaviors (Buck, 1985). In his analysis of primate expressions, Andrew (1965) noted that the employment of facial displays and other types of nonverbal communication is a function of the extent of socialization of the given species and the communicative demands of the environment and the concomitant need for behavioral coordination. Indeed, social species that require greater degrees of communication to establish effective coordination show more sophisticated repertoires of facial displays than do species that lead solitary lives (Buck, 1980).

Fridlund (1991b, 1994) later suggested that the classical view of facial displays as expressions of internal emotional states should be replaced by a behavioral ecology view, which emphasizes the (voluntary) use of facial expressions in the interest of the individual's social motives. According to this perspective, facial expressions are reflections of salient social motives, and they bear no necessary relation to the individual's emotional state. In this view, individuals who show the right displays at the right time will have a better chance of survival, regardless of whether their outward expressions reflect their privately experienced emotions. Thus, infant cries and smiles, for instance, can be seen as communications of behavioral intentions or as action requests that serve to secure caretaker attention and that require no experienced emotion.

My interest here is not in contrasting the emotional readout hypothesis with the behavioral ecology view of emotional expressions. In fact, the two views are to a large extent compatible (Buck, 1994; Frijda, 1995; Hess, Banse, & Kappas, 1995; Horstmann, 2003) – they simply emphasize different aspects of the emotion process. Whether facial displays are, at the extremes, automatic and involuntary readouts of internal emotional states or deliberate expressions of social motives, both views converge on the notion that emotional expressions can provide insight into the goals and desires of the expresser. Although the question of whether facial displays reflect felt emotions or social motives is relevant when it comes to theorizing about the evolution of facial expressions, it is not particularly critical from the point of view of understanding the *social effects* of emotions, because emotions and motivations can hardly be seen as separate entities (Parkinson, 2005). We feel emotions because we strive toward certain goals, and thus, by implication, emotions reflect underlying motivations (Frijda, 1986; Lazarus, 1991). What matters for the current purpose is that observers may distill relevant information from other people's facial expressions – be it about their internally experienced emotions, their social motives, or some combination of the two. For the sake of simplicity, I will use the words "emotional expression" and "emotional display" to refer to those verbal and nonverbal expressive patterns that can be mapped theoretically onto felt emotions based on their form, while realizing that not all such expressions necessarily always reflect internally felt emotions. I return to this distinction in Chapter 4, where I discuss the issue of emotional authenticity.

Emotional expressions as communicative tools

The fact that emotional expressions contain information about the expresser's internal feelings and/or motives implies that emotional expressions may function as communicative tools (Fridlund, 1994). This view can be traced back to Darwin's (1872) seminal work on the expression of the emotions in man and animals, in which he wrote:

> The movements of expression in the face and body, whatever their origin may have been, are in themselves of much importance for our welfare. They serve as the first means of communication between the mother and her infant; she smiles approval, and thus encourages her child on the right path, or frowns disapproval. We readily perceive sympathy in others by their expression; our sufferings are thus mitigated and our pleasures increased; and mutual good feeling is thus strengthened. The movements of expression give vividness and energy to our spoken words. They reveal the thoughts and intentions of others more truly than do words, which may be falsified. (Darwin, 1872, p. 359)

Darwin's thinking has stimulated a great deal of research into the possible communicative function and purpose of emotional expressions. Even though Darwin did not believe that the muscles of the face have evolved *because* they allow us to convey our emotions to others, he was convinced that emotional expressions reveal important information about the expresser and thus play a role in social communication.[1]

---

[1] This nuance relates to the distinction that is made in evolutionary biology between *signals* and *cues* (see Shariff & Tracy, 2011, for a discussion). Signals evolved specifically for the purpose of communication, whereas cues did not evolve to facilitate communication but convey information as a *byproduct* of another characteristic that serves a primary adaptive purpose, such as an intrapersonal physiological function (e.g., widening the eyes in fear to increase the scope of the visual field or scrunching the nose in disgust to reduce the intake of potentially contaminated air). Some scholars have proposed a two-stage model, suggesting that emotional expressions first emerged as cues and eventually transformed in form and function to become signals (e.g., Chapman, Kim, Susskind, & Anderson, 2009; Eibl-Eibesfeldt, 1989). As is the case for the emotional readout versus behavioral ecology debate discussed previously, this distinction is more germane to theorizing about the evolution of emotional expressions than to theorizing about their contemporary social consequences. For present purposes I will therefore treat the existence of the current repertoire of emotional expressions as a given and focus on how emotional expressions may be used as communicative tools to regulate social interaction.

The deliberate targeting of emotional expressions

Anecdotal observations and empirical findings converge to suggest that emotional expressions are often deliberately directed at observers so as to maximize the impact of the expressions as communication devices and tools of social influence (Côté & Hideg, 2011; Van Kleef, Van Doorn, Heerdink, & Koning, 2011). Consider the familiar examples of the waitress who smiles purposefully as a way of increasing her tip; the homeless person who expresses sadness in the hopes of extracting some change from passers-by; the father who shows disgust to discourage his three-year-old from spitting out his food; the boxer who shows anger to intimidate his opponent; or the toddler who trips and hurts his knee but only starts to cry when he detects a suitable audience (also see Fridlund, 1994). Examples such as these illustrate how commonly people use emotional expressions to communicate their appraisals, motives, and intentions to others. As discussed in greater detail in Chapter 4, such emotional expressions may vary in the extent to which they reflect the expresser's internal feeling states, but the communicative goals behind their expression may be largely the same.

Several independent programs of research also support the conclusion that emotional expressions may be used deliberately as part of a communication strategy. In what has become a classic study, Kraut and Johnston (1979) videotaped bowlers from the position of the pins at the end of the lane as well as from the perspective of the fellow bowlers waiting to take their turn. The researchers found that the bowlers exhibited more visible emotional displays when facing the audience than when facing the pins, suggesting that they intentionally directed their expressions toward the audience as a way of communicating their emotional evaluation of the ongoing events (e.g., strikes, misses). A study of the nonverbal behavior of gold medal winners at the Olympic Games similarly showed that happiness alone was not sufficient to generate smiling; rather, smiling was triggered by the presence of a social audience (Fernández-Dols & Ruiz-Belda, 1995).

Another illustrative study was reported by Bavelas, Black, Lemery, and Mullett (1986). In a carefully staged experiment, participants saw the experimenter drop a heavy television onto his apparently already bruised finger, while looking either at or away from the participant. Participants exhibited more visible signs of empathetic pain when they could establish eye contact with the experimenter than when they could not. When no eye contact was possible, participants' vicarious winces quickly faded away. This suggests that participants' emotional displays served the communicative goal of signaling empathy and mutual distress, presumably to soothe the victim's pain and/or to create a bond. Participants strategically timed their facial expressions so as to maximize their signaling value.

Modulation of emotional expressivity by the presence of others

Fridlund (1991b) later demonstrated that the *implicit* presence of an audience can be sufficient to catalyze facial expressions. Participants in this study watched an amusing film in one of four sociality conditions: (1) alone, (2) alone believing that a friend was nearby, (3) alone believing that a friend was nearby and watching the same film, or (4) in the physical presence of a friend. The sociality manipulation did not influence self-reported emotional reactions to the film, but it did affect facial displays as measured by facial electromyography (fEMG): Participants smiled more in the more social situations. It is noteworthy that smiling was equally potentiated in conditions 3 (implicit audience) and 4 (explicit audience), suggesting that merely imagining an audience is enough to trigger the social-communicative mind-set that increases emotional expressivity.

Interestingly, there appears to be an asymmetry in the degree to which individuals are inclined to express positive versus negative emotions as a function of the sociality of the situation. Whereas Fridlund (1991b) reported evidence that sociality potentiates positive facial expressions, other studies indicate that negative emotional expressions (e.g., of sadness) may actually be tempered by the presence of an audience (Jakobs, Manstead, & Fischer, 2001; but also see Chovil, 1991). Other work revealed that the presence of strangers inhibits the expression of emotions, whereas the presence of friends facilitates emotional expression (Buck, Losow, Murphy, & Constanzo, 1992). Although slightly different in its outlook, this work also demonstrates that people tend to adapt their emotional displays to characteristics of the social situation, presumably to maximize the communicative functionality of those displays.

As is the case for the interpretation of others' emotional expressions discussed above, the deliberate use of emotional expressions is common not only among human adults, but also among younger children and nonhuman primates. For instance, Jones and colleagues demonstrated that ten-month-old infants' smiling is strongly dependent on visual contact with the caregiver, with smiles being much less frequent in the absence of such contact (Jones & Raag, 1989; Jones, Collins, & Hong, 1991). Zeman and Shipman (1996) found that second graders communicated sadness to elicit support but suppressed anger for fear of negative social consequences. Furthermore, McCrone (1991) observed how chimpanzees deliberately and intelligently used emotional expressions to influence conspecifics. The chimpanzees' purposeful use of facial, vocal, and postural emotional expressions to sway the behavior of their interaction partners suggests that they possess at least a rudimentary understanding of how other individuals may respond to various types of emotional displays and, accordingly, of how emotional displays can be used as a form of communication.

Clearly, then, there is much more to emotions than their internal experience. More often than not, emotions are purposefully expressed (or suppressed) to communicate with others and to achieve certain goals, and their expression is skillfully managed so as to yield optimal social benefits (Planalp, 1999). This highlights the possibility that the communicative qualities of emotions are part of the reason why emotions have evolved in the first place. Indeed, Parkinson (1996) proposed that private outbursts of emotion may be developmentally secondary to the primary communicative function of emotional expressions. "Our emotional expressions," Parkinson suggested, "are often intended as communicative acts addressed to another person rather than being simple and direct reflections of an underlying mental state" (p. 676).

The functional equivalence of expressive modalities

Most research on the communicative nature of emotional expressions has focused on facial displays of emotion, as reflected in the preceding discussion. This focus has gone at the expense of attention paid to the informational and communicative functions of verbal, vocal, and postural emotional expressions (but see, e.g., Aviezer, Trope, & Todorov, 2012; Byron, 2008; Coyne, 1976; Sauter et al., 2010; Scherer, 1986; Van Kleef, De Dreu, & Manstead, 2004a; Wallbott, 1998). It is evident from the above that facial expressions of emotion play a pivotal role in regulating social interaction, but there is no reason to assume that they are unique in serving this function. On the contrary, if we accept the assumption that emotional expressions have evolved in part because of their communicative functionality, it stands to reason that the social signaling value of emotional expressions is similar across expressive modalities (Van Kleef et al., 2011).

Emotional expressions may provide information about the expresser's appraisal of the situation (Manstead & Fischer, 2001), his or her internal feeling state (Ekman, 1993), and his or her social motives and intentions (Fridlund, 1994). It seems likely, then, that such information can be conveyed via facial, verbal, postural, or paralinguistic cues, or through any combination of these expressive channels. Obviously, the suitability of the various forms of emotional expression depends on the situation. For instance, in modern life facial expressions are likely to be generally more effective in face-to-face contact, vocal expressions in phone conversations, and verbal expressions in e-mail exchanges. Such obvious boundary conditions aside, however, EASI theory postulates that the social-signaling value of emotions is functionally equivalent across expressive modalities. The *magnitude* of the interpersonal effects of various forms of emotional expressions may vary due to differences in the relative strength of expressions and the degree to which they are picked up by others, but the *direction* of the effects should be the same irrespective of the expressive channel, as long as the emotional expression is accurately perceived.

Proposition 2: The social-signaling function of emotional expressions is functionally equivalent across expressive modalities in that the direction (but not necessarily the magnitude) of the interpersonal effects of emotions is similar regardless of whether emotions are expressed in the face, through the voice, by means of bodily postures, and/or with words or symbols.

Emotional expressions as cues to social predispositions

The foregoing arguments and evidence support the notion that a key function of emotional expressions is to provide information to observers so as to help them disambiguate the situation and inform their actions. This begs the question of what type of information individuals may glean from others' emotional expressions. Building on the idea that (authentic) emotional expressions reflect a combination of internally felt emotions, concerns, motives, intentions, and states of action readiness (Frijda, Kuipers, & ter Schure, 1989; Keltner & Haidt, 1999; Oatley & Jenkins, 1992), EASI theory posits that people use the emotional expressions of others to gain insight into others' internal states as well as to draw inferences about the nature of the situation they are in.

Darwin (1872) proposed that, over the course of evolution, facial expressions of emotion eventually came to convey information not merely about expressers' internal feeling states, but also about their social intentions. It seems plausible that this communicative aspect of emotional expressions contributed to the adaptive success of human beings and thereby to the evolution of emotional expressions. One type of social information that has immediate repercussions for people's chances of survival concerns the degree to which other individuals they encounter are inclined toward cooperation or competition (Boone & Buck, 2003). It stands to reason, then, that one of the primary types of information people distill from others' emotional expressions pertains to cooperative versus competitive inclinations.

Along similar lines, Knutson (1996) argued that observers may extract information from others' emotional expressions regarding their dominance and affiliation motives (also see Frank, 1988). In support of this possibility, Knutson found in two experiments that perceivers inferred high degrees of dominance and affiliation from expressions of happiness, high degrees of dominance and low degrees of affiliation from expressions of anger and disgust, and low degrees of dominance from expressions of sadness and fear. These findings suggest that people do indeed use the emotional expressions of other individuals to infer fundamental traits that bear relevance to social interaction and that help them anticipate the behavior of other individuals.

Compatible findings were obtained in other research (e.g., Hareli & Hess, 2010; Hareli, Shomrat, & Hess, 2009; Hendriks & Vingerhoets, 2006; Hess, Blairy, & Kleck, 2000). For instance, Hareli and Hess found that a person who reacted with anger to blame was perceived as more aggressive, self-confident, and masculine, and as less gentle and warm than a person who reacted with sadness to the same situation, and Hendriks and Vingerhoets found that crying individuals were judged as less aggressive than individuals who expressed anger, fear, or no emotion. Interestingly, Hess and colleagues further found that basic inferences of dominance and affiliation were rather similar regardless of the ethnic group membership or the sex of the expresser (although these factors did influence perceptions to some extent). This speaks to the universality debate by suggesting that interpersonal trait inferences based on emotional expressions may be fairly similar across social and biological groups.

Another relevant line of research shows that emotional expressions may be used as cues regarding the expresser's hierarchical standing. Tiedens (2001) demonstrated that people who express anger (as opposed to sadness) are more likely to be seen as high in status and to be afforded status by others. Accurate perception of (and accommodation to) other people's positions in hierarchies is important for (social) survival because power, status, and dominance serve as heuristic solutions to coordination problems and thereby help to preempt conflict (Keltner, Van Kleef, Chen, & Kraus, 2008). Interestingly, Tiedens and Fragale (2003) showed that complementary responses to dominant nonverbal behaviors produced more comfortable interactions and greater interpersonal liking among interaction partners. Thus, granting power to individuals who display dominant nonverbal behavior (e.g., expressions of anger) by deferring nonverbally leads to smoother interactions.

It is noteworthy that the various types of inferences from emotional expressions discussed above all relate in one way or another to cooperation versus competition. It makes theoretical sense, in light of the presumed evolutionary history of emotional expressions, that the key types of information observers obtain from emotional expressions would have implications for survival. Of course emotional expressions can convey other, more specific types of information that depend on the social situation in which they are expressed, the object in relation to which they are expressed, and the person at whom they are directed. For instance, it would be quite straightforward to infer from a friend's laughter in the movie theater that she enjoys the film, and perhaps that she is a fan of the director. But the more general trait inferences that people may make on the basis of others' emotional expressions are likely to be relatively independent of the social setting, and these inferences probably relate to interpersonal tendencies that have immediate repercussions for the nature of the social interaction in terms of survival, bonding, and reproduction.

In line with this idea, recent research indicates that emotional expressions shape the construal of social situations in terms of cooperation versus competition. Van Doorn, Heerdink, and Van Kleef (2012) conducted a series of studies in which participants were asked to prepare for an interaction with another person with whom they would supposedly perform a joint task. Participants received information about the task (e.g., writing a paper, planning a vacation), and they were shown a picture of their future interaction partner. The partner's emotional expression was systematically varied to reflect anger, disappointment, happiness, or no emotion. Across studies, expressions of anger led participants to construe the anticipated interaction as more competitive compared to expressions of happiness or disappointment. Furthermore, greater cooperative intentions were attributed to the expresser when happiness or disappointment was expressed, compared to when anger was expressed. Similar effects were found when the counterpart's emotion was manipulated by means of verbal rather than facial expressions, and the effect held even when explicit information about the likely nature of the situation (cooperative or competitive) was provided.

Complementary evidence was obtained in another series of studies. Homan, Van Kleef, and Sanchez-Burks (2016) presented participants with sketches of work situations that showed the facial emotional expressions of two teammates. The teammates' emotional expressions were systematically varied so that both showed happiness or both showed sadness. Participants then indicated how they thought the interaction between the team members would unfold. Participants anticipated more cooperative interactions, greater interpersonal liking and trust, and less conflict when both partners showed happiness than when both showed sadness. Interestingly, Homan and colleagues further found that the effects of the teammates' emotional expressions on participants' expectations regarding the trajectory of their interaction were stronger when the teammates had different ethnic backgrounds and when their pictures had supposedly been taken after (rather than before) an initial meeting. These results suggest that emotional expressions take on heightened importance as cues of cooperation versus competition in situations that present greater ambiguity and/or potential for conflict, such as interactions between individuals from different cultural or ethnic backgrounds (Hewstone, Rubin, & Willis, 2002; Van Knippenberg, De Dreu, & Homan, 2004). Furthermore, the findings indicate that observers are more likely to use others' emotional expressions as a source of information to the degree that the emotional expressions are potentially relevant and diagnostic (i.e., when they arose as part of the current social interaction).

Together, these findings support the idea that people use others' emotional expressions to draw inferences regarding their dominant versus affiliative predispositions and to anticipate future levels of cooperation versus competition.

Proposition 3: People use others' emotional expressions to infer traits and dispositions that are relevant to (social) survival and success (e.g., dominance, affiliation) and to anticipate others' behavior (e.g., collaboration vs. exploitation) as well as the trajectory of social interactions (e.g., cooperative vs. competitive).

When emotional signaling fails

One way of illuminating the importance of emotional expressions in regulating our social lives is by considering what may happen when emotional communication is thwarted. In this section I briefly discuss a variety of clinical and subclinical conditions that may threaten individual well-being, the quality of social relationships, and general life success by undermining emotional signaling.

Clinical conditions

The importance of the social-informational function of emotional expressions for well-adapted social relations becomes painfully clear when one considers what can happen when emotional communication is frustrated. Brain damage, psychological disorders, and physical conditions can contribute to serious social-relational problems by undermining various aspects of emotional functioning. Such conditions may threaten well-being and the quality of social interaction by thwarting the perception and understanding of emotions, the expression of emotions, and/or the regulation of emotions. Although an in-depth treatment of such conditions falls outside the scope of this book, a brief digression can illustrate the importance of normal emotional functioning for effective communication and social adjustment.

Brain trauma

A large body of research has documented that various types of brain lesions can debilitate particular aspects of emotional functioning. For instance, the famous incident of Phineas Gage, who suffered major brain damage when a large iron rod was driven through his skull in an explosion, revealed associations between lesions to the prefrontal cortex and impaired emotional understanding, empathy, and impulse control, which severely compromised the quality of Gage's social relationships after the accident (Damasio, 1994). Other illustrative studies have demonstrated associations between amygdala lesions and impaired recognition of particular facial emotional expressions (Adolphs, Tranel, Damasio, & Damasio, 1994) and between cortical malfunctions and impairments in emotion regulation that may result in impulsive violence and aggression (Davidson, Putnam, & Larson, 2000). These and many other investigations point to the far-reaching social consequences of impaired emotional functioning.

Psychopathology

Various psychopathologies can severely undermine the quality of social life by impairing emotion recognition, emotional understanding, emotional expression, and/or emotion regulation (Blair, 2003). Difficulties surrounding the perception and understanding of other people's emotional expressions feature prominently in Mark Haddon's (2003) novel *The curious incident of the dog in the night time*. Upon discovering a dead dog in the garden, the main character introduces himself as follows (pp. 2–3):

> My name is Christopher John Francis Boone. I know all the countries of the world and their capital cities and every prime number up to 7,507. Eight years ago, when I first met Siobhan, she showed me this picture ☺ and I knew that it meant "sad," which is what I felt when I found the dead dog. Then she showed me this picture ☺ and I knew that it meant "happy," like when I'm reading about the Apollo space missions, or when I'm still awake at three or four in the morning and I can walk up and down the street and pretend that I am the only person in the whole world. Then she drew some other pictures [. . .], but I was unable to say what these meant. I got Siobhan to draw lots of faces and then write down next to them exactly what they meant. I kept the piece of paper in my pocket and took it out when I didn't understand what someone was saying. But it was very difficult to decide which of the diagrams was most like the face they were making, because people's faces move very quickly.

It is apparent from this passage that Christopher has difficulty recognizing more intricate expressions of emotion. This makes it challenging for him to understand how others are feeling and to relate to them in a socially appropriate way, as becomes clear in the rest of Haddon's book. Christopher most likely has some form of autistic spectrum disorder, a heterogeneous set of developmental disorders that are characterized, among other things, by difficulties in recognizing and responding to other people's emotional expressions (Uljarevic & Hamilton, 2013) and associated problems with social functioning (Volkmar, Chawarska, & Klin, 2005). These problems have been attributed to impairment in theory of mind exhibited by patients with autism spectrum disorders (Blair, 2003; Frith, 2001), that is, the ability to represent the mental states of others (i.e., their thoughts, beliefs, desires, and intentions; Leslie, 1987; Premack & Woodruff, 1978). Given that a lot of important information can be gleaned from emotional expressions, as we have seen above, the reduced ability to accurately perceive, represent, and/or understand other people's emotional displays poses a significant challenge for patients with autism spectrum disorders. Although specific disorders within the autism spectrum vary greatly in the degree to which they handicap patients' social skills (Volkmar et al., 2005), even high-functioning children and adults with autism often have fewer and lower-quality relationships and are more likely to experience feelings of loneliness (Bauminger & Kasari, 2000; Jobe & Williams White, 2007).

Other types of psychopathology influence patients' social-emotional lives by restricting the emotions they feel, the emotions they express, and/or the degree to which they are able to regulate their emotions. A prime example is unipolar depressive disorder, which is characterized by chronic low levels of experienced positive affect and heightened levels of experienced negative affect (Watson, Clark, & Carey, 1988). These internal affective states may be reflected in depressive speech patterns (Buck, 1984; Hargreaves, Starkweather, & Blacker, 1965; Scherer, 1986) and limited facial and postural expressions of positive emotion (Berenbaum & Oltmanns, 1992; Waxer, 1974), which may in turn be picked up by interaction partners (Keltner & Kring, 1998). Due in part to the negative affective reactions they elicit in other people (Coyne, 1976; Joiner, 1994), individuals suffering from depressive symptoms are more likely to experience social rejection by others (Joiner, Alfano, & Metalsky, 1992). Accordingly, depressed individuals tend to have fewer close relationships and smaller social networks (Gotlib, 1992; Nezlak, Imbrie, & Shean, 1994), enjoy less social support (Lara, Leader, & Klein, 1997), and experience more marital discord (Beach, Smith, & Fincham, 1994). Furthermore, the lack of positive emotional responsiveness of depressed parents may contribute to the development of long-lasting negative affective states in their children (Cohn & Tronick, 1983).

An example of a disorder that influences patterns of emotional expression is schizophrenia. Among other things, schizophrenia is characterized by diminished emotional expressivity, or "flat affect" (Berenbaum & Oltmans, 1992). Schizophrenic patients' inability to express their emotions robs their interaction partners of critical cues as to their internal feeling states, problems, and desires (Keltner & Kring, 1998). As a result of this impaired emotional signaling, patients stand a serious risk of missing out on social support that they might otherwise have received (Hooley, Richters, Weintraub, & Neale, 1987). Accordingly, compared to controls, schizophrenic patients tend to have smaller social networks (Hammer, 1986), exhibit poorer social adjustment (Mueser, Bellack, Morrison, & Wixted, 1990), and experience greater marital dissatisfaction (Hooley et al., 1987).

A final class of clinical conditions that is of interest here consists of disorders that impair patients' emotion regulation abilities and, thereby, their patterns of emotional experience and expression. A chief example of such a condition is the borderline personality disorder (BPD), which is associated (among other things) with emotional oversensitivity, affective instability, and extreme mood fluctuations (Farchaus-Stein, 1996; Lumsden, 1993). Patients may also experience intense feelings of anger and other negative emotions, which they find difficult to control (Farchaus-Stein, 1996; Soloff & Ulrich, 1981). Most important in the context of the current discussion is that these negative expressive patterns may be interpreted by interaction partners as negative information about the status of their relationship with the patient, which may trigger avoidance tendencies (Keltner & Kring, 1998). These avoidant reactions may in turn be perceived as signs of rejection by patients, thus further contributing to their negative emotional experience and expression. As a result of these and other social dynamics, BPD patients are more likely than healthy individuals to have hostile and conflict-ridden relationships (Benjamin & Wonderlich, 1994; Modestin & Villiger, 1989).

Physical constraints on emotional expressivity
Conditions outside the realm of psychopathology can also threaten the quality of social relationships by hampering emotional signaling. For instance, patients who suffer from Parkinson's disease often exhibit a stiffness in their facial musculature that impairs (spontaneous) emotional expressions (Smith, Smith, & Ellgring, 1996). This makes it difficult for interaction partners to gauge how the patient feels and what she or he wants, reducing the likelihood that they will respond adequately to the patient's needs. In addition, patients with Parkinson's disease tend to exhibit difficulties in decoding the emotional expressions of others

(Jacobs, Shuren, Bowers, & Heilman, 1995), which may reduce the quality of their social relationships.

Social interaction may also be compromised when individuals undergo a facelift or receive cosmetic injections of *botulinum toxin* type-A to combat visible signs of aging in the face. First, the reduced muscle activity in the face that results from these types of surgery logically undermines emotional expression. Second, emotional understanding may be impaired (Havas, Glenberg, Gutowski, Lucarelli, & Davidson, 2010), because the blocking of facial mimicry interferes with recognition of and (empathic) responses to others' emotional expressions (Hawk, Fischer, & Van Kleef, 2012; Niedenthal, Winkielman, Mondillon, & Vermeulen, 2009; Oberman, Winkielman, & Ramachandran, 2007).

Subclinical conditions: the perils of expressive suppression

Besides physical and psychopathological conditions that undermine emotional expressivity, people may develop maladaptive patterns of emotional suppression as a result of their upbringing and socialization. Even though such patterns may not meet the criteria of clinical pathologies, their social consequences can be far-reaching nonetheless. Several studies indicate that the discouragement of emotional expressivity among infants is associated with developmental problems at a later age. For instance, Eisenberg and Fabes (1994) found that parental punishment of children's displays of negative emotions was associated with children's avoidance of emotional expressions, particularly of anger. Such minimization of (negative) emotional expressions on the part of young children has been linked to insecure and avoidant attachment (Cassidy, 1994).

Other work has yielded complementary evidence for the important role of emotional expressions in parent–child relationships (Tronick, 1989). For instance, Roberts and Strayer (1987) reported that preschoolers whose parents accepted and encouraged their expressions of distress showed more social competence than children whose parents rejected their expressions of distress. Similarly, Gottman, Katz, and Hooven (1996) demonstrated in a longitudinal study that children whose parents accepted their (negative) emotional expressions at age 5 exhibited higher academic achievement at age 8. Findings such as these suggest that the expression of emotions is a cornerstone of healthy child development and the formation of secure attachment bonds and social competence.

The potential detriments of expressive suppression are not limited to young children (Gross & John, 2003). Early work by Gottman and Levenson yielded evidence that emotional withdrawal (which involves reduced emotional expressivity) of husbands is associated with declining marital satisfaction of both partners (Gottman & Levenson, 1988; Levenson & Gottman, 1985). More recent research by Butler and colleagues has demonstrated links between expressive suppression of emotions and physical indicators of stress as well as reduced rapport and inhibited friendship formation between conversation partners (Butler et al., 2003). Another study similarly found that emotional suppression predicted lower social support, less interpersonal closeness, and lower social satisfaction (Srivastava, Tamir, McGonigal, John, & Gross, 2009). One explanation of patterns such as these is that individuals who suppress the expression of internally felt emotions deny interaction partners critical information as to their internal states, which makes it difficult for partners to adequately respond to their situation.

Although positive emotional expressivity may be expected to have especially favorable consequences for the quality of social relationships (Mauss et al., 2011), negative emotional expressions serve a critical role in drawing attention to problems that need to be addressed. In the face of pertinent concerns, expressive suppression of negative emotions may therefore have detrimental consequences for wellbeing and social adaptation. Clearly, however, the uninhibited expression of negative emotions without regard for the social context is not likely to be very functional, either. Successful adaptation depends on the ability to flexibly enhance or suppress emotional expression in accord with situational demands (Bonanno, Papa, Lalande, Westphal, & Coifman, 2004). In other words, individual wellbeing and the quality of social relations depend on adequate emotion regulation (Bell & Calkins, 2000), which is one of the recurring themes of this book.

This brief foray into the effects of brain trauma, psychopathology, and physical and psychological constraints on emotional functioning is far from exhaustive, but it suffices to highlight the serious social difficulties that may arise when individuals experience problems with respect to perceiving the emotions of others and/or regulating and appropriately expressing their own emotions. Many of the adverse social consequences that are associated with these various conditions appear to result at least in part from compromised communication and social connectedness.

Conclusion

Various literatures converge to show that emotional expressions play a critical role in enabling effective communication and social coordination. Emotional expressions provide a wealth of information that allows observers to gauge the social intentions of the expresser and to adjust their own behavior accordingly. People deliberately target their emotional expressions at others who in turn use those expressions as a source of information when deciding how to respond. Considerable degrees of continuity in the encoding and decoding of emotional expressions across human cultures and across primate species point to the possibility that our emotional expressions have evolved because they fulfill critical social-communicative functions. Indeed, a host of clinical and subclinical conditions that undermine the social-communicative functions of emotions can have far-reaching consequences for the quality of social interactions.

If we accept the premise that emotional expressions contribute vitally to the regulation of social interaction, the next question is how this regulation occurs. In the following two chapters I discuss the various mechanisms that drive the social consequences of emotional expressions (Chapter 3) as well as the contingencies that govern the nature of these consequences (Chapter 4).

CHAPTER 3

Mechanisms involved in the social effects of emotions

> Just as an outstretched finger tends to direct attention wherever it points, a witnessed emotion encourages us to take account of its implied perspective on events.
>
> Parkinson, Fischer, and Manstead (2005, p. 179)

We have seen in the previous chapter that emotional expressions provide pertinent cues into the internal states of expressers. These cues play a critical role in social interaction by serving as communication devices that facilitate interpersonal coordination (Keltner & Haidt, 1999). Whenever individuals perceive the emotional expressions of others around them, they may be influenced by those expressions. Thus, a spouse may be more willing to put the garbage outside after her partner produced a sincere smile while asking the favor; a child may tidy up his room after his father gave him an angry glance; a shopper may donate some money to a good cause upon seeing the charity collector's disappointed reaction to impervious bystanders; a nego-tiator may stand her ground after learning that her opponent feels guilty about his last offer; an athlete may work harder for the team after being reprimanded by his coach. Such instances of social influence by means of emotional expressions are omnipresent (Van Kleef, Van Doorn, Heerdink, & Koning, 2011), but how exactly do they come about?

Common sense suggests that people may respond to other individuals' emotional expressions in a multitude of ways. For one thing, different emotional expressions may elicit different responses in observers, as is clear from the basic research on human infants and nonhuman primates discussed in the previous chapter (e.g., infants whose caregivers smiled were more likely to cross a visual cliff than infants whose caregivers looked fearful; Klinnert, Campos, Sorce, Emde, & Svejda, 1983). But even the exact same emotional expression may trigger a variety of responses through different mechanisms. These mechanisms underlying the social effects of emotional expressions are the focus of this chapter.

Building on the proposition that emotional expressions have evolved in part because of the informational value they represent to observers (as discussed at length in Chapter 2), I argue that the provision of informa-tion is at the heart of the processes that drive the social consequences of emotional expressions. The Emotions as Social Information (EASI) framework identifies two classes of mechanisms underlying the interpersonal effects of emotions: Emotional expressions may (1) trigger affective reactions in observers and/or (2) elicit inferential processes in observers (Van Kleef, 2009). Both types of processes provide information to observers that helps them better understand the feelings, desires, motives, and intentions of the person expressing the emotion, and to act accordingly. I discuss both classes of processes in turn.

Emotional expressions trigger affective reactions in observers

Emotional expressions can evoke various types of affective reactions in observers, which may subsequently inform their behavior. Affective reactions can take the form of *reciprocal* or *complementary* feeling states (Keltner & Haidt, 1999) as well as associated sentiments such as likes or dislikes (Frijda, 1994). For instance, one person's displays of distress may evoke reciprocal feelings of distress and/or complementary feelings of compassion in an observer (Batson, Fultz, & Schoenrade, 1987; Van Kleef et al., 2008), and these affective states may be accompanied by feelings of warmth or closeness and affectively laden behavioral tendencies, such as a desire to provide consolation to the distressed person. As another example, expressions of anger may inspire reciprocal anger and/or complementary fear in observers (Dimberg & Öhman, 1996; Dimberg, Thunberg, & Elmehed, 2000; Moody, McIntosh, Mann, & Weisser, 2007), which may motivate fight and flight responses, respectively. Affective reactions thus constitute a mediating mechanism between the emotional expressions of one person and the (behavioral) responses of another, as shown in Figure 3.1.

Reciprocal affective reactions and their underlying processes: emotional contagion, perspective taking, social appraisal, and embodiment

Most research in the realm of reciprocal affective reactions to emotional expressions revolves around the notion of emotional contagion, the

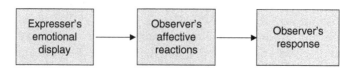

Figure 3.1 Affective reactions as a mediating mechanism between one person's emotional expression and another person's response.

tendency to "catch" other people's emotions in social interaction on a moment-to-moment basis (Hatfield, Cacioppo, & Rapson, 1994; Lundqvist & Dimberg, 1995). One type of emotional contagion occurs when individuals are exposed to others' nonverbal displays of emotion (e.g., facial, vocal, and postural expressions), which may be automatically and nonconsciously mimicked and produce congruent emotional states via various forms of afferent feedback (i.e., physiological feedback from facial, vocal, and postural movements; e.g., Adelmann & Zajonc, 1989; Hess & Blairy, 2001; Flack, 2006; Neumann & Strack, 2000; Wild, Erb, & Bartels, 2001). Hatfield, Cacioppo, and Rapson (1992) referred to this phenomenon as "primitive emotional contagion," which they defined as the "tendency to automatically mimic and synchronize movements, expressions, postures, and vocalizations with those of another person and, consequently, to converge emotionally" (pp. 153–154). Although direct evidence for the full mediating chain from emotion perception → mimicry → afferent feedback → emotional experience, as originally proposed under the conceptualization of primitive emotional contagion, is weak and inconclusive (see Hess & Fischer, 2013), there is abundant evidence that people do indeed often unintentionally take on the emotions of others, not just in the lab (e.g., Barsade, 2002) but also in real-life situations (e.g., Anderson, Keltner, & John, 2003; Totterdell, 2000).

Despite the equivocal status of mimicry and concomitant afferent feedback as explanatory mechanisms for primitive emotional contagion, the extant literature puts a lot of emphasis on these mechanisms, which sometimes goes at the expense of attention paid to other mechanisms of emotional contagion. Notably, however, Hatfield and colleagues (1992) proposed that emotional contagion can also occur via processes that do not require mimicry, such as classical conditioning and deliberate perspective taking (also see Elfenbein, 2014). Although these non-primitive forms of emotional contagion have received comparatively little research attention, there is growing evidence that emotional contagion can indeed occur in the absence of mimicry. For instance, several studies indicate that people can come to feel the anger and happiness of others even when these emotions are expressed verbally in computer-mediated interaction (Cheshin, Rafaeli, & Bos, 2011; Friedman et al., 2004; Van Kleef, De Dreu, & Manstead, 2004a). Such effects obviously cannot be accounted for in terms of mimicry and afferent feedback (i.e., primitive emotional contagion), because lack of visual or auditory access to the nonverbal emotional expressions of others precludes mimicry in the traditional sense.

Other research has found that people can come to feel the emotions of others when they deliberately take their perspectives and imagine what it would feel like to be in their shoes, even in the absence of visible signs of emotion. In a study by Hawk, Fischer, and Van Kleef (2011), participants watched a video clip of an actor performing a silly dance. Participants were instructed to watch the clip in an objective way or, in another condition, to try and take the actor's perspective. The actor either showed nonverbal signs of embarrassment (including gaze aversion; smiling; touching her face, hair, and clothing; and downward head movements; see Keltner, 1995) or remained cool and aloof while dancing. The actor's embarrassment displays and the perspective-taking instructions both produced reciprocal feelings of embarrassment in participants, and the effect of perspective taking was significant also when the actor emitted no visual signs of embarrassment. Thus, consistent with Hatfield and colleagues' (1992, 1994) ideas, this study indicates that emotional contagion can also occur via intentional perspective taking, and in the absence of mimicry.

Parkinson and Simons (2009) further reported evidence suggesting that emotions may spread both via traditional and relatively automatic forms of emotional contagion and via more deliberate cognitive processes of social appraisal (Manstead & Fischer, 2001), whereby individuals use the emotions of others to interpret their situation and then come to feel accompanying emotions as a result. Thus, one individual's anxiety may draw another person's attention to potentially threatening aspects of a common situation, thereby evoking reciprocal anxiety in that person. In a diary study on the role of emotions in decision making in naturalistic settings, Parkinson and Simons found that emotions spread between interactants. This emotional convergence was partially mediated by appraisals of risk and importance of the decisions, suggesting that more deliberate social appraisal processes can account for part of the variance. It is plausible that more automatic processes of emotional contagion accounted for another part of the variance, but this could not be established directly. Interestingly, transfer effects remained after controlling for participants' perceptions of the other person's emotion, indicating that emotional convergence does not require conscious registration of other people's emotions.

A final qualification of the traditional view of emotional contagion that is relevant here comes from work in the realm of embodiment, which views concordant responses to the emotional expressions of others as "simulations" that facilitate emotional convergence and understanding. According to embodiment theories, individuals process other people's emotional expressions by reactivating neural states involved in their own prior affective experiences (Barsalou, Niedenthal, Barbey, & Ruppert, 2003; Niedenthal, 2007). Building on this idea, Hawk, Fischer, and Van Kleef (2012) introduced the possibility of cross-channel imitation of discrete emotions. Specifically, they investigated whether perceivers engage facial muscles when hearing emotional vocalizations of others (also see Hietanen, Surakka, & Linnankoski, 1998; Magnée, Stekelenburg, Kemner, & De Gelder, 2007), and whether such muscle activity contributes to emotional convergence. In a series of experiments, Hawk and colleagues demonstrated that listening to others' discrete emotion vocalizations activates the same facial behaviors and subjective states that are involved in producing similar sounds oneself, and that cross-channel facial simulations of others' discrete emotion vocalizations are involved in processing these sounds and producing concordant emotional experiences.

Interestingly, even though primitive emotional contagion by definition occurs automatically and nonconsciously, the fact that emotions tend to spread between individuals appears to be well known. Consider the following lyrics by Louis Armstrong:

> *When you're smiling ... when you're smiling*
> *the whole world smiles with you*
> *When you're laughing ... when you're laughing*
> *the sun comes shining through*
>
> *But when you're crying ... you bring on the rain*
> *So stop your sighing ... and be happy again*
> *Yes, keep on smiling ... keep on smiling*
> *and the whole world smiles with you*

We all share such experiences, whether with positive or with negative emotions, and there appears to be considerable implicit awareness of the phenomenon of emotional contagion (although perhaps not of its mechanisms). Besides examples from popular culture, there is scientific evidence that people are aware of the occurrence of emotional contagion effects. Hendriks and Vingerhoets (2006) asked participants how they expected to feel if they were to meet other individuals showing various facial emotional expressions. Participants who imagined interacting with a crying person were more likely to anticipate experiencing sadness themselves than were participants who anticipated interacting with an angry, fearful, or emotionally neutral individual. This further underscores the fact that emotional contagion in the broader nonprimitive sense does not have to occur nonconsciously, something that was acknowledged early on by Hatfield and colleagues (1992, 1994) but that has been overlooked in much later research (also see Hess & Fischer, 2013). This is important, because it indicates that emotional contagion is a more encompassing phenomenon than it is often portrayed to be.

In short, there appears to be considerable flexibility in the motoric and affective systems involved in interpersonal emotion transfer (Hawk et al., 2012). Emotional contagion may occur consciously or nonconsciously, and it may involve mimicry and feedback processes, within- or cross-channel simulation, social appraisal, and/or deliberate perspective taking. This flexibility points to the possibility that various processes of emotional contagion have evolved to facilitate emotional transfer and understanding in diverse settings that may be conducive to different types of emotional convergence (e.g., facial mimicry is more effective in face-to-face interaction, while cross-channel mimicry is more effective when people are within hearing distance but cannot see each other's faces; Hawk, Van Kleef, Fischer, & Van der Schalk, 2009).

Complementary affective reactions: different yet matching feeling states

The EASI framework recognizes that, besides the reciprocal emotional experiences that may come about via emotional contagion and related processes, emotional expressions can also arouse complementary emotional experiences in observers. That is, individuals may respond with particular patterns of emotional expressions and experiences that are different from those displayed by the expresser yet match those expressions in terms of their meaning and motivational implications. For instance, expressions of sadness and distress may elicit sympathy (Batson et al., 1987; Eisenberg, 2000) or compassion (Van Kleef et al., 2008) in observers, expressions of anger may elicit fear (Dimberg & Öhman, 1996; Moody et al., 2007), and expressions of disappointment may elicit guilt (Lelieveld, Van Dijk, Van Beest, & Van Kleef, 2012, 2013). Although research on complementary emotional reactions is relatively scarce (compared to the abundance of studies on reciprocal emotional responses), there is evidence for the incidence and functionality of complementary emotional reactions.

Building on the assumption that the intricate facial musculature of human and nonhuman primates has evolved to produce expressions that signal information about the expresser's emotional state and/or social intentions (see Chapter 2), Dimberg and Öhman (1996) argued that people should exhibit a tendency to spontaneously react with specific emotional responses to particular facial expressions to facilitate understanding, communication, and behavioral adjustment. Besides support for reciprocal emotional expressions and experiences, Dimberg (1988) reported evidence that angry faces evoke more fear in observers than happy faces – a finding that fits well with an evolutionary account of human emotional expression. People who are disposed to experience a certain degree of fear when confronted with others' expressions of anger may be more likely to avoid potentially dangerous encounters.

Another type of complementary emotional response that may be highly functional for social adaptation occurs when observers experience sympathy, concern, or compassion when confronted with the emotional suffering of another person (Batson et al., 1987). As is the case with reciprocal affective reactions, such complementary affective reactions can emerge either relatively automatically (e.g., as conditioned responses) or as a result of more conscious processes such as cognitive perspective taking (Eisenberg, 2000). Several studies have shown that expressions of sadness, worry, and fear can elicit sympathetic emotions in observers, which may in turn motivate supportive responses (Eisenberg et al., 1989; Kennedy-Moore & Watson, 2001). Such complementary emotional responses and concomitant behavioral tendencies can be highly functional for the quality of social relationships (Côté, 2005; Keltner & Haidt, 1999). For instance, Van Kleef and colleagues (2008) found that strangers who were instructed to disclose episodes of emotional suffering felt more understood and appreciated and expressed a greater desire to befriend their conversation partner when the partner showed more signs of compassion in response to their suffering than when the partner exhibited less compassion.

Downstream consequences of affective reactions

The feeling states that result from exposure to other people's emotions have downstream consequences for observers' cognitions, motivations, and behaviors (Van Kleef, De Dreu, & Manstead, 2010). Cognitive effects can come about via various types of "affect infusion" (Forgas, 1995). For instance, according to the affect-as-information model (Schwarz & Clore, 1983), individuals may (mis)attribute their current affective state to the situation at hand, using their feelings as input to their social judgments and decisions – a "how do I feel about it?" heuristic (Schwarz & Clore, 1988; cf. Martin, Ward, Achee, & Wyer's [1993] mood-as-input model). Thus, if a traveler in a train catches a stranger's happiness and thereby comes to experience reciprocal positive feelings, she may judge the stranger and/or the situation as benign, which may facilitate mutual trust, understanding, and benevolence. Conversely, if she picks up a fellow traveler's irritability, she may judge the situation and the other traveler more negatively, possibly resulting in less constructive behavioral responses.

Affective reactions to the emotional expressions of others may also influence judgment and behavior by modulating an individual's representation of the object of judgment. According to affect-priming models (Bower, 1981; Forgas & Bower, 1987; Isen, 1987; Isen, Shalker, Clark, & Karp, 1978; Singer & Salovey, 1988), affective states selectively prime related concepts and memories that are part of an associative network, which facilitates their accessibility when making subsequent judgments and decisions. A good mood temporarily increases the likelihood that positive cognitions will be generated in response to subsequent stimuli, whereas a bad mood increases the accessibility of negative cognitions. Thus, if our traveler catches a fellow traveler's joy, she may begin to selectively focus on positive aspects of that person and/or the situation, which may fuel prosocial tendencies. Conversely, if she picks up a stranger's grumpiness, the increased salience of negative concepts may contribute to a more adversarial inclination toward that person.

It is also possible for the positive or negative valence of an emotional expression to become directly associated with a stimulus via evaluative conditioning (De Houwer, Thomas, & Baeyens, 2001). In this type of process an emotional expression can come to serve as the unconditioned stimulus that changes the subjective valence of a previously neutral conditioned stimulus. Such conditioning can theoretically be established with any object, concept, or person. Thus, our traveler may come to associate the stranger's joy or irritability with traveling by train, respectively resulting in a more positive or more negative attitude toward public transportation. Furthermore, the traveler may come to associate the stranger's emotional expressions with the stranger himself, which may in turn influence her impressions of the stranger. It is well established that joyful expressions generally inspire positive impressions in observers, whereas angry expressions engender negative impressions (Clark & Taraban, 1991). It is conceivable that such impressions are due in part to evaluative conditioning. Moreover, the impressions that people develop of others based on their emotional expressions may in turn shape social behavior. Thus, the traveler may be more willing to help the smiling stranger than the grumpy stranger, because the former instigates a more favorable impression, and people tend to be more willing to help others whom they like (Clark, Pataki, & Carver, 1996).

Besides the cognitive mechanisms of affect-as-information, affect priming, and evaluative conditioning, the emotions that individuals pick up from others can influence social judgment and behavior through more motivational processes of mood maintenance and negative state relief. The core assumption in this type of model is that people strive to promote and maintain positive mood states and to avoid experiencing negative mood states (Carlson, Charlin, & Miller, 1988). This fundamental desire motivates people in a negative mood to engage in behaviors associated with positive feelings (e.g., helping others) in order to relieve their negative feeling state (Schaller & Cialdini, 1988). Likewise, individuals in a positive mood are motivated to exhibit behaviors that produce positive feelings and to abstain from activities that entail the risk of spoiling the good mood (i.e., positive mood maintenance; Wegener & Petty, 1994). This means that when our traveler encounters a cheerful stranger, she may catch the stranger's happiness and become motivated to maintain the positive feeling by acting in a friendly and generous way. Alternatively, when the other expresses sadness, the traveler's mood may drop and she may become motivated to relieve herself of the negative feeling, for instance by engaging in some form of prosocial behavior (Van Kleef, De Dreu, & Manstead, 2010).

Finally, judgment and behavior may be influenced by complementary affective reactions to the emotional expressions of others. For instance, as indicated above, expressions of anger on the part of one individual may induce a sense of fear in another person (Dimberg & Öhman, 1996; Moody et al., 2007), which may in turn motivate that person to avoid interactions with the angry individual. As another example, expressions of sadness of one individual may induce feelings of compassion in another (Van Kleef et al., 2008), and such feelings may in turn motivate consolation and helping behavior in both children (Barnett, Howard, Melton, & Dino, 1982) and adults (Clark, Ouellette, Powell, & Milberg, 1987; Yee & Greenberg, 1998). In a similar vein, crying has been found to elicit helping (Cornelius, 1984; Hendriks, Croos, & Vingerhoets, 2008; cf. Labott, Martin, Eason, & Berkey, 1991). It seems plausible that complementary emotions of concern and compassion play a role in motivating such behavior.

In sum, a person's affective reactions to the emotional expressions of another individual may afford insight into the expresser and the situation by informing the observer's understanding of the other's emotional state (Keltner & Haidt, 1999). Thus, individuals may gain information about other people by monitoring their own affective reactions to the emotions of others, a method that is often practiced in psychotherapy (Hsee, Hatfield, & Chemtob, 1992). Moreover, an observer's reciprocal or complementary affective reactions to another person's emotional expressions may have downstream consequences for the observer's cognitions, attitudes, motivations, and actions vis-à-vis that person.

Proposition 4: Emotional expressions elicit reciprocal and complementary affective reactions in observers, which in turn inform observers' behavioral responses.

Emotional expressions elicit inferential processes in observers

EASI theory posits that observers can also glean information from others' emotional expressions via a more deliberate and cognitively effortful process, namely through the act of drawing inferences from another person's emotional expressions (Van Kleef, 2009). Specific emotions arise in response to appraisals of specific situations (Frijda, 1986; Lazarus, 1991). Because discrete emotions have such distinct appraisal patterns (Manstead & Tetlock, 1989; Smith, Haynes, Lazarus, & Pope, 1993), they provide a wealth of information to observers (Hareli & Hess, 2010; Keltner & Haidt, 1999; Van Kleef, 2009). For instance, emotional expressions may convey information about the inner states of the expresser (Ekman, 1993), his or her social intentions (Fridlund, 1994), and his or her orientation toward other people (Ames & Johar, 2009; Hess, Blairy, & Kleck, 2000; Knutson, 1996). In addition, emotional expressions inform observers about the expresser's appraisal of the situation (Manstead & Fischer, 2001). Weisbuch and Adams (2012) further suggested that emotional expressions function as forecasts of relevant impending events, which may in turn inform observers' responses.

The exact implications of an emotional display vary as a function of the situation, but the basic informational value of discrete emotions generalizes across situations (Van Kleef, 2009). For instance, according to appraisal theories (e.g., Frijda, 1986; Ortony, Clore, & Collins, 1988; Roseman, 1984; Scherer, Schorr, & Johnstone, 2001; Smith et al., 1993), anger arises when a person's goals are being frustrated and she or he blames someone else for it. Expressions of anger therefore signal appraisals of goal blockage and other blame. Conversely, happiness arises when goals have been met (or good progress is being made toward attaining them) and expectations are positive. Expressions of happiness therefore signal that the environment is appraised as favorable and benign. Guilt arises when a person feels that she/he has transgressed some social norm or moral imperative. Expressions of guilt therefore signal that one is aware of (and possibly troubled by) one's misdemeanor. Sadness arises when one faces an irrevocable loss and experiences low coping potential. Expressions of sadness therefore signal lack of control and helplessness. By the same logic, expressions of fear signal that there is something potentially threatening to a situation, expressions of pride signal that the expresser feels superior in some way, expressions of hope signal that there may be potential for favorable outcomes, expressions of disappointment signal that the expresser had expected a more favorable outcome or situation than she is currently facing, and so forth.

Individuals may thus distill useful pieces of information from others' emotional expressions. For instance, when one is the target of a colleague's anger, one may infer that one did something wrong, and this inference may in turn inform one's behavior (e.g., apologizing, changing one's conduct). When confronted with a sports coach's happiness, an athlete may conclude that things are going well, which may lead her to stay the course. When one's partner shows guilt after making a faux pas, one may infer that the partner cares about the relationship and is willing to make up for the mistake. And when confronted with a friend's sadness,

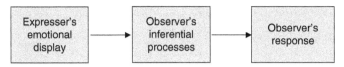

Figure 3.2   Inferential processes as a mediating mechanism between one person's emotional expression and another person's response.

one might infer that he faces a painful loss and experiences low coping potential, which may lead one to offer help or consolation. In short, besides affective reactions, inferential processes are a second mechanism underlying the social effects of emotional expressions (see Figure 3.2).

Despite the intuitive plausibility of the idea that individuals may infer relevant pieces of information from the emotional expressions of others, it is less clear at this point exactly how such inferences are drawn. There appears to be some consensus in the literature that people may access information about others by thinking consciously about the meaning and implications of their emotional expressions (Hareli, 2014; Hareli & Hess, 2010; Manstead & Fischer, 2001; Parkinson & Simons, 2009; Van Kleef, 2009). EASI theory maintains that such deliberate inferential processes depend on the individual's ability and motivation to engage in effortful information processing (Van Kleef, De Dreu, & Manstead, 2010; see Chapter 4). In line with this idea, neuroscientific evidence indicates that the neural processing of emotional expressions requires a certain degree of attention. One study showed that all brain regions that respond differentially to emotional versus nonemotional faces did so only when sufficient cognitive resources were available to process the faces (Pessoa, McKenna, Gutierrez, & Ungerleider, 2002). Another study found that the interpretation of others' emotions relies on cortical brain structures that are involved more generally in mental state attributions (Ochsner et al., 2004). Participants who were asked to judge others' emotional expressions showed increased activation in the medial prefrontal cortex, the medial occipital cortex, and the left lateral prefrontal cortex, which also includes Broca's area (a structure that plays a critical role in producing speech). These patterns suggest that developing an understanding of the emotions of others requires a fair amount of cognitive processing and perhaps a degree of conscious internal verbalization, although a crude understanding of the nonspecific implications of others' emotional expressions in terms of imminent threats and opportunities may require less conscious attention and cognitive processing (Weisbuch & Adams, 2012).

Social appraisal, reverse appraisal, and access to emotion knowledge

Drawing on appraisal theories (see Scherer et al., 2001), various authors have proposed that people extract information from the emotional expressions of another person about how that person is appraising the current situation. From this information they may then draw inferences regarding the expresser's personality, social motives, and intentions, which in turn inform their own behavior. This process has been variously referred to as "tracking" (Van Kleef et al., 2004a), "backtracking" (Elfenbein, 2007), "reverse engineering appraisals" (Hareli & Hess, 2010), "reverse appraisal" (de Melo, Carnevale, & Gratch, 2011), and "situation-oriented social appraisal" (Bruder, Fischer, & Manstead, 2014).

A number of studies provide support for the role of such processes in shaping responses to others' emotional expressions (e.g., Bayliss, Frischen, Fenske, & Tipper, 2007; de Melo, Carnevale, Read, & Gratch, 2014; Hareli & Hess, 2010; Parkinson, Phiri, & Simons, 2012; Scherer & Grandjean, 2008; also see Kaiser & Wehrle, 2001). Extending classic appraisal theories to the interpersonal domain, Scherer and Grandjean hypothesized that emotional expressions allow observers to infer information about all components of the emotion process the expresser is experiencing, including his or her felt emotions, appraisals, social appeals, and action tendencies. Participants in their study were asked to judge facial expressions of emotions from pictures on a number of dimensions. The authors found that judgments of experienced emotions yielded the highest accuracy scores, followed by inferences of appraisals. Inferred information regarding social appeals and action tendencies showed comparatively lower accuracy rates, and participants were less confident of these ratings than they were of their ratings of felt emotions and appraisals. This study suggests that appraisals can indeed be reliably inferred on the basis of emotional expressions.

In another study, Hareli and Hess (2010) investigated how people use the emotional expressions of others to arrive at inferences concerning their personality. They proposed that individuals reconstruct or "reverse engineer" the appraisals underlying another person's emotional reaction. As they put it, "people infer from the way an individual reacted in a given situation how that individual must have perceived the situation and use this inference to reach conclusions about that person's character" (p. 137). In a person perception study, the authors obtained evidence that the impact of an actor's emotional expressions on personality inferences were indeed, in some cases, mediated by appraisals. For instance, a person who reacted with anger in a particular situation was perceived as more aggressive than a person who remained emotionally neutral in the same situation, and this effect was mediated by participants' judgments of how the person appraised the situation (in this case, in terms of urgency).

Along similar lines, another study demonstrated that individuals may use others' emotional expressions to make sense of ambiguous situations, in particular to arrive at attributions of agency and responsibility. Consistent with the logic of reverse appraisal, individuals who witnessed expressions of regret in the context of an adverse situation inferred that the expresser was responsible for the situation, whereas those who observed expressions of anger inferred that another person was responsible (Van Doorn, Van Kleef, & Van der Pligt, 2015a). These findings indicate that emotional expressions can help people make sense of situations by informing attributions that correspond with the emotion's associated appraisal structure (e.g., self-blame for regret and other-blame for anger).

Perhaps the strongest support for a causal role of reverse appraisals in shaping responses to emotional expressions comes from a recent series of experiments by de Melo and colleagues (2014), who examined the effects of emotional expressions in the context of social decision making. In a first experiment, they tested the idea that the underlying information that is communicated by an emotional expression is more critical for the social effects of emotions than the emotional expression itself. In support of this assertion, the authors found that the same emotional displays had opposite consequences for behavior in a prisoner's dilemma depending on the cooperative versus competitive context in which they were shown, suggesting that it is the interpretation of another person's emotion in light of the social context that drives behavioral responses rather than the emotion per se (for a similar argument and findings, see Fischer, Manstead, & Zaalberg, 2003; Lanzetta & Englis, 1989; Van Kleef, De Dreu, & Manstead, 2010).

In a second study, de Melo and colleagues (2014) showed that textual information about another person's appraisals (e.g., "I like this outcome") had similar effects on expectations of cooperation as did corresponding facial displays of emotion (e.g., happiness). Follow-up studies further revealed the content of the appraisals observers distilled from others' emotional expressions in the context of interdependent decision making. Consistent with a reverse-appraisal framework, expressions of happiness were interpreted as a sign that the outcome was conducive to the expresser's goals, sadness was interpreted as a signal of goal obstruction, anger was interpreted as reflecting an appraisal of goal obstruction combined with other blame, and regret was perceived as a sign of goal obstruction combined with self-blame. Finally, the authors showed that these appraisals (partially or fully) mediated the effects of the emotional displays on participants' social decision making.

Such processes of reverse appraisal evidently rely on the emotion knowledge of individuals who observe another person's emotional expressions (an issue that will be discussed in greater depth in Chapter 4 in relation to emotional intelligence). If someone does not understand what kind of eliciting events may trigger anger, happiness, disappointment, regret, or any other emotion, it will be difficult for him or her to reverse engineer the appraisals that produced an expresser's emotions. In normally developing individuals, emotion knowledge is acquired through direct or indirect socialization (Fischer et al., 2003). Thus individuals learn how people generally react to particular emotional events, how they express their emotions, and what such expressions reveal (Shaver, Schwartz, Kirson, & O'Connor, 1987).

To the degree that such emotion knowledge is well learned and firmly embedded within individuals' mental representations of the associations among precipitating events, appraisal patterns, and emotional responses, individuals may be able to quickly access relevant information from associations stored in long-term memory when confronted with another person's emotional expressions. This implies that the act of drawing inferences from emotional expressions becomes less effortful to the degree that the relevant associations are well learned. This may be the case, for instance, when one is very familiar with the specific situation at hand and with the emotions it may trigger or when one knows the person expressing the emotion very well. In contrast, when the situation and/or the expresser is unfamiliar, more cognitive effort may be needed to retrieve information from memory, and inferences regarding the expresser's appraisals, motives, and intentions may be paired with a greater degree of uncertainty.

Downstream consequences of inferential processes

The information observers distill from others' emotional expressions via inferential processing may in turn influence their behavior. What form this influence takes depends on the situation (Van Kleef, De Dreu, & Manstead, 2010). Suppose a job candidate expresses disappointment upon hearing the potential employer's salary proposal. The employer may infer from the candidate's disappointment that she had expected a higher starting salary. This information may lead the prospective employer to increase the offer if he is eager to recruit the candidate, but the information may be ignored (or even prompt the employer to consider other options) if other suitable candidates are willing to accept the proposed starting wage.

Although several personality and situational variables may influence how an observer decides to act upon the information he or she has obtained from another person's emotional expressions, perhaps the most pervasive factor is the nature of the relationship between the expresser and the observer. EASI theory posits that behavioral consequences of inferential processes are shaped by the degree and nature of the perceived interdependence between the expresser and the observer. In the relatively rare event that individuals' outcomes are perceived as being in no way related to one another (i.e., pure independence), any information an observer may infer from the emotional expressions of another person is most likely to be ignored and will have no downstream consequences for behavior (as when the employer in the previous example decides to shift his attention to another candidate). More often, however, individuals in social interaction experience at least some degree of interdependence (Kelley & Thibaut, 1978; Rusbult & Van Lange, 2003).

Perceived interdependence is shaped to an important extent by features of the situation. Although most social situations contain a mixture of cooperative and competitive elements (Deutsch, 1973; Komorita & Parks, 1995; Schelling, 1960), some situations offer comparatively more cooperative than competitive incentives and thereby drive people toward cooperation; other situations offer more competitive than cooperative incentives and predispose individuals toward competition (Kelley et al., 2003; Rusbult & Van Lange, 2003; Weber, Kopelman, & Messick, 2004). For instance, friends planning a joint vacation, players in a soccer team, and colleagues working on an advertisement campaign may be expected to experience a degree of positive interdependence because they presumably share at least one important goal (i.e., having a nice vacation, winning a game, or developing a high-quality campaign). In other words, their relationship is likely to be predominantly cooperative: All can achieve their goals at the same time, and one person's success also implies success for the other. In contrast, a buyer and a seller negotiating the sale of a second-hand car, opposing politicians in a public debate, and two boxers preparing for the final game of a tournament find themselves in situations of negative interdependence. Their relationship is predominantly competitive, because one can only be successful at the expense of the other.

In addition to actual features of the situation, the perceived cooperativeness versus competitiveness of situations is shaped by chronic dispositional tendencies. Due to temperament or socialization, some individuals are more likely to emphasize the cooperative elements of a situation and to de-emphasize or ignore competitive incentives, whereas other individuals are more inclined to emphasize competitive rather than cooperative aspects of a situation (Carnevale & Pruitt, 1992; De Dreu, Beersma, Steinel, & Van Kleef, 2007; Deutsch, 1973; Komorita & Parks, 1995; Rusbult & Van Lange, 2003; Van Kleef & De Dreu, 2002). Thus, one and the same social situation may be perceived and interpreted quite differently in terms of cooperative versus competitive interdependence.

Perceived cooperative versus competitive interdependence influences how information conveyed through emotional expressions translates into behavior (Van Kleef, De Dreu, & Manstead, 2010). Consider the example of happiness. In cooperative settings, where parties' goals are positively correlated, one party's happiness implies that the other also has reason to be happy. Thus, in cooperative settings, the information that is conveyed by expressions of happiness (e.g., that things are going well for the expresser) is likely to elicit cooperative behavior in interaction partners. By contrast, in competitive settings, a partner's happiness may be taken as a sign that the other is gaining at one's own expense (Lanzetta & Englis, 1989), which may motivate competitive behavior. As another example, in cooperative situations displays of "appeasement" emotions such as guilt or regret may contribute to the quality of relationships by signaling remorse and caring and a promise of better behavior in the future (Baumeister, Stillwell, & Heatherton, 1994). As such, appeasement emotions can be expected to reduce destructive tendencies that might otherwise arise due to a social transgression. In competitive settings, by contrast, appeasement emotions may invite competition and exploitation. Because such emotions signal that the transgressor is willing to make amends, competitors may seek to exploit the situation to further their own goals (Van Kleef, De Dreu, & Manstead, 2010).

Proposition 5: Observers of emotional expressions may extract information from these expressions about the expresser's appraisal of and orientation vis-à-vis the situation and the people involved, which in turn shapes observers' behavioral responses to the emotional expressions.

The relationship between affective reactions and inferential processes

Affective reactions and inferential processes are the two key mechanisms that drive the social effects of emotional expressions according to EASI theory. It is important to note that the two processes are not always perfectly orthogonal, because under particular circumstances, the activation of one process may influence the other. For instance, affective states may influence information-processing depth (Schwarz, Bless, & Bohner, 1991) and thereby modulate inferential processes, and inferential processes may to some extent shape emotional reactions to the emotions of others (e.g., when one realizes that another person's anger is unfair, stronger negative emotional reactions may arise than if the anger were perceived as reasonable; Van Kleef & Côté, 2007).

Despite this potential for mutual influence, there are good reasons for distinguishing between affective reactions and inferential processes (Van Kleef et al., 2011). First, the two processes are clearly distinguishable theoretically, in the sense that one belongs to the family of cognitive processes and the other to the family of affective processes (cf. Zajonc, 1980). Affective processes and cognitive processes are regulated in different areas of the brain (e.g., the amygdala and the prefrontal cortex, respectively), even though there is also evidence of functional interaction between these areas (Salzman & Fusi, 2010). LeDoux (1998) proposed that "emotion and cognition are best thought of as separate but interacting mental functions mediated by separate but interacting brain systems" (p. 69). The separation of affective reactions and inferential processes in EASI theory is consistent with this position.

Second, there is a long and rich tradition in social and cognitive psychology of dual-process models that distinguish between responses to stimuli (e.g., persuasive messages) that are based primarily on thorough deliberation versus responses that are based on shallower heuristic, affective, or experiential processes. Influential examples are the elaboration-likelihood model (Petty & Cacioppo, 1986) and the heuristic-systematic model (Chaiken, 1980), among others (for reviews, see Chaiken & Trope, 1999; Evans, 2008). EASI theory extends this dual-process tradition by distinguishing between inferential processes and affective reactions to expressions of emotion.

Third, there is ample empirical evidence that affective reactions and inferential processes can be measured separately. As we will see in Part II of this book, affective reactions are typically operationalized in terms of moods, emotions, and sentiments toward the expresser of an emotion. Inferential processes are operationalized in terms of the information observers distill from others' emotional expressions and the conclusions and implications they infer from these expressions. These inferences often take the form of reverse appraisals (de Melo et al., 2011; Hareli & Hess, 2010), whereby observers use their emotion knowledge to infer from another person's emotional expressions what has happened to that person and what their own role in the situation is. For instance, based on the fact that anger often arises in response to perceived injustice, an observer may infer from another person's expressions of anger that that person feels unjustly treated, and if the anger is directed at the observer personally, that he or she is seen as the cause of the injustice. Reflecting this important conceptual distinction, affective reactions and inferential processes vary largely independently of one another, and they have distinct effects on people's behavioral responses to others' emotional expressions (Van Kleef et al., 2011). The processes involved in

Table 3.1 Processes involved in producing the social effects of emotions

	Affective Reactions	Inferential Processes
Main Types	Reciprocal affective states (e.g., anger→anger, sadness→sadness)	Inferences regarding the expresser's appraisal of the situation
	Complementary affective states (e.g., anger→fear, sadness→compassion)	Inferences regarding the expresser's personality
	Associated sentiments (e.g., likes and dislikes)	Inferences regarding the expresser's social motives and intentions
Eliciting Processes	Emotional contagion	Reverse appraisal
	Perspective taking	Accessing emotion knowledge
	Social appraisal	Social appraisal
	Embodiment	
Downstream Processes	Behavioral tendencies are shaped by affect infusion (e.g., affect-as-information, affect priming), evaluative conditioning, mood management motives, and likes and dislikes	Inferences regarding expresser and/or situation inform behavioral tendencies

shaping the social effects of emotional expressions are summarized in Table 3.1.

In some cases inferences and affective reactions lead to the same behavior. For example, the distress of a significant other signals that she is going through tough times and is experiencing difficulty coping with the situation (inferences) but also triggers mutual concern and compassion (affective reactions), both of which foster supportive behavior (Clark et al., 1996). In other cases, however, inferences and affective reactions motivate opposite behaviors. To return to the earlier example, a colleague's angry remark about one's delay may instigate reciprocal feelings of anger and antipathy (affective reactions), which may motivate destructive behavioral responses, but the colleague's anger may also lead one to realize that it is indeed annoying to come late to a meeting (inference), which may motivate one to be on time on the next occasion. Which process takes precedence in guiding behavioral responses to another's emotional expressions depends on a number of factors that are addressed in the next chapter.

Proposition 6: Affective reactions and inferential processes have mutually influential yet conceptually distinct and empirically separable effects on observers' behavioral responses to others' emotional expressions.

Conclusion

Building on and integrating previous lines of theorizing and research, EASI theory posits that emotional expressions bring about social effects by triggering affective reactions and/or inferential processes in observers. Affective reactions may take the form of reciprocal or complementary affective states and associated sentiments, which can come about via emotional contagion, perspective taking, embodiment, social appraisal, and/or evaluative conditioning. The resulting affective states may in turn produce downstream (behavioral) consequences via various cognitive affect infusion processes (e.g., affect-as-information, affect priming) as well as motivational processes of mood maintenance and negative state relief. Affective reactions can also take the form of sentiments such as likes or dislikes, which may motivate prosocial versus antisocial behavioral tendencies, respectively. Inferential processes involve more or less conscious acts of "reverse appraising" the emotional expressions of another person to arrive at inferences regarding how that person relates to the situation, which requires a certain amount of emotion knowledge and emotional understanding. The resulting inferences in turn inform behavior. Given that affective reactions and inferential processes often motivate different behavioral responses, a key challenge lies in understanding when one or the other process is prioritized. This question is addressed in the following chapter.

CHAPTER 4

Contingencies of the social effects of emotions

> Anyone can become angry – that is easy. But to be angry with the right person, to the right degree, at the right time, for the right purpose, and in the right way – that is not easy.
>
> Aristotle (350 BCE/2004)

Social-functional accounts of emotion postulate that emotional expressions play a vital role in regulating social interaction (e.g., Fischer & Manstead, in press; Frijda & Mesquita, 1994; Keltner & Haidt, 1999; Parkinson, 1996; Van Kleef, 2009). An implicit assumption underlying such accounts is that people accurately perceive others' emotions. No matter how informative emotions may be, and however critical their social-regulatory functions, if emotions are not expressed and/or fail to be perceived by others, their signaling function is evidently lost and social interaction may be jeopardized. If a former colleague does not express her disappointment about me missing her farewell party due to illness, I may erroneously conclude that she didn't mind my absence and, perhaps, that our relationship wasn't that close after all. And even if my colleague does express her disappointment I may fail to pick up on it, thereby potentially reaching the same misguided conclusion. Thus, logically, for any emotion to have potential social consequences, it must be expressed to and perceived by one or more other individuals. In this chapter I first consider factors that influence the encoding and decoding of emotional expressions, which may be conceived as general preconditions for any social effects of emotions to occur. Next I discuss factors that determine the relative influence of affective reactions and inferential processes in shaping the social effects of emotions.

General prerequisites for the social effects of emotions

The example above illustrates that the social functionality of emotions is undermined when there is noise on the line. Emotions that are felt may not be expressed, or they may be expressed in ways that deliberately or inadvertently alter the information they convey. Furthermore, emotions that are expressed as intended may be lost on observers who lack the attention or skill to accurately perceive and interpret the message. Generally speaking, then, emotional communication may be hampered by failure in the encoding stage and/or in the decoding stage. Besides the various physical conditions and psychopathologies discussed in Chapter 2, emotional communication is affected by subclinical variations in emotional expressivity (encoding) and emotion perception ability (decoding).

Encoding: the role of emotional expressivity

The first general precondition for any social effects of emotions is that the emotion be expressed in one way or another, be it through facial expressions, tone of voice, bodily postures, written or spoken words, and/or use of symbols such as emoticons. Even though people have a tendency to express the emotions they feel in one way or another, they do so to various degrees. At one extreme, experienced emotions may be expressed in an uncensored way, so that externally observable signs of emotion provide full insight into the individual's feelings. At the other extreme, individuals may completely suppress the expression of any experienced emotion, so that their nonverbal or verbal expressions provide no clues whatsoever as to their internal feeling states. Emotional expressivity is guided in part by implicit or explicit rules and scripts that may vary across situations (e.g., gender roles, organizational norms, and cultural customs and expectations; Ekman, 1993; Manstead, 1991), an issue I return to later in this chapter in relation to the appropriateness of emotional expressions. In addition, emotional expressivity varies as a function of chronic individual differences (Gross & John, 1997; Kring, Smith, & Neale, 1994). Thus, two people who feel equally angry may show their anger to very different degrees, depending on temperament and demands of the social context.

It seems obvious that people who express their emotions in more outwardly visible ways provide more relevant social information to others in their social environment than do individuals who hold back on their emotional expressions. Still, this notion is important from the perspective of a social-functional account of emotion. It implies that, other things being equal, people who interact with more emotionally expressive others should gain better insight into those others' needs, desires, goals, and intentions. Accordingly, emotional expressivity may contribute to mutual trust and cooperation (Boone & Buck, 2003). Furthermore, people who obtain a richer insight into the internal states of other individuals should be able to respond more appropriately to others' needs and expectations, thus contributing to smoother social interactions. In line with this idea, a study by Butler and colleagues (2003) showed that explicit instructions to suppress the expression of any felt emotions during face-to-face conversations increased levels of stress of both conversation partners, reduced rapport, and inhibited friendship formation.

Research in developmental psychology also points to the importance of emotional expressivity for well-adjusted social relationships. For instance, parental emotional expressivity has been linked to children's social-emotional competence (Boyum & Parke, 1995; Denham, Zoller, & Couchoud, 1994) and social adjustment (Bronstein, Fitzgerald, Briones, Pieniadz, & D'Ari, 1993). Moreover, parental expressivity has been associated with the quality of parent–child relationships (Eisenberg, Cumberland, & Spinrad, 1998), although effects are more consistent for positive expressivity than for negative expressivity (Eisenberg et al., 2001). These findings indicate that successful social communication requires skillful expression of emotion (Côté & Hideg, 2011). For emotions to have any social-communicative functionality, they must be expressed in ways that make them potentially observable by others.

Decoding: emotional intelligence and emotion perception ability

The second general prerequisite for any social effects of emotions to occur is that the emotional expressions be perceived by one or more others. Although this seems self-evident, it is important to briefly consider this notion in relation to the presumed social functions of emotions. Theoretical perspectives on the social effects and/or functions of emotions hinge on the implicit or explicit assumption that people perceive one another's emotional states, yet individuals vary in their ability to accurately recognize and interpret their own and others' emotions. Besides the clinical conditions discussed in Chapter 2, emotion perception ability is shaped by individual differences in emotional intelligence, which is defined as "the ability to monitor one's own and others' feelings, to discriminate among them, and to use this information to guide one's thinking and action" (Salovey & Mayer, 1990, p. 189). The influential four-branch ability model of emotional intelligence identifies four critical emotional abilities: to accurately perceive emotions in oneself and others, to use emotions to facilitate thinking, to understand emotional meanings, and to manage emotions (Mayer & Salovey, 1997). Two of these four branches (perception and understanding) are directly relevant to the decoding of emotional expressions.

Branch 1 in the ability model of emotional intelligence denotes basic emotion perception capability. It involves the capacity to recognize emotions from others' facial, vocal, and postural expressions (Mayer, Salovey, & Caruso, 2004). Perceiving emotions can be said to represent the most fundamental aspect of emotional intelligence, in the sense that it makes all subsequent processing of emotional information possible (Salovey & Grewal, 2005). Accurate perception of the emotions of other people is vital to adequate social responding. Indeed, decoding of emotional expressions has been identified as an important factor in the successful negotiation of interpersonal relationships (Elfenbein, Foo, White, Tan, & Aik, 2007). Moreover, emotional intelligence (and concomitant emotion perception ability) is a significant predictor of relationship quality (Lopes et al., 2004; Lopes, Salovey, & Straus, 2003; Malouff, Schutte, & Thorsteinsson, 2014).

Branch 3 in the four-branch model refers to emotional understanding, which directly relates to a central theme of this book – that emotions convey information. Although work on emotional intelligence has typically stressed the importance of understanding, analyzing, and reflecting on one's own emotions (Mayer et al., 2004), emotional understanding clearly is also critical for appreciating the emotions of others. Indeed, comprehending emotion language is part of emotional understanding (Salovey & Grewal, 2005). Moreover, comprehending where one's own emotions come from and how they develop over time probably informs an understanding of the antecedents, meaning, and implications of the emotions of others – an understanding that is vital to well-adjusted social relationships and general life success. In line with this idea, research has shown that the ability to understand emotions predicts leadership emergence in groups (Côté, Lopes, Salovey, & Miners, 2010).

In sum, emotions can only be expected to bring about social consequences when they are both successfully encoded by the sender and successfully decoded by the receiver, as determined by the sender's expressive tendencies and the receiver's emotion perception and understanding. Furthermore, it is conceivable that characteristics of sender and receiver interact to shape the success or failure of emotional communication. In this respect, Planalp (1999) proposed that emotional communication is likely to be more successful to the degree that the emotional expressivity of the sender and the emotional expressivity of the perceiver match. She suggested that an inexpressive person listening to a highly expressive person is akin to someone with a hearing aid turned up conversing with someone talking through a megaphone. The sender's emotional expression could easily come across as exaggerated, thus disrupting smooth interaction. Conversely, Planalp likened a highly expressive person listening to an inexpressive person to someone with her hearing aid turned down listening to someone whispering. In such a constellation, any emotional message from the sender could easily be missed by the receiver. In more general terms, it seems plausible that the expressive tendencies of the sender and the perceptive sensitivity of the receiver jointly determine the success of emotional communication.

Proposition 7: The informational value of emotions is more likely to be capitalized upon to the degree that emotions are (a) successfully encoded by the sender (as determined by the sender's emotional expressivity), (b) successfully decoded by the receiver (as determined by the receiver's emotion perception and understanding abilities), and (c) there is a match between the intensity of the sender's emotional expression and the receiver's perceptual sensitivity.

Factors shaping the impact of inferential processes and affective reactions

According to the Emotions as Social Information (EASI) theory, emotional expressions bring about social consequences by triggering affective reactions and/or inferential processes in observers. We have seen in Chapter 3 that affective reactions and inferential processes may fuel divergent social responses to the emotional displays of other people. For instance, expressions of anger may trigger intransigence or competition by evoking mutual feelings of hostility in others, or they may enforce compliance by signaling that the expresser is not prepared to take no for an answer. Displays of happiness may facilitate cooperation by eliciting reciprocal positive affect, or they may invite exploitation by signaling that the expresser is easygoing and willing to accommodate. Expressions of sadness or disappointment may elicit prosocial behavior by evoking feelings of compassion or empathic concern, or they may invite exploitation because they signal weakness (Van Kleef, De Dreu, & Manstead, 2010). In short, affective reactions and inferential processes often push people's behavior in different directions.

It is important to emphasize at this point that the influence of affective reactions and inferential processes is conceptualized in relative terms in the EASI framework (Van Kleef, Van Doorn, Heerdink, & Koning, 2011). Any given emotional expression may trigger a combination of affective reactions and inferential processes. In some cases, affective reactions and inferential processes may work in tandem to produce the same behavioral responses, such as when a close friend's distress evokes reciprocal distress and complementary compassion and at the same time signals that the friend is struggling to cope with a tough situation, both of which foster helping and consolation (Clark, Pataki, & Carver, 1996). In cases where affective and inferential processes motivate differential responses, however, as in the above examples, the social consequences of emotional expressions depend on the relative strength of the processes involved. To be able to understand and predict the interpersonal effects of emotions we must therefore identify factors that determine the relative impact of affective reactions versus inferential processes. EASI theory identifies two broad classes of moderating variables that shape the relative predictive power of these processes: the observer's information processing and the perceived appropriateness of the emotional display.

Information processing

Building on the idea that emotional expressions provide information, EASI theory postulates that the interpersonal effects of emotional expressions depend on observers' information-processing mode (Van Kleef, 2009). Dual-process models of human thinking and decision making maintain that individuals assess situations and render judgments either by means of quick, effortless, and heuristic information processing or through more effortful, deliberate, and systematic processing that involves rule-based inferences (Chaiken, 1980; Chaiken & Trope, 1999; Petty & Cacioppo, 1986; Smith & DeCoster, 2000). This has important implications for how individuals process the emotional expressions of others. Affective reactions are more immediate than inferences, and they require less cognitive processing (cf. Zajonc, 1980). This implies that affective reactions can occur even when individuals engage in shallow information processing, as long as they register the emotional expression. Inferential processes, in contrast, require a degree of cognitive deliberation. As discussed in the previous chapter, the amount of thought required to draw a particular inference from another person's emotional expression likely depends on how familiar the situation, the person, and the emotional expression are to the observer and whether the emotional expression's associated meanings are well learned and easily accessible from the observer's memory. Generally speaking, however, inferences require more information processing than affective reactions (Van Kleef, De Dreu, & Manstead, 2010).

It follows from the above that the predictive power of affective reactions relative to inferential processes should be greater to the degree that the observer of an emotional expression engages in shallower information processing. An observer in a relatively superficial information-processing mode can still pick up the emotions of others, because primitive emotional contagion is not mediated by conscious cognitive processes (Hatfield, Cacioppo, & Rapson, 1992; see Chapter 3), and the resulting affective state may in turn influence the observer's cognition and behavior (Forgas, 1995). The observer would be less likely to draw deliberate inferences from the other's emotional expressions, however, because this process requires conscious cognitive effort. By reverse logic, EASI theory posits that the relative predictive power of inferential processes increases to the extent that an observer engages in more thorough information processing (Van Kleef, 2009). This is not to say that affective reactions become irrelevant under conditions of thorough information processing. Rather, the *relative* influence of affective reactions on an observer's (behavioral) responses decreases as the influence of inferential processes increases.

An influential idea in theorizing on social cognition is that humans are "cognitive misers" who are motivated to employ their scarce mental-processing resources as economically as possible (Fiske & Taylor, 1991). Given the abundance of social information people encounter on an every-day basis, and given that their cognitive resources are limited, people are inclined to navigate the social world by relying on mental shortcuts and heuristics (Fiske, 1993; Tversky & Kahneman, 1974). Thorough informa-tion processing is effortful and cognitively taxing, and therefore indivi-duals only engage in it when there is a good reason to do so and when the required cognitive resources can be mobilized. In other words, systematic information processing requires both motivation and ability (Chaiken, 1980; Petty & Cacioppo, 1986).

Epistemic motivation
Thoroughness of information processing is influenced by an indivi-dual's *epistemic motivation*, that is, his or her willingness to expend effort to achieve a rich and accurate understanding of the world (Kruglanski, 1989). Such epistemic motivation is related to the perceived sufficiency of the information that is currently available to the individual (Chaiken, Liberman, & Eagly, 1989). The more a person feels that his or her current information and understanding regarding a particular issue are insuffi-cient to inform an optimal decision or an appropriate course of action, the more he or she will be motivated to engage in systematic processing of (additional) information that is pertinent to the issue at hand. Conversely, when the person feels that the current information and level of understanding are sufficient to reach a decision and guide behavior, epistemic needs are satisfied and no additional search for and processing of new information is required (De Dreu, Nijstad, & Van Knippenberg, 2008; Kruglanski, 1989; Kruglanski & Webster, 1996). In other words, individuals with higher epistemic motivation have a higher threshold of information sufficiency than individuals with lower epistemic motivation. As a consequence, people with higher levels of epistemic motivation tend to engage in rather deliberate, systematic information search and processing before making judgments and deci-sions, whereas those with lower levels of epistemic motivation are more likely to engage in shallower information processing.

Epistemic motivation and associated perceptions of information sufficiency are partly rooted in personality. For instance, individuals with a
higher need for cognition, lower need for cognitive closure, lower personal need for structure, and higher openness to experience have chroni-
cally higher epistemic motivation than their counterparts who score on
the opposite poles of these scales, and as a result they engage in more
deliberate information processing (De Dreu & Carnevale, 2003; Flynn,
2005; Homan et al., 2008; Neuberg & Newsom, 1993; Van Kleef,
Anastasopoulou, & Nijstad, 2010; Webster & Kruglanski, 1994). EASI
theory posits that these individuals are more likely to reflect on other
people's emotions, meaning that the effects of others' emotional expressions on their behavior are driven by deliberate inferential processes (as
opposed to more automatic affective reactions) to a greater degree than is
the case for individuals with lower levels of epistemic motivation (Van
Kleef, De Dreu, & Manstead, 2010).

Epistemic motivation also varies as a function of the situation. For
instance, epistemic motivation is increased when a task is perceived as
attractive or personally involving (Eagly & Chaiken, 1993; Petty &
Cacioppo, 1986), when one is held accountable for one's judgments and
decisions (Tetlock, 1992), when outcomes are framed as losses rather than
as gains (De Dreu, Carnevale, Emans, & Van de Vliert, 1994), and when a
situation is competitively rather than cooperatively structured (Van
Kleef, De Dreu, & Manstead, 2010). Conversely, epistemic motivation is
undermined by factors such as environmental noise (Kruglanski &
Webster, 1991), mental fatigue (Webster, Richter, & Kruglanski, 1996),
time pressure (De Dreu, 2003; Van Kleef, De Dreu, & Manstead, 2004b),
and power (De Dreu & Van Kleef, 2004; Fiske & Dépret, 1996; Keltner,
Van Kleef, Chen, & Kraus, 2008). By influencing epistemic motivation,
these factors influence the relative predictive strength of affective reactions and inferential processes, with inferential processes becoming progressively more influential as epistemic motivation increases.

Processing capacity
Besides motivation, a person's information-processing mode logically
depends on his or her ability to engage in effortful processing (Chaiken,
1980; Chaiken & Trope, 1999; Petty & Cacioppo, 1986; Smith & DeCoster,
2000). This ability is partly rooted in stable individual differences in
general intelligence and working memory capacity (Conway, Cowan,
Bunting, Therriault, & Minkoff, 2002; Engle, Tuholski, Laughlin, &
Conway, 1999; Vernon, 1983). In addition, the ability to engage in systematic information processing is determined by momentary variations
in (among other things) cognitive load and mental fatigue, which undermine people's information-processing capacity (Ford & Kruglanski, 1995;

Gilbert & Hixon, 1991; Lavie, 2010; Webster et al., 1996). Under increasing cognitive load, working memory capacity is reduced (Engle, 2002). As a result, cognitive control and the ability to engage in systematic information processing are undermined (Lavie, Hirst, De Fockert, & Viding, 2004). Thus, individuals who are under high cognitive load should be less likely to engage in thorough processing of another person's emotional expressions, meaning that affective reactions to the other's emotions take on heightened importance in driving behavioral responses.

Proposition 8: The relative influence of inferential processes (as compared with affective reactions) in shaping responses to emotional expressions becomes greater to the degree that the observer of the emotional expression is motivated and able to engage in thorough information processing; the relative influence of affective reactions increases to the degree that information processing motivation or ability is reduced.

The perceived appropriateness of emotional expressions

In addition to observers' information processing, a second key determinant of the relative influence of affective reactions and inferential processes in shaping responses to emotional expressions is the perceived appropriateness of the emotional expression (Van Kleef et al., 2011). Perceptions of inappropriateness arise when individuals feel that another person's emotional expression is somehow inconsistent with implicit or explicit norms or rules that are salient within a particular context. Violations of such norms can be qualitative (showing the wrong emotion) or quantitative (showing the right emotion with the wrong intensity). In other words, emotional expressions can be considered "appropriate" to the degree that they are "correct for the situation and in correct proportion to the evoking circumstances" (Shields, 2005, p. 7; see also Parrott, 2001).

To some extent, this is of course a subjective call. Who is the judge of whether an emotional expression is fitting within a particular situation? According to Shields (2005), there is a political dimension to this question in the sense that certain people (e.g., those belonging to a majority group within a society) may have an interest in condemning the emotional reactions of particular others (e.g., those belonging to a minority group), for instance to preserve the status quo. A painful example of such politics occurred in the Netherlands in the autumn of 2014, when an old discussion about "Black Pete" came back to life. Black Pete is the assistant of Saint Nicholas, who (according to Dutch tradition) celebrates his birthday on December 5th by giving presents and candy to children. Some Dutch citizens with Surinamese or Antillean roots feel hurt by the tradition because it reminds them of slavery, and they would like to modernize the tradition (e.g., by introducing White Pete). Some indigenous Dutch citizens have difficulties appreciating the sensitivity of the matter due to their different perspective, and they feel that the negative emotions of opponents are unwarranted. From a more objective standpoint, it is easy to see why Surinamese and Antillean Dutch inhabitants take offense at the role of Black Pete, and yet the White majority appears to dictate that strong negative emotional reactions to Black Pete are inappropriate because Black Pete is part of the Dutch cultural heritage. As Shields observed, "when members of the dominant group discuss issues concerning groups considered minority or 'special interest' groups, the question of 'Why are they always so angry?' almost invariably arises. The answer depends on who is in a position to write the rules as to what counts as a legitimate appraisal" (p. 9).

EASI theory posits that the relative influence of inferential processes in shaping behavioral responses to the emotional expressions of others decreases to the extent that the emotional expressions are perceived as inappropriate (Van Kleef, 2009). This idea resonates with Shields's (2005) argument that emotional expressions that are perceived as inappropriate are accorded less legitimacy, which implies that the appraisals that gave rise to the emotions are less likely to be taken into account. In other words, a person who deems another's emotional expression inappropriate rather than appropriate will be less inclined to engage in the effortful process of drawing inferences from the emotional expression about the expresser's appraisals of the situation, which makes it less likely that the person will reach the conclusion that behavioral change on his own part is required.

At the same time, the relative influence of (negative) affective reactions in driving responses to others' emotional expressions increases when emotional expressions are perceived as inappropriate (Van Kleef et al., 2011). Inappropriate emotions violate the shared reality of groups and societies, thereby potentially endangering group harmony, coordinated action, and the functioning of collectives (Kruglanski & Webster, 1991; Mannetti, Levine, Pierro, & Kruglanski, 2010; Marques, Abrams, Paez, & Martinez-Taboada, 1998). Beliefs about which emotions should be expressed in which circumstances are therefore interpreted in the interest of regulating the functioning of social groups (Shields, 2005). Accordingly, emotional displays that are perceived as inappropriate for the circumstances tend to evoke negative emotions in observers (Bucy, 2000), and (emotional) deviance is often socially sanctioned (Eidelman, Silvia, & Biernat, 2006; Marques et al., 1998).

It is important at this point to distinguish inappropriateness from unexpectedness. Perceptions of inappropriateness may stem from the observation of unexpected emotional expressions, such as when one sees a person laughing out loud during a sad speech at a funeral, or when one gets an angry reaction from the recipient of a gift. In such cases, the emotional reaction is probably perceived by most people as both unexpected and inappropriate. But not all unexpected emotional reactions will necessarily be deemed inappropriate. If one expects an irritated reaction from a colleague when arriving late to a meeting but receives a sincere smile instead, the colleague's emotional expression is unexpected but will probably not be seen as inappropriate. The reverse also applies: An emotional reaction does not need to be unexpected to be perceived as inappropriate. Some people habitually display domineering or contemptuous emotions, to a point where the expressions can be expected by others. But even if anticipated, the expressions are still likely to be seen as inappropriate because they violate prevailing norms.

The distinction between unexpectedness and inappropriateness is important in light of evidence that expectancy violations can, under particular circumstances, trigger increased information processing (Hamilton & Sherman, 1996; Stern, Marrs, Millar, & Cole, 1984). When something unanticipated happens, people may become motivated to engage in more thorough information processing to increase their understanding of the situation (i.e., lack of understanding may increase epistemic motivation; Chaiken et al., 1989; Kruglanski & Webster, 1996). There is also evidence, however, that negative affective reactions to expectancy violations are primary (Bartholow, Fabiani, Gratton, & Bettencourt, 2001; Olson, Roese, & Zanna, 1996) and that negative affective reactions to unexpected emotional expressions in particular are more likely to arise to the degree that the expressions are considered inappropriate (Bucy, 2000; Van Kleef & Côté, 2007). Consider the case of a person who starts laughing out loud during a funeral ceremony. Even though other mourners may at some level be curious about what caused the person to laugh, their sense that the amusement is utterly inappropriate for the situation is likely to make them experience strong negative affective reactions. Thus, even though inappropriate emotional displays have the potential to trigger information processing when they are unexpected, EASI theory posits that – generally speaking – negative affective reactions take precedence over inferential processes when individuals are confronted with inappropriate emotional expressions (Van Kleef et al., 2011).

In short, in light of the processes outlined above, EASI postulates that the relative influence of negative affective reactions (as opposed to inferential processes) in shaping responses to the emotional expressions of others increases to the degree that the emotional expressions are perceived as inappropriate. The perceived appropriateness of emotional expressions depends on a number of social-contextual factors, including characteristics of the situation (e.g., cultural norms regarding emotion expression, the cooperative vs. competitive nature of the situation), characteristics of the emotional expression (e.g., its authenticity, intensity, target), characteristic of the expresser (e.g., gender, status, group membership), and characteristics of the observer (e.g., agreeableness, extraversion, neuroticism). I discuss each of these in turn.

Characteristics of the situation: display rules, culture, and interdependence

The perceived appropriateness of emotional expressions is shaped to an important degree by "display rules," the often tacit social rules that dictate when, how much, and which emotions should be expressed to others (Ekman & Friesen, 1975; Shields, 2005). Display rules vary across situations and social groups, and they play an important role in regulating social interaction by shaping emotional expressions (Saarni, 1999). In general terms, display rules pertain to the appropriateness of an emotional expression within a particular context (Shields, 2005).[1] Perhaps the most basic and universal (albeit mostly implicit) expectation in this regard is that emotional expressions should reflect a proper appraisal of the situation (Parrott, 2001). A person who gets angry upon reaching a goal or starts laughing after a painful failure may be perceived by others as showing the wrong emotion for the situation, and this perception may evoke negative affective reactions.

More specific display rules vary as a function of culture, because different cultures put differential emphasis on values associated with cultural dimensions such as individualism-collectivism and power distance (Matsumoto, 1990). For example, in individualistic cultures, expressions of anger tend to be relatively acceptable. In the United States, Israel, and the Netherlands, expressions of anger are more likely to be interpreted as a sign of assertiveness and individuality than as a sign of aggression, provided that the expressions are not overly intense. In more collectivistic cultures, however, expressions of anger are not appreciated. In Japan, for instance, expressing anger tends to be perceived as rather inappropriate (except perhaps when the anger is directed at an outgroup; Matsumoto, 1990) because anger poses a threat to group harmony, which is highly valued in this cultural context (Kitayama, Mesquita, & Karasawa, 2006; Markus & Kitayama, 1991).

---

[1] A related concept is that of "feeling rules," which prescribe qualities of a person's privately experienced emotions (Hochschild, 1983). Both types of rules speak to the appropriateness of emotional reactions to events. I concentrate on display rules here because they relate more directly to the appropriateness of emotional expressions (as opposed to experiences).

Display rules also vary according to social and organizational customs. Situational scripts determine the extent to which certain emotional expressions are deemed appropriate in a given setting. Within a Western context, a person who displays happiness at a funeral violates a consensual script and can expect to meet with negative affective reactions and possibly social sanctions. Similarly, many organizations have implicit or explicit guidelines with regard to emotional expression (Rafaeli & Sutton, 1987). In some organizational settings, such as customer service professions, a lot of emphasis is put on providing "service with a smile" (Grandey, Fisk, Mattila, Jansen, & Sideman, 2005). Other occupational contexts, such as the construction industry, may be seen as relatively "rough" in terms of behavioral norms and expectations regarding emotional expression (Lindebaum & Fielden, 2011). The social-organizational context thus shapes emotional norms and display rules, which in turn determine to what extent a given emotional expression is likely to be perceived as appropriate or inappropriate within that context.

Furthermore, and in a somewhat related vein, the perceived appropriateness of emotional expressions depends on the interdependence structure of the situation (Van Kleef, De Dreu, & Manstead, 2010). In cooperative settings (e.g., colleagues working together on a task) there tends to be a relative emphasis on collaboration, trust, support, and social harmony, as compared with competitive settings (e.g., opponents in a hockey match), which more commonly evoke feelings of rivalry and antagonism. Accordingly, aggressive and domineering emotions such as anger may be rather inappropriate in a cooperative context, but relatively acceptable in more competitive settings, where aggression is part of the situational script. In short, situational characteristics affect the degree to which particular emotional expressions are likely to be perceived as appropriate or inappropriate, thereby shaping the relative influence of affective and inferential processes on responses to emotional expressions.

Characteristics of the emotional expression: authenticity, intensity, and target
The perceived appropriateness of emotional expressions also depends on characteristics of the emotional expression itself. Although it seems intuitively plausible that positive emotional expressions are generally perceived as more appropriate than negative emotional expressions, upon closer scrutiny it is more likely that the appropriateness of a particular emotional expression depends on the degree to which the expression fits situational norms and scripts. Even though cheerful emotional expressions are often well received, expressing joy after learning about the company's disastrous financial performance is likely to be perceived as unfitting. Similarly, even though expressions of anger may not be

appreciated in many situations, a friend who tells us about how unfairly she is treated by her boss would probably deem an angry response on our part more appropriate than an indifferent response. In general, then, an expresser's emotions are more likely to be perceived as appropriate by an observer to the degree that they fit the observer's appraisal of the situation and his or her expectations based on display rules and situational scripts (Shields, 2005). Nevertheless, several characteristics of emotional expressions may influence perceptions of appropriateness across social situations. These include the authenticity, intensity, and target of the expression.

For various reasons, people may decide to express emotions that they do not actually feel or to exaggerate or suppress felt emotions, for instance in order to comply with prevailing display rules and expectations or to get something done. For example, people may deliberately express happiness to make a positive impression, or express sadness to elicit support (Clark et al., 1996), even if they do not actually feel these emotions or feel them to a lesser extent than their displays would suggest. People may also purposefully upregulate anger in an attempt to influence others (Andrade & Ho, 2009; Fitness, 2000) and to further their own goals (Tamir, Mitchell, & Gross, 2008). For example, bill collectors reported that they displayed anger that they did not feel, because they had learned that expressing anger could compel certain debtors to pay (Sutton, 1991).

Emotions that are strategically expressed may come across as inauthentic depending how they were regulated. One way of regulating emotions is by means of antecedent-focused regulation or "deep acting," which involves regulating both one's subjective feelings and one's public displays of emotions (Côté, 2005; Grandey, 2003; Gross, 1998a; Hochschild, 1983). When individuals engage in this type of regulation, their subjectively felt emotions match their external displays of emotion, and hence emotional displays generated by deep acting tend to be perceived as authentic (Grandey, 2003; Hennig-Thurau, Groth, Paul, & Hemler, 2006). An alternative way of regulating emotions is through response-focused regulation or "surface acting," which involves modifying one's external displays of emotion without changing one's internal feeling state (Côté, 2005; Grandey, 2003; Gross, 1998a; Hochschild, 1983). This type of regulation creates a mismatch between publicly displayed and privately felt emotions. This discrepancy may be noted by observers, because feigned emotional displays appear different than spontaneous expressions of truly felt emotions (Ekman, 2003; Ekman, Friesen, & O'Sullivan, 1988). For instance, compared to genuine facial displays of emotion, feigned displays tend to be less symmetrical (Ekman, Hager, & Friesen, 1981; Hager & Ekman, 1985; Skinner & Mullen, 1991). Due to such subtle cues, surface-acted emotional expressions are likely to be perceived as less authentic than genuinely felt emotions (Côté, Hideg, & Van Kleef, 2013; Grandey et al., 2005).

In some cases, emotional expressions that appear inauthentic may also be deemed inappropriate (Rafaeli & Sutton, 1989). Relative to authentic emotional expressions, inauthentic emotional expressions are more likely to be perceived as dishonest, unethical, or manipulative attempts to influence others (Côté et al., 2013), and such perceptions may elicit negative affective reactions in observers (Van Kleef, Homan, & Cheshin, 2012). In line with this idea, individuals who habitually engaged in surface acting (and whose emotional expressions were therefore often inauthentic) reported lower-quality relationships (Gross & John, 2003) and received less social support (Srivastava, Tamir, McGonigal, John, & Gross, 2009) compared to individuals who less frequently engaged in surface acting. Other research found that surface acting emotions at work was negatively related to coworker ratings of "affective delivery," which encompasses sincerity, warmth, courtesy, and friendliness (Grandey, 2003). Furthermore, experimental work revealed that female interviewees who displayed inauthentic smiles during a simulated job interview were rated less positively and were less often short-listed for the job than were interviewees who displayed authentic smiles (Krumhuber, Manstead, Cosker, Marshall, & Rosin, 2009). In other studies, participants felt less trust toward and cooperated less with interaction partners who exhibited inauthentic rather than authentic smiles (Johnston, Miles, & Macrae, 2010; Krumhuber et al., 2007).

Anecdotal evidence from the political domain also indicates that inauthentic emotional expressions may elicit negative affective reactions in observers. During her campaign for the Democratic presidential nomination for US president in 2008, Hillary Clinton's voice trembled and her eyes got teary when she was asked how she managed to hang in there during the long and tiring campaign. Although some applauded her for showing humaneness, others doubted the genuineness of her displays: "After a political lifetime of keeping her emotions secret, why was Mrs. Clinton finally letting her guard down? Was it a spontaneous outburst or a calculated show?" (Kantor, 2008). As another case in point, in the wake of the British Petroleum oil spill in the Gulf of Mexico in 2010, U.S. president Barack Obama eventually showed anger about the incident on a television show after having been criticized for his calm response (Pareene, 2010). Obama drew considerable skepticism, however, because his display was perceived as inauthentic. Veteran newscaster Sam Donaldson commented: "It's not authentic. He is mister cool. He is *no drama Obama*. Someone told him, get out there and show your anger ... And we say, that's not him" (Chalian, 2010).

Not all feigned emotions may be perceived as equally inappropriate, however. It seems plausible that inauthentic positive emotional expressions (e.g., fake smiles) are generally more welcome than inauthentic negative expressions (e.g., fake tears). Nevertheless, an insincere smile can still be expected to elicit more negative affective reactions than a genuine smile, even if these negative reactions may be relatively mild. In addition, the perceived appropriateness of inauthentic emotional displays depends on the context. A fake smile may be perceived as relatively more appropriate in a customer service setting than in an intimate relationship, and feigned grumpiness may be more acceptable from a bouncer than from a doctor. Despite these nuances, inauthentic emotional expressions are more likely than authentic expressions to be perceived as inappropriate and, accordingly, to trigger negative affective reactions in observers.

Another characteristic of emotional expressions that shapes their perceived appropriateness is intensity. Emotional expressions are perceived as appropriate to the degree that they match situational expectations (Shields, 2005). Besides factors such as display rules and cultural influences, the appropriateness of an emotional expression in a given situation depends on the congruence between the severity of the eliciting event and the intensity of the emotion. An emotional expression whose severity does not seem to match the situation, for instance because the emotion appears too grave in light of its minor cause, may evoke negative affective reactions in observers due to its perceived inappropriateness (Van Kleef et al., 2012).

Parrott (2001) argued that the functionality of emotions depends on the accuracy of the appraisals that underlie them, proposing that emotions that are too intense (or not intense enough) for the eliciting event are likely to be dysfunctional. Although Parrott's argument focused primarily on the intrapersonal dysfunctionality of ill-calibrated emotional intensity, the argument can easily be extended to the interpersonal domain. A person who grieves intensely over a trivial loss or exhibits excessive enthusiasm over a minor success stands the risk of being perceived by others as mannered or inauthentic, which may trigger negative affective reactions. Conversely, someone whose emotional expressions apparently fail to reflect the severity of an event may elicit negative affective reactions in others because emotional unresponsiveness suggests a disregard for the significance of the situation.

In general terms, then, emotional expressions are more likely to elicit negative affective reactions to the degree that there is a greater discrepancy (whether positive or negative) between their intensity and the severity of the situation (Van Kleef et al., 2012). Thus, a customer who is confronted with an overly enthusiastic car salesman may experience distrust and negative affect that may prevent him from buying a car from that dealer. Likewise, a service worker who is confronted with a disproportionately angry customer may be less likely to invest effort in finding a way to accommodate the customer's request (Geddes & Callister, 2007).

A final characteristic of emotional expressions that warrants discussion here concerns the target of the expression. It is important to distinguish among the *cause* of an emotion (i.e., the eliciting stimulus, be it a person or an event), the *target* of the emotion (i.e., the person, object, or situation the emotion is directed at, which may or may not have caused the emotion), and the *observer* of the emotion (i.e., the person who witnesses the emotional expression, who may or may not be the cause of the emotion and who may or may not be its target). Consider the following example. Someone promises a friend to help him paint his new house, and then calls up on the agreed-upon day that he is too busy with something else and backs out. If the friend expresses his irritation about this decision during the same phone call, then the nonhelper is at the same time the cause of the emotion, the target of the emotion, and the observer of the emotional expression. Now consider another example. Someone painfully bangs his head on a kitchen cupboard and then angrily kicks his dog that happens to get in the way, in the presence of his wife. In this case the pain from the cupboard is the cause of the emotion, the dog is its momentary target, and the wife is the observer of the expression.

This distinction is relevant for the present argument, because certain emotional expressions are more likely to be perceived as inappropriate and to elicit negative affective reactions in an observer when the observer is also the target of the emotion. Consider the case of anger. As discussed previously, a given expression of anger may be seen as more or less appropriate depending on the circumstances and depending on its intensity. All else being equal, however, due to self-serving and ego-defensive biases in perception and attribution, people may perceive expressions of anger as relatively more uncalled for when they are themselves the target of the expressions than when another person is the target.

People have a well-documented tendency to overestimate the role of dispositional as opposed to situational factors in explaining their own success versus adversity, while they tend to make the opposite pattern of attributions with regard to the success and adversity of others (Bradley, 1978; Miller & Ross, 1975). Due to such self-serving attributions, observers may deem expressions of anger directed at a third party or common enemy more appropriate (e.g., more deserved) than the same expressions directed at themselves. This tendency may be further enhanced by the fact that people tend to underestimate the severity of social pain (as induced, among other things, by expressions of anger) unless they are actively experiencing it themselves (Nordgren, Banas, & MacDonald, 2011). Furthermore, ego-defense motives may lead people to perceive expressions of anger as less appropriate when they are directed at them personally rather than at their behavior or at some aspect of the situation. For these reasons, expressions of unwelcome emotions such as anger may be perceived as more inappropriate and elicit more negative affective reactions in observers when they are themselves the targets of the expressions than when they are not.

Characteristics of the expresser: gender, group membership, and status
Several characteristics of the expresser of an emotion also influence the extent to which the expression is likely to be perceived as (in)appropriate by observers. Stereotypes play an important role in this regard, the most pervasive of which relate to gender. Although gender stereotypes vary somewhat across cultures, there is a widely shared belief that women and men differ in the experience and expression of emotion (Condry & Condry, 1976; Fischer, 2000; K. Lewis, 2000; Plant, Hyde, Keltner, & Devine, 2000). The female role has traditionally been associated with "soft" and "caring" emotions, while the male role has been associated with "strong" and "dominant" emotions (Reddy, 2001; Shields, 2005). For instance, anger is often regarded as fitting the male rather than the female gender role, and accordingly expressions of anger tend to be perceived as more appropriate when emitted by men than by women (Eagly, Karau, & Makhijani, 1995; Kring, 2000; K. Lewis, 2000; Timmers, Fischer, & Manstead, 1998). Conversely, sadness is considered to be more gender endorsed for women than for men, and hence expressions of sadness by a woman are likely to be perceived as more appropriate than expressions of sadness by a man (Plant et al., 2000).

The perceived appropriateness of emotional expressions also depends on the group membership of the expresser and the observer. As discussed previously in the context of the example of "Black Pete," individuals tend to ascribe greater legitimacy to the appraisals of members of their ingroup than to the appraisals of members of the outgroup (Shields, 2005). Thus, whenever there is ambiguity or tension concerning the "correct" appraisal of a situation, observers are likely to deem the appraisals and concomitant emotional expressions of ingroup members more appropriate than those of outgroup members. This means that, all else being equal, the emotional expressions of outgroup members are more likely to elicit negative affective reactions in observers than the emotional expressions of ingroup members.

A final characteristic of the expresser that is relevant in the current context is his or her standing within the social hierarchy. Research by Tiedens and colleagues (Tiedens, 2001; Tiedens, Ellsworth, & Mesquita, 2000) has shown that high-status individuals are expected to respond with anger (rather than sadness or guilt) to negative outcomes and with pride (rather than appreciation) to positive outcomes. Accordingly, people with lower relative standing in hierarchies reported controlling their expressions of anger more than did those with higher relative standing (Diefendorff, Morehart, & Gabriel, 2010). By reverse logic, individuals are perceived as having higher status and power when they display anger and pride than when they show sadness, guilt, shame, or appreciation (Shariff, Tracy, & Markusoff, 2012; Tiedens, 2001; Tiedens et al., 2000). Tiedens and colleagues suggested that expressions of anger and pride are seen as reflecting appraisals of other-blame and controllability (which are consistent with a powerful role), whereas expressions of guilt and appreciation reflect appraisals of self-blame and low control (which are consistent with a powerless role). Interestingly, people also believe that high-status individuals have more legitimate right to be angry in adverse situations than low-status individuals, a belief that may be fueled by the implicit assumption that individuals in higher positions are more competent than those in lower positions and therefore less likely to be responsible for any negative outcomes (Tiedens et al., 2000).

Given such stereotypes, expressions of "dominant" and social-distancing emotions such as anger and pride can be expected to be perceived as relatively more appropriate when shown by higher-status people, whereas expressions of "supplication" emotions such as sadness and disappointment, "appeasement" emotions such as guilt and shame, and "submissive" emotions such as gratitude and appreciation may be perceived as more appropriate when shown by lower-status people. Although research in this domain is scarce, there is some indirect evidence for the case of anger. Kuppens, Van Mechelen, and Meulders (2004) found that people more often overtly expressed their anger at individuals who had lower rather than higher status than themselves, while they more often suppressed their anger toward higher-status than toward lower-status individuals. This suggests that people estimate the likelihood of getting away with expressions of anger in light of their relative status vis-à-vis the target, anticipating that expressions of anger will be perceived as less appropriate and will arouse more negative reactions to the degree that their relative status is lower.

Characteristics of the observer: agreeableness, extraversion,
and neuroticism

The perceived appropriateness of emotional expressions is also influ-enced by characteristics of the observer. Some observer characteristics cannot be seen in isolation from expresser characteristics, as is the case for instance with group membership. As such, the arguments about group membership in the previous paragraph also apply to the observer. People are more likely to perceive the emotional expressions of others as appro-priate rather than inappropriate when they belong to the same rather than a different group. Similarly, the status of expresser and observer may be conceptualized in relative terms. This means that the foregoing argu-ments about the expresser's status are also relevant when it comes to the effects of the observer's status, except that the direction of the effects is the opposite. Thus, observers may deem others' expressions of anger and pride more appropriate to the degree that they themselves have lower status.

Besides such relative factors, perceptions of appropriateness are shaped by more stable personality attributes of the observer. In this respect it is useful to consider conceptual relationships between discrete emotions and personality dimensions. Personality traits reflect patterns of goals and values that are relatively stable and consistent across situa-tions and over time (Roberts & Robins, 2000; Roccas, Sagiv, Schwartz, & Knafo, 2002). Emotional expressions signal appraisals, social motives, and intentions that may be more or less compatible with such goals. In general terms, EASI postulates that emotional expressions are more likely to be perceived as appropriate by observers to the extent that the social signals that are conveyed by the expression fit with the goals and values of the observer, as shaped in part by his or her personality.

A considerable amount of variance in personality is captured by the classic Five-Factor Model, which encompasses extraversion, agreeable-ness, conscientiousness, neuroticism, and openness to experience (Costa & McCrae, 1988; McCrae & Costa, 1987). Several of these factors are relevant in the context of the present argument. Consider the case of agreeableness. Individuals who score high on agreeableness have a strong desire to achieve and maintain social harmony and to avoid con-flict, whereas low-agreeable people have less of such a desire (McCrae & Costa, 1987). Highly agreeable people should therefore be more likely to perceive expressions of anger as inappropriate and to respond negatively to such expressions, because such expressions may create hostility and conflict and thereby undermine the social harmony that agreeable people value and strive for (Graziano, Jensen-Campbell, & Hair, 1996; Suls, Martin, & David, 1998). Even though agreeable individuals may be reluc-tant to directly confront the anger expresser in the interest of securing social harmony, their elevated perceptions of inappropriateness may become manifest in their responses to angry people in less explicit ways (e.g., in the form of reduced compliance or helpfulness). Conversely, highly agreeable individuals should welcome expressions of happiness (perhaps more so than their less agreeable counterparts), because such expressions inspire trust (Stouten & De Cremer, 2010) and facilitate social connection (Clark & Taraban, 1991), and as such are compatible with agreeable individuals' preference for harmonious relations.

Extraversion also seems relevant when it comes to predicting the perceived appropriateness of emotional expressions. Extraverted people are outgoing, talkative, emotionally expressive, and energetic, whereas introverted people are more reserved, solitary, and less emotionally expressive (Costa & McCrae, 1988; McCrae & Costa, 1987). It stands to reason, then, that extraverted people would generally appreciate others' emotional expressions more than would introverted people, particularly when the expressions are relatively intense. Compared to extraverted individuals, introverted individuals may be more likely to perceive others' emotional expressions as unwarranted and inappropriate in light of their own standards of restrained emotional expression.

Finally, there are some interesting conceptual links between neuroticism and emotional expression. Neuroticism is associated with the experience of negative affective states, such as anxiety and depression. Individuals who are low on neuroticism are more emotionally stable and less susceptible to anxiety-provoking situations (Costa & McCrae, 1988; McCrae & Costa, 1987). It is conceivable, therefore, that neurotic individuals are better able than their less neurotic counterparts to relate to others' anxiety, and that they would perceive displays of anxiety by others as more appropriate because they resonate with their own patterns of emotional experience and expression. Similarly, people with a chronic prevention focus, who are preoccupied with avoiding negative outcomes and prone to experience agitated emotions (Higgins, 1997, 1998), may perceive others' displays of anxiety and agitation as more appropriate than individuals with a chronic promotion focus, who are more focused on attaining positive outcomes. In short, the perceived appropriateness of any emotional expression is likely to depend on the match between the signals that are conveyed by the expression and the salient goals and values of the observer, as rooted in his or her personality. These arguments can be summarized in the following proposition.

Proposition 9: The relative influence of negative affective reactions (as compared with inferential processes) in shaping observers' responses to others' emotional

expressions increases to the degree that observers perceive the emotional expres-
sions as inappropriate rather than appropriate, which depends on characteristics
of the situation, the emotional expression, the expresser, and the observer; the
relative influence of inferential processes increases to the degree that emotional
expressions are perceived as appropriate.

Conclusion

EASI theory posits that emotional expressions exert interpersonal effects
on observers by triggering affective and/or inferential processes in observers, as discussed in Chapter 3. The theory identifies two general preconditions of such effects. The first prerequisite for any social effects of
emotions to occur is that the emotions be encoded in a way that makes
them perceptible by others (i.e., through facial expressions, tone of voice,
bodily postures, written or spoken words, and/or use of symbols such as
emoticons), which depends on the emotional expressivity of the expresser. The second precondition is that the emotional expression be detected
and decoded, which depends on the emotional intelligence and associated emotion perception abilities of the observer.

The theory further specifies two classes of moderators that determine
the relative predictive strength of observers' affective reactions and inferential processes in shaping (behavioral) responses to others' emotional
expressions. The first moderator is the observer's information-processing
depth, which is shaped by dispositional characteristics as well as situational factors that determine information-processing motivation and ability. The second moderator is the perceived appropriateness of the
emotional expression, which is shaped by characteristics of the situation,
the expression, the expresser, and the observer. These various moderators
are summarized in Table 4.1.

EASI posits that the predictive strength of inferential processes relative
to affective reactions increases to the extent that the observer of an emotional expression is motivated and able to engage in thorough information processing and perceives the emotional expression as appropriate.
Conversely, the relative predictive power of inferential processes
decreases to the extent that the observer's information processing is
reduced and/or she or he perceives the emotional expression as inappropriate. In this regard it is important to bear in mind the critical
distinction between unexpectedness of emotional expressions (which
may enhance careful scrutiny) and inappropriateness of emotional
expressions (which may trigger negative affective reactions), as elaborated above. By specifying the various ways in which emotional expressions may bring about social effects and the contingencies that govern the

Table 4.1 Moderators of the social effects of emotions

General Preconditions of the Social Effects of Emotions
- *Encoding: Expresser's emotional expressivity*
- *Decoding: Observer's emotional intelligence and emotion perception ability*

Moderators of the Relative Influence of Inferential Processes and Affective Reactions
- *Observer's information processing*
  Epistemic motivation
    – Dispositional characteristics (e.g., need for cognitive closure, need for cognition, personal need for structure, openness to experience)
    – Situational characteristics (e.g., involvement, accountability, loss framing, environmental noise, mental fatigue, power)
  Processing capacity
    – Dispositional characteristics (e.g., general intelligence, working memory capacity)
    – Situational characteristics (e.g., cognitive load, mental fatigue)
- *Perceived appropriateness of the emotional expression*
  Characteristics of the situation (e.g., culture, display rules, cooperative vs. competitive interdependence)
  Characteristics of the expression (e.g., authenticity, intensity, target)
  Characteristics of the expresser (e.g., gender, status, group membership)
  Characteristics of the observer (e.g., agreeableness, extraversion, neuroticism)

relative primacy of these processes, EASI theory enables specific predictions about the social effects of emotional expressions across domains of life.

Now that the basic tenets of EASI theory have been laid out, we can move on to consider the empirical record. In the following chapters I provide a comprehensive overview of research on the social effects of emotions. I organize my review according to the five main domains of research in which the social effects of emotions have been investigated so far, namely close relationships, group life, conflict and negotiation, customer service and consumer behavior, and leadership.

PART II

Social effects of emotions: the empirical record

CHAPTER 5

Social effects of emotions in close relationships

> There was a time when you let me know
> what's really going on below
> but now you never show it to me, do you?
> *Leonard Cohen*

The theoretical framework of Emotions as Social Information (EASI) outlined in the previous section of this book emphasizes the social functionality of emotions. Emotional expressions help to regulate social interaction by eliciting reciprocal and/or complementary emotional responses in others and by providing insight into the expresser's inner feelings, desires, motives, and intentions (Keltner & Haidt, 1999; Van Kleef, 2009). Theorizing about the functionality of emotional expressions has highlighted the role of emotional expressions in developing and maintaining well-adjusted personal relationships (Keltner & Kring, 1998; Parkinson, Fischer, & Manstead, 2005). This is for good reasons, because emotions and relationships are inextricably intertwined. There is abundant evidence that emotions predominantly arise in social situations (Anderson & Guerrero, 1998; Planalp, 1999), and, more specifically, in the context of close relationships (Berscheid & Ammazzalorso, 2001). I therefore begin my review of research on the interpersonal effects of emotions by considering the domain of close relationships. If emotional expressions are indeed functional, their benefits should surely be apparent in situations in which interaction partners are concerned about each other's welfare and are motivated to understand each other's predicaments, to alleviate each other's distress, and to secure a healthy and stable relationship.

The functionality of emotions in close relationships

There are good reasons to believe that emotions are an essential ingredient of healthy social relationships, and particularly of close relationships. Clark and Taraban (1991) found that emotions are more frequently experienced and expressed in "communal" relationships (which are characterized by relatively high levels of intimacy and trust) than in "exchange" relationships (which are characterized by lower levels of closeness and a more transactional mind-set). In one experiment, participants were paired with either a friend (communal relationship) or a stranger (exchange relationship) with whom they expected to have a conversation. When asked what they would prefer to talk about with the other person, participants in the friend condition indicated a greater preference for emotional topics than did participants in the stranger condition. In another experiment, participants were led to desire either a communal relationship or an exchange relationship with another person who expressed happiness, sadness, irritability, or no emotion. When the other person expressed no emotion, participants rated the person as equally likeable in the exchange condition as in the communal condition. When the person expressed happiness, sadness, or irritability, however, participants liked the person significantly more in the communal than in the exchange condition. These findings suggest that emotional expressions play a special role in close relationships, and that positive as well as negative emotions may be functional. This conclusion is underscored by the fact that people are strongly inclined to share their emotional experiences with others, especially with close ones (Rimé, Finkenauer, Luminet, Zech, & Philippot, 1998).

Whereas the idea that positive emotional expressions benefit close relationships is not particularly provocative, the possibility that negative emotional expressions have favorable consequences in such a context is more controversial (Locke & Horowitz, 1990; Sommers, 1984). Nevertheless, there is evidence that the expression of negative emotions is associated with positive relationship outcomes. A series of studies by Graham and colleagues suggests that expressing negative emotions (e.g., distress, nervousness, anxiety, annoyance) helps to elicit support, build new relationships, and heighten intimacy in existing close relationships (Graham, Huang, Clark, & Helgeson, 2008). In a vignette study, participants indicated that they would provide more support to a person who expressed a negative emotion that she or he felt than to a person who did not express a felt negative emotion. A longitudinal field study among college students further revealed that the self-reported willingness to express negative emotions was a positive predictor of friendship formation and intimacy, and received support from roommates. Findings such as these suggest that negative emotional expressions can indeed have beneficial consequences in close relationships.

As elaborated in the previous chapter, the social functionality of emotions (whether positive or negative) hinges on the willingness and capacity of interaction partners to express their own emotions and to attend to, register, interpret, and respond to the emotional expressions of the other. When emotions fail to be expressed or registered, vital information may be lost, and social responding, coordination, and mutual understanding

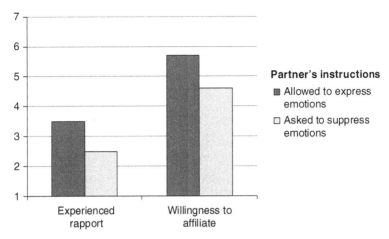

Figure 5.1 Effects of emotional expression versus suppression in face-to-face interaction on conversation partners' self-reported experience of rapport and willingness to affiliate (on a scale of 0–10; based on Butler et al., 2003, Study 2).

may be impeded. This implies that lack of emotional expressivity poses a threat to social relationships, because failure to express experienced emotions robs one's interaction partner of the opportunity to respond to one's situation.

In line with this idea, Butler and colleagues demonstrated experimentally that the suppression of felt emotions in conversations can have deleterious consequences for both interaction partners (Butler et al., 2003). The authors conducted two laboratory studies in which dyads of previously unacquainted women discussed an upsetting topic in face-to-face conversations. Unbeknownst to the conversation partner, one of the participants was either instructed to suppress any felt emotions, or was not given such instructions and was therefore presumably allowed to freely express any felt emotions. The authors found that emotional suppression increased stress in both conversation partners, as reflected in cardiovascular responses. Moreover, partners of emotion suppressors experienced less rapport and reported a lower willingness to affiliate with their conversation partner (as shown in Figure 5.1), suggesting that expressive suppression can hinder friendship formation. A longitudinal field study by Srivastava, Tamir, McGonigal, John, and Gross (2009) similarly showed that emotional suppression predicted lower social support, less interpersonal closeness, and lower social satisfaction among college students, as reflected in self-reports as well as peer reports.

Together, these studies indicate that emotional suppression may jeopardize the quality of social relationships.

Other research has examined the effects of perceptive abilities. Mayer, DiPaolo, and Salovey (1990) demonstrated that the ability to perceive affective content in ambiguous visual stimuli (e.g., reproduced faces, abstract designs) was positively associated with the ability to respond empathically to others. Expanding on this finding, Schutte and colleagues (2001) examined links between self-reports of emotional intelligence and the quality of social relationships. Across a series of studies, they found that self-reported emotional intelligence was positively correlated with empathic perspective taking, general social skills, cooperative responses toward partners, and relationship closeness and affection. Moreover, they found that partners of individuals with higher self-ratings of emotional intelligence reported greater marital satisfaction than partners of individuals with lower self-rated emotional intelligence. Later studies yielded compatible findings, indicating that emotional intelligence and concomitant emotion perception ability predict relationship quality (Lopes et al., 2004; Lopes, Salovey, & Straus, 2003; Malouff, Schutte, & Thorsteinsson, 2014).

The functionality of emotional expressions further depends on the perceived appropriateness of the expressions (see Chapter 4). Emotional expressions are more likely to have beneficial consequences for social relationships to the degree that they are perceived as fitting for the circumstances. In other words, people should express the right emotions at the right time and in the right way. When people express emotions that do not fit the circumstances or when they display overly intense emotions, observers are more likely to perceive the emotions as inappropriate (Shields, 2005), which undermines observers' tendency to process the meaning and implications of the emotional expressions (Van Kleef, 2010). Thus, the ability to regulate emotions is an important prerequisite for the functionality of emotional expressions in close relationships. Accordingly, research has documented links between emotion regulation ability and relationship quality, as reflected in self-reports and peer reports of interpersonal sensitivity and reciprocal friendship nominations among college students (Lopes, Salovey, Côté, & Beers, 2005).

Emotional convergence in interpersonal relationships

Social-functional analyses of emotion emphasize the role of emotional expressions in the coordination of social interactions (e.g., Fischer & Manstead, in press; Frijda & Mesquita, 1994; Keltner & Haidt, 1999; Van Kleef, 2009). One way in which such coordination may be enhanced is through emotional convergence (Anderson, Keltner, & John, 2003; Butler,

Table 5.1 Emotional similarity at Time 1 (in correlations) of couples who were still together at Time 2 (six months later) and those who had broken up.

	Correlation between Partners' Emotions at T1		
	Positive Emotion	Negative Emotion	Total Emotion
Couples still together at T2	.32*	.43**	.30*
Couples broken up at T2	−.05	−.02	−.06

* $p < .05$; ** $p < .01$. Based on Anderson et al. (2003, Study 1).

2011). Emotional similarity has been proposed to facilitate coordinated thoughts and actions, mutual understanding, and interpersonal closeness and attraction (Hatfield, Cacioppo, & Rapson, 1994; Keltner & Kring, 1998; Preston & de Waal, 2002; Schachter, 1959). Anderson and colleagues (2003) reasoned that if emotional similarity is so vital to personal relationships, relationship partners should become more emotionally similar over time as they develop a long-term bond, and such convergence should be positively associated with favorable relationship outcomes.

Anderson and colleagues (2003) examined these possibilities in a series of studies among opposite-sex dating couples and same-sex dormitory roommates. In one study, pairs of roommates were invited to the laboratory and shown positive and negative emotionally evocative film clips in separate rooms, after which their emotional reactions were recorded. The researchers compared the emotional reactions of the students within and across pairs. They found that independent emotional reactions to the film clips were more similar between roommates than between nonroommates. Other studies reported by Anderson and colleagues revealed that the similarity between romantic partners' emotional reactions to events increased over a period of six months, and that such emotional convergence predicted relationship satisfaction. Moreover, as shown in Table 5.1, partners who were more emotionally similar at Time 1 were more likely to be together at Time 2. Later studies produced compatible evidence for the occurrence of emotional convergence, not only in terms of subjective feelings but also in terms of facial expressions and appraisals (Bruder, Dosmukhambetova, Nerb, & Manstead, 2012).

The tendency of romantic partners to converge emotionally over time appears to be so strong that uninvolved observers can pick up on the similarities in emotional expressiveness between romantic couples. De Waal (2009) described a study on the facial resemblance of married couples, in which participants were shown pictures of men and women and were asked to indicate who was married to whom. Some of the pictures had been taken on the partners' wedding day, whereas other pictures had been taken twenty-five years later. Participants could not determine above chance who had married whom based on the pictures taken on the wedding day, but they were able to do so based on the pictures that had been taken twenty-five years later. Interestingly, the observable expressive similarities were greater among couples who indicated that they were happily married. This study suggests that the growing emotional similarity between people in close relationships becomes engrained in their everyday facial expressions, and that such similarity is associated with relationship success.

In light of the apparent benefits of emotional convergence in interpersonal relationships, it is interesting to consider factors that may modulate such convergence. In this regard, research has examined the role of power (Van Kleef et al., 2008). Several studies have shown that people who feel more powerful are less motivated to pay attention to individuating information about other people, because they feel less of a need to fully understand others as they do not depend as much on others as low-power people do (for reviews, see e.g. Fiske & Dépret, 1996; Keltner, Van Kleef, Chen, & Kraus, 2008). To examine the possibility that power reduces responsiveness to the emotions of other people, Van Kleef and colleagues prompted unacquainted same-sex dyads to talk about instances in their life that had caused them great suffering and distress. Participants with a higher sense of power exhibited lower emotional responsiveness to the distress of their conversation partner than did participants with a lower sense of power, as reflected in lower levels of distress and compassion and physiological markers of autonomic emotion regulation (i.e., respiratory sinus arrhythmia reactivity). Accordingly, participants who had told their emotional story to a high-power partner felt less of a social connection with the partner than did those who had talked to a low-power partner.

Social consequences of emotional expressions for relationships

It is clear from the above that emotional responsiveness and convergence are important for smooth social interaction, and that lowered emotional responsiveness may jeopardize the quality of social relationships. But how about the specific effects of discrete emotional expressions? In the remainder of this chapter I consider the interpersonal effects of four broad classes of emotions or "emotion families" (Ekman, 1992) that have been studied in the context of close relationships: affiliative emotions such as happiness, supplication emotions such as sadness and disappointment, dominant and other-blaming emotions such as anger, and appeasement emotions such as guilt, embarrassment, and interpersonal regret (see Van

Kleef, De Dreu, & Manstead, 2010, for a more elaborate discussion of these particular classes of emotions).[1]

Affiliation: displays of happiness facilitate social bonding

The first class of emotions that is relevant in the context of close relationships consists of positive emotions that are associated with opportunity and affiliation, of which happiness is a prime example. Happiness arises when people feel that they are making good progress toward the realization of their goals (Lazarus, 1991). Happiness is associated with a state of pleasure, security, and generosity, which is manifested in outgoingness and approach-related behaviors. It is also associated with well-being and a broadening of momentary thought-action repertoires, which enables individuals to identify and seize opportunities to build enduring (social) resources (Fredrickson, 1998, 2001).

Numerous studies have documented associations between happiness and success in various domains of life, including marriage, friendship, income, work performance, and health (for an extensive review, see Lyobomirsky, King, & Diener, 2005). There is growing evidence that these links exist not only because success makes people happy, but also because happiness engenders success. In a meta-analytic review of cross-sectional, longitudinal, and experimental studies, Lyobomirsky and colleagues obtained converging support for the effects of happiness on various indicators of success in life. Their model emphasized the intrapersonal effects of positive affect on cognition, well-being, and success, suggesting that the success of happy people stems from the fact that the frequent experiences of positive emotions propel them toward active goal pursuit, and that happy people can capitalize on skills and resources that they acquired during previous episodes of pleasant moods. This conclusion resonates with a famous quote by Bertrand Russell: "The good life, as I conceive it, is a happy life. I do not mean that if you are good you will be happy – I mean that if you are happy you will be good" (Russell, 1951).

Although research has established associations between happiness and various measures of life success, it has devoted relatively little attention

---

[1] Obviously, love is also a prominent affective state in close relationships. It is debatable, however, whether love should be considered an emotion, because the common conception of love does not qualify as an acute and relatively short-lived response to a concrete eliciting event; rather, love is a long-lasting feeling of closeness, caring, and attachment, or, in Ekman's (1992) terms, an "emotional attitude" that typically involves multiple emotions. Some have argued for a distinction between a "momentary surge of love" (which would qualify as an emotion) and "relational love" (which would not; Shaver, Morgan, & Wu, 1996). Given that research has almost exclusively focused on relational love, a discussion of this literature falls outside the scope of this book.

to the interpersonal effects of happiness. Nevertheless, many of the positive consequences that have been associated with happiness can also be explained from an interpersonal perspective. It seems plausible that people who are prone to experience positive emotions enjoy social benefits because they more frequently *express* these positive emotions in the presence of others. These positive emotional displays may elicit favorable responses from others, which in turn help the expresser to build (social) resources, garner goodwill and support from others, seize opportunities, and ultimately achieve success in social and occupational life. In this section I consider evidence that speaks to this possibility.

At the interpersonal level of analysis, expressions of happiness signal a desire to affiliate, socialize, and play (Fridlund, 1994). Indeed, as discussed in Chapter 2, several scholars have argued that smiles can be seen as communicative acts aimed at facilitating affiliation and social bonding (Fridlund, 1991b; Hess, Banse, & Kappas, 1995; Jakobs, Manstead, & Fischer, 1999a, 1999b; Kraut & Johnston, 1979; Manstead, Fischer, & Jakobs, 1999). In line with this idea, research has documented that people commonly smile deliberately in order to get others to like them and to establish or maintain social bonds (Clark, Pataki, & Carver, 1996; Godfrey, Jones, & Lord, 1986; Rosenfeld, 1966).

In the context of social relationships, expressions of happiness and related emotions tend to trigger positive responses in observers (Fischer & Manstead, in press; Van Kleef, De Dreu, & Manstead, 2010). Sincere smiles signal that a person is nonthreatening, friendly, and playful, and thereby invite others to approach (Frijda & Mesquita, 1994; Keltner & Kring, 1998). Expressions of happiness are associated with increased liking (Clark & Taraban, 1991; Shaver, Schwartz, Kirson, & O'Connor, 1987), and smiling people are more likely than their nonsmiling counterparts to be ascribed positive traits such as kindness, humor, intelligence, and honesty (Hess, Beaupré, & Cheung, 2002; Reis et al., 1990). Furthermore, studies have shown that expressing happiness and related positive emotions can have favorable outcomes at work in terms of supervisor evaluation and coworker support (Staw, Sutton, & Pelled, 1994). Accordingly, employees have been found to exaggerate their expressions of positive emotions toward their bosses (Duck, 1986).

Other work has shown that individuals high on trait positive affect enjoy more intimate social contact with others and trigger their interaction partners to engage in higher-quality exchanges (Berry & Hansen, 1996). Individuals prone to positive affect tend to be socially engaged with others (Watson, 1988), and their positive emotions may spread to those around them via processes of emotional contagion (Hatfield et al., 1994). Given that feelings of happiness promote prosocial behavior (George & Brief, 1992; Isen, 1987), expressions of happiness can thus contribute to mutually

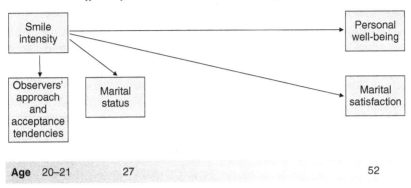

Figure 5.2 Women's smiles in college yearbook photographs taken around the age of 20 positively predict observers' approach and acceptance tendencies, marital status at age 27, and personal well-being and marital satisfaction at age 52 (based on Harker & Keltner, 2001).

rewarding social interactions that serve to build and strengthen social bonds (Harker & Keltner, 2001). Indeed, the expression of positive emotions during conflict discussions has been found to predict relationship satisfaction and a reduced likelihood of relationship dissolution (Carstensen, Gottman, & Levenson, 1995; Gottman & Levenson, 1992). Accordingly, individuals who are prone to experience (and therefore presumably express) positive emotions are more likely than their less cheerful counterparts to be involved in a romantic relationship (Berry & Willingham, 1997).

The positive outcomes associated with expressions of happiness were nicely highlighted in a longitudinal study of the relationship between smiling and life success. Harker and Keltner (2001) examined photographs of female college students from college yearbooks of 1958 and 1960. The researchers coded the women's faces for smiles using the Facial Action Coding System developed by Ekman and Friesen (1976, 1978), focusing on the activation of the zygomatic major (which pulls up the corners of the lips) and the orbicularis oculi (which raises the cheeks and creates crow's feet next to the eyes) muscles. Smile intensity was then used to predict various aspects of the women's life trajectories. The key findings of the study are visualized in Figure 5.2. Women who smiled more in their yearbook pictures were perceived as more pleasant company (as reflected in observers' approach and acceptance tendencies), were more likely to be married by age 27, and reported greater personal well-being and marginally higher marital satisfaction by age 52 (i.e., 30 years after their yearbook pictures had been taken). Although it is impossible to determine how these positive effects came about, it seems plausible that at least some of the positive outcomes associated with smiles can be attributed to the affiliative signals they convey and the favorable responses they elicit from interaction partners. In short, expressions of happiness may contribute to life success because they facilitate the formation of social bonds.

Supplication: displays of sadness and related emotions elicit social support

The second class of emotions that is germane to close relationships consists of emotions that arise when individuals face a loss (sadness), when outcomes fall short of expectations (disappointment), or when negative events may occur (worry, fear). Although these emotions have different secondary appraisal components (Lazarus, 1991; Smith, Haynes, Lazarus, & Pope, 1993), they share a *supplication* function (Van Kleef, De Dreu, & Manstead, 2010) – that is, they serve as a call for help (Clark et al., 1996; Eisenberg, 2000; Eisenberg & Miller, 1987; Kennedy-Moore & Watson, 2001; Timmers, Fischer, & Manstead, 1998). Sadness has been found to increase perceptions of neediness and dependency (Clark & Taraban, 1991), and worry and fear have been shown to communicate a need for assistance (Côté, 2005; Eisenberg, 2000; Kennedy-Moore & Watson, 2001; Yee & Greenberg, 1998). Accordingly, displays of supplication emotions trigger prosocial tendencies in observers (Barnett, Howard, Melton, & Dino, 1982; Clark, Ouellette, Powell, & Milberg, 1987; Labott, Martin, Eason, & Berkey, 1991; Small & Verrochi, 2009; Yee & Greenberg, 1998).

In an illustrative study described by Clark and colleagues (1996), participants were invited to the lab supposedly to take part in a text-proofing experiment together with two other students. Participants were led to believe that they would work in a group of three, and that one person would be allowed to leave early while the other two would proofread each other's work. The experimenter explained to each participant that the other two students were hoping that they would be allowed to leave early, and that the participant could choose who would be dismissed and who would have to stay. Participants then received the work of the other students, which included self-reports of how they were supposedly feeling at the time. The results showed that fellow students who were described as sad were more likely to be selected by participants to leave the experiment early than those who were described as nonemotional or angry. In another study, Clark and colleagues (1987) found that expressions of sadness had stronger effects on helping among individuals desiring a communal relationship than among

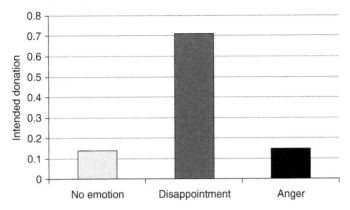

Figure 5.3 Intended donations (in euros) to a charity collector as a function of the collector's emotional expression (based on Van Doorn et al., 2015b, Study 2).

those desiring a more business-like exchange relationship, suggesting that the expression of supplication emotions is particularly effective in close relationships.

Other studies have investigated the interpersonal effects of emotional expressions on compliance with explicit requests for help (Van Doorn, Van Kleef, & Van der Pligt, 2015b). In one experiment, participants were asked to imagine that while out shopping they encountered a charity collector. After the participant had donated 50 cents, the charity collector paused in front of them, as if he expected an additional donation. Participants were shown a picture of the collector's face, which expressed either anger, disappointment, or no emotion. As shown in Figure 5.3, participants in the disappointment condition were willing to more than double their initial donation, while those in the neutral and angry conditions did not intend to make an additional donation. In fact, several participants in the anger condition indicated that they wanted to *take back* their initial donation. The difference between the disappointment and anger conditions was mediated by the perceived appropriateness of the charity collector's emotional expression, which was higher in the case of disappointment than in the case of anger.

In another experiment by Van Doorn and colleagues (2015b), participants played a computer-simulated donation game. They first made a donation in a practice round, upon which they were informed that previous players had on average made either low or high allocations (i.e., a descriptive norm; Cialdini, Reno, & Kallgren, 1990). Then they received a message from their "partner," who asked them to be more generous in the real game than they had been in the trial round. This request was paired with anger or disappointment about the participant's allocation in the trial round, or with no emotion. In the absence of an emotional expression participants conformed to the descriptive norm, giving more or less generously according to what others had given in the past. When the partner had expressed disappointment, participants donated substantially more regardless of the norm; when the partner had expressed anger, participants donated substantially less regardless of the norm. The difference between the anger and disappointment conditions was again mediated by perceived appropriateness.

These studies demonstrate that expressing emotions as part of a request can affect targets' willingness to comply with the request. Interestingly, the predictive value of emotional expressions outweighed that of an explicit descriptive norm, indicating that emotional expressions can be a powerful source of social influence (Van Kleef, Van Doorn, Heerdink, & Koning, 2011). The studies also corroborate EASI theory's proposition that the effectiveness of emotional expressions in engendering social influence depends on their perceived appropriateness within the social context. In the context of a request for help, expressions of disappointment are perceived as more appropriate than expressions of anger, which explains why the former are effective whereas the latter are not.

A particular way of expressing sadness is by crying (Vingerhoets, Cornelius, Van Heck, & Becht, 2000). Similar to other displays of sadness, crying communicates to others that one is suffering and in need of attention or support (Cornelius & Labott, 2001; Nelson, 2005), and the visible presence of tears may further strengthen this signal. Cornelius and colleagues found that tearful faces were rated as sadder than the same faces with the tears digitally removed (Cornelius, Nussbaum, Warner, & Moeller, 2000). They also reported that participants were more inclined to comfort a crying person than a noncrying person (Cornelius & Lubliner, 2003). Similar findings were reported by Hendriks and Vingerhoets (2006). Compared to individuals expressing anger, fear, or no emotion, crying individuals were perceived as less emotionally stable and less aggressive. Participants reported feeling more sadness themselves upon seeing crying faces as compared to faces showing other emotional expressions, and they reported a greater inclination to provide emotional support in response to crying than noncrying faces. In another study, participants reported that they would express less anger toward a crying person than toward a noncrying person (Hendriks, Croon, & Vingerhoets, 2008), suggesting that tears may not only elicit social support but also buffer against aggression.

Interestingly, however, participants in the latter study also judged crying individuals less positively than noncrying individuals, and they reported experiencing more negative emotions in the presence of crying individuals (Hendriks et al., 2008). This raises the question of why people are inclined to provide support to crying people: Is it because they wish to alleviate the crying person's negative state or their own negative state (Batson, O'Quin, Fultz, Vanderplas, & Isen, 1983; Cialdini et al., 1987)? The broader altruism-versus-egoism debate is beyond the scope of this book, but this more specific question is relevant to theorizing about the downstream consequences of affective reactions to the emotional expressions of others (see Chapter 3). The data reported by Hendriks and colleagues are consistent with an interpretation in terms of negative state relief, according to which the motivation to help a suffering person is fueled by the desire to relieve one's own distress (Cialdini et al., 1987). The altruism account cannot be ruled out, however, because it is unclear whether the reciprocal sadness that observers of others' crying tend to experience is a key mediating mechanism or a mere by-product, leaving open the possibility that altruistic considerations are (partly) responsible for the effect.

Dominance and blame: how displays of anger shape close relationships

The third group of emotions that is of interest here consists of negative emotions associated with the (deliberate) frustration of goals. A prominent example is anger, which arises when a person's goals are thwarted and he or she blames someone else for it. Anger is associated with a tendency to aggress against the person (or object) seen as responsible for the goal blockage and with a desire to bring about change (Averill, 1982; Fischer & Roseman, 2007). Anger is facilitated when the individual perceives attack as a viable option to restore the unfavorable situation (Lazarus, 1991). Perhaps in part because of the associated action tendencies of coercion and attack, anger signals power and dominance (Tiedens, 2001). Anger is commonly expressed in close relationships, most notably when partners feel unjustly treated (Averill, 1982; Fitness & Fletcher, 1993; Shaver et al., 1987).

How do expressions of anger influence the development of close relationships? Research into this question is relatively scarce, and the evidence is mixed. Some studies point to the potential benefits of expressing anger in close relationships. Averill (1982) asked respondents to describe situations in which they had been angry at somebody else or someone else had been angry at them. The majority of the respondents indicated being angry at someone else on average once or twice a week, with the anger being targeted mostly toward close relatives (e.g., parent, child), romantic partners, and friends. Participants generally experienced the episodes of anger as negative, both when they were the expresser and when they were the target of the anger. Nevertheless, 62 percent of the expressers and 70 percent of the targets deemed the anger episode useful, because it had prompted partners to address a relational problem. Another study revealed that a common response tendency to expressions of anger in intimate relationships is to talk things over rather than express aggression (Fehr, Baldwin, Collins, Patterson, & Benditt, 1999), which helps explain why expressions of anger can be beneficial in close relationships.

Further evidence for the functionality of anger in personal relationships comes from a study by Fischer and Roseman (2007). They invited participants to describe instances in which they had felt either anger or contempt toward someone else and to indicate what they were hoping to accomplish by expressing the emotion and how the interaction had evolved. A common theme in participants' responses was that they expressed anger to make clear that the other person had done something wrong, and that they hoped to change the other person's behavior and/or make the other apologize. Another common theme in participants' stories was that their anger had had favorable long-term consequences, despite eliciting initial negative affective reactions from the partner. A prototypical anger episode started with short-term attacks (mostly verbal aggression) but often resulted in reconciliation and relationship improvement later on. Consistent with Fehr and colleagues' (1999) findings, respondents reported that their displays of anger had led to constructive conversations that were geared toward resolving relational problems. Fischer and Roseman concluded that, compared to contempt, anger is characterized more by short-term verbal attack, longer-term reconciliation and reparation of harm done, and ultimately higher relationship quality.

The conclusions that can be drawn from this study are somewhat limited by the fact that anger was contrasted only with contempt. Contempt is a particularly toxic emotion in close relationships – it is the emotion that is most predictive of marriage dissolution (Gottman, 1993). This raises the question of whether expressions of anger are more or less beneficial than expressions of emotions that are less destructive than contempt, such as sadness or disappointment. In this respect, a study on the communication of negative emotions in marital conflicts revealed that statements communicating anger evoked more antagonistic tendencies in partners than did statements communicating distress (Kubany, Bauer, Muraoka, Richard, & Read, 1995). The authors of this study concluded that, compared to expressions of distress, the explicit verbalization of anger may actually be maladaptive because it undermines social support and contributes to marital dissatisfaction (also see Guerrero, La Valley, & Farinelli, 2008, for a similar conclusion).

Given the mixed evidence and the different comparison emotions involved in the extant body of research, it is unclear at this point how beneficial expressions of anger really are in the context of close relationships. It stands to reason that any functionality of anger displays is subject to boundary conditions, many of which may relate to the perceived appropriateness of the anger expression. EASI theory predicts that positive consequences of anger expressions are more likely to the degree that the target perceives the partner's anger as reasonable and appropriate in light of the situation (Van Kleef et al., 2011). In such cases, anger should be more likely to elicit inferential processes that may be beneficial for the relationship (e.g., the target may come to realize that she or he did something wrong). In contrast, expressions of anger can be expected to threaten the quality of relationships to the degree that the target perceives the anger as inappropriate, for instance because it seems uncalled for given the situation, or because it is too intense, expressed too frequently, or expressed in an overly confronting way. In such instances, displays of anger are more likely to trigger negative affective reactions in the target (e.g., hostile feelings). Although research is lacking, it has been proposed that frequent expressions of anger may have detrimental effects both at the intrapersonal level and at the interpersonal level, as they may solidify a hostile attitude, overshadow other emotions that are potentially more advantageous, and/or instigate a vicious cycle of hostility (Tavris, 1984).

Besides the perceived appropriateness of anger expressions, EASI theory points to the importance of information processing. Again, research is lacking, but it seems plausible that the consequences of anger expressions in close relationships depend in part on the target's information-processing depth. When information processing is high, individuals are more likely to consider the various implications of their partner's anger and to draw inferences as to how their own behavior might have given rise to the anger and how they might alleviate the situation by changing their conduct. In contrast, when information processing is low, affective reactions take on heightened prominence in driving behavioral responses to expressions of anger. In such cases expressions of anger would be more likely to instigate a vicious cycle of anger and hostility that may pose a serious threat to the relationship.

Consistent with this argument, a recent series of studies revealed that the effects of anger expressions in close relationships depend on the communal motivation of the target of the anger (Yoo, Clark, Lemay, Salovey, & Monin, 2011). In one study, married couples reported on the communal strength of their marriage, the expression of anger within their relationship, and their relationship satisfaction. Lower communal motivation was associated with more negative evaluations of angry partners and with reduced relationship satisfaction. In another study, college students reported on the communal strength of their best friendships and on the anger expressions that occurred within those friendships. In addition to replicating the previous study, the data revealed effects on the provision of social support. Lower communal motivation was associated with less support provided to angry partners, whereas higher communal motivation was associated with greater support. Even though these studies did not directly consider the role of information processing, it is conceivable that greater communal motivation is associated with a stronger motivation to consider and reflect upon the meaning and implications of a partner's anger, which would promote inferential processing and behavioral adaptation in response to a partner's anger expressions rather than hostile reactions and conflict escalation. Future research is needed to examine this possibility directly.

Appeasement: expressions of guilt and related emotions restore relationships

The fourth class of emotions that is pertinent to close relationships consists of emotions such as guilt, embarrassment, and interpersonal regret. Such emotions serve an *appeasement* function in that they communicate submissiveness and signal that one is aware that one did something wrong and is willing to make up for it, thereby pacifying observers of social transgressions (Castelfranchi & Poggi, 1990; Keltner, 1995; M. Lewis, 2000; Miller & Leary, 1992). Especially in predominantly cooperative settings such as close relationships, expressions of appeasement reduce tendencies among observers to "move against" the expresser, thus defusing conflict and competition and contributing to the restoration of threatened relationships (Van Kleef, De Dreu, & Manstead, 2010).

Baumeister, Stillwell, and Heatherton (1994) made a powerful case for the inherently interpersonal nature and social functionality of guilt, which arises in social relationships as a result of the (perceived) infliction of harm, loss, or distress on a relationship partner. Baumeister and colleagues suggested that feelings of guilt are stronger, more prevalent, and more influential in close relationships than in distant ones (cf. Clark et al., 1996), and they argued that (the expression of) guilt strengthens social bonds in three partly interrelated ways. First, guilt may contribute to healthy relationships by showing that one cares about the relationship and is willing to make amends for a transgression. Second, guilt may restore relationships by redistributing emotional distress and alleviating emotional imbalances that arose within the relationship due to some misdemeanor. Third, the deliberate evocation of guilt in a relationship partner may produce desired behavioral changes and discourage future transgressions. Although direct evidence for effects on relationship quality is scarce, expressions of guilt have been found to increase perceptions of perspective taking (Leith & Baumeister, 1998), cooperativeness, likeability, and interpersonal sensitivity, and to decrease perceptions of competitiveness, self-centeredness, and hostility (Van Kleef, De Dreu, & Manstead, 2006), suggesting that displays of guilt are indeed beneficial for social relationships.

Whereas guilt is associated with actions that harm others, embarrassment arises from transgressions of conventions that govern public interactions (Keltner, 1996). Despite this difference in the antecedents of guilt and embarrassment, the social functions of both emotions appear to be similar. Displays of embarrassment and related expressions such as blushing signal that one feels bad about a faux pas and imply that one will conform to social norms in the future (Goffman, 1967; Keltner, Young, & Buswell, 1997; Leary, Britt, Cutlip, & Templeton, 1992). Such signals may facilitate social bonding. An early study by Semin and Manstead (1982) showed that displays of embarrassment after a social transgression had equally favorable effects on evaluations of likeability as actual restitution behavior, suggesting that visible signs of embarrassment can help to maintain or restore cooperative relations. Embarrassment displays have further been found to evoke sympathy, positive evaluations, and helpful behavior in others (Keltner & Anderson, 2000; Miller, 2004; Miller & Leary, 1992).

A review by Keltner and Buswell (1997) highlighted interesting parallels between the functions of nonhuman appeasement and human embarrassment. In terms of antecedents, social situations that may evoke nonhuman appeasement and human embarrassment as well as related phenomena such as blushing include interactions with high-status individuals (de Waal, 1986, 1988; Keltner et al., 1997) and strangers (Tangney, Miller, Flicker, & Barlow, 1996), the distribution of resources (Öhman, 1986), and being the center of (undesirable) social attention (Leary et al., 1992). In terms of behavioral consequences, nonhuman appeasement and human embarrassment involve similar responses that may have evolved to reduce social threats and restore cooperative relationships, such as submissive and affiliative behaviors (de Waal, 1986, 1988; Eibl-Eibesfeldt, 1989; Keltner, 1995).

A final appeasement emotion that merits discussion is interpersonal regret.[2] The favorable social consequences of interpersonal regret were demonstrated in a study by Zeelenberg, Van der Pligt, and Manstead (1998), who found that feelings of interpersonal regret can

---

[2] I use the adjective "interpersonal" to distinguish the feeling of regretting something that happened to *another person* from the more commonly studied feeling of regretting something that happened to the self (Gilovich & Medvec, 1995).

motivate "behavioral repair work." In one study, they coded cases from a Dutch television show called "I Am Sorry" – a show that provides people with the opportunity to undo regrets arising in close relationships by apologizing and offering flowers to the target of the regret. Zeelenberg and colleagues found that apologies were indeed often motivated by interpersonal regrets, especially those stemming from action rather than inaction. Apologies, in turn, signal interpersonal sensitivity and a willingness to appreciate another person's perspective – important relationship repairing qualities that facilitate reconciliation (Steiner, 2000; Tavuchis, 1991). Empirical evidence indicates that apologizing after a transgression or explicitly communicating regret may reduce blame and punishment (Darby & Schlenker, 1982), increase forgiveness (Bachman & Guerrero, 2006), reduce aggression (Ohbuchi, Kameda, & Agarie, 1989), and enhance liking and positive impressions (Darby & Schlenker, 1982; Ohbuchi et al., 1989; Van Kleef, De Dreu, & Manstead, 2006). Thus, just like expressing guilt and embarrassment, expressing interpersonal regret and making an apology can prevent hostile responses and help sustain close relationships.

Conclusion

The research reviewed in this chapter indicates that emotions have critical social functions and consequences in close relationships. Expressions of affiliation emotions such as happiness facilitate social bonding. Displays of supplication emotions such as sadness, disappointment, worry, and fear help to garner social support. Expressions of dominant emotions such as anger may serve to identify relational problems and enforce changes in a partner's behavior. And displays of appeasement emotions such as guilt, embarrassment, and interpersonal regret contribute to the quality of close relationships by signaling that one cares about the relationship, feels bad about a transgression, and is willing to make up for it.

Even though most research on the social effects of emotions in close relationships has not been designed with the aim of disentangling affective reactions from inferential processes, examples of both mechanisms appear throughout this literature. In the case of affiliative emotions such as happiness, extant research mostly points to a role for affective processes. People tend to prefer interactions with cheerful others because such exchanges lift their own spirits and contribute to constructive social relationships (Clark et al., 1996; Hatfield et al., 1994). Research to date has not paid close attention to inferential processes that may be triggered by expressions of happiness, but several studies indicate that observers make positive trait inferences based on displays of happiness (Hess et al., 2002; Reis et al., 1990). Future studies could investigate such inferential processes in greater depth.

Research on the social effects of sadness and related supplication emotions contains examples of both affective reactions (e.g., personal distress; Cialdini et al., 1987) and inferential processes (e.g., inferences of neediness and dependence; Clark & Taraban, 1991). Displays of sadness, disappointment, worry, and fear help to garner social support by communicating dependence and lack of coping potential as well as by instilling distress in observers, which observers then aim to alleviate through prosocial behavior. It is not clear at this point to what extent behavioral responses to displays of supplication in close relationships are driven by affective reactions versus inferential processes. From a practical point of view this may not be a problem, because the affective reactions and inferential processes that are triggered by displays of supplication are likely to produce similar behavioral tendencies. From a theoretical point of view, however, it would be desirable to gain a deeper understanding of the relative importance of affective and inferential processes.

Studies on anger and similar dominance-asserting emotions have also documented a role for negative affective reactions (e.g., reciprocal anger, hostile tendencies; Guerrero et al., 2008; Kubany et al., 1995) as well as more constructive inferential processes (e.g., inferences that there is a problem that requires attention; Averill, 1982; Fischer & Roseman, 2007). To date, no study has compared the relative influence of negative affective reactions and inferential processes in response to expressions of anger in the context of close relationships. As a result, no firm conclusions can be drawn regarding the functionality of anger expressions in determining relationship quality. EASI theory would predict that expressions of anger are more likely to produce beneficial outcomes to the extent that the target is more motivated and able to engage in thorough information processing and the anger is perceived as appropriate. Research is needed to test this prediction.

Finally, work on appeasement emotions such as guilt, embarrassment, and interpersonal regret has documented evidence for the occurrence of inferential processes as triggered by emotional displays of appeasement (e.g., inferences of interpersonal concern; Van Kleef, De Dreu, & Manstead, 2006). There is also some evidence that expressions of guilt and embarrassment elicit positive affective reactions in observers (Baumeister et al., 1994), which might be fueled by the inference that the expresser cares about the relationship despite his or her transgression. Here, too, more research is needed to better disentangle the role of affective and inferential processes.

In sum, there is some evidence for the role of affective and inferential processes in shaping responses to emotional expressions in close relationships, but more research is welcome. In particular, future studies are needed to examine the proposed moderating influences of the observer's information-processing motivation and ability and the perceived appropriateness of the emotional expression. Such research is especially critical for our understanding of the (dys)functionality of anger in close relationships, because the affective versus inferential processes that are triggered by expressions of anger motivate opposite behavioral tendencies (i.e., hostility vs. reconciliation, respectively).

CHAPTER 6

Social effects of emotions in groups

A certainty in the mystery of managing effective work groups is that groups are emotional. By understanding their emotionality, we may come closer to understanding the mystery.

Barsade and Gibson (1998, p. 98)

Being innately social animals, humans spend a considerable proportion of their lives in various types of groups. Groups are a natural breeding ground for emotions (Barsade & Gibson, 1998). Social interactions are the primary elicitors of emotions (Anderson & Guerrero, 1998; Parkinson, 1996; Planalp, 1999), and the opportunity for such emotionally evocative encounters increases exponentially with the size of social groups. Whether we think of work groups, school classes, groups of friends, sports teams, or any other type of interacting social collective, emotional influences abound in groups (Kelly & Barsade, 2001). This makes the group setting ideal for studying the social effects of emotional expressions – or so one would think. Despite the fact that group processes are at the heart of what defines much of social and organizational psychology and adjacent disciplines, empirical research on the social effects of emotional expressions in groups is relatively scarce. This is all the more surprising given that the study of emotions in groups got off to an early start.

Scientific interest in the interplay of emotions and group dynamics dates back at least to Le Bon's (1895) classic work on the role of the "group mind" in crowd behavior. Le Bon argued that any individual who is immersed in a large group for a sufficient period of time will sooner or later find him- or herself in a special state characterized by increased emotionality, impulsiveness, incapacitated reasoning, and lack of critical judgment. Similarly, McDougall (1923) characterized the experience of crowd membership as being "carried away by forces" which one is "powerless to control" (p. 57). These overpowering forces were thought to create collective emotional attributes that transcend the consciousness of the individual group members (Barsade & Gibson, 1998).

Contemporary views on the role of emotions in groups are considerably more positive (Van Kleef & Fischer, 2016). Over the past two decades, several theorists have proposed that emotions fulfill critical social functions in groups that help their members to address the various problems associated with living and working in groups (Keltner & Gross, 1999). For instance, emotions have been proposed to play a role in the development and maintenance of interpersonal bonds and group cohesion, the allocation of roles and responsibilities among group members, the resolution of problems associated with deviance and defection, and the coordination of collective efforts toward the achievement of shared goals (e.g., Barsade & Gibson, 1998; Fischer & Manstead, in press; Frijda & Mesquita, 1994; Keltner & Haidt, 1999; Spoor & Kelly, 2004).

Although few scholars doubt the importance of emotions for understanding group processes, empirical research on the social consequences of emotions in groups is still in its infancy. The relatively immature status of this field may be due in part to inherent characteristics of groups that render them difficult, time-consuming, and costly to study. Surely, these difficulties have hampered progress in group research more generally. Over forty years ago, Steiner (1974) lamented the fact that social psychology was becoming increasingly individualistic and that interest in the group as a system had given way to a focus on intrapersonal processes, exclaiming in the title of his article: "Whatever happened to the group in social psychology?" Countering the suggestion that group research was dead, Levine and Moreland (1990) later noted that "groups are alive and well, but living elsewhere" (p. 620). Indeed, the study of (small) groups now occurs predominantly in the field of organizational science, where the importance of the group as a social system is clearly recognized.

The focus in this chapter is on small groups engaging in actual or simulated interaction rather than on larger and more abstract collectives such as organizations, nations, or groups defined by demographic characteristics such as age, gender, ethnicity, or socioeconomic status. Although the role of emotions is also being studied quite fruitfully in the context of larger collectives and intergroup relations (Iyer & Leach, 2008), most notably in the interrelated areas of group-based emotions (e.g., Doosje, Branscombe, Spears, & Manstead, 1998), intergroup emotions theory (e.g., Mackie, Devos, & Smith, 2000; Smith, Seger, & Mackie, 2007), and collective action (e.g., Van Zomeren, Spears, Fischer, & Leach, 2004), this research tends to focus on the social origins and consequences of emotional *experience* rather than on the social consequences of emotional *expressions*. As such this work falls outside the scope of this book, which is chiefly concerned with the social effects of emotional expressions.

The functionality of emotions in group life

Several theorists have argued that emotions serve vital functions in groups, which may have played a role in promoting group survival over evolutionary history (Keltner & Gross, 1999; Keltner, Haidt, & Shiota, 2006; Spoor & Kelly, 2004). For example, some scholars have proposed that emotions such as fear, hatred, disgust, and contempt function to sharpen group boundaries (Frijda & Mesquita, 1994; Heise & O'Brien, 1993; also see Dunham, 2011). Suggestive evidence for this idea is provided by research in the area of terror management, where it has been found that the experimental induction of fear of death (i.e., mortality salience) increases ingroup solidarity and outgroup derogation (Greenberg et al., 1990). Other work has shown that expressions of contempt serve a social-distancing function (Fischer & Roseman, 2007), which may contribute to clear group boundaries by keeping outgroup members at a distance, both psychologically and physically.

Other scholars have proposed that the differential experience and expression of emotions help group members define and negotiate their respective roles and statuses within the group (Clark, 1990; Collins, 1990). Consistent with this idea, research has revealed associations between status and the expression of discrete emotions such as anger, sadness, embarrassment, contempt, pride, and fear (Keltner, Young, Heerey, Oemig, & Monarch, 1998; Tiedens, Ellsworth, & Mesquita, 2000). Reflecting such associations, expressions of anger and pride tend to be perceived by observers as signals of high status, whereas displays of sadness and gratitude are perceived as signs of low status (Tiedens, 2001; Tiedens et al., 2000). The actual or stereotypical association between discrete patterns of emotional responding and particular power roles contributes to a sense of role clarity, predictability, and stability in groups that may serve as a heuristic solution to conflict and that may facilitate the achievement of group goals (Keltner, Van Kleef, Chen, & Kraus, 2008).

Finally, theorists have proposed that collective emotional behavior helps group members deal with group-related problems (Keltner & Gross, 1999). Some evidence for this claim is provided by a study on chimpanzee groups (de Waal, 1996). The chimpanzees in this study were observed to engage in exuberant affiliation immediately prior to the allocation of scarce resources. The shared and cultivated positive emotions presumably served to strengthen social bonds that might be threatened by conflict over the distribution of scarce resources. Such behavior is not too different from the routines exhibited by diplomats involved in complicated international negotiations, in which a considerable amount of time tends to be devoted to building and sustaining positive emotions and rapport prior to discussing contentious issues.

Upon reviewing the primarily theoretical body of work on the presumed functionality of emotions in group life, Spoor and Kelly (2004) proposed that emotions serve a coordination function in groups. They suggested that this coordination function may become manifest in two different ways. First, when they become shared, emotions may facilitate coordinated action by fostering group bonds and group loyalty. Second, emotional expressions may provide information about the group and the current situation to other group members, which may help to coordinate joint activities and goal pursuit (also see Chapter 2 for a discussion of emotional expressions as communicative signals). These presumed functions of emotions in groups show interesting conceptual parallels with the two mechanisms underlying the social effects of emotions identified in Emotions as Social Information (EASI) theory (i.e., affective reactions and inferential processes). In the next sections I review research that speaks to various types of affective reactions and inferential processes in groups and I consider the consequences of these phenomena for group functioning in cases where such data are available.

Affective reactions, affective composition, and group functioning

A considerable proportion of the empirical research on emotions in groups has been concerned with the question of when and how emotions become shared in groups. The lion's share of research has focused on various types of affective convergence. After reviewing this research, I discuss studies on the related phenomena of affective divergence and affective diversity.

Affective convergence, group emotion, and group affective tone

A recurring theme in empirical work on the role of emotions in groups is the notion that individual group members' emotions may, over time, become shared by other members of the group. Such affective similarity among group members arises from the combination of bottom-up affective compositional effects (e.g., individual group members' emotions) and the group's top-down affective context (e.g., an emotionally evocative situation the group members are in together; Barsade & Gibson, 1998; Kelly & Barsade, 2001). The resulting affective state of the group has been variably referred to as "group affective tone" (e.g., Collins, Lawrence, Troth, & Jordan, 2013; George, 1990; Sy, Côté, & Saavedra, 2005) or "group emotion" (e.g., Kelly & Barsade, 2001; Smith et al., 2007). Several theorists have proposed that the sharedness of emotions among group members promotes group functioning and survival. For instance, Dezecache et al. (2013) argued that the (nonconscious) attunement to and spreading of emotional signals in groups is a form of spontaneous cooperative behavior that functions to share survival-value information to conspecifics, and Spoor and Kelly (2004) suggested that the sharedness of emotions among group members facilitates bonding and coordinated action toward joint goals.

In some of the earliest studies on affective convergence within teams, Totterdell and his associates examined whether the emotional states of team members become linked over time. In a first study, Totterdell, Kellett, Teuchmann, and Briner (1998) investigated in teams of community nurses how people's moods are influenced by the collective mood of their teammates. They found a significant association between the nurses' moods and the collective moods of their teammates, which could not be accounted for by shared hassles. In a second study Totterdell and colleagues (1998) found similar evidence for mood linkage within a team of accountants.

A later study demonstrated a similar form of affective convergence in sports teams. Totterdell (2000) had players from two professional cricket teams provide ratings of their moods during a competitive match between the teams. The results showed that the players' moods were more strongly correlated with the current aggregate mood of their own team than with the aggregate mood of the other team or with the aggregate mood of their own team at other times. Mood linkage was not affected by the score of the game. In Kelly and Barsade's (2001) terms, these various studies point to the workings of bottom-up (rather than top-down) processes of affective convergence in groups.

Compatible findings were reported by Bartel and Saavedra (2000), who investigated affective convergence in work groups. The authors compared observers' reports of group mood with group members' own mood ratings. Groups converged for eight distinct mood categories, and observers' ratings of work group mood were positively correlated with the groups' aggregated self-report scores. The study also revealed that moods characterized by high arousal (e.g., cheerful enthusiasm, hostile irritability) yielded more accurate observer assessments and were more likely spread among the group members than moods characterized by low levels of arousal (e.g., serene warmth, depressed sluggishness).

Interestingly, later work has demonstrated that the emotions of one group member can even spread to the rest of the group in situations where nonverbal cues are very difficult or impossible to perceive. For instance, a study on virtual teams yielded evidence of emotional contagion in the absence of visual access to nonverbal emotional displays (Cheshin, Rafaeli, & Bos, 2011). When confronted with a confederate who expressed anger or happiness via text messages, other team members caught the emotion and in turn displayed that emotion via text messages to other teammates, thus reinforcing the emotional state within the team. Another study found that displays of joy and fear by one person were involuntarily transmitted via a second person to a third one, even if the third person could not explicitly recognize the second person's emotional expression (Dezecache et al., 2013).

Clearly, then, moods and emotions can spread among group members, resulting in affective convergence. But how does the resulting affective state of the group shape group processes and outcomes? Several studies have identified effects of the shared emotional states of group members on various indices of group functioning. For instance, an early field study by George (1990) revealed that positive group affective tone (i.e., shared positive affect) in work groups was negatively related to absenteeism, while negative group affective tone (i.e., shared negative affect) was negatively associated with prosocial behavior. A longitudinal field study of workgroups of government employees similarly showed that positive affective tone was negatively associated with group absence rates (Mason & Griffin, 2003). Other studies revealed favorable effects of positive group affect on group efficacy (Gibson, 2003), customer service performance (George, 1995), and group creativity (Grawitch, Munz, & Kramer, 2003).

Research also speaks to the consequences of affective convergence for group interaction. In a seminal laboratory study, Barsade (2002) examined the downstream effects of emotional contagion on cooperation and conflict in ad hoc groups. Participants in groups that included a confederate who displayed positive emotions reported more pleasant moods later on than did those in groups with a confederate showing negative emotions. Moreover, the extent to which group members caught the confederate's affective state was predictive of levels of cooperation and conflict, with dispersion of positive affect leading to greater cooperation and reduced conflict in the group, as summarized in Figure 6.1. In a similar vein, Sy and colleagues (2005) demonstrated in a study of ad hoc laboratory groups that positive group affective tone was associated with better group coordination.

In another lab experiment, Klep, Wisse, and Van der Flier (2011) compared the consequences of dynamically versus statically emerging group-level affective states. In the dynamic condition, groups of students watched an emotionally evocative film clip together, and they were encouraged to share their emotional responses to the film with one another. This procedure facilitated interactive affective sharing processes, such as emotional contagion, affective comparison, and deliberate social sharing of emotions. In the static condition, students watched the same film clip in individual cubicles before they joined their fellow group members. Group members were thus exposed to the same situation, but interactive affective sharing processes were precluded. Klep and colleagues found that group affect arising from the dynamic and interactive

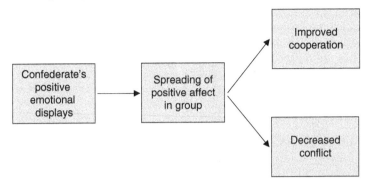

Figure 6.1   Effects of a confederate's positive emotional displays on the positive affective state of the group and downstream consequences for cooperation and conflict (based on Barsade, 2002).

exchange of emotions through emotional contagion and deliberate social sharing (cf. bottom-up compositional effects in the model proposed by Kelly & Barsade, 2001) improved feelings of group belongingness and information sharing on a later group task compared to statically created group affect. This study suggests that the process through which emotions become shared in groups adds explanatory value above and beyond the sharedness per se, a conclusion that resonates with theoretical arguments about the functionality of emotional contagion and related processes (e.g., Hatfield, Cacioppo, & Rapson, 1994; Keltner & Haidt, 1999; Spoor & Kelly, 2004; see Chapter 3).

Although most research speaks to the favorable consequences of shared positive affect, there is also some evidence for potential benefits of shared negative affect. Locke and Horowitz (1990) examined the effects of similarity versus dissimilarity among dyad members in levels of dysphoria, a mild form of depression. They found that people in homogeneous dyads (in which both partners were dysphoric or both partners were nondysphoric) were more satisfied with the interaction than were people in heterogeneous dyads. Individuals in heterogeneous dyads also perceived each other as colder and spoke about increasingly negative topics as the interaction progressed. Although it is unclear to what extent these dyadic effects generalize to larger groups, this study suggests that the sharedness of emotions can contribute to smoother group interactions, even if the shared emotions are (mildly) negative.

Additional evidence for the potential benefits of shared negative affect comes from an experimental study on group decision making (Kooij-de Bode, Van Knippenberg, & Van Ginkel, 2010). Drawing on classic findings that negative affect is associated with more extensive information processing and greater openness and attention to new information (Forgas, 1995; Forgas & George, 2001; Schwarz & Bless, 1991), the authors argued that the presence of negative affect in groups may be important in tasks in which information is distributed among members and thus needs to be shared and elaborated for optimal team performance (also see Van Knippenberg, Kooij-de Bode, & Van Ginkel, 2010). In line with this idea, they found that negative affectivity stimulated group information processing and decision quality in groups in which information was distributed among group members, but not in groups in which information was fully shared. Other research in different task settings has found adverse effects of negative group mood for team performance (Jordan, Lawrence, & Troth, 2006), suggesting that the favorable effects observed by Kooij-de Bode and colleagues are indeed limited to particular circumstances.

Complicating matters further, some scholars have suggested that shared positive affect can be harmful to groups in certain circumstances because it may undermine the critical mind-set that is required for certain types of performance (George & King, 2007). Indeed, one study found that high positive affective tone was detrimental to creative task performance in teams whose members were less likely to express divergent opinions and thoroughly explore different options (Tsai, Chi, Grandey, & Fung, 2012). This suggests that positive affective tone is a potential liability for groups who are prone to "groupthink" (Janis, 1972), the phenomenon that a strong drive toward consensus leads members of highly cohesive decision making groups to suppress dissent and neglect alternative decisions or courses of action.

These arguments and findings suggest that the functionality of positive versus negative affective tone in groups depends on particularities of the situation, including the nature of the task the group is carrying out. The aforementioned study by Klep and colleagues (2011) provides some evidence for this possibility. Consistent with prior theorizing and research on the intrapersonal effects of emotions on individual cognition (e.g., Amabile, Barsade, Mueller, & Staw, 2005; Ashby, Isen, & Turken, 1999; Forgas, 2000; Fredrickson, 2001; Isen, 2004; Schwarz & Bless, 1991), they found that shared positive affect enhanced performance on a task that required breadth of cognitive scope and creativity, whereas shared negative affect boosted performance on a task that demanded analytical information processing and attention to detail.

Affective divergence and affective diversity

Based on the preceding review, affective convergence appears to be more prevalent within groups than affective divergence. Nevertheless, several situational characteristics may contribute to affective divergence. An early study by Lanzetta and English (1989) revealed that patterns of affective convergence versus divergence depend on the cooperative versus competitive nature of social relationships. Participants who expected a cooperative interaction with another person were more likely to mimic the other person's smiles versus grimaces, thus producing converging affective states. Participants who expected a competitive interaction, however, were more likely to respond to the other person's emotional expressions with complementary rather than reciprocal affective reactions, matching smiles with grimaces and vice versa.

Although not a group study, this experiment suggests that affective convergence in groups is more likely to occur to the degree that group members' goals are cooperatively linked (Van Kleef, De Dreu, & Manstead, 2010), and that affective divergence becomes more likely to the degree that goals are competitively linked. This conclusion is in line with Totterdell's (2000) finding that cricket players' moods were more strongly correlated with the aggregate mood of their own team members (with whom they had a cooperative relationship) than with the mood of the other team's members (with whom they had a competitive relationship).

Related work speaks to the role of group membership in shaping processes of affective convergence versus divergence. In a series of experiments involving affective priming and lexical decision tasks, Weisbuch and Ambady (2008) examined affective reactions to the emotional expressions of ingroup versus outgroup members (operationalized in terms of race as well as sports team endorsement). They observed relatively more positive affective reactions to fear expressions and more negative affective reactions to joy expressions among outgroup perceivers compared to ingroup perceivers, indicating differential affective divergence as a function of group membership.

Compatible evidence was reported by Van der Schalk and colleagues (2011). In two experiments they used facial electromyography (fEMG), coding of facial displays based on the Facial Action Coding System (FACS; Ekman & Friesen, 1978), and self-reports of emotion to examine patterns of mimicry in response to emotional expressions by ingroup and outgroup members. Across the board, the studies yielded evidence that displays of anger and fear by outgroup members were mimicked to a lesser extent than displays of the same emotions by ingroup members. Specifically, FACS data revealed greater activation in participants' facial

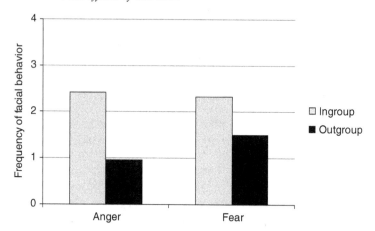

Figure 6.2 Frequency of facial behavior in FACS action units AU4 (associated with anger) and AU5 (associated with fear) in response to anger and fear displays as a function of the expresser's ingroup versus outgroup membership (based on Van der Schalk et al., 2011, Study 2).

"action units" AU4 (associated with anger) and AU5 (associated with fear) when participants viewed emotional displays of anger and fear by ingroup as opposed to outgroup members (see Figure 6.2). In addition, participants' self-reports yielded some evidence of divergent affective reactions to outgroup anger and fear displays, with outgroup anger evoking fear and outgroup fear evoking aversion.

Given that certain situational factors can produce patterns of affective divergence as opposed to convergence, the question that arises is how such affective divergence shapes group dynamics. Few studies speak to this question, and the studies that have been performed paint an inconsistent picture. Barsade, Ward, Turner, and Sonnenfeld (2000) investigated the effects of mean group trait affect and affective homogeneity versus heterogeneity on group processes in a sample of top management teams of large corporations. They found that emotional similarity in trait positive affectivity (which logically predicts state positive affect) predicted more favorable self-reported team processes and even marginally better corporate financial performance. Affectively diverse groups that scored low on mean group positive trait affectivity experienced the greatest task and emotional conflict and the least cooperation. This study thus suggests that affective diversity undermines group functioning.

There are also reasons to believe, however, that affective diversity may have beneficial consequences for groups. Spoor and Kelly (2004) suggested, for instance, that heterogeneous affect can function as a signal of a changing environment. Affective heterogeneity can thus conceivably alert group members to important events that require their attention. It is also possible that affective diversity would make group members aware of the fact that their appraisals of the situation differ. Although differential appraisals of the same situation could undermine coordinated group action, awareness of diverging views and perceptions may also motivate group members to take each other's perspectives and to exhibit better information exchange in an attempt to develop a more accurate understanding of the situation (Jehn, Northcraft, & Neale, 1999; Van Knippenberg, De Dreu, & Homan, 2004).

There is indeed some evidence that affective diversity can prompt better group decision processes. Tuncel and Doucet (2005) examined the impact of mood diversity on confirmation bias and decision accuracy in four-person groups working on a hidden-profile task (a group task in which the discovery of the correct solution requires pooling of unshared information rather than seizing on shared information; Stasses & Titus, 1985). They found that mood diversity in groups was positively related to decision accuracy. This effect could be explained in terms of the degree of consideration given to individual pieces of disconfirming information, which was greater in affectively diverse rather than homogeneous groups. This study suggests that affective diversity can counteract groupthink (Janis, 1972). Given that group cohesiveness is one of the key antecedents of groupthink, a certain degree of affective diversity may contribute to more rational group decision making by motivating group members to critically evaluate alternative viewpoints.

Finally, returning to the idea that emotional expressions help group members to negotiate their respective roles and statuses within the group (Clark, 1990; Collins, 1990; Keltner & Haidt, 1999), affective heterogeneity may be beneficial for groups to the degree that diverse emotional expressions are associated with differential levels of dominance versus submission (Elfenbein, 2007; Keltner et al., 2008). Displays of emotions such as sadness, fear, and embarrassment are associated with submissiveness and low status (Keltner et al., 1998; Knutson, 1996; Tiedens et al., 2000), whereas emotions such as anger and to some degree happiness are associated with dominance and high status (Hess, Blairy, & Kleck, 2000; Knutson, 1996; Tiedens, 2001). Tiedens and Fragale (2003) showed that interactions in which dominant nonverbal behaviors of one partner (e.g., expanded bodily postures) were complemented with submissive nonverbal behaviors by the other (e.g., constricted bodily postures) were experienced as more comfortable and inspired greater interpersonal liking than interactions that were characterized by less nonverbal complementarity. This suggests that complementary affective reactions to emotional displays (e.g., fearful, embarrassed, or guilty responses to expressions of anger) may contribute to coordinated and well-adjusted group interactions by clarifying group members' relative standing. Research is needed to examine this possibility.

Emotional expressions and inferential processes in groups

Although most research on the role of emotions in groups has been concerned with affective reactions to emotional expressions and/or the effects of the affective composition of groups (as discussed above), a handful of studies have considered the role of inferential processes driven by emotional expressions in group settings. In some of these studies third-person observers were asked to judge various aspects of a group's interaction from an outsider's perspective, whereas other studies investigated what types of inferences group members themselves draw on the basis of the emotional displays of their fellow group members. I discuss both types of research in turn.

Outside observers' inferences from group members' emotional displays

In a pioneering study, Magee and Tiedens (2006) found that outside observers inferred certain characteristics of three-person groups based on the valence and the consistency of the emotions displayed by the group members in a picture. Specifically, participants perceived a greater degree of common fate when all group members displayed either positive (happiness) or negative (sadness) emotions than when they displayed different emotions, as can be seen in Figure 6.3. This effect of emotional consistency on perceptions of common fate was mediated by inferences of psychological similarity. Furthermore, as also shown in the figure, groups were perceived as more cohesive when all members displayed happiness than when they displayed sadness or showed variance in their emotions. This effect of emotional valence on perceptions of group cohesion was mediated by inferences of interpersonal liking. Interestingly, the emotion composition effects were stronger than the effects of the race or sex composition of the group. This led the authors to conclude that "information about the feelings of group members could be a preferred basis for judgments about group characteristics" (p. 1705).

Additional support for this general conclusion was obtained in later research using a similar procedure. Homan, Van Kleef, and Sanchez-Burks (2016) showed participants pictures of the facial emotional expressions of the members of a two-person team, of which both members showed either happiness or sadness. Participants anticipated more cooperative interactions, higher satisfaction, greater interpersonal liking and trust, and less conflict when both teammates showed happiness than

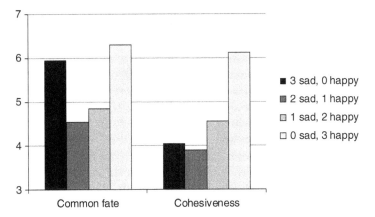

Figure 6.3 Observers' ratings of group members' common fate and cohesiveness (on a scale of 1–9) as a function of the group members' constellation of facial emotional expressions (based on Magee & Tiedens, 2006, Study 1).

when both showed sadness – inferences that are consistent with the effects of positive and negative group affect on actual conflict and cooperation reported by Barsade (2002). The study further revealed that emotional expressions triggered stronger inferences when there was greater ambiguity surrounding the future success or failure of the team (i.e., when the team was racially diverse; Van Knippenberg et al., 2004) and when the emotional expressions were more likely to reflect team processes rather than dispositional tendencies toward positive or negative emotionality (i.e., when the pictures had supposedly been taken after rather than before the team interaction).

Group members' inferences from their fellow members' emotional displays

A few studies have examined the inferential processes and concomitant behavioral reactions exhibited by members of a group (as opposed to outside observers) in response to the emotional displays of one or more fellow group members. For instance, Cheshin, Israely, and Rafaeli (2015) investigated the effects of expressions of anger versus happiness of a confederate in a computer-mediated team interaction. They found that the confederate's expressions of anger reduced the self-efficacy as well as the performance of the other teammates. In interpreting these findings, the authors suggested that targets of the confederate's anger may have inferred that their performance was inadequate, which in turn undermined their self-efficacy. This conclusion complements earlier evidence that positive affect in teams is associated with greater team efficacy (Gibson, 2003).

Another recent line of research has begun to address the possibility that emotional expressions in groups help to delineate group boundaries and assist groups in negotiating problems of deviance and lack of consensus. Heerdink and colleagues proposed that emotional expressions fulfill this function by acting as signals of group members' inclusionary status (Heerdink, Van Kleef, Homan, & Fischer, 2015). Inclusion in social groups is of vital importance to human survival and well-being. Given the evolutionary significance of group life (Cosmides & Tooby, 1992; Dunbar, 1992), it would be adaptive for human beings to be sensitive to moment-to-moment variations in the extent to which fellow group members accept them (Baumeister & Leary, 1995). Heerdink and colleagues argued that individuals use the emotional expressions of their fellow group members as implicit signals of acceptance versus rejection.

In six experiments employing the affect misattribution paradigm (Payne, Cheng, Govorun, & Stewart, 2005), Heerdink et al. (2015) examined to what extent observers associate expressions of anger, happiness, sadness, fear, or no emotion with three different operationalizations of inclusionary status that vary in terms of abstractness (i.e., acceptance vs. rejection, warm vs. cold, and close vs. distant). A meta-analysis on the experiments revealed that angry expressions were most strongly associated with rejection and that happy expressions were most strongly associated with acceptance, regardless of the particular operationalization of inclusionary status. These results extended earlier findings showing that displays of happiness are construed as a signal of affiliation, whereas displays of anger are seen as a signal that one's behavior is inappropriate and needs to be adapted (Averill, 1982; Cacioppo & Gardner, 1999; Clark, Pataki, & Carver, 1996; Fischer & Roseman, 2007).

If people use their fellow group members' emotional displays to gauge their moment-to-moment levels of acceptance in the group, a question that arises is what the behavioral consequences of such inferences may be. Given humans' fundamental desire to be included in social groups (Baumeister & Leary, 1995), individuals who realize that their group membership is in doubt may become motivated to change their behavior so as to secure their future acceptance in the group (Williams, 2007). One way of promoting acceptance is by showing increased conformity, that is, changing one's behavior to match the responses of others (Cialdini & Goldstein, 2004). Accordingly, Heerdink, Van Kleef, Homan, and Fischer (2013) hypothesized that individuals who are confronted with expressions of anger on the part of their fellow group members experience pressure to conform to the apparent group norm, because expressions of anger signal potential rejection.

In one of the studies conducted to test this idea, Heerdink and colleagues (2013) asked participants to recall an incident in which their opinion had differed from that of the majority of the group they belonged to. After describing the situation, participants reported which emotions the majority of the group members had shown and how this had made them feel. The more anger the majority had expressed, the more the participant had felt rejected. Conversely, the more happiness the majority had expressed, the more the participant had felt accepted. These inferences of inclusion versus rejection in turn predicted the extent to which participants experienced pressure to conform to the majority position.

A follow-up study demonstrated effects of emotional expressions on actual conformity in a face-to-face interaction study in which three-person groups worked together on a problem-solving task (Heerdink et al., 2013). The researchers manipulated the emotion expressed by the majority by instructing two of the three group members to express either anger, happiness, or no emotion in response to ideas voiced by the third (focal) group member. Conformity was operationalized as the relative influence of the focal group member on the ultimate group decision, based on the logic that conformity of the focal member to the preference of the majority should be reflected in relatively lower influence of the focal member on the group decision. The results showed that participants who were confronted with an angry majority had less influence on the ultimate group decision compared to those who were confronted with a neutral or happy majority. The effect of the majority's emotional displays on the focal group member's conformity was mediated by the focal member's inferences of rejection.

Related research indicates that emotional expressions may similarly contribute to the learning of (group) norms. Specifically, Hareli and colleagues found that norm violators who were confronted with expressions of anger were better able to successfully infer the norm for correct behavior than were those who were confronted with expressions of sadness or neutral emotion (Hareli, Moran-Amir, David, & Hess, 2013). Together, these studies suggest that particular patterns of emotional responding assist groups in reinforcing desired behavior of individual members (e.g., rewarding welcome ideas with expressions of happiness) and discouraging undesired behavior (e.g., sanctioning deviance with expressions of anger).

Contingencies of the social effects of emotional expressions in groups

We have seen in the preceding sections that emotional expressions can evoke reciprocal and/or complementary affective reactions in fellow group members. We have also seen that individuals may draw inferences from group members' emotional expressions about characteristics of the group and its interaction as well as about their own standing in the group. These findings beg the question of when affective reactions or inferential processes are primary in driving behavioral responses to emotional expressions in groups. Even though no studies to date have directly examined the relative influence of both types of process, there is some evidence for moderating influences on affective reactions as well as on the behavioral consequences of inferential processes.

Identification, entitativity, and affective convergence

Perhaps the most proximal predictor of affective convergence in groups is the receptiveness of the individual group members to emotional contagion (Hatfield et al., 1994). Such receptiveness depends on individual differences as well as on situational factors and group characteristics. The cricket study by Totterdell (2000) revealed that team members who scored higher on the dispositional susceptibility to emotional contagion were more likely to converge affectively with their team members than were those who scored lower on susceptibility to contagion. Similarly, a longitudinal study of the affective linkages among team members' affective states in the context of a team performance task revealed that the strength of affective linkages was moderated by individual differences in team members' susceptibility to emotional contagion (Ilies, Wagner, & Morgeson, 2007).

Other studies point to situational factors and group characteristics that shape individuals' receptiveness to affective convergence. For instance, the studies by Totterdell and colleagues revealed greater affective convergence among team members who were more committed to the team, who perceived the team climate as more positive, who were engaged in collective rather than individual activities, and who experienced fewer hassles with fellow teammates (Totterdell, 2000; Totterdell et al., 1998). Along similar lines, other work has demonstrated stronger affective convergence among collectivistic (Ilies et al., 2007) and more identified group members (Tanghe, Wisse, & Van der Flier, 2010) than among individualistic and less identified individuals. Interestingly, the latter study also yielded some evidence that the effects of group affective tone on group effectiveness were stronger in higher identifying groups.

The common denominators in these studies appear to be the individual group members' level of identification with and commitment to the group and the concomitant entitativity or "groupiness" of the group. The various studies suggest that greater levels of identification, commitment, and entitativity increase individuals' susceptibility to affective convergence with their fellow group members, whereas lower levels of identification, commitment, and entitativity reduce the likelihood of affective convergence.

This tentative conclusion resonates with the insights stemming from research on affective divergence, which has shown that divergent affective responses to others' emotional displays are more likely when people anticipate or experience a competitive rather than a cooperative interaction (Lanzetta & Englis, 1989) or when they are part of a different rather than the same social group (Van der Schalk et al., 2011; Weisbuch & Ambady, 2008). The conclusion also aligns with research on power and emotional convergence among dating partners and college roommates (Anderson, Kelner, & John, 2003). This work revealed that individuals are less likely to converge with the affective states of their interaction partners to the degree that they feel more powerful in their relationship. Together with emerging insights that power increases people's subjective psychological distance from others (Magee & Smith, 2013), this finding, too, suggests that affective convergence hinges on a sense of togetherness, identification, and commitment. This moderating role of groupiness in shaping affective convergence among individuals resonates with the presumed evolutionary benefits of affective sharing for groups (cf. Spoor & Kelly, 2004).

Inferences of rejection, motivation to be accepted, and conformity

We have seen that the emotional expressions of group members can trigger inferential processes in fellow group members as well as outside observers regarding group members' psychological similarity and common fate (Magee & Tiedens, 2006), satisfaction, interpersonal liking, trust, cooperation, and conflict (Homan et al., 2016) and inclusionary status (Heerdink et al., 2015). Research so far has not paid a great deal of attention to potential moderators of the link between such inferential processes and behavioral responses in groups. The only available evidence to date comes from the work by Heerdink and colleagues (2013) on the effects of emotional expressions on conformity in groups. Viewing conformity as strategic behavior aimed at gaining (re)acceptance in groups, they argued that the effects of group members' emotional expressions on conformity of deviant individuals should be moderated by social-contextual factors that determine deviant individuals' motivation to be accepted by the group.

In one of Heerdink et al.'s (2013) studies participants read about a situation in which they were attempting to decide on a holiday destination with three of their friends. It turned out that the three friends all had the same holiday destination in mind, but the participant preferred a different destination. The majority did not agree with the participant's proposal. Depending on the condition, the majority expressed anger, enthusiasm, or no emotion about the situation. The researchers also manipulated the availability of an alternative group with which participants could go on holiday, reasoning that expressions of anger might prompt conformity in the absence of a salient alternative, but not in the presence of an alternative. Expressions of anger by the majority led to greater inferences of rejection on the part of the deviant than did expressions of enthusiasm, with neutral expressions falling in between. These rejection inferences in turn motivated participants to conform when no alternative group was available, whereas they motivated participants to leave the group when such an alternative was available.

In another study, Heerdink and colleagues (2013) examined the effects of emotional expressions in the context of a computer-simulated group discussion about aesthetic preferences. In one condition, participants learned that their responses on several questionnaires indicated that they were very prototypical members of the group, meaning that their personality overlapped strongly with the personalities of the other group members. In the other condition they learned that they were peripheral members of the group, because their personality structure was different from that of the other group members. Participants then privately rated a number of abstract paintings. To generate discussion, their ratings were supposedly sent to the other group members, who were preprogrammed to express different preferences than the participant.

Next, all group members sent a few messages to the rest of the group to initiate the discussion. Depending on the condition, participants received messages expressing anger or happiness about their deviating opinion, with emotions being communicated by means of words and emoticons. Then participants rated the paintings for a second time, and this time their ratings could supposedly be viewed by the rest of the group. As can be seen in Figure 6.4, participants who occupied a prototypical position in the group were not influenced by their group members' emotional expressions, presumably because they felt little fear of social exclusion and, consequently, experienced little pressure to change their opinion. However, participants who occupied a peripheral position in their group were almost three times more likely to conform to the majority's position after receiving angry reactions than after receiving happy reactions. Strikingly, Heerdink et al. (2013) found that these patterns of conformity were still manifest three weeks later. Both immediate and longer-term conformity of peripheral group members were mediated by inferences of rejection, which were higher after expressions of anger than after expressions of happiness. These findings speak to some of the moderating conditions that determine whether and how individuals use the emotional expressions of their group members to inform their own behavior.

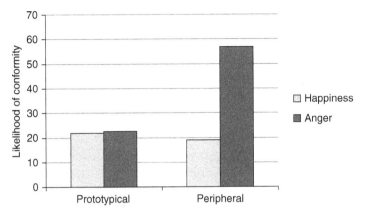

Figure 6.4 Percentage of participants conforming to the majority's position as a function of the majority's expressions of happiness versus anger and the participant's prototypical versus peripheral position in the group (based on Heerdink et al., 2013, Study 5).

Conclusion

Various theorists have proposed that emotions play a vital role in regulating group behavior (e.g., Barsade & Gibson, 1998; Keltner & Haidt, 1999; Spoor & Kelly, 2004; Van Kleef & Fischer, 2016). Although empirical research on the role of emotions in groups is still in a relatively early stage, several studies speak to the various ways in which emotional displays influence behavior in groups. There is a tendency in the literature to view emotions in groups as functional, and much of the work reviewed in this chapter certainly fuels that conception. Observers may extract pertinent information from group members' emotional expressions about various characteristics and processes that may be critical to the group's success or failure (Homan et al., 2016; Magee & Tiedens, 2006). Individual members may use their fellow group members' emotional displays to draw inferences regarding their own standing in the group (Heerdink et al., 2013). To the degree that emotions become shared in groups, the resulting affective state of the group may facilitate coordinated action by fostering group bonds and creating a shared mind-set for approaching joint tasks (Barsade, 2002; Sy et al., 2005). Even affective diversity may be functional in particular circumstances (Tiedens, Sutton, & Fong, 2004), for instance because it may alert group members to their differential appraisals of events, which may prompt critical discussion.

As tempting as it may be to construe all of these phenomena in terms of their usefulness for groups, we should be cautious not to fall prey to a functionality fallacy. Several of the effects mentioned in the previous paragraph could just as well be framed as constituting a potential liability to group success. For instance, although high levels of affective homogeneity in groups may facilitate joint goal pursuit, they may also imperil the group's success by contributing to groupthink. Conversely, even though affective heterogeneity could function as a signal of divergent goals or views that may spark much-needed renegotiation of the group's mission, it may also debilitate the group's capacity to render joint decisions. As is true for the broader literature on the social functionality of emotions, the presumed functions of emotional expressions should be critically scrutinized in light of the available evidence and weighed against evidence of dysfunctional outcomes (see Parrott, 2001).

In the quest to better understand the beneficial and detrimental effects of emotions in groups, it will be important to take into account moderating influences that govern the (dys)functionality of various patterns of emotional expression and affective composition. Although previous research has begun to consider some of these moderators (e.g., Heerdink et al., 2013; Klep et al., 2011; Tanghe et al., 2010), much more work is needed to map out the intricate contingencies of the functionality of emotional expressions in groups. In doing so, future theorizing and research would do well to examine the effects of discrete emotional expressions (rather than diffuse displays of positive or negative mood) and to consider these in the context of the group's goals and in relation to any problems the group may be facing in attaining those goals.

Different emotions (or families of emotions) have been proposed to serve different social functions, which may help to address various types of problems that can emerge in group life (Keltner & Gross, 1999; Morris & Keltner, 2000; Van Kleef, De Dreu, & Manstead, 2010). Logically, then, the functionality of a particular emotional display should depend on the degree to which it helps to remedy a current problem in the group. For instance, a group that has difficulties reaching consensus on a task that requires unanimity might benefit from affective convergence, because the resulting group emotion would help members to approach the decision problem with similar mind-sets. A positive affective tone would be particularly conducive to reaching consensus, because the sharedness of positive emotions reduces conflict and increases cooperation (Barsade, 2002). However, when a group's capacity to take decisions is hampered by a power vacuum or a lack of role clarity, differential displays of high-status (e.g., anger, pride) versus low-status (e.g., embarrassment, guilt) emotions by different group members may facilitate coordination by instilling a rudimentary sense of hierarchy that may serve as a heuristic solution to decision making. The functionality of particular patterns of emotional responding should thus be considered in conjunction with the main problems that stand in the way of group success.

Along similar lines, future research should consider the effects of emotional expressions and affective compositions in relation to the current goals and tasks of the group. When the task requires cooperation, cognitive broadening, and/or creativity, groups may be best off when they develop a positive affective tone (Barsade, 2002; Grawitch et al., 2003; Klep et al., 2011). When the task requires careful planning, analytical information processing, and critical evaluation of ideas, groups may be better off when they develop a (mildly) negative affective tone (Forgas, 2000; Klep et al., 2011; Kooij-de Bode et al., 2010; Schwarz & Bless, 1991). Logically, then, group performance on tasks that require a combination of cognitive broadening and critical evaluation may benefit from affective heterogeneity.

Given the many complexities and contingencies surrounding the effects of emotions in groups, it stands to reason that group success depends on the degree to which group members are able to regulate the emotions in the group in a way that is conducive to group functioning. This means that a group's functioning should be enhanced to the degree that its members have higher levels of emotional intelligence (Elfenbein, 2005; also see Chapter 4). Group members with higher levels of emotional intelligence are more likely than their less emotionally intelligent counterparts to appreciate how the group's emotional state influences its mode of operation (Côté, 2007), and they should be better able to regulate their own (Gross, 1998b) and/or their fellow group members' emotions accordingly (Niven, Totterdell, & Holman, 2009). Some support for these ideas is provided by studies in which group member emotional intelligence was identified as a positive predictor of team performance (Chang, Sy, & Choi, 2012; Jordan, Ashkanasy, Härtel, & Hooper, 2002; Jordan & Troth, 2004), although the processes by which emotional intelligence may benefit team success remain unclear. Other work has found that the ability to accurately perceive the collective affective state of a group of individuals (i.e., emotional aperture; Sanchez-Burks & Huy, 2009) is positively associated with leadership performance (Sanchez-Burks, Bartel, Rees, & Huy, 2016).

In conclusion, it is clear from the current body of evidence that emotions have pervasive effects on group functioning. Consistent with the EASI framework, several studies point to the reciprocal and complementary affective reactions that may be elicited by emotional expressions in groups, as well as to the situational factors that shape the nature of these effects. Other studies have begun to document various types of inferential processes and the contingencies that govern their occurrence and their impact on group members' behavior. What remains unclear is how the affective reactions and inferential processes that may arise in groups relate to each other, and how the relative strength and downstream consequences of these processes for behavior and group functioning are shaped by the social context. Addressing these issues constitutes a big challenge for future research on emotions in groups. Awaiting such efforts, we can draw insights regarding the interplay between moderating influences and mediating mechanisms from the literature on emotion in conflict and negotiation, which is considered in the following chapter.

CHAPTER 7

Social effects of emotions in conflict and negotiation

> To make a good salad is to be a brilliant diplomatist – the problem is entirely the same in both cases. To know how much oil one must put with one's vinegar.
>
> Oscar Wilde

Conflict is an inevitable fact of life. Whether we focus on interactions between individuals, groups, organizations, or nations – conflicts are omnipresent. Salespersons disagree with potential buyers about the price of their merchandise. Divorcing partners quarrel about the conditions of their breakup. Organizational departments hold conflicting views about the distribution of company resources. Companies fight over the terms of a merger. Diplomats argue about the time frame of a cease-fire. The divergent interests that lie at the heart of social conflict often give rise to intense emotions, which may in turn strongly influence conflict development (Barry & Oliver, 1996; Morris & Keltner, 2000; Van Kleef & Sinaceur, 2013).

The most common and constructive way of dealing with conflict is through negotiation, which can be defined as a discussion between two or more parties aimed at resolving a (perceived) divergence of interests (Pruitt & Carnevale, 1993). The outcomes of negotiations can be highly consequential. When negotiators create high-quality agreements that satisfy all parties' interests, they create order and stability, foster harmony, reduce the probability of future conflict, and stimulate economic prosperity. When negotiators create poor agreements, or fail to agree, they leave dissatisfied, create frustration and annoyance, face continued conflict and disharmony, and undermine productivity (De Dreu, Beersma, Steinel, & Van Kleef, 2007; Rubin, Pruitt, & Kim, 1994). Given that conflicts are inherently emotional, attempts to resolve them through negotiation are also likely to be pervaded by emotions.

How do emotions shape conflict and negotiation? Are they a liability or an asset? It turns out that both professional negotiators and management scholars differ widely in their beliefs about the functionality or dysfunctionality of emotions in negotiation (Thompson, Medvec, Seiden, &

123

Kopelman, 2001). Some believe that negotiators should remain emotion-ally detached, because showing emotions could be construed as a sign of weakness and an indication that one has departed from the path of rationality. Accordingly, negotiation training programs are often aimed at teaching negotiators how to control (in practice, suppress) their emo-tions rather than instructing them how to use emotions to their advantage (Leary, Pillemer, & Wheeler, 2013; Raiffa, 1982).

Others believe that negotiators are better off adopting a positive emo-tional approach (Thompson et al., 2001). As discussed before, research shows that positive emotions help to establish and maintain social bonds (Harker & Keltner, 2001), facilitate interpersonal understanding (Fischer & Manstead, in press), and foster cognitive flexibility (Fredrickson, 1998; Isen, 1987). Nourishing positive emotions could therefore be beneficial in negotiations, whose success often depends on mutual understanding, perspective taking, and creativity (Pruitt & Carnevale, 1993). Indeed, it is not uncommon for professional negotiators and diplomats to spend a considerable amount of time building a positive emotional atmosphere before getting down to business.

Still other people believe that a negative emotional approach is more likely to be effective in negotiations (Thompson et al., 2001). Expressing emotions such as anger may serve to create a sense of urgency, portray an image of intransigence, and lend credibility to ultimatums and threats (Frank, 1988; Schelling, 1960). Consider the following quote from Richard Holbrooke, a US diplomat who mediated in the war between Bosnia-Herzegovina and Serbia.

> Karadzic . . . said that our draft proposal was unacceptable. Suddenly, Mladic erupted. Pushing to the center of the circle, he began a long, emotional diatribe . . . This was the intimidating style he had used with the Dutch commander at Srebenica, with Janvier, and with so many others. He gave off a scent of danger . . . I did not know if his rage was real or feigned, but this was the genuine Mladic, the one who could unleash a murderous rampage. (Holbrooke, 1999, pp. 150–151)

Such emotional expressions are common in negotiations, especially when the stakes are high. As reflected in the disparate views on the utility of emotion in conflict and negotiation, however, the effects of emotional expressions on negotiation processes and the resolution versus escalation of social conflict are not easy to predict. This is due in part to the intricate mixed-motive nature of many conflict settings, where parties simulta-neously experience incentives to compete so as to maximize their own outcomes and to cooperate in order to secure an agreement (Schelling, 1960).

The mixed-motive setting provides a particularly interesting arena for examining the interpersonal effects of emotional expressions. On the one hand, the intrinsically emotional nature of social conflict paves the way for emotional expressions that may evoke affective reactions in counterparts. On the other hand, strategic considerations lead parties in social conflict to pay close attention to the meaning and implications of their counterpart's emotional expressions, because an accurate interpretation of such expressions could help them to develop a strategic advantage (Van Kleef, De Dreu, & Manstead, 2010). As we shall see in this chapter, Emotions as Social Information (EASI) theory provides a useful framework for understanding this tension between affective and inferential processes and for analyzing the interpersonal consequences of emotional expressions in social conflict.

Affective reactions and their behavioral consequences

Systematic empirical research on the interpersonal effects of emotions in conflict and negotiation was kick-started by a series of studies on the interpersonal effects of anger versus happiness. Although later studies have also considered other emotions, this literature is still characterized by a predominant focus on a small subset of emotions. As a result, evidence pertaining to the role of affective reactions to emotional expressions in negotiations also stems primarily from studies on anger and happiness. I discuss this literature first and then consider more recent studies on other emotions.

Anger and happiness elicit reciprocal affective reactions

Researchers have used a variety of correlational and experimental research methods to examine the interpersonal effects of emotional expressions in negotiations, employing computer-mediated negotiation simulations, observation and coding of actual face-to-face or online negotiations, pictures and videos of emotional expressions, and emotional expressions delivered by professional actors. Despite the diversity of research methods, these studies consistently show that expressions of anger and happiness tend to trigger reciprocal affective reactions in negotiation partners.

An initial investigation of the interpersonal effects of emotions in negotiations focused on the effects of verbal expressions of anger and happiness in a computer-mediated negotiation task (Van Kleef, De Dreu, & Manstead, 2004a). In the course of the negotiation, participants received emotional messages from their (simulated) opponent (e.g., "This negotiation pisses me off"; or "I feel good about this negotiation"). Participants who received angry messages became angrier themselves as well, whereas those who received happy messages from their opponent became happier. Similarly, in a study of online dispute resolution negotiations, negotiators whose partners expressed anger in their written messages reported experiencing more anger themselves compared to those whose partners sent emotionally neutral messages (Friedman, Anderson, Brett, Olekalns, Goates, & Lisco, 2004). These findings are consistent with research on affective convergence in other domains (Anderson, Keltner, & John, 2003; Hatfield, Cacioppo, & Rapson, 1994; Totterdell, 2000).

Convergent evidence further indicates that affective reactions to emotional expressions in negotiations are not limited to reciprocal emotional experiences but extend to interpersonal impressions and concomitant behavioral tendencies. In several studies, participants who were confronted with angry negotiation counterparts developed a more negative impression of their counterpart than did those who dealt with a happy or nonemotional counterpart (Van Beest, Van Kleef, & Van Dijk, 2008; Van Kleef et al., 2004a). Moreover, participants who interacted with an angry rather than a happy negotiation partner were less satisfied with the negotiation afterward and were less willing to engage in future interactions with the same partner (Kopelman, Rosette, & Thompson, 2006; Van Kleef, De Dreu, & Manstead, 2004b).

Such affective reactions to emotional expressions have been repeatedly demonstrated to shape subsequent negotiation behavior. For instance, Friedman and colleagues (2004) found that electronically mediated dispute resolution negotiations were more likely to break down when negotiators expressed anger, especially when the other party had a strong negotiation position due to a favorable reputation. Similarly, Kopelman and colleagues (2006) showed that negotiators who expressed negative affect at the bargaining table were less likely to secure a deal than were those who expressed positive affect.

Later studies revealed additional negative consequences of anger expressions in negotiation. In a series of experiments on multiparty coalition formation, Van Beest and colleagues (2008) found that negotiators who expressed anger during coalition negotiations were less likely to be accepted in a profitable coalition by the other negotiators than were those who refrained from expressing anger. Another series of experiments showed that bargainers who express anger run a greater risk of being deceived by their counterparts (Van Dijk, Van Kleef, Steinel, & Van Beest, 2008). In both sets of studies, the adverse consequences of anger expressions were mediated by participants' negative affective reactions to their counterparts' expressions of anger (negative impressions and reciprocal anger, respectively).

Finally, a study by Wang and colleagues demonstrated that the negative affective reactions that are triggered by expressions of anger in negotiations may lead negotiators to try and sabotage their angry counterparts in ways that may only become apparent after the negotiation is over (Wang, Northcraft, & Van Kleef, 2012). The authors hired a professional actor to play the role of an angry or emotionally neutral negotiation partner. Participants exhibited greater overt concessionary behaviors when the actor expressed anger rather than no emotion during the negotiation. However, negative affective reactions (in this case, feelings of mistreatment) led participants to sabotage their angry counterpart in a covert manner by secretly assigning more unappealing tasks to the actor in an ostensibly unrelated study.

Few studies have examined the role of complementary (as opposed to reciprocal) affective reactions to emotional expressions in negotiation (e.g., fearful responses to anger expressions). A line of research by Lelieveld and colleagues has begun to shed some light on this issue. A series of computer-mediated bargaining experiments showed that angry messages emitted by high-power negotiators evoked complementary fear in targets (which in turn led them to make larger concessions), whereas angry messages by low-power negotiators evoked reciprocal anger in targets (which led them to make smaller concessions; Lelieveld, Van Dijk, Van Beest, & Van Kleef, 2012). Presumably, a powerful counterpart's anger elicited fear because it was perceived as a threat. In contrast, expressions of anger by a weaker counterpart constituted less of a threat and evoked reciprocal anger, as in the earlier research discussed above. In short, expressions of anger and happiness generally trigger reciprocal affective reactions in negotiation partners, with the complementary feelings of fear elicited by powerful negotiators' expressions of anger being a notable exception.

Disappointment and sadness elicit complementary guilt and compassion

Relatively little is known about the types of affective reactions that may be evoked by emotions other than anger and happiness, but a few studies have begun to consider the affective reactions that are elicited by expressions of disappointment and sadness. Evidence for the effects of expressions of disappointment comes from a number of studies by Lelieveld and colleagues. Two computer-mediated bargaining studies revealed that counterparts' expressions of disappointment elicited complementary guilt in participants (Lelieveld et al., 2012). These feelings of guilt in turn led participants to make more generous offers, consistent with previous research on the intrapersonal effects of guilt on cooperation in social dilemmas (Ketelaar & Au, 2003). In another study, the effects of expressions of disappointment on feelings of guilt and resultant concessions were especially apparent when the disappointment was targeted at the participant as a person rather than at the participant's offer (Lelieveld, Van Dijk, Van Beest, Steinel, & Van Kleef, 2011). Finally, a recent series of experiments suggests that the elicitation of complementary feelings of guilt in observers may be a necessary ingredient for the beneficial effects of expressions of disappointment to emerge. In four computer-mediated experiments involving verbal as well as nonverbal manipulations of emotional expression, a counterpart's expressions of disappointment only led participants to make more generous offers under conditions that were conducive to eliciting guilt (e.g., when the expresser was an ingroup rather than an outgroup member; Lelieveld, Van Dijk, Van Beest, & Van Kleef, 2013).

Compatible findings were obtained in a recent series of experiments by Sinaceur, Kopelman, Vasiljevic, and Haag (2015) on the interpersonal effects of sadness in negotiations. Sinaceur and colleagues argued that displays of sadness can be effective in negotiations because they may evoke complementary feelings of empathy and compassion in targets that may in turn lead them to adopt a more cooperative stance with the expresser. In three experiments involving face-to-face interaction, the authors found that displays of sadness were indeed effective, but only when they elicited empathy and compassion in the target. Such affective reactions only arose when features of the social situation provided reasons to experience other-concern for the expresser, for instance when recipients perceived the expresser as having low power, when they anticipated a future interaction with the expresser, or when they construed their relationship with the expresser as collaborative. In all three experiments the positive effect of sadness expression was mediated by the recipients' complementary feelings of empathy and compassion.

Inferential processes and their behavioral consequences

Besides providing support for the occurrence and downstream consequences of affective reactions, negotiation studies have produced robust evidence for the important role of inferential processes in shaping behavioral responses to the emotional expressions of negotiation partners. As was the case with affective reactions, early studies primarily focused on inferences drawn from expressions of anger versus happiness, whereas later studies shifted the focus to other emotions such as guilt and disappointment. I review both sets of studies in turn.

Anger versus happiness: inferences of ambition, toughness, threat, and credibility

Early studies using the computer-mediated negotiation paradigm described previously uncovered reliable effects of opponents' expressions of anger versus happiness on inferences drawn by the receiving negotiator (Van Dijk et al., 2008; Van Kleef et al., 2004a, 2004b). Participants who received angry messages generally inferred that the opponent had an ambitious negotiation limit, and to avoid costly impasse they made relatively large concessions. Conversely, negotiators who received happy messages inferred that the opponent's limit was low, felt less need to concede to avoid impasse, and therefore made smaller concessions. Behavioral responses to the emotional expressions of the counterpart in these studies were consistently mediated by inferences regarding the counterpart's limits.

Other evidence indicates that people may take advantage of their knowledge of other people's incidental feeling states. Andrade and Ho (2007) found that proposers in an ultimatum bargaining game were more likely to make unfair offers when they knew that the receiver was in a good rather than a bad mood, presumably because they suspected that the good mood would make the receiver more lenient. Klapwijk, Peters, Vermeiren, and Lelieveld (2013) replicated and extended these findings using a sample of adolescents, reporting evidence that the tendency to make unfair offers to happy recipients is stronger among individuals with a selfish orientation than among those with a prosocial orientation. This finding suggests that the effects of emotional expressions are modulated by the observer's social motives (also see Van Kleef & Van Lange, 2008).

Another set of studies showed that the inferences that negotiators draw from their counterpart's emotions continue to influence behavior in later encounters with the same person. In a second negotiation with an opponent who had previously expressed anger, negotiators conceded again because they believed that the other had high limits, even when that person expressed no emotion during the second encounter (Van Kleef & De Dreu, 2010). This finding suggests that, unless overruled by new information, the situation-specific inferences that people draw from others' emotional expressions may be consolidated in memory in the form of more stable personality judgments (cf. Hess, Blairy, & Kleck, 2000; Knutson, 1996).

Additional evidence for the role of inferential processes was obtained in two experiments by Sinaceur and Tiedens (2006). In a scenario study and in a face-to-face negotiation experiment (in which one of the negotiators was instructed to display either anger or no emotion), they found that participants conceded more to angry as opposed to nonemotional counterparts. Furthermore, Sinaceur and Tiedens demonstrated that the effect of anger was mediated by the focal negotiator's appraisal of the opponent's toughness, with angry opponents appearing tougher and therefore eliciting larger concessions than nonemotional counterparts.

These findings are fully compatible with those obtained using the computer-mediated negotiation paradigm (Van Dijk et al., 2008; Van Kleef et al., 2004a, 2004b).

A later study by Sinaceur and colleagues revealed that the effects of anger expressions on concession making are also mediated by threat perceptions (Sinaceur, Van Kleef, Neale, Adam, & Haag, 2011). Expressions of anger were construed by participants as conveying an implied threat, which explained why participants conceded more to angry as opposed to nonemotional opponents. The authors also found that explicit threats had similar effects on concession making as expressions of anger, providing additional evidence for a mediating role of threat-related inferences.

Along similar lines, a study on complaints in a customer service setting showed that expressing anger when complaining may lead to greater compensation because anger enhances the credibility of the complainant when there is room for doubt (Hareli et al., 2009). This finding is compatible with the preceding studies and in line with Frank's (1988) proposition that displays of anger lend credence to threats and ultimatums. Together, these studies show that negotiators may use the emotional expressions of their counterparts to draw inferences about crucial aspects of the counterpart's negotiation position and intentions. Moreover, from a practical point of view, the mediating roles of inferences regarding negotiation limits, toughness, threat, and credibility appear to be comparable.

Extending these findings, Adam and Shirako (2013) investigated in a series of experiments how the cultural background of the expresser modulates the inferences of toughness and threat that observers draw from expressions of anger. Based on the stereotype that East Asian individuals are relatively emotionally inexpressive whereas European Americans are relatively emotionally expressive, they argued and showed that expressions of anger emitted by East Asian negotiators trigger stronger inferences than the same expressions shown by European American negotiators. As in previous research, these inferences of toughness and threat were in turn positively associated with concession making. Interestingly, the authors further found that these effects occurred only among negotiators who endorsed the stereotype of East Asians being less emotionally expressive. These experiments suggest that emotional expressions of people who are believed to be relatively inexpressive are perceived as more diagnostic and informative about their intentions, resulting in stronger inferences and downstream consequences for behavior.

Most research on the effects of emotional expressions in negotiations (and on the interpersonal effects of emotions in general) has considered either one-shot expressions or sequences of expressions of the same emotion. Recently, researchers have begun to examine the social consequences of changing emotions in negotiations (Filipowicz, Barsade, & Melwani, 2011; Sinaceur, Adam, Van Kleef, & Galinsky, 2013). This work is pertinent to the notion of inferential processes, because it demonstrates that the information negotiators derive from a counterpart's emotional expressions depends on the emotional "background" against which a particular expression is shown.

In a series of computer-mediated and face-to-face negotiation experiments, Filipowicz and colleagues (2011) found that participants made larger concessions to counterparts who first expressed happiness and later expressed anger than to counterparts who expressed steady-state anger. This effect of "becoming angry" could be explained in terms of inferential processes. The emotional transition from happiness to anger elicited greater situational attributions (i.e., participants inferred that the expressed emotion was a response to their own actions), whereas steady-state anger elicited greater dispositional attributions (i.e., participants inferred that the expressed emotion was a result of the counterpart's personality). These findings speak to the notion that emotions derive part of their meaning and informational value from the fact that they change, and that such changes in and of themselves have a signaling function (Frijda, 1986; Kuppens, Oravecz, & Tuerlinckx, 2010; Scherer, 2009).

Related research was inspired by the "madman strategy" that formed an important component of former US president Richard Nixon's international diplomacy. When dealing with foreign adversaries such as the Soviet Union or the North Vietnamese government, Nixon allegedly liked to portray himself as mad, emotionally unstable, and volatile (Kimball, 2004). Apparently, he believed that such an image would help him to get his opponents to comply, because in the eyes of the enemy a madman would probably be willing to escalate the conflict (Frank, 1988; Schelling, 1960). Similar strategies were purportedly used by Soviet premier Nikita Khrushchev (Gaddis, 2005) and, several centuries before, Queen Elizabeth I of England (Loades, 2006). Moreover, the above quote from Richard Holbrooke suggests that at least part of the influence of Bosnian Serb army chief Ratko Mladic (a.k.a. the "Butcher of Bosnia") in the peace negotiations about former Yugoslavia stemmed from his sudden and unpredictable eruptions of anger.

To test the potential effectiveness of such strategies, Sinaceur and colleagues (2013) explored the effects of emotional inconsistency and unpredictability in negotiations. In a computer-mediated negotiation simulation as well as in a face-to-face negotiation study, they found that participants made larger concessions to counterparts who exhibited emotional inconsistency (i.e., alternating several times between expressing anger and happiness) than to counterparts who consistently showed anger or happiness. This happened because participants who were confronted with an emotionally inconsistent counterpart came to experience a sense of unpredictability and lack of control over their outcomes. Thus, in keeping with Nixon's intuition, projecting an aura of volatility can elicit compliance from negotiation partners.

Finally, there is some evidence that the impact of emotional expressions on inferences and behavior is not limited to distributive negotiation situations in which one person's gain equals the other person's loss. Pietroni and colleagues (Pietroni, Van Kleef, De Dreu, & Pagliaro, 2008) demonstrated that the inferences negotiators draw from their counterpart's emotional expressions can result in better joint outcomes in an integrative negotiation task (i.e., a negotiation that allows for "win-win" solutions that satisfy both parties' wishes beyond the value of a mere compromise; De Dreu, 2010; Pruitt & Carnevale, 1993; Thompson, 2001). In a computer-mediated negotiation simulation, negotiators inferred from a counterpart's verbal and nonverbal expressions of anger versus happiness associated with different negotiation issues that the other attached relatively high versus low value to the respective issues. In tasks with integrative potential, these inferences led participants to stand firm on their own high-value issue and to give in on the issue that appeared to be more important for the counterpart, thereby arriving at mutually satisfying win-win solutions (Pietroni et al., 2008).

Supplication versus appeasement: inferences of giving too little versus too much

A few studies have examined the types of inferences negotiators may draw from emotional expressions of emotions other than anger and happiness. In the first of these studies, Thompson, Valley, and Kramer (1995) investigated how an opponent's signs of disappointment versus happiness affect a focal negotiator's judgments regarding negotiation success. The authors found that, independent of objective negotiation performance, participants inferred that they had been more successful when their opponent expressed disappointment rather than happiness. This finding indicates that negotiators take their counterpart's disappointment as a signal that the other was hoping for more, suggesting that they themselves did a good job in extracting concessions from the other.

Using the aforementioned computer-mediated negotiation paradigm, Van Kleef, De Dreu, and Manstead (2006) examined the interpersonal effects of emotions that may arise as a result of the appraisal that one has taken too much or received too little in a negotiation. Specifically, the experiments focused on the effects of disappointment, worry, guilt, and regret on inferences, demands, and concessions. In a first experiment, participants made smaller concessions to opponents who expressed appeasement emotions (guilt or regret) than to opponents who expressed supplication emotions (disappointment or worry). Additional experiments revealed that participants interpreted the other's expressions of disappointment as a signal that the other had received too little, whereas they took expressions of guilt as a sign that the other had claimed too much. These studies indicate that different negative emotional expressions may give rise to different inferences, which in turn motivate different behavior.

Research on the effects of emotional expressions in social dilemma games has yielded compatible evidence. In one set of studies, participants interpreted another player's expressions of guilt about previous contributions to a public good as a sign that the other would contribute more to the public good in a next round (Wubben, De Cremer, & Van Dijk, 2009b). In public-good dilemmas, which are characterized by strong cooperative incentives, such inferences led to greater cooperation on the part of participants who witnessed others' expressions of guilt. When mutual cooperation is the most advantageous strategy for the group, emotional cues suggesting that others will cooperate (such as those provided by expressions of guilt) provide a clear impetus to cooperate oneself. In more competitively structured negotiation settings, in contrast, emotional cues suggesting that one's counterpart will cooperate may elicit a tendency to exploit the guilty counterpart so as to maximize one's own outcomes without risking an impasse. Accordingly, expressions of guilt by a fellow player motivated cooperation in social dilemmas (Wubben et al., 2009b) but elicited competition in negotiations (Van Kleef, De Dreu, & Manstead, 2006).

Compared to the effects of guilt, the effects of disappointment are remarkably consistent across different types of conflict settings involving differential incentives for cooperation versus competition. A growing number of studies speak to the effectiveness of expressing disappointment in various types of negotiations (Klapwijk et al., 2013; Lelieveld et al., 2011, 2012, 2013; Van Kleef, De Dreu, & Manstead, 2006; Van Kleef & Van Lange, 2008) as well as various types of social dilemmas (Van Doorn, Van Kleef, & Van der Pligt, 2015b; Wubben, De Cremer, & Van Dijk, 2009a). It is interesting to note that, besides triggering inferential processes in observers that may spur greater cooperation (Van Kleef, De Dreu, & Manstead, 2006), expressions of disappointment may also elicit complementary feelings of guilt that similarly motivate cooperative behavior (Lelieveld et al., 2012, 2013). This makes disentangling the role of affective reactions and inferential processes more complicated in the case of disappointment, also because the emergence of complementary feelings of guilt may in fact be mediated by the inference that the other had hoped for more, as per appraisal theories of emotion (e.g., Frijda, Kuipers, & ter Schure, 1989; Roseman, 1984; Scherer, Schorr, & Johnstone, 2001; Smith, Haynes, Lazarus, & Pope, 1993).

Incidentally, anecdotal evidence also supports the potential effectiveness of expressing disappointment in bargaining situations. Anyone who has ever bought a souvenir from a private shop in a Third World country will be familiar with the theatrical displays of disappointment that may result when the salesperson considers one's initial bid too low (perhaps even when the offer is actually quite generous). More often than not this strategy proves effective in securing a higher price, be it because the disappointment signals that the salesperson had hoped for a better price, because the disappointment elicits complementary feelings of guilt, or both.

Affective reactions versus inferential processes

A considerable body of research speaks to the affective reactions and inferential processes that are triggered by the expression of various discrete emotions in negotiations, including anger, happiness, disappointment, worry, guilt, and regret. Although affective reactions and inferential processes were discussed in separate sections here, some of the aforementioned studies have considered affective reactions and inferential processes in conjunction (e.g., Van Dijk et al., 2008; Van Kleef et al., 2004a, 2004b). This is helpful, because it allows for a more integrative analysis of the interpersonal effects of emotional expressions.

For instance, Wubben and colleagues (2009a) argued that expressions of anger and expressions of disappointment may both be interpreted as signs that the expresser is unsatisfied and wants a better deal, but that expressions of anger are more likely than expressions of disappointment to elicit negative affective reactions (also see Lelieveld et al., 2012; Van Doorn et al., 2015b). Thus, the cooperative tendencies that may be fueled by inferences drawn from a counterpart's expressions of anger may be offset by the negative affective reactions that are triggered by those same expressions (e.g., reciprocal anger, negative impressions). In that sense, expressing disappointment may entail less risk, because it arouses less negative affective reactions in negotiation partners than anger does. In fact, expressions of disappointment may elicit complementary feelings of guilt that in turn promote cooperation (Lelieveld et al., 2013). In other words, in the case of expressed disappointment, affective reactions and inferential processes jointly push targets toward greater cooperation.

This is not the case for other emotional expressions. In the case of expressed anger or happiness, for instance, affective reactions and inferential processes drive opposite behavioral tendencies. Negative affective reactions fueled by expressions of anger (e.g., reciprocal anger, negative impressions) may motivate competitive behavior (Friedman et al., 2004; Kopelman et al., 2006), but inferences regarding the opponent's high limits and toughness may inform strategic cooperation to secure an agreement (Van Dijk et al., 2008; Van Kleef et al., 2004a). Conversely, positive affective reactions evoked by expressions of happiness (e.g., reciprocal happiness, increased liking) may motivate cooperative behavior, but inferences regarding the opponent's low ambition level and potential weakness may invite exploitation (Van Kleef et al., 2004a).

Given that inferential processes and affective reactions may motivate opposite behaviors in conflict and negotiation, it is important to understand when one process takes precedence over the other. As discussed in detail in Chapter 4, EASI theory postulates that the relative predictive strength of affective and inferential processes triggered by emotional expressions depends on the perceiver's information-processing ability and motivation and on social-contextual factors that determine the perceived appropriateness of the emotional expression. I now turn to empirical research on these moderating influences.

The role of information processing

Building on the idea that emotional expressions provide information to observers about the expresser's goals, intentions, and interpretation of the situation (see Chapters 2 and 3), EASI theory posits that the interpersonal effects of emotional expressions depend on observers' motivation and ability to process the information inherent in the emotional expressions. Specifically, EASI maintains that the relative predictive power of inferential processes versus affective reactions in shaping one's behavioral responses to others' emotional expressions increases to the degree that one's information-processing motivation and ability are higher.

Several negotiation studies support this idea. An early series of experiments revealed that the interpersonal effects of anger and happiness in negotiations depend on the target's information processing (Van Kleef et al., 2004b). In a first experiment, the authors examined the moderating role of need for cognitive closure, a personality variable that reflects chronic individual differences in the tendency to search for and process new pieces of information (Kruglanski & Webster, 1996; Webster & Kruglanski, 1994). Participants with a low need for cognitive closure (which indicates relatively high information-processing motivation)

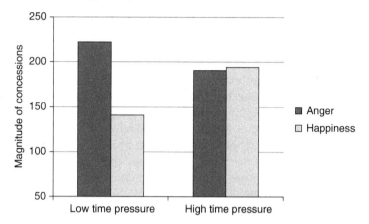

Figure 7.1   Magnitude of concessions (in points) made over the course of a negotiation as a function of the counterpart's expressions of anger versus happiness and time pressure. The total amount of points to be divided was 760 (based on Van Kleef et al., 2004b, Study 2).

made larger concessions to angry counterparts than to happy counterparts. However, participants with a high need for closure (which reflects relatively low information-processing motivation) were unaffected by their counterpart's emotional expressions.

In a second experiment the authors manipulated participants' information-processing motivation by varying time pressure (Van Kleef et al., 2004b). Participants who negotiated under low time pressure reported higher information-processing motivation and spent more time pondering the emotional messages of their counterpart than did those who negotiated under high time pressure. Accordingly, participants under low time pressure were more strongly influenced by their opponent's emotional expressions, making larger concessions to angry than to happy opponents (see Figure 7.1). Additional analyses revealed that the effects of emotional expressions under low (but not under high) time pressure were mediated by participants' inferences regarding the counterpart's limits, as in previous research discussed above.

Other studies indicate that the interpersonal effects of anger and happiness are moderated by power, which is known to influence the degree to which individuals are motivated to process information about other people (for reviews, see Fiske & Dépret, 1996; Keltner, Van Kleef, Chen, & Kraus, 2008). Across several studies involving various operationalizations of power (e.g., in terms of organizational position, control over others, or independence from others), lower-power negotiators were consistently more strongly affected by their counterpart's emotional expressions than were higher-power negotiators (Friedman et al., 2004; Overbeck, Neale, & Govan, 2010; Sinaceur and Tiedens, 2006; Van Dijk et al., 2008; Van Kleef et al., 2004b; Van Kleef, De Dreu, Pietroni, & Manstead, 2006).

The critical role of information processing has also been demonstrated in the context of intergroup conflict, where negotiations tend to be conducted by group representatives. A series of experiments showed that representatives who occupied a peripheral position within their constituent group engaged in more thorough information processing compared to more prototypical group representatives, especially when they were held accountable by their fellow group members (Van Kleef, Steinel, & Homan, 2013). Peripheral representatives also reported greater motivation to acquire and process relevant information about the negotiation situation and the opponent, presumably because they believed that doing well in the negotiation could help them to improve their position in the group. By contrast, prototypical group members were less motivated to engage in thorough information processing because their position in the group was already secure. Accordingly, peripheral group representatives used their opponent's expressions of anger versus happiness as information to guide their own negotiation behavior, whereas prototypical group representatives were largely uninfluenced by their opponent's emotional expressions.

Once again, there are few studies that have addressed the role of information processing in relation to emotions other than anger and happiness. Moreover, the available evidence is suggestive rather than conclusive. One study revealed that participants with a more selfish, calculating, and strategizing personality were more responsive to their counterpart's expressions of disappointment (Van Kleef & Van Lange, 2008). These individuals were more motivated to take the other's emotions into account because they feared that failing to do so might endanger their own outcomes (i.e., the other might reject their offer). As a result, they conceded more to a disappointed counterpart than to a nonemotional one. In other experiments the differential effects of expressions of disappointment versus guilt on concessions were moderated by trait as well as state trust (Van Kleef, De Dreu, & Manstead, 2006). Participants with higher levels of trust used their counterpart's emotional expressions to guide their own negotiation strategy, offering larger concessions to disappointed counterparts than to guilty ones. Participants with lower levels of trust, in contrast, explicitly discounted the opponent's emotional expressions, and as a result they did not behave differently toward disappointed versus guilty opponents.

Although the evidence pertaining to disappointment and guilt is indirect in the sense that information processing was not directly manipulated in these experiments, the findings converge with the more explicit evidence pertaining to the moderating influence of information processing on the interpersonal effects of anger and happiness considered above. Across the board, negotiators who are less motivated to engage in thorough information processing (be it due to dispositional tendencies or due to characteristics of the situation) are less likely to draw inferences from their counterpart's emotional expressions.

The role of appropriateness

Besides information processing, the interpersonal effects of emotional expressions are modulated by the perceived appropriateness of those expressions. EASI theory posits that the relative impact of inferential processes decreases to the degree that emotional expressions are perceived as inappropriate, while the relative impact of (negative) affective reactions increases. As discussed in detail in Chapter 4, the perceived appropriateness of emotional expressions is shaped by characteristics of the situation, the observer, the expression, and the expresser. The current empirical record speaks to the first three factors, which I discuss in order. Again, most of the evidence stems from studies on anger.

Regarding characteristics of the situation, several studies indicate that aspects of the negotiation setting and/or the broader social context shape the perceived appropriateness of expressions of anger in negotiations. For instance, Van Kleef and Côté (2007) examined the effects of anger in the presence or absence of an explicit display rule that prohibited expressions of anger. In the absence of such a display rule, participants deemed expressions of anger relatively appropriate. When there was an explicit norm prohibiting expressions of anger, however, participants perceived their counterpart's expressions of anger as inappropriate, which fueled strong negative affective reactions (i.e., feelings of revenge and a desire to retaliate). Accordingly, participants in the display rule condition adopted a more competitive stance when their opponent expressed anger, but only when they felt sufficiently powerful to strike back at their opponent.

Another relevant situational characteristic is the type of issue that is being negotiated. Studies have shown that people are relatively willing to give in on issues that involve interests such as money or time, but that they are more resistant to compromising on issues that are related to their personal values about what is right and wrong (Bazerman, Tenbrunsel, & Wade-Benzoni, 2008; Druckman, Broome, & Korper, 1988; Harinck, De Dreu, & Van Vianen, 2000; Wade-Benzoni, Hoffman, Thompson, Moore, Gillespie, & Bazerman, 2002). Accordingly, Harinck and Van Kleef (2012) found that expressions of anger in the context of a value conflict were deemed more inappropriate than expressions of anger in the context of a conflict of interests. For instance, participants who imagined receiving an angry reaction from their employer upon asking for a few extra days off deemed the anger more inappropriate when they wanted the extra days off to take care of a sick relative (a matter of personal values) than when they wanted the extra days off to go on a brief holiday (a matter of personal interests). As a result, participants who were confronted with expressions of anger in a value conflict expressed less willingness to make concessions and a greater desire to retaliate against their opponent. Along similar lines, another study found that displays of anger resulted in reduced concession making among negotiators who attached moral significance to the negotiation issue at hand (Dehghani, Carnevale, & Gratch, 2014).

Other work speaks to the role of characteristics of the situation as well as the observers in that situation. Kopelman and Rosette (2008) found that East Asian negotiators, who generally value humility and deference, were more likely to accept an offer from a counterpart who displayed positive emotions and less likely to accept an offer from a counterpart who expressed negative emotions, as compared to Israeli negotiators, who hold humility and deference in comparatively lower regard. Along similar lines, Adam, Shirako, and Maddux (2010) examined the effects of verbal expressions of anger across cultures. In a series of computer-mediated negotiation experiments, they found that European American participants conceded more to angry than to neutral opponents, whereas Asian American participants conceded less to angry than to neutral opponents, as visualized in Figure 7.2. The authors reasoned that this pattern arose because Asian American participants deemed expressions of anger more inappropriate than did European American participants. Accordingly, a follow-up study revealed that the effect of culture was mitigated when the appropriateness of anger expressions was manipulated directly through instructions, as in the aforementioned study by Van Kleef and Côté (2007) on the moderating role of display rules.

There is also some evidence for a moderating influence of characteristics of the emotional expression itself. We have seen before that, across the board, expressions of anger are more likely to be viewed as offensive and inappropriate by perceivers than expressions of disappointment (Van Doorn et al., 2015b; Wubben et al., 2009a). Other work has shown that the relative predictive strength of inferential processes and affective reactions on negotiation behavior is shaped by the way in which emotions are expressed (Lelieveld et al., 2011; Steinel, Van Kleef, & Harinck, 2008). Steinel and colleagues differentiated between emotions that are directed toward a negotiator's offer and emotions that are directed toward the negotiator as a person. When emotional messages were directed at the participant's offer, participants conceded more to an angry

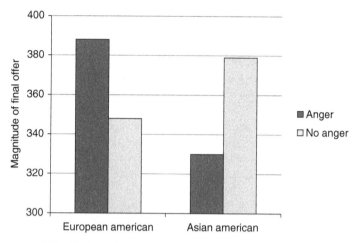

Figure 7.2 Magnitude of participants' final offers in a negotiation as a function of the opponent's emotional expression and participants' cultural background. The total amount of points to be divided was 760 (based on Adam et al., 2010, Study 2).

opponent than to a happy one because they interpreted the anger as a sign of high limits. However, when the emotions were directed at the negotiator as a person, participants conceded less to an angry opponent than to a happy one, presumably because they felt affronted by the opponent's angry remarks (although such mediation was not examined in this study).

Finally, there is evidence that the effects of emotional expressions in negotiations depend on the perceived authenticity of the expressions (Côté, Hideg, & Van Kleef, 2013). Emotional expressions resulting from antecedent-focused regulation or "deep acting" match one's actual emotional experience and are therefore perceived as authentic; in contrast, emotional expressions resulting from response-focused regulation or "surface acting" do not match one's internal emotional state and are therefore perceived as less authentic (Côté, 2005; Grandey, 2003; Grandey, Fisk, Mattila, Jansen, & Sideman, 2005; Gross, 1998a; Hochschild, 1983). Côté and colleagues (2013) conducted a face-to-face negotiation study and a video-mediated negotiation study, in both of which trained actors were employed to enact the various emotional expressions. As can be seen in Figure 7.3, deep-acted expressions of anger led participants to make considerable concessions on their asking price for a second-hand car, consistent with findings from previous research discussed above. However, surface-acted expressions of anger

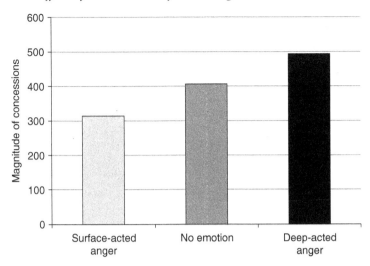

Figure 7.3 Concessions (in dollars) in a negotiation about a second-hand car as a function of the counterpart's emotional displays. There was a discrepancy of $1,100 between the seller's initial asking price and the buyer's initial offer (based on Côté et al., 2013, Study 2).

undermined trust and thereby decreased rather than increased participants' concessions, presumably because the inauthentic anger expressions were perceived as unethical, manipulative, or otherwise inappropriate influence attempts.

There is currently no empirical evidence concerning the role of expresser characteristics in shaping the perceived appropriateness of emotional expressions in negotiations. It is conceivable that factors such as the expresser's sex would play a role in this regard. In light of widespread stereotypes regarding gender and emotion, displays of anger by men might be deemed more appropriate in negotiations than displays of anger by women (Eagly, Karau, & Makhijani, 1995; Kring, 2000; K. Lewis, 2000), whereas displays of sadness by women may be perceived as more appropriate than displays of sadness by men (Plant, Hyde, Keltner, & Devine, 2000). Thus, all things being equal, male negotiators might have better chances of success when they express anger rather than sadness, whereas female negotiators may be more successful when they express sadness rather than anger. However, there may also be instances in which emotional expressions that deviate from prevailing gender stereotypes actually result in favorable negotiation outcomes for the expresser because they are perceived as more diagnostic, analogous to Adam and Shirako's (2013) finding that expressions of anger by East Asians elicited greater concessions than expressions of anger by European Americans. Future research is needed to examine these and other issues related to expresser characteristics.

Emotional intelligence in conflict and negotiation

The preceding review reveals that pretty much every emotion can have positive as well as negative consequences when expressed in the context of a conflict or negotiation. In keeping with central tenets of EASI theory, the consequences of emotional expressions depend on the perceiver's information-processing motivation and ability and on the perceived appropriateness of the expressions. From a practical point of view, this makes the use of emotions as tactical gambits in negotiation a delicate endeavor.

From the perspective of the expresser, harvesting the potential benefits of emotional displays in negotiations requires a deep understanding of the social effects of emotions and careful calibration of one's emotional displays to the situation, the counterpart, and the issue at hand. From the perspective of the perceiver, the ability to accurately detect the emotions of one's negotiation partner may provide an edge because insight in the counterpart's negotiation position and goals allows one to optimize one's own strategy. In other words, using emotions to one's advantage in conflict and negotiation would seem to require a certain degree of emotional intelligence – "the ability to monitor one's own and others' feelings, to discriminate among them, and to use this information to guide one's thinking and action" (Salovey & Mayer, 1990, p. 189; see Chapter 4 for a more elaborate discussion).

Empirical work does indeed point to effects of emotional intelligence in negotiations, but the evidence is less consistent than one might expect. Several studies converge in showing that emotional intelligence predicts relevant psychological negotiation outcomes. Negotiators who interacted with a more emotionally intelligent counterpart reported more positive negotiation experiences (Foo, Elfenbein, Tan, & Aik, 2004), higher satisfaction with the outcome of the negotiation (Mueller & Curhan, 2006), greater trust and rapport (Kim, Cundiff, & Choi, 2014), better liking of their negotiation partner (Mueller & Curhan, 2006), and a greater willingness to engage in future transactions with the partner (Kim et al., 2014; Mueller & Curhan, 2006). Effects of emotional intelligence on objective negotiation outcomes are less reliable, however. In one study, emotion recognition ability predicted better objective negotiation outcomes, both in terms of creating value and in terms of claiming value (Elfenbein, Foo, White, Tan, & Aik, 2007). In another study, however, individuals who scored higher on emotional intelligence achieved poorer objective outcomes than their counterparts (Foo et al., 2004). Yet another study revealed no effects of emotional intelligence on joint gain (Kim et al., 2014).

These inconsistent findings present a puzzle that has yet to be resolved. One potential explanation lies in the fact that researchers have used different measures of emotional intelligence (e.g., emotion detection skills vs. more general assessments of emotional intelligence, self-report vs. ability-based measures) and different operationalizations of negotiation outcomes (e.g., individual vs. joint outcomes), which renders direct comparisons across studies difficult and potentially misleading. A partly related explanation resides in the mixed-motive nature of negotiations, which provides incentives for cooperation as well as competition (Schelling, 1960). Research has shown that emotional intelligence allows individuals to be more successful in the social domain (Mayer, Salovey, & Caruso, 2004), but how people use their emotional skills in interpersonal interactions depends on their chronic or momentary social goals (Côté, DeCelles, McCarthy, Van Kleef, & Hideg, 2011; Kilduff, Chiaburu, & Menges, 2010). Thus, negotiators with more selfish, Machiavellian inclinations may mobilize their emotional intelligence to obtain the best possible outcome for themselves and/or to weaken their partner's position, whereas those with a more prosocial disposition may use their emotional skills to enhance joint outcomes.

Conclusion

The research discussed in this chapter shows that discrete emotional expressions have pervasive effects on behavior in conflict and negotiation. Consistent with EASI theory, these interpersonal effects are driven by both affective reactions and inferential processes. The relative predictive strength of these two mechanisms depends on the target's information-processing motivation and ability and on social-contextual factors that determine the perceived appropriateness of the emotional expressions, such as display rules, cultural norms, and the way in which emotions are expressed. In addition, several studies point to the role of emotional intelligence in shaping both psychological and monetary negotiation outcomes, although the current empirical record is inconclusive with regard to the latter.

So far research on the effects of emotional expressions in conflict and negotiation has almost exclusively focused on negotiations between two individuals (but see Van Beest et al., 2008, discussed above, for a rare study on the effects of emotional expressions in multiparty coalition negotiations). Although a great deal can be learned from studies on interpersonal negotiations, many high-stakes conflicts and negotiations occur between groups of people rather than between individuals. It is therefore important to extend future investigations of the effects of emotional expressions to the domain of intergroup conflict. Recent research indicates that emotional expressions are indeed relevant in this context. De Vos, Van Zomeren, Gordijn, and Postmes (2013) found that the communication of anger in intergroup conflict can reduce destructive conflict tendencies compared to the communication of contempt or no emotion, because anger signals that the expresser is motivated to maintain positive long-term intergroup relations.

Intergroup negotiations are typically conducted by representatives who negotiate on behalf of a constituency. This introduces an additional set of features that do not apply in interpersonal negotiation, including social dynamics associated with the relationship between the representative and the constituent group. Van Kleef and colleagues (2013) found that group representatives who occupied a peripheral position within their group were more responsive to the emotional expressions of the outgroup representative because they were more motivated than their prototypical counterparts to engage in thorough information processing and to gain a rich understanding of the social situation. These initial investigations attest to the potential impact of emotional expressions in intergroup conflict, but more research is needed to develop a fuller understanding of the nature and contingencies of these effects.

Regardless of the level of analysis we adopt (interpersonal or intergroup), it will be clear from the present analysis that there is no simple answer to the question of whether emotions are helpful or harmful in negotiations. Expressions of anger can help to extract concessions from an opponent by signaling that one is unwilling to compromise, but they can also elicit strong negative affective reactions and retaliation. Displays of happiness may contribute to smooth interactions and interpersonal liking, but they also suggest that one is willing to settle for less. Signs of guilt may help to repair a damaged business relationship, but they may also invite exploitation.

Clearly, then, the functionality of emotional displays in negotiations depends on a complex interplay of factors, including the particular emotion being displayed, the social context within which it is displayed, and parties' negotiation goals. For instance, expressions of anger may be highly effective when they are perceived as appropriate for the situation, the target is at least somewhat dependent on the expresser, and the primary goal of the expresser is to serve his or her own immediate (monetary) interests. Conversely, displays of anger are likely to be counterproductive when they are perceived as inappropriate, when the target has a more powerful position, and/or when the expresser's goal is to establish a fruitful long-term relationship. Similar trade-offs and contingencies determine the functionality of displays of other discrete emotions.

In sum, emotional displays play a critical role in conflict and negotiation, and whether they constitute an asset or a liability depends on how they are used. Emotionally intelligent and strategically savvy negotiators use their own and their partners' emotional displays to their advantage to craft optimal deals. In line with Oscar Wilde's metaphor in the opening quote of this chapter, a key to success lies in the right mix of emotional expressions. The proper dosage of oil and vinegar results not only in a tasty salad, but also in optimal negotiation outcomes.

CHAPTER 8

Social effects of emotions on consumer behavior and customer service

Your most unhappy customers are your greatest source of learning.
Bill Gates

Anyone who has ever received or provided some kind of customer service – that is, everyone who reads this – is likely to recall several service encounters that left an emotional mark. Whether we walked away happy and satisfied or angry and frustrated, and whether we were in the role of service provider or receiver, we are likely to remember the emotional tone of the episodes. Like any social interaction, encounters between service employees and customers are rife with emotional triggers, and the resulting emotional expressions shape momentary interactions as well as future intentions. A tired grocery shopper may catch a cashier's cheerfulness and feel satisfied and re-energized. A customer in a shopping center who is annoyed by a service employee's bad temper may decide not to come back to the store and to share her bad experience with her friends. A nurse may feel uplifted by a patient's heartfelt gratitude for the care received, which may increase her job satisfaction and well-being. A waiter in a touristy restaurant who is routinely confronted with disrespectful diners may develop health problems and decide to quit his job.

Examples such as these are all too familiar, both the positive and the negative, and they testify to the importance of emotions in the service industry. It is not surprising, then, that organization scholars have long been interested in the role of emotions in customer service and consumer behavior. This is for good reasons. Consistent with the general finding that people's satisfaction with various aspects of their lives is influenced by their momentary affective states (Schwarz & Clore, 1983), research on consumer behavior has documented that (positive) affective states can bias product attitudes. For instance, consumers experiencing positive affect have been found to report more favorable attitudes toward products than those in neutral moods (Batra & Stayman, 1990; Edell & Burke, 1987). Moreover, in keeping with anecdotal observations, satisfaction with the service delivery process of both service providers and customers is influenced by the emotional tone of their encounters. Service providers' emotional displays can influence customers' emotions and their satisfaction with the service (Hoffman, 1992). Customers' emotional expressions can influence service providers' well-being and job satisfaction (Grandey, Dickter, & Sin, 2004). Moreover, service representatives may use the emotional reactions of customers as cues about how they are doing (Mattila & Enz, 2002).

Research on the role of emotions in customer service has been strongly influenced by Hochschild's (1983) seminal book *The managed heart*, in which she introduced the concept of emotional labor. Hochschild defined emotional labor as "the management of feeling to create a publicly observable facial and bodily display" (p. 7) as a part of one's job. Such emotional labor may involve surface acting, deep acting, or the expression of genuinely felt emotions (Ashforth & Humphrey, 1993). As discussed in Chapter 4, surface acting (or emotion-focused regulation) involves creating outward expressions of emotions that one does not privately experience, whereas deep acting (or antecedent-focused regulation) involves changing one's internally felt emotions so as to be able to express genuinely felt emotions that are required in a particular situation (Côté, 2005; Grandey, 2003; Gross, 1998b; Hochschild, 1983).

Many jobs in the service industry are characterized by social-emotional requirements that dictate the expression of certain emotions and/or the suppression of other emotions as part of the work role, with specific emotional expectancies depending on particularities of the occupational culture, the discrete emotion in question, and the target of the emotional display (e.g., a coworker or a customer; Diefendorff & Greguras, 2009). A common assumption in the literature is that service workers' effectiveness and well-being depend on their ability to meet such emotional requirements (Ashforth & Humphrey, 1993; Hochschild, 1983). Displaying organizationally incentivized emotions to clients, customers, or patients has been conceptualized as a type of labor because it often requires the deliberate and effortful adjustment and/or portrayal of emotions that one may not necessarily feel so as to meet the demands of the professional context (James, 1989).

Over three decades of research since the publication of Hochschild's (1983) book have produced a rich body of data on the role of emotions in customer service (Grandey, Diefendorff, & Rupp, 2013). A considerable proportion of this work is concerned with the impact of various emotion regulation strategies (e.g., deep acting vs. surface acting) on outcomes such as service providers' job satisfaction, well-being, and burnout (e.g., Beal, Trougakos, Weiss, & Dalal, 2013; Grandey, 2003; Zapf & Holz, 2006). A meta-analysis of this research revealed that surface acting was more strongly associated with decreases in service workers' job satisfaction and well-being than deep acting (Hülsheger & Schewe, 2011). This literature speaks to intrapersonal rather than interpersonal effects of emotions, and, as such, an elaborate discussion falls outside the scope of this book. The present discussion focuses on the social consequences of emotional displays in customer service.

Many social interactions are symmetrical in the sense that interacting parties fulfill similar roles (e.g., the role of spouse, group member, or negotiation partner). Thus, in most research on the role of emotions in close relationships, groups, and conflict and negotiation discussed in the preceding chapters, emotional influences between people can theoretically be assumed to flow in both directions following similar patterns, except when there are considerable power differences between interactants. This is different in the case of customer service (and in the case of leader–follower relations, which are the topic of the next chapter), because service providers and customers play markedly different roles. Due to their different roles, customers and service employees respond somewhat differently to each other's emotions, and accordingly research has addressed different types of processes and outcomes, depending on whether the primary focus was on the customer or on the service provider. In light of these differences, I treat the two streams of research separately. I first consider research on the effects of service providers' emotional expressions on customers, followed by a discussion of studies on the effects of customers' emotional expressions on service workers. Next I consider the effects of third parties' emotional expressions on consumers' product attitudes. Finally, I discuss research on interpersonal emotion regulation and emotional intelligence in the context of customer service and consumer behavior.

Effects of service providers' emotions on customers

The idea that service providers' emotional expressions may influence the judgments and behaviors of their customers has been present in the literature for quite a while (Hochschild, 1983; Rafaeli & Sutton, 1987, 1989). There is a widespread belief among laypersons, service professionals, and scholars that the emotional displays of service representatives influence customers' emotional experiences and satisfaction with the service provided. Much theorizing and research in this area has been guided by the straightforward assumption that service representatives' positive emotional displays contribute to favorable service outcomes, whereas negative emotional displays contribute to unfavorable outcomes. There is a slight imbalance in the literature, however, in the sense that the effects of positive emotional expressions have received greater research attention than the effects of negative emotional expressions. In particular, researchers have shown interest in the impact of

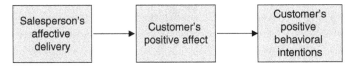

Figure 8.1   The effects of positive "affective delivery" of salespeople on customers' favorable intentions vis-à-vis the store are mediated by customers' positive affect (based on Tsai & Huang, 2002).

displays of positive emotion by service providers on various indices of customer satisfaction.

Service with a smile

The proverbial "service with a smile" is an explicit or implicit job requirement in many customer service settings, certainly in the United States. Accordingly, it occupies a prominent position in the customer service literature. An early study on the effects of smiling behavior by waitresses in a cocktail lounge revealed that greater smiling was associated with larger tips by male customers (Tidd & Lockard, 1978). Another study found that service friendliness (which involved behaviors such as greeting, smiling, and looking at customers) was a positive predictor of customer satisfaction (Brown & Sulzer-Azaroff, 1994).

Later studies have provided more direct support for the idea that positive emotional expressions by service personnel enhance customers' service experiences and contribute to favorable behavioral intentions vis-à-vis the store. For instance, Pugh (2001) examined the effects of bank tellers' positive emotional displays (e.g., smiling) on customers' emotions and judgments. He found that customers who observed positive emotions reported more positive affect and more favorable evaluations of service quality. Tsai and colleagues (Tsai, 2001; Tsai & Huang, 2002) found that when salespeople in the retail shoe business displayed positive emotions, customers reported a higher likelihood of revisiting the store and spreading positive word of mouth. Barger and Grandey (2006) found that smiling behavior of food service providers during encounters with customers was related to favorable perceptions of service quality and greater customer satisfaction. Futhermore, Tsai and Huang (2002) obtained some evidence for the frequently assumed mediating role of customers' affective reactions, as visualized schematically in Figure 8.1. They demonstrated that positive "affective delivery" of salespeople, which includes friendliness and service with a smile, instigated positive in-store moods in customers, which in turn contributed to customers' favorable behavioral intentions vis-à-vis the store (i.e., willingness to return to the store and to pass positive comments to friends).

These findings align with lay conceptions about the benefits of smiling for customer service outcomes. Within the same realm, other studies have examined the somewhat less obvious consequences of various strategies aimed at producing the much-appreciated service with a smile. This research speaks to the differential effects of more versus less authentic displays of positive emotion.

Emotional labor and the authenticity of service providers' emotional displays

Customers and service managers expect employees to provide service with a smile, but naturally employees do not always experience positive emotions. Job-related emotional expectations and requirements may therefore lead service workers to portray positive emotions that they do not actually feel (Hochschild, 1983). An important determinant of the effectiveness of such positive emotional displays is the degree to which customers perceive them as genuine and authentic (Grandey, Fisk, Mattila, Jansen, & Sideman, 2005). In a study involving videotaped simulated hotel check-in encounters with a trained actress as the service representative, Grandey and colleagues found that authenticity of the service provider's positive emotional displays enhanced perceptions of friendliness and customer satisfaction, but only when the service provider performed well (see Figure 8.2). In a second study, the perceived authenticity of an employee's emotional displays enhanced customer satisfaction, regardless of task performance. Together, these studies suggest that authentic smiles contribute to perceptions of service quality, even though they may not compensate for objectively bad service performance.

In line with theorizing about the effects of emotion regulation strategies on the perceived authenticity of emotional expressions (see Chapter 4), several studies indicate that customers' perceptions of the authenticity of service workers' emotional expressions and customers' responses to those expressions depend on how the expressions were regulated. For instance, Grandey (2003) found that deep acting on the part of service workers was positively associated with ratings of affective delivery (the extent to which the service was perceived as friendly and warm), whereas surface acting was negatively related to affective delivery. Affective delivery, in turn, has been associated with favorable service outcomes (Pugh, 2001; Tsai, 2001).

Service employees' emotional labor strategies of deep acting versus surface acting have been shown to influence other indices of service

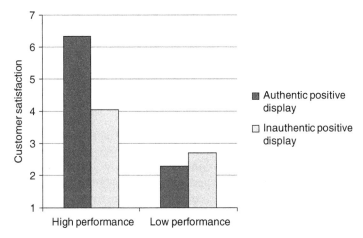

Figure 8.2 Customer satisfaction as a function of a service provider's authentic versus inauthentic positive emotional displays and the quality of the service provider's performance (based on Grandey et al., 2005, Study 1).

quality as well. When analyzing dyadic survey data from a large number of service interactions between employees and customers, Groth and colleagues found that deep acting was positively associated with perceptions of customer orientation, ratings of service quality, and customers' loyalty intentions, whereas surface acting was not (Groth, Hennig-Thurau, & Walsh, 2009). Their data further revealed that these effects were stronger among customers who were more accurate at detecting employees' emotion regulation strategies. This suggests that customers with higher levels of emotional intelligence are better at discriminating between sincere and insincere expressions of positive emotion by service providers, which makes them more likely than their less emotionally intelligent counterparts to respond favorably to sincere smiles but also to respond unfavorably to insincere smiles.

Experimental research provides complementary insights. In a study involving simulated service encounters in which actors played the roles of service employees, Hennig-Thurau and colleagues investigated how customers' emotions and satisfaction with the service are shaped by employees' smiling behavior and their use of a deep acting or a surface acting emotion regulation strategy (Hennig-Thurau, Groth, Paul, & Gremler, 2006). The authors hypothesized that authentic displays of happiness (as produced by deep acting) trigger more positive emotions in customers than inauthentic displays of happiness (as produced by surface acting), because customers appreciate honesty and authenticity. In support of this idea, participants who were confronted with deep-acted happiness displays by a service employee were more likely to adopt the positive emotion of that employee than were those who encountered surface-acted happiness displays. Moreover, deep-acted displays of happiness resulted in greater customer satisfaction and experienced rapport with the service employee than surface-acted displays.

The general pattern that emerges from these studies is that deep acting on the part of customer service representatives has favorable consequences for customers' emotions, satisfaction, and future intentions vis-à-vis the store, whereas surface acting has negative consequences. This conclusion was also borne out by a meta-analysis, which revealed a negative relationship between surface acting and various indices of service quality such as task performance and customer satisfaction, and a positive relationship between deep acting and service quality (Hülsheger & Schewe, 2011).

The exact mechanisms through which deep acting and surface acting exert their positive and negative effects in customer service settings have not yet been uncovered. Hennig-Thurau and colleagues (2006) highlighted the fact that customers (much like people in general) desire to be treated honestly. This idea resonates with a key proposition of Emotions as Social Information (EASI) theory about the adverse effects of emotional expressions that are perceived as inappropriate (see Chapter 4). Inauthentic emotional expressions may be perceived as dishonest or manipulative influence attempts (Côté, Hideg, & Van Kleef, 2013). The perceived inappropriateness of such influence tactics may inspire negative affective reactions in customers that may lead them to turn against the service employee and/or the company that they represent (Rafaeli & Sutton, 1989; Van Kleef, Homan, & Cheshin, 2012).

Although few studies have explicitly considered the notion of appropriateness of emotional displays in customer service, there is some evidence that service employees' emotional expressions are more likely to have beneficial effects to the degree that they are perceived as normative by customers. Menon and Dubé (2000) reported a study on the effects of salespersons' positive (joy and delight) and negative (anxiety and anger) emotions as a function of the normative emotional expectations of customers. They found that emotional responses of salespersons that met or exceeded customers' expectations led to greater customer satisfaction than emotional responses that fell short of expectations. This was true for the positive as well as the negative emotions. More direct evidence for the role of the perceived appropriateness of service workers' emotional displays comes from a recent line of research on the effects of emotional intensity in customer service.

The intensity and perceived appropriateness of service providers' emotional displays

As elaborated in Chapter 4, the perceived appropriateness of emotional displays depends on the degree to which they are "correct for the situation and in correct proportion to the evoking circumstances" (Shields, 2005, p. 7). Besides displaying the "wrong" emotion for the context (e.g., cheerfully telling a customer that the reserved product she came to pick up has not been delivered), service employees may express emotions whose intensity does not match the implicit script for that particular situation (e.g., bursting out in tears while explaining that the reserved product is not in store). EASI posits that emotional expressions whose intensity violates situational scripts may evoke negative affective reactions and concomitant behavior in observers because such expressions are perceived as inappropriate (Van Kleef et al., 2012).

Building on these ideas, Cheshin and colleagues examined whether and how service providers' displays of emotions of varying intensities have diverging effects on relevant customer service outcomes (Cheshin, Amit, & Van Kleef, 2015). To enable a meaningful investigation of the effects of positive (happiness) as well as negative (sadness) emotions of varying intensities, the authors created customer service settings that were somewhat ambiguous in terms of their emotional meaning. That is, participants who inquired about a specific product (i.e., a particular book or DVD) were told by the service representative that that particular item was currently not in store, but that an interesting alternative was available. Given that this situation involves both bad news and good news, the service employee could credibly display either sadness about the lack of availability of the requested item or happiness about the availability of the alternative. In light of the relatively minor importance of the situation, however, highly intense emotional expressions of either emotion would likely violate customers' implicit normative scripts for that situation, meaning that intense expressions should be perceived as relatively inappropriate compared to mild expressions, thereby potentially undermining perceptions of service quality.

In an initial laboratory study conducted to test this possibility, Cheshin et al. (2015) found that verbal expressions of high-intensity (as opposed to low-intensity) sadness and happiness led participants to evaluate a service provider's emotion as more inauthentic and inappropriate, and to deem the service provider as less trustworthy. In a second experiment, the authors replicated the effect of emotion intensity on trust and

obtained evidence that the impact of emotion intensity extends to evaluations of service quality. Satisfaction with the service was somewhat
higher when the employee expressed happiness rather than sadness,
but above and beyond that effect, participants reported significantly
greater satisfaction in both mild emotion conditions than in both intense
emotion conditions. The effect of the intensity of emotional expressions
on satisfaction with the service was mediated by perceptions of the
employee's trustworthiness.

Finally, Cheshin and colleagues (2015) replicated their experimental
findings in a field study. Shoppers were handed out flyers inviting them
to try a new movie recommendation web service in return for a free DVD.
Upon indicating their favorite movie genre online, respondents received
a message from an employee of the (fictitious) web company, who
explained that movies in that particular genre were currently not in
stock, but that the system had identified an alternative movie for them
that they might also find interesting to watch. The message contained a
verbal expression of either mild or intense happiness or sadness. Again,
respondents indicated trusting the service representative more and being
more satisfied with the service after receiving a message containing a
mild rather than an intense emotional expression. Moreover, participants
in the mild expression conditions were more likely to have watched their
free DVD ten days after receiving it than were those in the intense
expression conditions.

Summary

Several studies indicate that positive emotional displays by service providers are associated with favorable outcomes such as customer satisfaction, intentions to return to the store, positive word of mouth, and tipping
behavior. Furthermore, there is ample evidence that emotional displays
that are perceived as authentic and/or appropriate are more likely to
have a favorable impact on customers, whereas emotional displays that
are perceived as inauthentic and/or inappropriate are more likely to have
unfavorable consequences. This evidence supports the moderating role of
the perceived appropriateness of emotional expressions as postulated in
EASI theory. To date, no studies have examined the role of information
processing (another key moderator of the social effects of emotions
according to EASI theory), and, as such, no evidence for such moderation
is currently available from this domain of research.

Evidence for behavioral consequences of service representatives' emotional displays is scarce, which is most likely due to the obvious difficulties associated with measuring behavior in customer service settings.
Most studies that aimed to speak to behavior included measures of

customers' behavioral intentions (e.g., intentions to return to the store or to spread positive word of mouth), which are likely to be relatively strongly correlated with momentary affective reactions to a service encounter. Evidence for such affective reactions abounds, with numerous studies pointing to effects of service providers' emotional expressions on customers' emotional states, impressions of the service representative, and/or satisfaction with the service. The potential mediating role of more deliberate inferential processes has not received systematic attention in research on the impact of service workers' emotional displays on customers. However, scholars have begun to consider the role of inferential processes in studies on the effects of customers' emotional expressions on service providers.

Effects of customers' emotions on service providers

Reflecting the qualitatively different roles and behaviors associated with consumers and service providers, research on the impact of customers' emotional expressions on service workers has focused on different types of processes and outcomes than research on the effects of service workers' emotional expressions on customers. Some of these studies focused primarily on service providers' affective and behavioral reactions to customers' emotional expressions, whereas other studies focused on the cognitive consequences of customers' emotional expressions. I discuss these two types of research in turn.

Affective and behavioral consequences of customers' emotional displays

Service providers are confronted with emotional expressions of customers on a daily basis. Although employees are likely to encounter positive as well as negative emotional displays of customers, research has focused mostly on the consequences of negative displays such as anger (Miron-Spektor & Rafaeli, 2009). Customers may express anger or become rude, hostile, or aggressive in encounters with service representatives, for instance when complaining about unsatisfactory service. Research shows that verbal abuse by customers is more prevalent than verbal abuse by coworkers or supervisors, and that customer verbal aggression predicts service representatives' well-being over and above verbal aggression by fellow organization members (Grandey, Kern, & Frone, 2007). In a field study by Grandey and colleagues (2004), call center employees in the United States reported being confronted with customer verbal aggression on average ten times a day. The higher the frequency of customer aggression and the more employees appraised the encounters as stressful, the more emotionally exhausted they felt. Emotional exhaustion in turn predicted absenteeism. Similarly, a field study among hotel employees in Cyprus showed that customer verbal aggression predicted emotional exhaustion, which in turn undermined service recovery performance and job satisfaction and increased turnover intentions (Karatepe, Yorganci, & Haktanir, 2009).

These effects of customer anger and verbal aggression align with research on the effects of customer mistreatment and interactional injustice, even though this work did not explicitly address the role of emotional expressions. In an experimental study, Rupp and Spencer (2006) investigated the consequences of customer interactional unfairness, which involves personal attacks on service employees and a general lack of dignity and respect in the way they approach employees. Participants played the role of customer service representatives in a workplace simulation, during which they were confronted with either interactionally fair or interactionally unfair customers. Results showed that unfairly treated participants experienced more anger than did those who were treated fairly, which made it more difficult for them to comply with display rules. A study involving daily survey data from call center employees in China further showed that customer mistreatment significantly predicted customer-directed sabotage, which involved behaviors such as hanging up on customers, intentionally putting them on hold for a long period of time, and purposefully transferring their calls to the wrong department (Wang, Liao, Zhan, & Shi, 2011).

There is some evidence that service employees' responses to customers' incivility depend on their own chronic positive or negative affectivity. One study found that a higher frequency of customer aggression was associated with reduced well-being and job satisfaction especially among employees with higher levels of trait positive affect (Goussinsky, 2011). Although the exact dynamics responsible for this effect are unclear, it is conceivable that customer aggression is perceived as particularly rude and inappropriate by employees who tend to adopt a more positive emotional approach in social interactions themselves. At the same time, employees high on trait negative affectivity have been found to be more likely to lash out to rude customers by purposefully sabotaging them (Wang et al., 2011). These studies suggest that service employees high on positive versus negative affectivity respond quite differently to customer verbal aggression. The former may privately suffer more from the perceived mistreatment, whereas the latter may be more likely to actively take revenge.

Recent work by Glikson and colleagues provides more direct evidence for the role of perceived appropriateness in shaping service providers' responses to customers' expressions of anger (Glikson, Rafaeli, & Wirtz, 2015). The authors examined the combined effects of the intensity of anger displays and culture on customer service representatives' reactions to angry customers. In a lab simulation conducted in Israel (individualistic culture) and Singapore (collectivistic culture), they found that perceptions of appropriateness of anger displays (based on the intensity of the anger) differed between the two cultures, and that responses to the anger differed accordingly. Students acting as service representatives had the option of replying to an angry customer's message immediately or putting it off until later. They could also decide whether or not to offer monetary compensation to the customer. Israeli participants handled the complaints of customers who showed high-intensity anger more quickly than those of customers who showed low-intensity anger, whereas Singaporean participants did not differ in this respect. Moreover, Israelis offered higher compensation to customers emitting high-rather than low-intensity anger displays, whereas Singaporeans gave less compensation to customers showing high-intensity anger. Although the precise mechanisms underlying these effects remain to be uncovered, it seems plausible that the negative responses of Singaporean participants to intense expressions of anger were due in part to negative affective reactions triggered by the perceived inappropriateness of the emotional displays (Van Kleef et al., 2012).

Another recent experimental study provides compatible evidence for the role of perceived appropriateness of emotional expressions. Cheshin and colleagues examined how customers' expressions of anger shape service providers' tendencies to offer compensation depending on the intensity of customers' anger displays (Cheshin, Glikson, Van Kleef, & Rafaeli, 2015). Participants played the role of service representatives of a resort company, in which capacity they were confronted with several customer complaints. Some of the complaints were delivered in an emotionally neutral fashion, whereas others were accompanied by expressions of anger. Using a trained actress, the tone of the angry complainant's voice was experimentally varied to express anger at different levels of intensity. In the mild anger expression condition the complainant's tone of voice remained polite and composed, but her annoyance about the situation was clearly articulated. In the moderate anger condition the complainant's tone of voice was noticeably aggravated. In the intense anger condition the complainant's tone of voice was very angry indeed, and the voice message ended with the sound of the phone slamming. After listening to the complaints, participants had to decide how to allocate an assigned amount of compensation money among all complaints received. Participants offered higher compensation in response to mildly or moderately angry complaints than in response to nonemotional complaints. However, they offered less compensation to the intensely angry complainant. The effects of anger expressions on compensation were mediated by participants' perceptions of the inappropriateness of the complainant's expressions, which were exacerbated in the intense anger condition.

Cognitive consequences of customers' emotional displays

Analogous to the various other domains of social interaction covered in this book, the emotional expressions of customers may also trigger inferential processes in service employees, for instance regarding the quality of their service. Quite sensibly, consumers' appreciation of the service they receive has been found to correlate with their experienced and expressed emotions, with positive affect being associated with favorable service assessments and negative affect with negative assessments (Gardner, 1985; Mattila & Enz, 2002). Thus, customers' emotional expressions may provide useful information about how they evaluate the service. Accordingly, Mattila and Enz (2002) proposed that "a customer's displayed emotions might be one of those discriminating cues that enable contact employees to enhance their own performance" (p. 274). Or, as Bill Gates put it in the opening quote of this chapter, unhappy customers may be a service company's greatest source of learning.

Although direct tests of the role of inferential processes in the context of customer service are scarce, there is some evidence that service employees use customers' emotional displays as a source of information about the quality of their service. Hareli and colleagues (2009) examined how emotional expressions of customers influence service representatives' inferences regarding the credibility of a complaint. They found that when a situation was ambiguous and the complaint left room for doubt, displays of anger (compared to sadness) on the part of the customer bolstered perceptions of injustice and enhanced the perceived credibility of the complaint in the eyes of the service provider. Besides speaking to inferential processes associated with emotional displays in customer service, this finding corroborates the more general theoretical notion that emotional expressions take on heightened diagnostic importance under more ambiguous circumstances, where more direct information about the expresser's situation and/or intentions is lacking (Van Kleef, De Dreu, & Manstead, 2010).

Another study examined how exposure to angry customers may influence service workers' task performance and problem-solving capabilities (Miron-Spektor, Efrat-Treister, Rafaeli, & Schwarz-Cohen, 2011). In a series of experiments, Miron-Spektor and colleagues obtained evidence that expressions of anger by customers enhance service providers' performance on relatively straightforward analytical tasks that can be completed by following a well-rehearsed routine, but undermine performance on more complex problem-solving tasks that require flexible switching between different alternative representations of the problem and engaging more unconventional perspectives. The authors concluded that observing anger motivates people to apply dominant responses to well-known problems and situations, while interfering with their ability to perform complex problem-solving tasks. Interestingly, the experiments also produced some evidence that more indirect expressions of anger through sarcastic remarks can have a positive effect on complex thinking and problem-solving performance. The authors suggested that the incongruent information that is inherent in sarcasm stimulates complex thinking and attenuates the negative effects of anger on individuals' problem-solving capacities.

Along related lines, another series of studies provides evidence that customer verbal aggression can have debilitating effects on service providers' cognitive performance (Rafaeli et al., 2012). Customers' verbal aggression was found to impair the recognition memory and working memory of service workers and, accordingly, to reduce their recall of customers' requests. The authors further reported evidence for detrimental effects of customer verbal aggression on the quality of service employees' cognitive task performance. In line with the general pattern that emotional expressions of more powerful parties have a greater impact than do those of less powerful parties (Keltner, Van Kleef, Chen, & Kraus, 2008), the negative impact of customer verbal aggression on cognitive performance was especially pronounced when the aggression was exhibited by high-status customers.

Summary

Several studies point to the cognitive, affective, and behavioral consequences of customers' emotional expressions for service providers. Reflecting a strong interest in adverse (health) consequences for service workers, this literature has focused almost exclusively on the effects of customer expressions of anger and related displays of hostility or aggression. This predominantly cross-sectional body of research has documented robust associations between displays of anger and hostility by customers and negative affect, emotional exhaustion, and decreased job satisfaction of service employees, which are sometimes reflected in absenteeism, turnover intentions, or customer-directed sabotage. Given that much of this research has employed cross-sectional research designs, some caution is warranted when interpreting the findings. For instance, it is difficult to completely rule out the possibility that employees who are emotionally exhausted and unsatisfied with their jobs evoke more negative emotional displays from customers than employees who are happy with their jobs, although such reverse causality is less likely in some studies due to the inclusion of various control variables and/or the use of longitudinal designs.

There is also some evidence that customer displays of anger can enhance service outcomes (e.g., compensation for prior unsatisfactory service), provided that service providers perceive the expressions as appropriate for the context. When displays of anger are overly intense or in violation of culturally determined display rules, anger expressions are more likely to undermine rather than improve service quality. Research has further documented cognitive and performance consequences of customers' emotional expressions, most notably anger. Expressions of anger have been found to increase the perceived credibility of customer complaints in the eyes of service workers. Moreover, there is evidence that customer expressions of anger may motivate service personnel to perform better, but only on relatively well-learned tasks and/or when the anger is displayed in an indirect way. Direct expressions of anger have been found to undermine performance on more complex tasks, and displays of aggression have been shown to impair memory capacity and cognitive performance.

This body of research provides evidence for the role of affective reactions as well as inferential processes in the context of customer service. In addition, several studies speak to the role of the perceived appropriateness of customers' emotional expressions. Relatively few studies have examined the ways in which affective reactions and inferential processes shape service providers' behavior, and so far no research has explicitly investigated contingency factors that shape the relative impact of both processes on behavior. EASI would predict that service providers are more likely to use customers' emotional displays to draw inferences regarding the quality of their service to the degree that they are more motivated and able to engage in thorough information processing, but to date no evidence for this possibility exists. Moreover, the almost exclusive focus on anger renders the generalizability of the emerging patterns to other emotions uncertain at this point. Interestingly, some evidence regarding the effects of emotions other than anger is provided by research on the influence of third parties' emotional displays on product attitudes.

How third parties' emotional expressions shape consumers' attitudes

We have seen that consumers' satisfaction with service encounters and their attitudes toward products and stores are shaped by their own emotional state as well as by the emotional expressions of service providers. There is also evidence that such attitudes are influenced by emotional expressions of impartial third parties who have no vested interest in making a profit or selling a particular product. Various streams of research in the areas of social psychology and consumer behavior converge to show that third parties' emotional expressions can influence product attitudes by eliciting affective reactions and/or inferential processes in perceivers.

Fundamental social-psychological research indicates that the positive or negative valence of emotional expressions may become directly associated with a stimulus via evaluative conditioning (De Houwer, Thomas, & Baeyens, 2001). In this type of process, an emotional expression can come to serve as the unconditioned stimulus that changes the subjective valence of a previously neutral conditioned stimulus. As a case in point, Murphy and Zajonc (1993) showed that subliminal exposure to happy or angry facial expressions led participants to judge neutral Chinese ideographs more and less favorably, respectively. Other studies found compatible effects of subliminal affective priming with emotional expressions (e.g., Winkielman, Zajonc, & Schwarz, 1997) as well as of classical conditioning involving emotional expressions (e.g., Baccus, Baldwin, & Packer, 2004).

There is also some suggestive evidence that third parties' emotional expressions can influence perceivers' voting behavior. Mullen and colleagues (1986) found that the positivity of a newscaster's facial expressions while referring to one of the 1984 presidential candidates predicted viewers' voting behavior. Regular viewing of a newscaster who exhibited "biased" facial expressions in favor of a particular political candidate was associated with an increased likelihood of voting for that candidate (Ronald Reagan). Besides issues of reverse causality and the potential role of third variables, it is unclear from this study how the effects of the newscaster's emotional displays on viewers' voting behavior came about. Later studies shed more light on the underlying mechanisms that may be responsible for the effects of sources' emotional displays on perceivers' attitudes, providing direct evidence for the mediating role of affective reactions as well as inferential processes.

One study focused on the role of affective reactions in shaping attitudinal responses to others' emotional displays. Specifically, Howard and Gengler (2001) examined the effects of emotional contagion on product evaluations in two experiments. They found that participants developed a more favorable attitude toward a product when another person whom they liked showed positive as opposed to neutral emotional displays while evaluating the product. The authors further demonstrated that these effects were mediated by emotional contagion: Participants caught the positive emotions of the expresser, which in turn influenced their product attitudes.

Another series of experiments speaks to the role of inferential processes in the relationship between emotional expressions and attitudes (Van Kleef, Van den Berg, & Heerdink, 2015). One experiment showed that attitudes about a Dutch television show were influenced by a source's verbal emotional expressions of happiness versus sadness in response to plans to discontinue the show. Participants reported more favorable attitudes toward the show after reading a sad reaction to the intended discontinuation than after reading a happy reaction. Presumably, participants inferred from the source's negative emotional reactions to the intended discontinuation of the show that the show was valuable and should be continued. In another experiment, participants viewed a specially developed news bulletin about Greenpeace that contained interviews with people on the street, one of whom expressed either anger or happiness about Greenpeace by means of facial expressions and vocal intonation. Participants who watched the happy source later reported a marginally more positive attitude about Greenpeace than they had reported at the beginning of the experimental session, whereas those who had watched the angry source reported a significantly more negative attitude than before.

Additional experiments provided complementary evidence for the moderating role of information-processing motivation and ability (Van Kleef et al., 2015). One study showed that participants' opinions about the ideal mix of textbooks and research articles in the psychology curriculum were more strongly influenced by another participant's emotions (as expressed by means of emoticons) to the degree that they had a stronger dispositional tendency to engage in thorough information processing. Another experiment revealed that a source's facial expressions of sadness versus happiness only influenced participants' attitudes about a particular topic when they had ample cognitive resources available. As shown in Figure 8.3, the source's emotional display influenced participants' attitudes when they were placed under low cognitive load, but the effect was mitigated when participants were put under high cognitive load (i.e., when they had to memorize a ten-digit telephone number). These findings suggest that people use others' emotional expressions as pieces of information upon which to base their attitudes about various issues, provided that they are sufficiently motivated and able to engage in thorough information processing.

Interpersonal emotion regulation

Reflecting the important role of customers' emotions in shaping their product attitudes and service experience (Batra & Stayman, 1990; Edell & Burke, 1987), the last two decades have witnessed a growing interest in

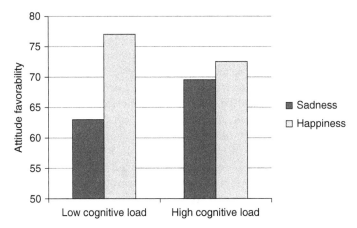

Figure 8.3 Attitude favorability (on a scale of 0–100) as a function of the emotional display of the source of a persuasive communication and the perceiver's cognitive load (based on Van Kleef et al., 2015, Study 3).

interpersonal emotion management strategies, that is, the ways in which individuals may regulate the emotional states of others (Francis, 1997; Little, Kluemper, Nelson, & Gooty, 2012; Niven, Totterdell, & Holman, 2009; Williams, 2007). This theoretical development is of particular relevance to the service industry, because there are obvious incentives for service providers to engage in attempts at increasing customers' positive affect and/or reducing their negative affect (Little, Kluemper, Nelson, & Ward, 2013; Lively, 2000; Locke, 1996). Indeed, besides regulating one's own emotional experiences and expressions (Gross, 1998b; Parkinson & Totterdell, 1999), a key part of emotional performance in the service industry consists of managing the emotional experience of customers and clients (Gabriel, Cheshin, Moran, & Van Kleef, in press). Examples of such interpersonal emotion management are medical personnel trying to alleviate the distress of patients (Francis, Monahan, & Berger, 1999) and customer service personnel attempting to increase customers' positive affect so as to improve their satisfaction with the service and increase the likelihood of (future) business (Locke, 1996).

Shifting the empirical focus to such interpersonal emotion management, recent research has begun to examine how interpersonal emotion regulation strategies employed by customer service representatives influence customers' emotions. Building on previous work on emotion regulation (e.g., Gross, 1998b; Williams, 2007), Little and colleagues (2013) distinguished between problem-focused emotion regulation strategies (changing, removing, or altering a problem to remove its emotional impact or reappraising a situation or problem in a more positive way) and emotion-focused regulation strategies (directing the target's attention to something more pleasant or modulating the target's emotional response tendencies). Based on their analysis of customer service calls, the authors concluded that problem-focused strategies reduced the intensity of customers' negative emotions and increased the intensity of positive emotions, whereas emotion-focused strategies had the opposite effects on customers' emotions.

Interestingly, the study by Little and colleagues (2013) also revealed that customers' initial emotions influenced the regulation strategy adopted by the service representative. Ironically, negative emotions expressed by the customer reduced the use of the more effective problem-focused emotion regulation strategies and increased the use of the less effective emotion-focused regulation strategies. This suggests that customers who enter a service encounter in a negative emotional state set in motion a self-perpetuating cycle of negative emotions and ineffective regulation strategies (above and beyond the spreading of negative affect via emotional contagion; Hatfield, Cacioppo, & Rapson, 1994), which may undermine the quality of the service and reduce the likelihood of future business and positive word of mouth.

As discussed previously, regulating their own emotions can come at a cost to employees in the form of emotional exhaustion and health impairments, particularly when emotions are regulated by means of surface acting (Hülsheger & Schewe, 2011). Interestingly, however, results of a field study among prisoners and staff members in a therapeutic prison as well as a laboratory study involving a student sample yielded evidence that interpersonal emotion-enhancing regulation strategies are positively associated with the regulator's own well-being (Niven, Totterdell, Holman, & Headley, 2012). This finding suggests that employees who are adept at upregulating others' positive emotions benefit not only in terms of their service performance but also in terms of their personal health.

In short, there is emerging evidence that interpersonal emotion regulation is critical to service performance as well as to the well-being of service providers and customers. It is also clear, however, that some interpersonal emotion regulation strategies are more effective than others and that there is considerable variation in the degree to which individuals are inclined to use particular strategies. It stands to reason that service employees who are more aware of the intrapersonal and interpersonal consequences of various emotion regulation strategies and who are more capable of using the right strategies in the right circumstances are more successful than are those who have lesser insight in and/or ability to recruit appropriate interpersonal emotion regulation strategies. This suggests that the well-being and service performance of service employees depend on their emotional intelligence.

Emotional intelligence in the service industry

It is clear from the above that employees in the consumer business are faced with a difficult challenge. They are expected and encouraged to express positive emotions during service encounters with customers (Hochschild, 1983), and failure to comply with such expectations may undermine customer satisfaction (Pugh, 2001; Tsai, 2001). However, when service employees show positive emotions that they do not feel and that therefore come across as inauthentic, customer satisfaction may also be compromised (Grandey et al., 2005; Groth et al., 2009). Research suggests that the best way out of this dilemma is for service workers to engage in emotion regulation strategies such as deep acting (or antecedent-focused emotion regulation) that help them to actually experience the positive emotions that the job requires them to display. Compared to surface acting, deep acting results in more favorable customer impressions, and it is associated with better health outcomes (Grandey, 2003). Clearly, however, not all employees are equally capable of mobilizing effective emotion regulation strategies. It seems plausible that the ability to do so depends on employees' emotional intelligence, particularly their emotion regulation abilities (Côté, 2005).

Indirect evidence for the influence of emotional intelligence on emotion regulation comes from a study on the relation between age and the selection of emotion regulation strategies (Dahling & Perez, 2010). Throughout their lives, individuals' understanding of their own and others' emotions and of ways to manage them gradually increases. Indeed, there is evidence that older people have, on average, higher emotional intelligence than younger people (Mayer, Caruso, & Salovey, 1999; Van Rooy, Alonso, & Viswesvaran, 2005). Accordingly, older individuals may use more effective emotion regulation strategies than their younger counterparts (Gross & John, 2003). Consistent with this argument, Dahling and Perez found that older service employees were less likely to employ surface acting and more likely to engage in deep acting and the expression of naturally felt emotions. Even though emotional intelligence was not measured in this study, the findings are suggestive of the possibility that higher levels of emotional intelligence allow service personnel to recruit more effective emotion regulation strategies.

Other work provides more direct evidence for the role of emotional intelligence in customer service. One stream of research examined whether emotional intelligence can act as a buffer of the adverse effects of emotional labor on service workers' well-being. These studies have yielded mixed evidence. A longitudinal study involving a sample of nurses and police officers revealed that emotion recognition (as measured with an ability test) moderated the relationship between emotional labor and work engagement (Bechtoldt, Rohrmann, De Pater, & Beersma, 2011). Specifically, service employees with relatively poor emotion recognition skills who engaged in surface acting or deep acting reported lower work engagement four weeks later, whereas those with higher emotion recognition skills did not. A survey among frontline employees of five-star hotels in Korea similarly suggested that emotional intelligence (assessed using a self-report measure) buffers the relationship between emotional labor and employee emotional exhaustion and service recovery performance (Kim, Yoo, Lee, & Kim, 2012). However, another survey among employees of eight different customer service organizations did not yield evidence that self-reported emotional intelligence moderates the relationship between emotional labor strategies and emotional exhaustion, affective well-being, and job satisfaction (Johnson & Spector, 2007).

Another stream of research has linked various aspects of emotional intelligence to the perceived quality of service performance. In one study, emotion recognition skills (as assessed with an ability-based measure) predicted performance on a managerial assessment center, which included activities such as team meetings and individual speeches (Bommer, Pesta, & Storrud-Barnes, 2011). Importantly, the effects of emotion recognition emerged above and beyond effects of general mental ability and conscientiousness. Several field studies uncovered similar effects of emotional intelligence in naturalistic settings. In these studies, salespersons' self-reported emotional intelligence was associated with their perceived customer orientation (Rozell, Pettijohn, & Parker, 2004); the emotional intelligence of physicians (as rated by nurses) was a positive predictor of the patient's trust in the physician (Weng, 2008); the self-reported emotional competence of financial advisers was related to customer evaluations (both directly and via customers' positive affective states during the encounters; Giardini & Frese, 2008); casino hosts' self-reported emotional intelligence was positively associated with their adaptability and service performance in encounters with "premium players" (Prentice & King, 2013); and customer perceptions of employee emotional competence were positively associated with customer satisfaction and loyalty (Delcourt, Gremler, Van Riel, & Van Birgelen, 2013).

Together, these studies paint a fairly consistent picture of the generally favorable effects of emotional intelligence on the well-being and performance of service employees. A word of caution is in order, however, when it comes to drawing firm conclusions from the observed patterns. Many of the investigations reviewed above employed self-report or peer-report measures of emotional intelligence, presumably because it is often unfeasible to administer extensive ability-based emotional intelligence tests in field research. There is a debate in the literature about the extent to which such measures tap actual emotional abilities (Côté, 2010). People are notoriously biased in their evaluations of their own abilities (Dunning, Heath, & Suls, 2004), and self-evaluations of emotional abilities are no exception – nearly 80 percent of people believe that they are among the top 50 percent most emotionally intelligent individuals (Brackett, Rivers, Shiffman, Lerner, & Salovey, 2006). People may thus portray their own levels of emotional competence as more favorable than they really are, whether knowingly or unknowingly, for instance due to self-serving biases or social desirability concerns. Peer ratings of emotional intelligence do not suffer from this problem, but they may be subject to halo effects (Nisbett & Wilson, 1977). That is, observers may provide higher emotional intelligence ratings of people whom they like than of people whom they dislike. In light of these potential limitations, more studies involving ability-based measures are needed to further substantiate the positive impact of emotional intelligence on customer service encounters.

Conclusion

Emotional expressions play a pivotal role in the consumer industry. Service encounters and consumer behavior are influenced by the emotional expressions of service representatives, customers, and third parties. The general pattern that emerges from this literature is that positive emotional displays have favorable consequences (provided that they are perceived as authentic), whereas negative emotional displays have unfavorable consequences (although some studies reported favorable effects of customer anger on particular aspects of service employees' performance). Another clear theme concerns the generally beneficial interpersonal effects of service workers' deep acting and the generally detrimental effects of surface acting. Finally, there is growing evidence that various aspects of the service process benefit from greater levels of emotional intelligence on the part of service employees, presumably because employees with higher emotional intelligence are better able to detect the emotions of their customers, to control their own emotional responses, and to regulate their customers' emotions in beneficial ways. Even though the empirical record is thus fairly consistent, there are a number of interesting asymmetries in this literature and several intriguing issues remain to be addressed.

First, research on the effects of customers' emotional expressions on service workers has focused almost exclusively on the consequences of negative emotional expressions by customers (most notably anger and verbal aggression), which have been found to undermine service employees' job satisfaction, increase emotional exhaustion, and predict absenteeism, among other things. Surprisingly little is known about how customers' positive emotional displays influence service employees' job satisfaction, well-being, and performance. Based on EASI theory, it can be predicted that encounters with cheerful customers have a favorable impact on service workers' well-being (an effect that may be mediated by affective reactions), while customers' positive emotional expressions may lead to complacency of service representatives when confronted with customer complaints (an effect that may be mediated by inferential processes).

Second, research on the effects of service workers' emotional expressions on customers has focused almost exclusively on the effects of positive emotional displays. The general finding is that positive displays of service representatives have favorable consequences for customers' satisfaction, intentions to return to the store, and likelihood of spreading positive word of mouth, with favorable effects being more likely to the degree that the positive emotional expressions are perceived as authentic. Interestingly, the influence of negative emotional expressions of service workers has remained largely unaddressed – a state of affairs that is understandable in light of the prevailing display rules in the service industry. Nevertheless, it would be valuable to investigate how customers respond to service representatives' negative emotional expressions, even if those may be relatively rare in cultures that emphasize service with a smile. It seems reasonable to assume that displays of anger by employees in such (service) cultures trigger strong negative affective reactions in customers that in turn undermine their intentions to purchase products or come back to the store. However, such effects may be less apparent in cultures that put less emphasis on positive emotions in the service setting. Expectations of service with a smile are higher in the United States than in many other countries, whereas the French are comparatively accepting of anger expressions in service encounters (Grandey, Rafaeli, Ravid, Wirtz, & Steiner, 2010). Given the adverse consequences of inauthentic emotional expressions, a question that arises is whether customers in certain cultural contexts might prefer an authentically depressed or grumpy service employee to an inauthentically cheerful one.

Third, most research in this area has been limited to the consequences of displays of happiness or positive affect and anger or verbal aggression – very few studies have examined other emotions. It therefore remains unclear whether different positive and negative emotions have differential effects on service outcomes. It is conceivable, for instance, that expressions of socially engaging emotions (Kitayama, Mesquita, & Karasawa, 2006) such as happiness or gratitude on the part of a service provider have more favorable effects on customers than displays of socially disengaging emotions such as pride, even though all of these emotions share a positive valence. It is also conceivable that customers' expressions of disappointment versus anger about a dissatisfying service outcome may result in differential compensation. Expressions of disappointment may be effective because they are less affronting for service workers, but expressions of anger may be effective because they signal greater urgency.

Finally, the literature on emotions in the service industry reflects a strong interest in the role of affective reactions (e.g., emotional contagion) as mediating links between emotional expressions and responses. The role of inferential processes has so far received relatively little attention. Moreover, whereas there is emerging evidence that the effects of emotional expressions depend on the perceived appropriateness of the expressions (as determined by the authenticity and intensity of the emotional displays), so far no studies have examined the possible moderating role of the perceiver's information-processing motivation or ability on the effects of customers' or service workers' emotional expressions. As such, there is currently no support for EASI's predictions about information processing in this context. Such evidence is provided by research on the role of emotions in leader–follower relations, to which I turn in the next chapter.

CHAPTER 9

Social effects of emotions in leadership

> The key to your impact as a leader is your own sincerity. Before you can inspire with emotion, you must be swamped with it yourself. Before you can move their tears, your own must flow. To convince them, you must yourself believe.
>
> Winston Churchill

Winston Churchill was far ahead of his time when he emphasized the importance of emotions for successful leadership. In the first half of the twentieth century, few people appreciated affective phenomena, and emotions were especially viewed with suspicion in the context of political discourse. Although the appreciation of emotions in science and society alike has increased dramatically since Churchill's time, the role of emotions in leadership is still a matter of considerable controversy. Just as professional negotiators and mediators are strongly divided when it comes to the utility of emotions in deal making and dispute resolution, both managers and management scholars differ widely in terms of the value they accord to emotions in leadership.

One group sees emotions as a sign of weakness, reasoning that people who get emotional lack control over the situation and are therefore unfit for a leadership position. Emotions are thought to taint judgments and interfere with effective leadership by inspiring impulsive behavior and irrational decisions. For instance, Jackall (1988) argued that managers "need to exercise iron self-control and have the ability to mask all emotion and intention behind bland, smiling, and agreeable public faces" (p. 47), because letting emotions enter the equation is "seen as irrational, unbenefitting men or women whose principle claim to social legitimacy is dispassionate rational calculation" (p. 49). Others, in contrast, share Churchill's belief that emotions are an essential part of leadership, arguing that a leader can use his or her emotions to motivate and inspire followers to perform to the best of their abilities (Humphrey, Pollack, & Hawver, 2008). As is so often the case in the social sciences, there is no simple answer to this dilemma. Rather, emotional expressions can contribute to or undermine successful leadership depending on a variety of factors, as we shall see in this chapter.

170

Leadership refers to the process of influencing others to accomplish a goal (Yukl, 2010). As influential agents in organizations, leaders play a crucial role in promoting, managing, supporting, and developing individual and team effectiveness. Given that emotional expressions are a prominent source of social influence (Côté & Hideg, 2011; Van Kleef, Van Doorn, Heerdink, & Koning, 2011), it stands to reason that leaders' emotional expressions have an impact on subordinates. In fact, there is evidence that leaders' emotional displays have a greater impact on followers than does the content of their messages (Newcombe & Ashkanasy, 2002). Accordingly, the idea that emotions play a prominent role in the leadership process has been around for several decades, perhaps most notably in the literature on charismatic and transformational leadership (Bass, 1985). Systematic empirical research on the role of emotional expressions in leadership emerged only relatively recently. Nevertheless, there is now a considerable body of evidence that speaks to the effects of emotional expressions in leadership. In this chapter I review and integrate research on the effects of leaders' emotional expressions on followers' emotions, cognitions, and behavior.

In analyzing the effects of leaders' emotional expressions on followers, it is useful to distinguish between subjective and objective indices of leader effectiveness. Subjective perceptions of leader effectiveness are likely to be influenced by several factors besides the leader's actual (objectively measured) success in attaining organizational goals, such as followers' own emotional states, their liking of the leader, and the degree to which they experience a sense of similarity or identification with the leader (Bono & Ilies, 2006; Hogg, 2001; Howell & Shamir, 2005; Van Knippenberg & Hogg, 2003). As a result, discrepancies may arise between objective and subjective measures of leadership effectiveness.

Subjective ratings of (leadership) performance tend to be heavily influenced by affective states such as positive or negative moods and interpersonal liking (Brown & Keeping, 2005; Duarte, Goodson, & Klich, 1994; Tsui & Barry, 1986). In terms of Emotions as Social Information (EASI) theory, subjective ratings of a leader's performance can therefore be expected to be relatively strongly influenced by followers' affective reactions to the leader's emotional displays (as opposed to inferential processes triggered by those displays). For instance, an employee may perceive his leader as effective because he likes her, even though the leader's actual success in motivating and guiding followers to attain organizational goals is low. Conversely, an employee may rate her leader as ineffective due to a lack of interpersonal rapport, even if the leader is actually quite successful in promoting organizational goals. Below I first discuss research on the effects of leaders' emotional displays on followers' subjective perceptions of leadership quality. Subsequently,

I review research on the effects of leaders' emotional expressions on objective measures of leader effectiveness, such as follower performance.

Leaders' emotional displays and perceptions of leadership quality

As noted above, professionals are divided with respect to the question of whether a leader should show emotions to inspire followers or rather suppress emotions to avoid signaling weakness or lack of professionalism. Despite this disagreement, there are reasons to believe that followers generally prefer more emotionally expressive leaders over less expressive leaders. This makes sense from the perspective that emotions provide social information (Van Kleef, 2010). Emotions arise in response to events that are perceived as relevant to a person's concerns (Frijda, 1986). By reverse logic, observers may infer from others' emotional reactions to particular events that those events are appraised by the expresser as relevant to his or her goals. Such signals may be effective in mobilizing followers, especially when the leader and followers have the same goals. Conversely, a company leader who remains unmoved regardless of whether the company is doing well or poorly may be perceived by followers as showing little commitment to the cause. Such inadvertent signals may have detrimental consequences for a leader's credibility and support. This suggests, then, that followers may have a preference for leaders who show at least some emotion when important events take place.

Historical developments in the political domain are consistent with the idea that emotional expressivity contributes to a leader's popularity. For instance, many historians attribute the rise of Adolf Hitler to his highly persuasive public speeches, which were characterized by intense expressions of negative emotions such as anger and hatred. Conversely, attesting to the social power of positive emotions, Martin Luther King Jr. managed to mobilize large crowds for his fight against racial inequality in the United States by passionately declaring his hope and vision for peaceful and equal relationships between European Americans and African Americans ("I have a dream"). Nelson Mandela used a very similar positive emotional style during his inaugural speech as president of South Africa in 1994, during which he vehemently expressed the hope for "a glorious life for all." And Barack Obama is widely believed to have owed his first presidential election in 2008 in large part to the positive emotions he showed in the course of his campaign in conjunction with his hopeful vision of a better country ("Yes we can!").

Such affective displays reflect strong commitment and motivation on the part of a leader to attain a particular goal or vision, which may contribute to perceptions of charisma and effectiveness (Humphrey

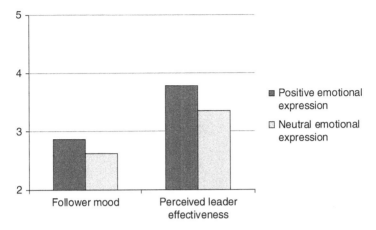

Figure 9.1 Positivity of followers' moods (on a scale of 1–7) and perceptions of leader effectiveness (on a scale of 1–5) as a function of the leader's emotional expressions (based on Bono & Ilies, 2006, Study 4).

et al., 2008). This reasoning would imply that positive and negative emotional expressions are equally effective in inspiring perceptions of leadership quality. Nevertheless, the available evidence points to a valence asymmetry, in that positive emotional expressions generally inspire more favorable perceptions of leaders than negative emotional expressions. An early study by Newcombe and Ashkanasy (2002) revealed that leaders who expressed positive affect in the context of performance feedback were rated more positively by their followers than were leaders who expressed negative affect. Similarly, a study by Rubin, Munz, and Bommer (2005) showed that leaders who scored higher on trait positive affectivity were perceived as more "transformational" by their followers.

These effects of leaders' positive emotional expressions on followers' perceptions were replicated and extended in a multimethod investigation conducted by Bono and Ilies (2006). Two correlational studies in a natural work setting revealed that leaders' positive emotional expressions were associated with ratings of leaders' charisma. Moreover, two experimental studies involving videotapes of leaders who varied their displays of positive emotion showed that leaders' positive emotional expressions were linked to the mood states of followers as well as to the perceived effectiveness of the leader (see Figure 9.1). Compatible effects were reported in several later studies (Chi, Chung, & Tsai, 2011; Damen, Van Knippenberg, & Van Knippenberg, 2008b; Eberly & Fong, 2013; Erez, Misangyi, Johnson, LePine, & Halverson, 2008; Johnson, 2008), attesting to the robustness of the relationship between leader positive emotional displays and follower perceptions of leadership quality.

Interestingly, a study by Johnson (2008) indicated that the effects of leaders' emotional expressions on the favorability of followers' responses to the leader were stronger among followers who were more susceptible to emotional contagion. This indicates that the effects of leaders' emotional expressions on subjective perceptions of leadership quality can be explained at least in part by followers' affective reactions to the leaders' emotions, as was also suggested by Bono and Ilies (2006). Furthermore, Damen and colleagues (2008b) found that the impact of leaders' positive emotional expressions on followers' attributions of charisma depended on the arousal level of the emotion, with higher-arousal emotions such as anger and enthusiasm engendering greater emotional contagion and concomitant ratings of charisma than lower-arousal emotions like relaxedness and sadness. Similarly, Connelly and Ruark (2010) found that positive emotional expressions with high "activating potential" (e.g., pride) elicited more favorable reactions from followers than positive emotional expressions with low activating potential (e.g., contentment). In light of Damen et al.'s findings, it is conceivable that this difference arose because more activating positive emotional expressions triggered stronger affective reactions in followers.

Representing the other side of the coin, a study by Glomb and Hulin (1997) revealed that leaders who expressed anger were rated less favorably than leaders who did not express anger. Other studies showed that negative leader affect displayed during the delivery of performance feedback generally produced lower perceptions of leader effectiveness than did positive leader affect (Gaddis, Connelly, & Mumford, 2004; Newcombe & Ashkanasy, 2002), although negative affect was appreciated more when it was congruent with the type of feedback (i.e., negative rather than positive) the leader delivered (Newcombe & Ashkanasy, 2002). Related work on performance feedback delivered by coworkers rather than leaders similarly revealed a negative influence of displays of contempt on interpersonal relations, as manifested in greater expressed verbal aggression by the target of the contempt (Melwani & Barsade, 2011).

Across the board, then, people exhibit a preference for leaders with a positive emotional style (Dasborough & Ashkanasy, 2002). It seems plausible that this valence asymmetry is due at least in part to the fact that subjective perceptions of leadership effectiveness are rather susceptible to the influence of followers' affective reactions to their leader's emotional displays, which tend to be more favorable in the case of positive rather than negative emotional displays. Nevertheless, there is some evidence that negative emotional displays may be appreciated under particular circumstances. For instance, Connelly and Ruark (2010) found that even though followers responded unfavorably to negative emotional expressions of "transactional" leaders, they responded relatively favorably to negative emotional displays of "transformational" leaders. Whereas transactional leadership is based on a give-and-take exchange relationship, transformational leadership hinges on followers' identification with the leader's personality, inspirational vision, and challenging goals (Bass, 1985; Bass & Riggio, 2005). Connelly and Ruark's data suggest that transformational leaders have more leeway to express negative emotions without running the risk of undermining followers' perceptions of their effectiveness.

There is also some evidence that discrete negative emotional expressions of leaders may have differential effects on followers' evaluations of the leader. In this regard, Madera and Smith (2009) examined followers' perceptions of leaders as a function of the specific negative emotion the leader expressed in the context of an organizational failure. Participants in their study reported more positive evaluations after the leader had expressed sadness rather than anger. Additional analyses indicated that this difference was mediated by participants' own negative affective reactions to the leader, which were stronger when the leader expressed anger than sadness.

A study on perceptions of public leaders further revealed that leaders' negative facial displays were perceived by observers as more honest, credible, and trustworthy than were leaders' positive emotional displays (Bucy, 2000; but see Eberly & Fong, 2013, for evidence that positive emotions inspire greater perceptions of sincerity). Moreover, active negative emotions such as anger have been shown to signal decisiveness, competence, dominance, and power (Tiedens, 2001). Such perceptions may in turn fuel attributions of leadership ability (Anderson & Kilduff, 2009; Lord, De Vader, & Alliger, 1986). For instance, Tiedens (2001) found that participants exhibited greater endorsement of politicians who expressed anger rather than sadness, because expressions of anger were perceived as a sign of competence.

These various studies indicate that leaders' negative emotional displays can have favorable effects on followers' evaluations of leadership quality, but these positive effects are subject to numerous boundary conditions. Moreover, the empirical record is somewhat inconsistent in that some evidence suggests that expressions of sadness contribute to more favorable perceptions of leadership quality than expressions of anger (Madera & Smith, 2009), whereas other work indicates that displays of anger signal greater competence and leadership effectiveness than displays of sadness (Tiedens, 2001).

It seems plausible that the effects of a leader's emotional displays on followers' perceptions of leadership quality depend in part on the target of the leader's emotions. The perceived appropriateness of expressions of anger in the eyes of followers may be higher when the emotion is directed at a situation or a third party (e.g., a common enemy) rather than at the followers themselves. Consequently, the potential for detrimental effects is higher when leaders direct their anger toward followers. Followers may prefer a leader who expresses sadness or disappointment (rather than anger) at them for failing to reach an organizational target, because these emotions are less confrontational and affronting. However, followers may prefer a leader who expresses anger (rather than sadness or disappointment) at an outside party who fails to deliver on promises, because a leader who expresses anger signals a stronger intention to confront the outside party than a leader who expresses low-activation emotions such as sadness or disappointment. As Malcolm X once put it, "usually when people are sad, they don't do anything. They just cry over their condition. But when they get angry, they bring about a change." Positive motivational effects would therefore seem more likely when the leader's anger is directed outside of the leader's immediate group or organization. In line with this logic, Waples and Connelly (2008) reported evidence that leader expressions of anger that were directed toward competitors had positive effects on follower performance.

In a related vein, research has explored how attributions of leadership quality are shaped by the perceived appropriateness of leaders' emotional displays. Leaders' emotional displays may be perceived as inappropriate when they are incongruent with prevailing norms, expectations, and/or situational scripts (see Shields, 2005). According to EASI theory, such perceptions of inappropriateness drive negative affective reactions that undermine leader endorsement (Van Kleef, Homan, & Cheshin, 2012). In keeping with this idea, K. Lewis (2000) obtained some evidence that leaders are rated more positively when their emotional displays are congruent with gender stereotypes. More specifically, female leaders who expressed anger were evaluated more negatively than male leaders who expressed anger, presumably because expressions of anger are more fitting with the male rather than the female gender stereotype. At the same time, however, the study also showed that expressions of sadness undermined perceptions of leadership quality of both male and female leaders, perhaps because displays of sadness signal a lack of control over the situation that is incongruent with the general leadership stereotype, regardless of gender.

Perceptions of inappropriateness may also arise from inauthentic emotional expressions (Van Kleef et al., 2012), and there is some evidence that such perceptions undermine leader endorsement. For instance, Newcombe and Ashkanasy (2002) found that leaders were evaluated less favorably when followers perceived a mismatch between leaders' actions (in this case the provision of positive vs. negative performance feedback) and their displayed emotions, which may have been interpreted as a sign of inauthenticity. Other studies revealed that followers whose leaders more frequently displayed sincere emotions reported higher job satisfaction (Fisk & Friesen, 2012), and that leaders and followers who engaged in more sincere emotional exchanges reported having a higher-quality relationship (Glasø & Einarsen, 2008). Although this evidence is suggestive rather than conclusive, it is consistent with the possibility that leader emotional displays that appear inauthentic or insincere are perceived as inappropriate and thereby undermine leader support.

In short, several studies indicate that leaders' emotional expressions influence various subjective indices of leader effectiveness. In addition, there is some evidence that the effects of leaders' emotional displays on perceptions of leadership quality depend on the perceived authenticity and appropriateness of the emotional displays. These effects appear to be driven at least in part by followers' affective reactions to their leaders' emotional expressions, with positive and appropriate displays generally eliciting positive affective reactions, and negative and inappropriate displays eliciting negative affective reactions. However, as indicated above, subjective perceptions of leadership quality may not correspond with actual leadership effectiveness. Followers may prefer leaders who show positive emotions, but negative emotions may actually be more effective under certain circumstances. In the next section I consider research on the effects of leaders' emotional expressions on actual follower performance, which is typically seen as the ultimate index of leadership effectiveness (Kaiser, Hogan, & Craig, 2008).

Leaders' emotional displays and followers' performance

Leaders differ widely in the emotional strategies they employ to boost their followers' performance. As noted before, some leaders view emotions as a hindrance, whereas others see them as useful. Moreover, anecdotal evidence indicates that there is great variation in the emotions leaders show in their attempts to motivate followers. The examples of Nelson Mandela and Barack Obama discussed above illustrate the potential effectiveness of a generally positive emotional style. In contrast, people such as former Apple chairman Steve Jobs (who oversaw the development of several groundbreaking personal computer products and turned Apple into a world-leading company) and celebrity chef and restaurateur Gordon Ramsay (whose various restaurants obtained a total of fifteen Michelin stars) embody a predominantly negative – yet equally successful – emotional style.

Empirical evidence regarding the effectiveness of positive versus negative emotional expressions in leadership is also somewhat mixed,
although there is more evidence for favorable rather than unfavorable
effects of positive emotional displays. In a pioneering study of the role of
affective processes in leadership, George and Bettenhausen (1990) examined how leaders' affective states shaped customer service performance.
They found that service workers were more likely to engage in customer
helping, sold more products, and were less likely to leave the organization when their leader scored higher on state positive affectivity. The
authors proposed that these effects might be due to emotional contagion
between the leader and followers, such that subordinates take over the
positive mood of the leader and therefore perform better.

Other studies directly compared the effects of leaders' positive and
negative affective displays on follower affect, perceptions, and behavior.
For instance, Gaddis and colleagues (2004) found that leaders who delivered failure feedback in a positive emotional tone instigated better team
performance than leaders who displayed negative affect while delivering
the feedback. Compatible findings were reported by Johnson (2009), who
examined the effects of leaders' positive versus negative affect on followers' performance on a hiring task. In the first part of her study Johnson
manipulated participants' moods and asked them to record a leadership
speech in which they explained how to perform the task. In the second
part of the study a new sample of participants watched one of the
speeches recorded in the first part of the study, completed ratings of the
leader, and performed the hiring task. Participants in the positive mood
condition reported experiencing more positive and less negative affect
themselves, compared to those in the negative mood condition.
Moreover, participants in the positive mood condition rated their leaders
as more charismatic and performed better on the hiring task than did
participants in the negative mood condition. These effects could be
explained in part in terms of followers' affective reactions to the leader.
More specifically, as shown in Figure 9.2, the favorable effects of leader
positive mood on ratings of charisma were partially mediated by follower
positive affect, whereas the effects on task performance were partially
mediated by follower negative affect. Although the differential mediating
roles of positive versus negative affective reactions in this particular
study present somewhat of a puzzle, it is clear from these various investigations that leaders' displays of positive emotions can have favorable
consequences for follower performance.

There is also evidence, however, that negative emotional expressions
can enhance performance, albeit from slightly different contexts.
Melwani and Barsade's (2011) study on feedback delivery by coworkers
revealed favorable effects of expressions of contempt on performance,

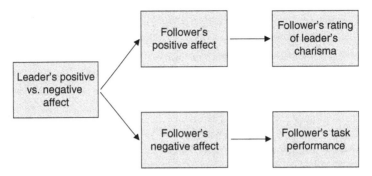

Figure 9.2 Effects of a leader's positive versus negative mood on followers' ratings of the leader's charisma and followers' task performance are mediated by followers' affective state (based on Johnson, 2009).

even though contempt had obvious negative repercussions for the interpersonal relationship between the feedback deliverer and the feedback recipient. Displays of contempt send toxic signals of low regard that can be fatal for social relationships (Fischer & Roseman, 2007; Gottman, 1993), but these very same signals may also serve as incentives for performance because they motivate recipients of contempt to demonstrate their worth so as to recover their self-esteem.

Further evidence for the potential beneficial performance effects of negative emotional expressions comes from a study on the effects of teachers' emotional expressions on students' learning performance (Van Doorn, Van Kleef, & Van der Pligt, 2014). In a first experiment, participants were given a list of 100 word pairs. After they had spent fifteen minutes studying the combinations, baseline recognition was measured. Recognition scores were ostensibly sent to the participant's "instructor," who then conveyed learning tips in an angry or happy tone via a video connection. In the happy condition, the instructor (a trained actor) looked cheerful, spoke with an enthusiastic tone of voice, and smiled often; in the angry condition, he frowned a lot, spoke with an angry tone of voice, clenched his fists, and made irritable gestures. Participants then took their word list home and were instructed to spend a minimum of five minutes a day memorizing the combinations. Upon return to the lab one week later, participants in the anger condition exhibited better recognition than participants in the happy condition, even though they had perceived the angry instructor as less warm and competent, and this effect was independent of participants' self-reported affect. This suggests that the effect was not carried by interpersonal impressions or felt affect, but rather by the informational value of the emotional expressions. In a second experiment the effect was replicated using a recall task, although in this case expressions of anger only enhanced the performance of students who were in a promotion (rather than a prevention) focus.

In a rare study comparing the effects of different negative emotional expressions in a leadership context, Johnson and Connelly (2014) examined followers' affective reactions to their leaders' expressions of anger versus disappointment as well as the downstream behavioral consequences of these affective reactions. They found that expressions of disappointment by a leader providing informal feedback primarily elicited complementary feelings of guilt, whereas expressions of anger primarily triggered reciprocal feelings of anger. These affective reactions mediated the effects of the leader's emotional displays on participants' behavioral responses, including positive and negative organizational behaviors and various indices of task performance. Thus, expressions of disappointment had beneficial consequences, but expressions of anger were detrimental. Interestingly, these results closely parallel findings regarding the effects of expressions of anger versus disappointment in negotiations (e.g., Lelieveld, Van Dijk, Van Beest, & Van Kleef, 2012; see Chapter 7).

Other research points to the possibility that the effects of leaders' positive versus negative emotional displays on followers' performance depend on the performance criterion. Sy, Côté, and Saavedra (2005) invited groups of participants to the lab, and randomly selected one of them to play the role of leader. This person watched a film clip that induced either a positive or a negative mood. The leader then joined the rest of the team and coached them as they built up a tent together while blindfolded. The study revealed that one aspect of team performance benefited from a leader's positive mood, while another aspect benefited from a leader's negative mood (see Figure 9.3). Specifically, teams that were exposed to a leader in a positive mood developed a positive group affective tone, and as a result they exhibited better coordination than teams with a leader in a negative mood. However, teams with a leader in a negative mood expended more effort, presumably because they inferred from the leader's negative mood that their performance was unsatisfactory (although such mediation was not examined in this study). In line with this intuition, a qualitative study by Lindebaum and Fielden (2011) revealed that leaders in the construction business deliberately use expressions of anger to ensure that projects are finished on time.

Another recent study indicates that the effectiveness of positive versus negative emotional displays of leaders depends on the type of assignment followers are charged with. Building on theorizing and research on the intrapersonal consequences of emotional states for various types of

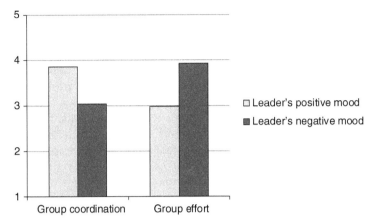

Figure 9.3 Effects of a leader's positive versus negative mood on observer-rated group coordination and effort on a scale of 1–5 (based on Sy et al., 2005).

performance (e.g., Forgas, 1995; Weiss & Cropanzano, 1996), Visser, Van Knippenberg, Van Kleef, and Wisse (2013) argued that both expressions of happiness and expressions of sadness on the part of a leader can be effective, depending on whether the task that followers are assigned to execute requires creative or analytical performance. People in a positive affective state broaden their thought-action repertoires (Fredrickson, 1998, 2001). Accordingly, the experience of positive affect is associated with greater creativity (Amabile, Barsade, Mueller, & Staw, 2005; Ashby, Isen, & Turken, 1999; Isen, 2004), especially when it concerns high-activation positive affect (De Dreu, Baas, & Nijstad, 2008). Conversely, the experience of negative affect is associated with an analytical mode of information processing that is characterized by considerable attention to detail and careful and logical analysis of the available information (Forgas, 2000; Schwarz & Bless, 1991). Consistent with these associations, Visser and colleagues demonstrated in a first study that a leader's displays of happiness enhanced followers' creative performance, whereas a leader's displays of sadness enhanced followers' analytical performance. A second study showed that these effects were mediated by follower positive affect. Interestingly, this study further demonstrated that subjective ratings and objective measures of leadership effectiveness do not always correspond. Participants uniformly rated the happy leader as more effective than the sad leader, even though the sad leader actually instigated better performance on the analytical task.

These studies allow for a number of conclusions. First of all, experimental research and field studies converge to show that leaders' emotional displays influence followers' emotions, perceptions of the leader, and task performance in theoretically meaningful ways. Second, several studies point to the role of affective reactions in bringing about these effects: Followers who are confronted with a leader's positive emotional expressions tend to experience more positive emotions than those who are confronted with a leader's negative emotional displays, and these reciprocal affective reactions in turn shape subjective ratings of the leader's effectiveness as well as actual task performance (but matters become somewhat more complicated when we consider the case of disappointment, which may elicit complementary feelings of guilt that can have favorable consequences; Johnson & Connelly, 2014; Lelieveld et al., 2012). Third, it is clear from the more recent studies discussed above that the effects of leaders' emotional displays on followers' performance depend on the performance criterion and on the type of task that is performed. Given the apparent variability in followers' responses to leaders' emotional displays, it is conceivable that such responses are also modulated by followers' information processing and by the perceived appropriateness of the leader's emotional expressions, as suggested by EASI theory.

The role of followers' information processing

First evidence for a moderating role of information processing was obtained in a study by Van Kleef and colleagues (2009). Four-person teams collaborated on a task, during which they received standardized feedback from their leader via a video-conferencing setup. The feedback was delivered either in an angry tone or in a happy tone, by means of facial expressions, vocal intonation, and bodily postures. In reality the leader was a trained actor, and the emotional speeches had been prerecorded. Teams consisting of members with low levels of dispositional information-processing motivation (operationalized in terms of personal need for structure; Neuberg & Newsom, 1993) performed better when the leader expressed happiness, whereas teams consisting of members with high information-processing motivation performed better when the leader expressed anger (see Figure 9.4). In line with EASI theory, inferential processes (i.e., inferences about performance quality) mediated behavioral responses to the leader's emotional expressions among followers with high information-processing motivation. Furthermore, affective reactions (i.e., positive vs. negative emotions and liking of the leader) mediated responses to the leader's emotions among followers with low information-processing motivation.

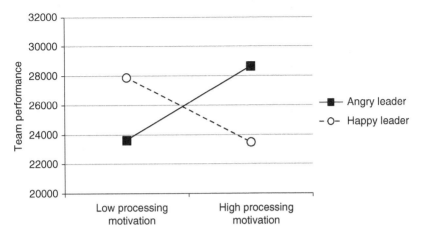

Figure 9.4 Team performance as a function of a leader's displays of anger versus happiness and team members' information-processing motivation. Team performance scores were automatically calculated by the computer software through which the task was administered, and they ranged from 11,796 to 40,586 points (based on Van Kleef et al., 2009).

Compatible findings were reported in a study concerning the effects of emotional expressions on individual creative performance (Van Kleef, Anastasopoulou, & Nijstad, 2010). Participants played the role of "generator of ideas" working with another participant in the role of "evaluator." After the participant had generated ideas, a prerecorded video message appeared on the participant's computer screen, in which the evaluator (a trained actor) provided feedback and tips in either an angry or neutral way. Participants with low information-processing motivation (again operationalized in terms of personal need for structure; Neuberg & Newsom, 1993) reported less motivation and task engagement after their evaluator had expressed anger rather than no emotion, and they generated fewer ideas as a result. Participants with high information-processing motivation, in contrast, became more engaged and motivated to perform well after the evaluator had expressed anger, and as a consequence they generated more ideas.

Similar effects were observed in a field study on the effects of music teachers' emotional expressions on students' musical performance (Van Kleef, Stamkou, & Larsen, 2014). At the start of the study, the researchers measured students' information-processing motivation using the personal need for structure scale (Neuberg & Newsom, 1993). Later on in the study students rated the perceived positive and negative emotional expressions of their teacher (as shown during the last music lesson), while the teacher rated the student's musical performance on a standardized assignment at the end of that lesson. The results revealed that students with lower levels of information-processing motivation performed better to the degree that their teacher had expressed more positive and less negative emotion during the lesson. Conversely, students with higher information-processing motivation performed better to the extent that their teacher had expressed more negative and less positive emotion. Thus, even though scholars and practitioners alike tend to emphasize the importance of positive, "nurturing" emotions for successful learning and performance, this study indicates that negative emotional expressions may, under particular circumstances, have more favorable consequences for performance (also see Van Doorn et al., 2014, for a similar conclusion).

Finally, a field study among leaders and followers employed in firms across a variety of industries (Chi & Ho, 2014) provided a conceptual replication of the moderating role of information processing by employing a different operationalization. Instead of looking at information-processing motivation per se, these authors examined the moderating influence of followers' levels of conscientiousness (Costa & McCrae, 1988; McCrae & Costa, 1987). Building on EASI theory and extending previous research discussed above (e.g., Sy et al., 2005; Van Kleef et al., 2009), Chi and Ho suggested that conscientious followers are more likely than their less conscientious counterparts to perceive their leaders' negative emotional expressions as signals of insufficient task progress. In support of this idea, the researchers found that greater levels of negative emotional expression on the part of leaders increased the performance of followers high on conscientiousness but decreased the performance of followers low on conscientiousness.

The role of the perceived appropriateness of leaders' emotional displays

The research discussed above demonstrates that leaders' expressions of anger and related negative emotions can be effective in increasing followers' performance to the degree that the expressions are processed by followers and thus trigger inferences regarding the adequacy of their performance. However, expressions of anger may undermine performance when they fail to trigger inferential processes and instead elicit negative affective reactions. EASI theory posits that the relative influence of inferential processes and affective reactions depends not only on observers' information-processing tendencies but also on the perceived appropriateness of the emotional expressions. This notion has implications for understanding the impact of leaders' emotions on organizational success.

Numerous factors may influence the degree to which a leader's emotional displays are perceived as appropriate by followers. As discussed in detail in Chapter 4, the perceived appropriateness of emotional expressions is shaped by characteristics of the situation, the expression, the expresser, and the observer. The exact same emotional reaction may be relatively appropriate in one situation, but rather inappropriate in the next. For instance, a leader's expressions of anger may be perceived as relatively appropriate in the context of a follower's low effort or substandard performance, but as rather inappropriate in the context of high effort or adequate performance. In addition, perceptions of appropriateness are influenced by factors such as the intensity or authenticity of the emotional expression, the gender and status of the expresser, and the personality and cultural background of the observer, among other things (Van Kleef et al., 2012).

Several studies support the idea that the effects of leaders' emotional displays depend on the perceived appropriateness of those displays. First, there is some evidence that the effects of leaders' emotional expressions on followers' performance are shaped by characteristics of the situation that may lead followers to perceive the leader's emotions as more or less appropriate. Initial suggestive evidence came from research by Gaddis and colleagues (2004). They found that followers typically performed worse when their leaders expressed negative emotions; however, this effect was attenuated when the leader expressed the negative emotions in a challenging context, in which negative emotions were presumably merited.

A more direct test of the role of situation-dependent appropriateness of emotional expressions was provided in a recent study by Koning and Van Kleef (2015), who examined the effects of happy versus angry expressions of leaders on followers' organizational citizenship behavior (OCB). OCB involves behaviors that benefit an organization but fall outside of formal job requirements and reward structures and as such have a rather voluntary nature (Bateman & Organ, 1983; Smith, Organ, & Near, 1983). The voluntary nature of OCB has implications for the degree to which particular emotional expressions of a leader are likely to be perceived as (in)appropriate by followers. Whereas expressions of anger might be relatively appropriate when emphasizing legitimate demands for adequate job-prescribed task performance, anger would seem less fitting in the context of voluntary behaviors such as OCB. When expressed in such a context, a leader's anger may therefore trigger strong negative affective reactions in followers due to the perceived inappropriateness of the anger display, and these negative affective reactions may in turn lower followers' willingness to perform OCB.

Two studies reported by Koning and Van Kleef (2015) supported this reasoning. A scenario study among employees of various organizations revealed a decrease in respondents' self-reported willingness to perform OCB after a leader expressed anger rather than happiness. A subsequent lab experiment showed that participants expended less effort working overtime on a task after having been confronted with an angry rather than a happy reaction from a leader on their prior performance. In both studies, the detrimental effects of anger on voluntary behavior were stronger when the anger was perceived as inappropriate (i.e., when participants had expended a lot of effort on the previous task) than when it was perceived as relatively appropriate (when participants had not put in much effort). Furthermore, in line with EASI theory, the effects were mediated by participants' negative affective reactions (i.e., reduced liking of the leader). These studies support the idea that a leader's emotional expressions may be perceived as more or less appropriate depending on the situation, and that such appropriateness perceptions shape followers' behavioral responses to leaders' emotional expressions.

Other studies provide evidence that the impact of a leader's emotional displays on follower performance depends on characteristics of the followers. For instance, Damen and colleagues examined the effects of (in) congruence between the leader's emotional expressions and followers' trait affectivity (Damen, Van Knippenberg, & Van Knippenberg, 2008a). They found that low positive affectivity followers functioned better under an angry leader, whereas high positive affectivity followers functioned better under an enthusiastic leader. This was reflected in the amount of work followers performed on behalf of the leader and in their compliance with the leader's requests (see Figure 9.5). Although not examined in this study, it is conceivable that these effects are driven by differences in the perceived appropriateness of the leader's emotional expressions, as shaped by the follower's own affective tendencies. Specifically, individuals who are prone to experience and express positive emotions themselves may be more sensitive to others' expressions of anger and may be more likely to deem such expressions inappropriate because they clash with their own emotional styles.

Along related lines, another study examined how followers' reactions to a leader's emotional displays are shaped by their desire for social harmony, as operationalized in terms of individual differences in agreeableness (Van Kleef, Homan, Beersma, & Van Knippenberg, 2010). The rationale behind this study was that agreeable individuals are more likely to perceive expressions of anger as inappropriate, because anger threatens the social harmony that they value (Costa & McCrae, 1992; McCrae & Costa, 1987). In a first experiment, participants read a scenario about a leader who expressed anger or no emotion about their performance, with

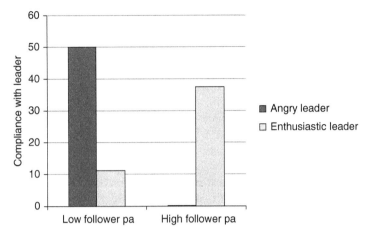

Figure 9.5 Likelihood of followers' compliance with a leader (in percentages) as a function of the leader's emotional displays and followers' trait positive affectivity (PA; based on Damen et al., 2008a, Study 2).

emotion being manipulated via pictures of facial expressions. Participants high on agreeableness reported lower work motivation in the anger condition than in the neutral condition, while those low on agreeableness reported higher motivation in the anger condition than in the neutral condition. In a second experiment, four-person teams received angry or happy feedback from their leader via a video setup. Teams consisting of high-agreeable followers performed better when the leader expressed happiness, whereas teams of low-agreeable followers performed better when the leader expressed anger.

The field study on emotional expression and musical performance described previously (Van Kleef et al., 2014) provides converging results. This study also yielded evidence that the effects of leaders' (in this case teachers') emotional expressions are moderated by followers' (in this case students') agreeableness. Specifically, more agreeable students performed better to the degree that their teacher expressed more positive rather than negative emotion during their music classes, whereas less agreeable students performed better to the degree that the teacher expressed more negative rather than positive emotion.

Together, these various studies indicate that the effects of leaders' emotional expressions on followers' performance depend on characteristics of the followers that may render them more or less likely to perceive negative emotional expressions (especially expressions of anger) as inappropriate, although it is important to note that perceptions of appropriateness were only explicitly assessed in some of these studies. Moreover, a recent field study among employees of various firms in Taiwan produced contradictory results, showing that leader expressions of anger had more beneficial performance consequences for high- rather than low-agreeable followers (Chi & Ho, 2014). These inconsistent findings may stem from the different cultural contexts within which the studies were conducted. The study by Chi and Ho was performed in a collectivistic culture (Taiwan), whereas the study by Van Kleef, Homan, and colleagues (2010) was situated in an individualistic culture (the Netherlands). Research on the effects of emotional expressions in negotiations (see Chapter 7) has shown that people from East-Asian versus European American cultural backgrounds respond quite differently to expressions of anger (Adam, Shirako, & Maddux, 2010). Follower agreeableness and cultural background appear to interact in ways that remain to be explored in greater depth. More generally, incorporating the role of culture in studies on emotion in leadership represents a key challenge for future research.

To the degree that individuals with particular personality characteristics (such as a strong desire for social harmony) are more likely to work in certain types of organizations or industries than in others (due to attraction, selection, and attrition processes; Schneider, 1987), the moderating role of follower characteristics can also be analyzed at the organizational or industry level. For instance, workers may self-select into particular occupations based on their own values and norms. In some occupations, a positive and constructive interpersonal approach is rewarded (e.g., in customer service professions), whereas other occupations may be seen as relatively "rough" in terms of behavioral norms and expectations regarding emotional expression (e.g., the army and the construction industry; see Lindebaum & Fielden, 2011). Such social-occupational contexts shape behavioral norms and display rules, which determine to what extent a given emotional expression is likely to be perceived as appropriate or inappropriate by employees working within that particular context. As a result, emotional cultures emerge that may shape both the prevalence and the consequences of particular emotional expressions.

There is also some evidence that followers' responses to their leaders' emotional expressions depend on characteristics of the leader. Connelly and Ruark (2010) demonstrated that negative emotional expressions of transformational leaders produced higher-quality performance than did negative emotional expressions of transactional leaders. The authors suggested that followers of transformational leaders performed well because they accepted negative emotional expressions as an integral part of the strategies by which transformational leaders motivate and inspire their followers. In other words, they may have perceived expressions of anger emitted by transformational leaders as more appropriate than expressions of anger emitted by transactional leaders.

The research reviewed above is consistent with the idea that properties of the situation, the expresser, and the observer of an emotional expression determine the perceived appropriateness of the display, which in turn has downstream consequences for observers' behavioral responses. What appears to be missing so far in research on the role of emotion in leadership is evidence pertaining to the influence of characteristics of the expression itself. As discussed in Chapter 4, there are good reasons to assume that behavioral responses to emotional expressions depend on the (perceived) authenticity of those expressions. This notion is particularly relevant to leadership, because leaders may face numerous incentives to regulate their emotional expressions. For instance, normative expectations (e.g., display rules) as well as strategic considerations (e.g., attempts to motivate followers) may bring leaders to express emotions that they do not actually feel, to exaggerate the intensity of the emotions they feel, or to suppress the emotions they feel (Fitness, 2000; Humphrey et al., 2008; Lindebaum & Fielden, 2011). Such attempts at emotion regulation may result in more or less authentic displays, depending on (among other things) how the emotional expression is regulated.

Emotional expressions that result from antecedent-focused regulation or "deep acting" tend to be perceived as authentic, because in this case the expresser's external displays of emotion match his or her internal feelings (Grandey, 2003; Gross, 1998a; Hennig-Thurau, Groth, Paul, & Hemler, 2006). In contrast, emotional expressions that result from response-focused regulation or "surface acting" tend to appear rather inauthentic, because the expresser's external displays of emotion do not match his or her internal state (Côté, 2005; Grandey, 2003; Gross, 1998a; Hochschild, 1983; see Chapter 4 for a more in-depth discussion). Inauthentic-looking emotional expressions may be deemed inappropriate (Rafaeli & Sutton, 1989; Van Kleef et al., 2012), especially when they are interpreted as opportunistic and manipulative attempts to influence others (Gardner & Martinko, 1988). Inauthentic emotional expressions may therefore contribute to negative follower impressions of the leader (Gardner, Fischer, & Hunt, 2009), which may in turn undermine followers' motivation and performance.

Although research so far has not examined effects of the perceived authenticity of leaders' emotional displays on followers' performance, there is some evidence that inauthentic emotional expressions on the part of leaders undermine the quality of the leader–follower relationship (Glasø & Einarsen, 2008). This observation is consistent with research in other domains of organizational behavior, for instance in the realm of consumer behavior and customer service (see Chapter 8). Grandey and colleagues found that the perceived authenticity of service providers' emotional displays was positively associated with customers' satisfaction and liking of the service provider (Grandey, Fisk, Mattila, Jansen, & Sideman, 2005). In another study, customers perceived service employees who displayed authentic positive emotions as having a stronger customer orientation, rated the quality of service more positively, and showed higher loyalty intentions (Groth, Hennig-Thurau, & Walsh, 2009). It seems plausible that similar processes are at play in the context of leader–follower interactions, and that such processes shape followers' behavioral responses to their leaders' emotional displays. However, research is needed to confirm this possibility.

Leadership and emotional intelligence

We have seen that leaders' emotional displays can have favorable or unfavorable consequences for perceptions of leadership quality and for actual follower performance, depending on the specific emotion in question, the task at hand, the information-processing style of the followers, and the perceived appropriateness of the leaders' emotional displays. Given these contingencies, it seems plausible that individuals who are better able to adjust their emotions to the demands of the situation and the people involved in it are more likely to rise to leadership positions. Effective leadership requires flexible and knowledgeable use of emotional strategies to ensure that any emotional displays on the part of a leader have maximal positive and minimal negative impact on followers. This implies that leaders who exhibit better understanding of emotion and better emotion regulation abilities should be better able to lead others effectively. In addition, leaders who have the ability to accurately perceive and understand others' emotions may gain considerable knowledge about others' feelings, goals, and desires, which should allow them to influence and manage others more effectively. In other words, adequate leadership requires a certain level of emotional intelligence (Ashkanasy & Tse, 2000; George, 2000; Pescosolido, 2002).

In keeping with this logic, several studies have shown that various components of emotional intelligence are positively associated with attributions of leadership and with follower satisfaction (Byron, 2007; Côté, Lopes, Salovey, & Miners, 2010; Kellett, Humphrey, & Sleeth, 2002, 2006; Rubin et al., 2005; Walter, Cole, Van der Vegt, Rubin, & Bommer, 2012; Wolff, Pescosolido, & Druskat, 2002). For instance, Côté and colleagues (2010) found that people who are capable of accurately perceiving, using, understanding, and managing their own and others' emotions (as measured with an ability-based measure) are more likely to emerge as leaders in small groups. The researchers followed project teams over the course of a ten-week collaboration. At the end of the project, team members reported to what extent the various members of the team had manifested themselves as leaders. The results showed that team members with higher overall emotional intelligence were more likely to be perceived as leaders than those who scored lower on emotional intelligence, even after controlling for differences in personality and cognitive intelligence. Of the various components of emotional intelligence, the ability to understand emotions was most consistently associated with leadership emergence in this study. Other studies found that leadership emergence was similarly predicted by the ability to perceive emotions (Kellett et al., 2002; Walter et al., 2012; Wolff et al., 2002) and the ability to express emotions (Kellett et al., 2006). These studies indicate that people prefer to afford leadership roles to emotionally intelligent individuals.

Other research has examined whether emotional intelligence is also related to leadership effectiveness, as one would expect based on the above findings. Several studies indeed provide evidence for positive associations between emotional intelligence and various operationalizations of leadership effectiveness. In one study, higher emotional intelligence of leaders (assessed using an ability-based measure) predicted higher effectiveness, as measured objectively as well as through manager and subordinate ratings of leadership effectiveness (Rosete & Ciarrochi, 2005). This association held when controlling for personality and cognitive intelligence, indicating that emotional intelligence explains unique variance. Compatible associations between leaders' emotional intelligence and subordinates' ratings of leadership effectiveness were obtained in other research (e.g., Kerr, Garvin, Heaton, & Boyle, 2006).

Another way of looking at the influence of emotional intelligence on leadership effectiveness is by examining the impact of leaders' emotional intelligence on team functioning. Managing team members' emotions is a crucial aspect of successful leadership (George, 2000; Pescosolido, 2002). By managing the emotions of team members, leaders can shape relational processes within teams (Jordan & Troth, 2002). For instance, higher levels of leader emotional intelligence have been linked with higher levels of trust in teams (Chang, Sy, & Choi, 2012). It stands to reason, then, that leaders' (lack of) emotional intelligence takes on heightened importance in difficult situations, for instance when team members have divergent perspectives on the task, or when teams are characterized by low cohesion or high levels of conflict. Such difficulties are more likely to arise in diverse teams, which are made up of members with different demographic or educational backgrounds and/or different personalities (Van Knippenberg, De Dreu, & Homan, 2004). Adequate emotion management should thus be especially critical in the context of diverse teams, where (negative) emotions are more likely to arise due to a greater prevalence of personality clashes and conflicts (Homan & Jehn, 2010).

To test this argument, Homan, Van Kleef, Côté, and Bogo (2014) examined the effects of leaders' emotional intelligence on the functioning of diverse teams. In a longitudinal quasi-experiment, they followed groups of students over a period of nine weeks. In the first week, the researchers assessed the emotion management skills of all students using an ability-based measure. The highest and the lowest scorers on the test were designated as team leaders, and the rest of the students were randomly assigned to teams. In the second week, the researchers measured the individual team members' conscientiousness (McCrae & Costa, 1987), which they used to operationalize the personality diversity in the teams. In the weeks that followed, the team members reported on the degree of cohesion and conflict within their team. At the end of the period, team performance on a final assignment was graded. Results revealed an interaction between team personality diversity and leader's emotion management ability on team conflict and cohesion. Teams with high levels of personality diversity experienced fewer conflicts and greater cohesion when their leader had high rather than low emotion management ability, which in turn resulted in better performance. Teams low on personality diversity exhibited no differential team processes or performance as a function of the leader's emotion management skills. This suggests that the importance of leaders' emotional intelligence for team performance depends on the type of teams they manage (see also Walter, Cole, & Humphrey, 2011). Emotional intelligence may be especially critical under circumstances that impede smooth interaction.

Conclusion

A growing body of research attests to the importance of emotions in leadership. The emotions that leaders show, and the ways in which they regulate those emotions, influence followers' emotions, cognitions, perceptions, and behavior in theoretically meaningful ways. It is also clear from the extant literature that there is no simple answer to the question of whether or not leaders should express their emotions, or whether they should express positive or negative emotions to maximize subordinates' performance. In accordance with EASI theory, the effects of leaders' emotional expressions depend on followers' information processing and on the perceived appropriateness of the leader's emotional expressions.

The moderating role of followers' information processing is evident primarily in studies that focused on followers' performance as an index of leadership effectiveness. Some of these studies also point to discrepancies between followers' subjective ratings of their leader's effectiveness (which are heavily influenced by followers' affective reactions to the leader's emotional displays) and followers' actual performance in response to the leader's emotional expressions (which is shaped not only by followers' affective reactions, but also by inferential processes that may be triggered by the leader's emotional displays). These findings point to the importance of separating subjective and objective performance indices in research on leadership as well as to the importance of measuring both inferential and affective processes to inform a better understanding of the intricacies of the social effects of emotions.

The critical role of the perceived appropriateness of leaders' emotional expressions is evident in research that focused on followers' subjective ratings of leadership effectiveness as well as in studies that incorporated more objective indices of effectiveness (e.g., actual follower performance). There is evidence that the perceived appropriateness of leaders' emotional expressions depends on characteristics of the situation (e.g., whether or not followers had expended much effort), characteristics of the leader (e.g., whether she or he uses a transactional or a transformational leadership style), and characteristics of the followers (e.g., whether they score high or low on agreeableness). It seems plausible that characteristics of the emotional expression (e.g., intensity, authenticity) also matter, but research is needed to examine this.

Finally, it is clear from the research discussed in this chapter that leadership effectiveness hinges critically on leaders' emotional skills. Leaders with higher levels of emotional intelligence are more likely to become aware of the unspoken thoughts and feelings of their followers by "eavesdropping" on their emotional displays, which should put them in a better position to lead their followers effectively. Emotionally intelligent leaders are also better able to manage the emotions of their subordinates so as to make team processes run smoothly and facilitate performance. Furthermore, emotionally intelligent leaders are better able to manage their own emotions and to adjust their emotional style to the situation and to the demands of their subordinates. Such qualities should increase the likelihood that followers perceive the leader's emotional expressions as appropriate, which in turn has consequences for follower performance and team functioning. In sum, careful tailoring of emotional displays is a key to leadership effectiveness and organizational success.

So far, research on the role of emotions in leadership has focused on the effects of leaders' emotions on followers. Even though this focus makes sense in light of the fact that leaders are key agents of social influence, it seems plausible that the emotional expressions of followers can also shape leadership effectiveness and performance (Tee, Ashkanasy, & Paulsen, 2013) by evoking emotions in the leader and/or signaling important information to the leader regarding followers' appraisals of the situation. When shifting the focus from leader to follower, several interesting new research questions emerge. For instance, do followers deliberately use their emotions to influence their leaders and to get things done? How does the effectiveness of such strategies depend on the specific emotion that is expressed, on the leader's information-processing motivation and ability, and on the perceived appropriateness of the emotional display in the eyes of the leader? How do the emotional expressions of followers shape leaders' affective states and well-being (e.g., enthusiasm, burnout, depression, annoyance)? When and how do leaders use the emotional displays of their followers to inform their decisions and actions? And how are such processes modulated by the emotional intelligence of leader and follower? Examining these and other questions will contribute to a deeper understanding of the role of emotions in leader–follower relations and of the social effects of emotions in general.

PART III

Conclusions, implications, and new directions

CHAPTER 10

Critical evaluation, theoretical integration, and implications

Experience without theory is blind, but theory without experience is
mere intellectual play.

Immanuel Kant

Emotional expressions have a pervasive influence on our lives. The
chapters in Part II of this book document how emotional displays shape
critical processes and outcomes in a wide variety of social and organizational contexts, including close relationships, group decision making,
conflict and negotiation, consumer behavior and customer service, and
leadership. Besides a shared interest in the mechanisms and contingencies that govern the social effects of emotions, these different fields of
inquiry are each characterized by their own unique research questions
and foci, which are rooted in the diverse traditions from which these
fields have emerged. Different emphases across domains of research also
reflect logical differences in the types of variables that are relevant in a
particular context. Quite sensibly, the literature on the effects of emotional expressions in personal relationships reflects a strong interest in
relationship outcomes. Research on emotions in groups tends to focus on
group-level variables such as group affective tone and decision quality.
Studies on emotions in conflict and negotiation often include objective
indices of individual or joint negotiation performance. Researchers interested in the role of emotions in consumer behavior and customer service
commonly address outcomes such as service providers' job attitudes and
well-being or customers' satisfaction. Finally, leadership scholars tend to
concentrate on the effects of leaders' emotional expressions on subjective
and/or objective measures of leadership effectiveness.

Besides inherent differences in the types of variables that are of interest
to scholars in different areas of investigation, research traditions differ in
terms of the prevailing approaches to studying the social effects of emotions. For instance, research on the effects of emotional expressions on
relationship outcomes or negotiation behavior has traditionally shown a
strong interest in discrete emotional expressions. In contrast, research on
the social effects of emotions on group processes, customer service, and
leadership started out with a predominant focus on more diffuse affective

states, which has only recently begun to be complemented with an interest in the differential effects of discrete emotional expressions. As a result of such inherent differences, the conclusions that can be drawn regarding the nature, mechanisms, and contingencies of the social effects of emotions differ somewhat across domains of research.

In this chapter I aim to transcend the boundaries between the different research domains by highlighting key principles that should hold across domains and by examining the support for and implications of these principles. First I provide a brief summary of Emotions as Social Information (EASI) theory, which is followed by a critical evaluation of its current empirical support. Next I discuss the key differences and commonalities between EASI theory and a number of other relevant theoretical perspectives. I conclude by outlining implications of the EASI framework for theory and research.

Summary of EASI theory

EASI theory seeks to illuminate the social effects of emotions. The theory is rooted in a social-functional approach to emotion, which assumes that emotions play a vital role in regulating social interaction (Fischer & Manstead, in press; Frijda & Mesquita, 1994; Keltner & Haidt, 1999; Parkinson, 1996; Van Kleef, 2009). Moving beyond the traditional questions of how our emotions arise and how they influence our own thinking and behavior, EASI theory provides an account of how one person's emotional expressions influence the feelings, thoughts, and actions of *others*. A fundamental assumption underlying the theory is that social life is ambiguous and that people therefore turn to others' emotions to inform their understanding of the situation and the people involved in it so as to determine a fitting course of action. Such disambiguation should be facilitated to the degree that individuals express the emotions that they experience (encoding) and accurately perceive the emotional expressions of others (decoding).

EASI theory specifies two distinct processes through which emotional expressions regulate social life, as discussed in detail in Chapter 3. First, emotional expressions may elicit affective reactions in observers (i.e., reciprocal and complementary emotions and sentiments about the expresser). Second, emotional expressions may trigger inferential processes in observers (i.e., inferences about the source, meaning, and implications of the expresser's emotion). In some cases affective reactions and inferential processes motivate similar behavioral tendencies. For instance, the distress of a relationship partner may be interpreted as a sign that help is required (inference) but it may also trigger reciprocal feelings of distress and/or complementary feelings of compassion in the observer (affective reactions), both of which foster supportive behavior. In other cases inferences and affective reactions motivate opposite behaviors. For instance, when faced with an angry opponent in conflict, one's own reciprocal anger may fuel competition and retaliation, but one's inference that the other is upset because his or her limits have been reached may encourage strategic cooperation. When affective reactions and inferential processes motivate different (behavioral) responses to emotional expressions, responses depend on the relative strength of inferential processes and affective reactions.

The relative strength of affective and inferential processes is shaped by two broad classes of moderators, which were discussed in depth in Chapter 4. First, building on the basic assumption that emotional expressions constitute a source of information, EASI theory posits that the social effects of emotional expressions are modulated by the observer's information-processing motivation and ability, which in turn depends on dispositional characteristics (e.g., need for cognitive closure, personal need for structure) and on situational characteristics (e.g., time pressure, cognitive load). The deeper the observer's information processing, the stronger the relative predictive power of inferential processes. Conversely, the shallower the information processing, the stronger the relative predictive power of affective reactions.

Second, the social effects of emotional displays are proposed to depend on social-contextual factors that shape the perceived appropriateness of the displays in light of the social context. Such perceptions of (in)appropriateness depend on characteristics of the situation, the emotional expression itself, the expresser, and the observer. EASI theory posits that emotional expressions are more likely to trigger inferential processes to the degree that they are perceived as appropriate. Conversely, emotional expressions are more likely to elicit (negative) affective reactions to the degree that they are perceived as inappropriate.

EASI theory is schematically summarized in Figure 10.1. The non-shaded boxes to the left of the figure represent variables that are situated in the expresser, whereas the shaded boxes represent variables that are located in the observer. The solid arrows from left to right represent the two mechanisms underlying the social effects of emotions, namely observers' affective reactions and inferential processes. The boxes in the heart of the model capture proximal moderators of the social effects of emotions. Of these, the expresser's emotional expressivity and the observer's emotion perception ability are necessary prerequisites for any social effects of emotions to occur, because emotions that are not expressed in perceptible ways and emotional expressions that are not registered cannot bring about social effects through either of the mechanisms stipulated here. The observer's information processing and the perceived

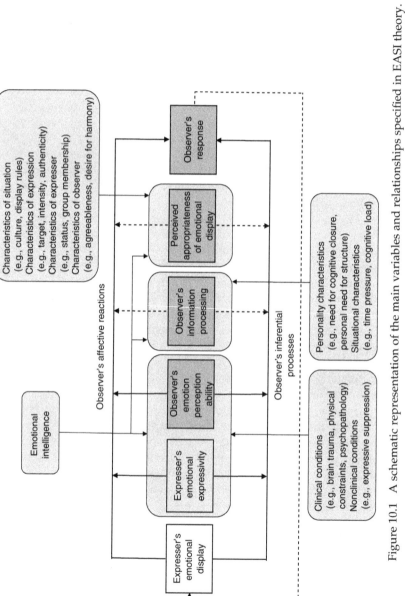

Figure 10.1   A schematic representation of the main variables and relationships specified in EASI theory.

appropriateness of the emotional display shape the relative predictive power of affective reactions and inferential processes, as denoted by the dashed arrows. The boxes outside the core of the model contain more distal moderating influences that exert their impact via the proximal moderators that are at the heart of the model.

A critical evaluation of the empirical support for EASI theory

The number of variables (especially distal ones) and relationships specified in EASI theory is too numerous to be tested within a single study, but dozens of studies speak to various parts of the theoretical framework. Because the empirical record on the social effects of emotions in various domains of research has already been discussed in detail in the foregoing chapters, the following discussion focuses on the general patterns that emerge from the various literatures reviewed in Part II.

EASI theory is rooted in a rich tradition of theorizing and research on emotion, and as such some of the assumptions and propositions that underlie the theory are not unique to the EASI framework. For instance, the idea that emotional expressions fulfill important social-communicative functions has been discussed in great depth in previous writings that have inspired the EASI framework (e.g., Buck, 1994; Keltner & Haidt, 1999; Parkinson, Fischer, & Manstead, 2005). Evidence for the possibility that emotions have evolved because of their social-communicative functions has also been discussed at length in earlier work (see Fridlund, 1994). I therefore limit the current discussion to the more unique aspects of EASI theory.

The functional equivalence hypothesis

Building on the argument that emotions facilitate social interaction by providing relevant information to interaction partners, EASI theory posits that expressions of the same emotion that are emitted via different expressive modalities (i.e., in the face, through the voice, by means of bodily postures, with words, or via symbols such as emoticons) should have comparable effects, provided that the emotional expressions can be perceived by others. Clearly, as discussed in Chapter 2, the suitability of the various expressive channels within a given interaction context depends on situational affordances that influence the effectiveness of verbal, nonverbal, or vocal communication (e.g., facial expressions are likely to be especially effective in face-to-face interaction, vocal expressions in phone conversations, and verbal expressions in e-mail exchanges). Such obvious boundary conditions aside, EASI theory postulates that the social-signaling value of emotions is functionally equivalent across expressive modalities in that the direction (but not necessarily the magnitude) of the interpersonal effects of emotional expressions is the same irrespective of the expressive channel through which they are emitted, as long as the emotional expression is accurately perceived. This is referred to as the functional equivalence hypothesis in the EASI framework.

To date, little research has directly (i.e., within a single study) compared the social effects of emotional expressions across expressive modalities beyond basic questions of decoding accuracy, with some notable exceptions in the literature on emotional contagion.[1] Separately, however, the various expressive modalities have been thoroughly investigated. It is therefore possible to cautiously compare the social effects of emotions expressed through different channels across studies. When doing so, it is useful to draw a distinction between similarity in the *direction* of effects (i.e., qualitative equivalence), which is predicted by EASI theory, and similarity in the *magnitude* of effects (i.e., quantitative equivalence), which is not implied.

It is important to note that comparisons of the magnitude of effects across studies (e.g., as reflected in effect sizes) are likely to be invalid, or at least not very informative, because researchers' choices of particular expressive modalities are often informed by (and therefore confounded with) characteristics of the study's setting that render one or the other expressive modality more feasible or suitable to study. For instance, a field study into the effects of emotional expressions on online dispute resolution would almost necessarily rely on coding of written emotional expressions, whereas a laboratory experiment on the effects of emotional expressions in conversations between marital couples could more easily incorporate nonverbal emotional displays in the study's design. There is little point in comparing the magnitude of the effects of verbal and nonverbal emotional expressions between such studies, because obvious differences between the research settings and procedures obfuscate the interpretation of any differences or similarities.

---

[1] It is worth mentioning that several studies have investigated the effects of inconsistencies between two simultaneously active expressive channels, such as when a sad message is delivered with a smiling face (e.g., Argyle, Alkema, & Gilmour, 1972; Bugental, 1974; Krumhuber & Manstead, 2009; Mehrabian & Ferris, 1967). Although this research provides insight into the relative weight observers attach to particular expressive channels within a particular context, it does not speak directly to the notion of functional equivalence. The functional equivalence hypothesis holds that the direction of the interpersonal effects of emotional expressions is similar across expressive modalities, but it makes no assumptions about the relative influence of simultaneous expressions via different channels.

Although comparing the magnitude of effects is thus problematic, the direction of effects can be meaningfully compared across studies involving different expressive modalities. The research on the social effects of emotions reviewed in the previous chapters has used a variety of procedures to manipulate emotional expressions. Some studies relied on verbal expressions of emotion, which were often delivered in the context of (simulated) computer-mediated interactions (e.g., Adam, Shirako, & Maddux, 2010; Bono & Ilies, 2006; Friedman et al., 2004; Melwani & Barsade, 2011; Van Kleef, De Dreu, & Manstead, 2004a). Other studies used pictures of facial emotional expressions (e.g., Hess, Blairy, & Kleck, 2000; Van Doorn, Heerdink, & Van Kleef, 2012) or film clips containing emotional expressions in face, voice, and posture (e.g., K. Lewis, 2000; Van Kleef et al., 2009). Still other studies utilized face-to-face paradigms, in which confederates were trained or naïve participants were induced to emit certain emotional expressions in interaction with another person (e.g., Barsade, 2002; Sinaceur & Tiedens, 2006; Sy, Côté, & Saavedra, 2005; Wang, Northcraft, & Van Kleef, 2012). Yet other research (often conducted in the field) involved self-reports of emotions and/or perceptions or coding of emotional expressions as they arose in the context of ongoing social interactions (Anderson, Keltner, & John, 2003; Averill, 1982; Grandey, 2003; Pugh, 2001; Tsai, 2001). Finally, some reports contain a combination of studies that involved written emotion messages, emoticons, pictures of facial displays, film clips containing facial, vocal, and postural expressions, and/or emotional expressions shown in face-to-face interaction (e.g., Bono & Ilies, 2006; Heerdink, Van Kleef, Homan, & Fischer, 2013; Sinaceur & Tiedens, 2006; Tiedens, 2001; Van Kleef, Van den Berg, & Heerdink, 2015).

Importantly, all these different procedures have yielded highly consistent effects. Even though the reviews in the preceding chapters revealed some inconsistent findings, these inconsistencies do not appear to arise from a focus on different expressive modalities. As it stands, there is no evidence of differential effects of emotions expressed through different expressive modalities. Moreover, support for the key relationships stipulated in EASI theory is provided by all types of studies, regardless of the expressive modalities that were examined. When it comes to their interpersonal effects, it appears that different channels of emotional communication are functionally equivalent, at least as far as the direction of their effects is concerned. Clearly, however, more direct evidence from comparative studies would be valuable.

The mediating roles of affective reactions and inferential processes

EASI's notion that emotional expressions may elicit affective reactions and/or inferential processes in observers emerged in part from a synthesis of earlier work in which various instances of such effects had already been demonstrated. Unsurprisingly, then, evidence for the effects of emotional expressions on various types of affective reactions and inferential processes on the part of observers is overwhelming – such evidence comes from all five of the research domains reviewed in this book.

Far fewer studies speak directly to the mediating role of affective reactions and/or inferential processes between emotional expressions and observers' (behavioral) responses. With regard to the role of affective reactions, evidence for mediation has so far been obtained in the context of close relationships (e.g., Anderson et al., 2003), group decision making (e.g., Barsade, 2002), negotiation (e.g., Friedman et al., 2004; Van Kleef & Côté, 2007), customer service and consumer behavior (e.g., Barger & Grandey, 2006), and leadership (e.g., Sy et al., 2005; Van Kleef et al., 2009). As such, there is reasonable support for the mediating role of affective reactions postulated by EASI theory, but more research is needed to further consolidate this conclusion.

Direct support for the presumed mediating role of inferential processes between emotional expressions and (behavioral) responses has only begun to emerge in the last decade. The most robust evidence comes from studies on group decision making (e.g., Heerdink et al., 2013), research on negotiation and social dilemmas (e.g., de Melo, Carnevale, Read, & Gratch, 2014; Sinaceur & Tiedens, 2006; Van Kleef et al., 2004a), and leadership (e.g., Van Kleef et al., 2009). Although several authors have argued and shown that emotional expressions provide information about individuals' goals and desires in close relationships (e.g., Clark, Pataki, & Carver, 1996; Eisenberg, 2000; Kennedy-Moore & Watson, 2001; Yee & Greenberg, 1998), direct evidence for a mediating role of such inferences in the link between emotional expressions and behavioral responses is scarce (for a rare example, see Yee & Greenberg, 1998; also see Bruder, Dosmukhambetova, Nerb, & Manstead, 2012). The customer service literature has also not paid great attention to the role of inferential processes, although some suggestive evidence has been reported in this domain as well (Hareli et al., 2009).

The moderating roles of information processing and perceived appropriateness

The EASI framework accords prominent moderating roles to the information-processing motivation and ability of the observer of an emotional display and to the perceived appropriateness of the emotional display. Support for the moderating influence of information processing has slowly begun to accumulate over the past decade. Current evidence comes from the literatures on group decision making (e.g., Heerdink et al., 2013), conflict and negotiation (e.g., Van Kleef, De Dreu, & Manstead, 2004b; Van Kleef, Steinel, & Homan, 2013), and leadership (e.g., Chi & Ho, 2014; Van Kleef et al., 2009). Evidence from the area of customer service and consumer behavior is limited to one study on persuasive communication (Van Kleef et al., 2015), and research in the realm of close relationships has so far not explicitly considered the role of information processing at all. Thus, although the existing data converge to show that the social effects of emotional expressions are modulated by the observer's motivation and ability to engage in thorough information processing, more evidence from different social settings is needed to further bolster confidence in the robustness of this pattern.

Empirical support for the moderating role of the perceived appropriateness of emotional displays has also begun to materialize only relatively recently. There is considerable evidence from various domains that emotional expressions that are perceived as inappropriate for the situation give rise to negative affective reactions in observers (e.g., Grandey, Fisk, Mattila, Jansen, & Sideman, 2005; Hennig-Thurau, Groth, Paul, & Gremler, 2006; Menon & Dubé, 2000; Van Kleef & Côté, 2007). EASI theory further posits that the *relative* influence of negative affective reactions (as compared with inferential processes) in shaping observers' responses to others' emotional expressions becomes greater to the degree that observers perceive the expressions as inappropriate. This proposition can only be directly examined in studies that involve a measure of both affective reactions and inferential processes. Such studies are rare, however, which is due in part to a disproportionate reliance on affective processes in several of the research domains in which the social effects of emotions have been studied. Especially the literature on group decision making and the literature on customer service have traditionally shown a strong interest in the mediating role of affective reactions. The body of research that is currently available is consistent with the proposition that negative affective reactions become more influential in shaping (behavioral) responses to emotional expressions to the degree that the expressions are perceived as inappropriate (e.g., Adam et al., 2010; Harinck & Van Kleef, 2012; Hennig-Thurau et al., 2006; Koning & Van Kleef, 2015; Lewis, 2000; Van Doorn, Van Kleef, & Van der Pligt, 2015b; Van Kleef & Côté, 2007), but additional research is needed to examine more directly whether the predictive power of inferential processes simultaneously decreases.

In sum, there is growing support for the key premises of EASI theory. The framework has emerged from a synthesis of early research on the social effects of emotions, which has in more recent years been complemented with evidence from studies that were specifically designed to test central tenets of the theory. Thus there is now a reasonable body of empirical evidence for the presumed functional equivalence of expressive channels, for the mediating roles of affective and inferential processes, and for the moderating influences of information processing and of social-contextual factors that shape the perceived appropriateness of emotional expressions. Clearly, however, because the EASI framework has evolved only recently, several aspects of the theory await further empirical attention. I discuss these issues in Chapter 11.

How does EASI theory relate to other approaches? Differences, commonalities, and integration

A key premise of EASI theory is that emotional expressions provide information to observers that may shape their behavior. Other central components of the theory include the mediating roles of affective reactions and inferential processes and the moderating influences of information processing and social-contextual factors that shape the perceived appropriateness of emotional expressions. Some of these ideas also appear in various other theoretical perspectives. It is therefore useful to consider the commonalities and differences between EASI theory and other models.

Affect-as-information, affect infusion, mood-as-input, and the dual-process tradition

The notion that emotions provide information is far from new (see, e.g., Damasio, 1994; Frijda, 1986; Oatley & Johnson-Laird, 1987). This idea has been featured in numerous influential emotion models, including (but not limited to) the affect-as-information model (Schwarz & Clore, 1983), the affect infusion model (Forgas, 1995), and the mood-as-input model (Martin, Ward, Achee, & Wyer, 1993). The key distinction between EASI theory and these approaches lies in the level of analysis. Whereas earlier frameworks are concerned with the question of how individuals' attitudes, cognitions, and behaviors are influenced by information individuals may obtain from their own emotions (whether consciously or nonconsciously), EASI theory is concerned with the question of how individuals are influenced by information they glean from the emotional expressions of others. Given its different level of analysis (i.e., interpersonal as opposed to intrapersonal), EASI theory is fully compatible with the earlier models.[2] Besides adopting a different level of analysis, EASI

---

[2] Due to their focus on intrapersonal affective influences, the earlier models are not particularly relevant for understanding the inferential processes that may underlie the interpersonal effects of emotions. However, the various processes of affect infusion

theory extends the intrapersonal models by specifying conditions that influence the relative impact of affective versus inferential processes in shaping the social effects of emotions.

Building on the idea that emotional expressions are a source of information, EASI theory posits that the interpersonal effects of emotions are modulated by observers' information-processing motivation and ability. Similar notions of information-processing motivation and ability feature prominently in dual-process models of social information processing and persuasion (see, e.g., Chaiken & Trope, 1999), as well as in Forgas' (1995) affect infusion model and Kruglanski's unimodel (e.g., Kruglansi & Thompson, 1999), all of which are again situated at the intrapersonal level of analysis (i.e., they illuminate how attitudes, judgments, and behavior are shaped by a person's own affective state). In contrast, EASI theory is situated at the interpersonal level of analysis (i.e., it seeks to explain how one person's attitudes, judgments, and behavior are shaped by the emotional expressions of others). Given the different foci and levels of analysis, the perspectives are complementary rather than mutually exclusive.

EASI is also different from some of the classic dual-process models in that it does not assume that people process information (in this case about others' emotions) either peripherally *or* systematically (e.g., Petty & Cacioppo, 1986; cf. Chen & Chaiken, 1999). Rather, it posits that individuals may simultaneously experience affective reactions to the emotional expressions of others *and* engage in inferential processing to interpret the meaning and implications of the emotional expressions. Given that both processes may occur at the same time and to varying degrees, responses to others' emotional expressions cannot be meaningfully conceptualized on a single bipolar continuum (cf. Kruglanski & Thompson, 1999). EASI theory builds on the dual-process tradition by distinguishing between inferential processes and affective reactions to expressions of emotion and by specifying conditions under which one or the other process becomes relatively more influential.

Finally, it should be noted that EASI theory's scope is somewhat different than that of the traditional dual-process theories. Although differences in focus exist among the classic models, they share a concern with understanding processes of social information processing and persuasion, broadly defined. Although EASI theory can be and has been applied to questions of persuasion and related phenomena such as

that are described in the intrapersonal models are relevant for understanding how observers' responses to others' emotional expressions are shaped by the impact of their own affective states on their cognitions, attitudes, and behavior, as detailed in Chapter 3.

compliance and conformity (Heerdink et al., 2013; Van Doorn et al., 2015b; Van Kleef et al., 2015), its scope is broader in the sense that it also speaks to the effects of emotional expressions in other domains of social interaction that have traditionally not been the focus of work in the realm of dual-process theories, including (but not limited to) close relationships, group decision making, conflict and negotiation, customer service, and leadership and coaching. At the same time, EASI's scope is narrower than that of classic dual-process models in that it is concerned specifically with the effects of emotional expressions, whereas traditional models seek to understand the effects of both affective and nonaffective communications.

Emotional contagion, social appraisal, and reverse appraisal

Although the interpersonal approach to emotions is relatively young compared to the long history of theory and research on intrapersonal effects, several models and ideas have been proposed that speak to different aspects of the social effects of emotional expressions. The oldest of these is emotional contagion theory (Hatfield, Cacioppo, & Rapson, 1994), which seeks to explain when and how emotions spread between individuals. The concept of emotional contagion is incorporated in EASI theory's notion of affective reactions. Besides (primitive) emotional contagion, however, these affective reactions may also include sentiments about the expresser of an emotion, such as increased or decreased liking of happy versus angry people (see Chapter 3 for an in-depth discussion). Existing models of emotional contagion are therefore relevant to understanding some of the affective reactions individuals may experience when they are confronted with the emotional expressions of others. However, these models are less useful when it comes to understanding inferential processes that may be triggered in perceivers of emotional expressions. The focus on such inferential processes constitutes a unique aspect of EASI theory.

Another notion that has bearing on the social effects of emotions is the concept of social appraisal (Bruder, Fischer, & Manstead, 2014; Fischer, Manstead, & Zaalberg, 2003; Manstead & Fischer, 2001; Mumenthaler & Sander, 2012; Parkinson, 2001). Social appraisal can be defined as "the appraisal of behaviors, thoughts, or feelings of one or more other persons in the emotional situation, in addition to the emotional event per se" (Manstead & Fischer, 2001, p. 222). Social appraisal speaks to the influence of other individuals on one's own emotional experiences and expressions. Two key facets of social appraisal can be distinguished (Bruder et al., 2014; Evers, Fischer, Rodriguez Mosquera, & Manstead, 2005).

First, other people's emotional or behavioral reactions to events may influence one's own appraisals of those events, which in turn shape one's emotional experience. More specifically, an individual's appraisal of an emotional event may be influenced by the apparent appraisals other individuals make of the same event. In support of this idea, one study showed that participants' reactions to a poor grade depended on the emotional responses of fellow students to the same event, with angry reactions by participants becoming more likely when other students responded with anger and sad reactions becoming more likely when other students responded with sadness (Fischer, Rotteveel, Evers, & Manstead, 2004).

Second, social appraisal speaks to the imagined consequences of expressing particular emotions in the presence of others (Manstead & Fischer, 2001). That is, individuals may anticipate how others will react to their own emotional expressions and/or how such reactions may affect the attainment of their personal goals. In line with this idea, Evers and colleagues (2005) reported evidence indicating that women are less likely than men to express their anger because women are more likely to believe that negative social consequences will ensue when they show their anger.

The notion of social appraisal is pertinent to understanding social factors that shape the experience and expression of emotions. Theorists working with this concept have stressed that emotional episodes do not unfold in a social vacuum that contains only the emotional stimulus and the focal individual but are always embedded in a larger social context (Fischer et al., 2003). The notion of social appraisal captures how people's emotional experiences and expressions are shaped by and regulated in light of the perceived and anticipated reactions of other individuals in the social context, which are appraised in relation to people's social objectives.

The first facet of social appraisal shows some resemblance with EASI theory's notion of inferential processes, although the two perspectives have different foci. The social appraisal account is primarily concerned with the question of how people's emotional experiences and expressions in response to relevant events are shaped by the reactions of others, which may or may not be emotional in nature. EASI theory is not primarily concerned with the determinants of emotional reactions to events but rather with the question of how people's (behavioral) responses to others' emotional expressions are shaped by affective and inferential processes that are triggered by those expressions. A commonality between the social appraisal account and the EASI framework is the emphasis on the social context. However, whereas the social appraisal account emphasizes the influence of (anticipated) reactions of others to one's own emotional expressions, EASI theory stresses the importance of the perceived appropriateness of other people's emotional expressions in light of the social context.

A related notion that is of relevance here is that of reverse appraisal, which was discussed in detail in Chapter 3. The concept of reverse appraisal refers to the interpretation of other people's appraisals based on their emotional expressions (de Melo et al., 2014). This process has previously been referred to as "tracking" (Van Kleef, De Dreu, & Manstead, 2004a), "backtracking" (Elfenbein, 2007), and "reverse engineering appraisals" (Hareli & Hess, 2010). The process is also implied in social appraisal theory (Manstead & Fischer, 2001), which describes how individuals integrate information gleaned from others' emotional expressions into their own appraisals of a situation (i.e., "situation-oriented social appraisal"; Bruder et al., 2014). Although different researchers have used different terms to refer to this process, the basic idea is the same: Individuals use others' emotional expressions to inform their own interpretations of situations and events. This notion is central to the inferential processes stipulated in EASI theory.

As was the case with the other theoretical accounts discussed above, the relationship of EASI theory to accounts of emotional contagion, social appraisal, and reverse appraisal is one of complementarity rather than mutual exclusiveness – the models have been developed to address different types of questions. For instance, the social appraisal account seeks to understand how emotional expressions are modulated by the social context, whereas EASI theory aims to illuminate how the social context shapes responses to emotional expressions. As such the various models can exist next to one another. Nevertheless, the shared focus of these perspectives on interpersonal rather than intrapersonal emotional processes raises the question of whether they can be combined into a unifying theoretical account. Parkinson and Simons (2009) noted that "neither social appraisal nor emotion contagion can provide an all-purpose theory of interpersonal emotional influence, and the challenge facing future research is to specify when and how each of these processes operates and how the two processes might interact with each other" (p. 1083). EASI theory aspires to provide such an integrative theoretical account by accommodating relevant aspects of emotional contagion, social appraisal, and reverse appraisal and specifying how the relative impact of affective reactions (which are fueled in part by emotional contagion and social appraisal) and inferential processes (which rely in part on reverse appraisal) are shaped by people's information-processing motivation and ability and the perceived appropriateness of emotional expressions in light of the social context.

Affective events theory and the dual threshold model of anger

A prominent framework in the organizational literature is affective events theory (AET; Weiss & Cropanzano, 1996), which was developed to explain how affectively laden work events influence job satisfaction and performance. AET holds that features of the work environment can give rise to affective reactions (i.e., moods and emotions), which in turn shape job satisfaction and performance. The theory played an important role in stimulating research on affective phenomena in the workplace by according a mediating role to affective states in explaining how organization members respond to their work environment. This focus on affective reactions represents a commonality with EASI theory. The main difference between the theories resides in their level of analysis. AET aims to explain the emergence and intrapersonal consequences of affective states, whereas EASI describes the interpersonal consequences of emotional expressions. Besides this critical distinction, there are differences in the scope of the theories. AET is concerned specifically with the role of affective states in shaping job-related attitudes and behaviors, whereas EASI seeks to explain the interpersonal effects of emotions across domains of life.

Another perspective from the organization sciences that merits discussion here is the dual threshold model of anger (Geddes & Callister, 2007). This model posits that emotion recognition and organizational display rules jointly create two thresholds that determine outcomes of anger episodes in the workplace. The *expression threshold* is crossed when individuals express rather than suppress their anger at work, so that the anger can be perceived by others. The *impropriety threshold* is crossed when expressed anger violates organizational emotion display norms. The general argument of the dual threshold model is that anger can only be expected to have favorable consequences at work when (1) it is expressed and (2) the expression does not cross the impropriety threshold. Anger that is suppressed cannot have beneficial consequences because it is not registered by others, and anger that crosses the line is likely to backfire because it is unfitting for the situation. Just like EASI theory, the dual threshold model is situated at the interpersonal level of analysis – it seeks to explain the social consequences of emotional expressions. Furthermore, the two perspectives share an interest in the perceived appropriateness of emotional expressions. However, whereas the scope of the dual threshold model is limited to the effects of expressions of anger in work settings, EASI theory speaks to the effects of expressions of any emotion across a wide range of social and organizational settings. Furthermore, EASI accords a critical moderating role to perceivers' information-processing motivation and ability, whereas the dual threshold model does not.

In sum, EASI theory shares some elements with a number of existing models, but it differs from these models in notable ways. EASI complements traditional perspectives that speak to the intrapersonal consequences of affective experiences (e.g., the affect-as-information model, the affect infusion model, affective events theory, and the various dual-process accounts) by illuminating the interpersonal consequences of emotional expressions. EASI further provides a way to integrate key elements of various approaches that are relevant to understanding the social effects of emotions. It borrows insights from emotion contagion theory and translates the dual-process models' notions of information-processing motivation and ability to the interpersonal level of analysis by considering how information processing shapes responses to *others'* emotional expressions as opposed to one's own affective experiences. EASI's scope is narrower than that of some other models (most notably those in the dual-process tradition) in that it does not incorporate the effects of nonaffective communications but is limited to the effects of emotional expressions. EASI is broader in scope than other models (e.g., emotion contagion theory, the dual threshold model, and the social appraisal and reverse appraisal approaches) in that it incorporates both affective and inferential processes, identifies moderating influences on the relative priority of both processes, is not limited to one particular emotion, and speaks to the effects of emotional expressions across social and organizational domains.

Implications for theory and research

In this section I discuss some of the implications of the view of emotions as social information and of the empirical research reviewed here. Several implications for the respective research domains reviewed in Part II have already been considered. I therefore focus the current discussion on more overarching theoretical considerations and implications for research.

Evolution and the social functionality of emotions

Theorists differ in terms of the functionality they ascribe to emotions. Some argue that emotions are merely an evolutionary by-product of the neural regulation of the autonomic nervous system (e.g., Porges, 1999). Others have proposed that emotions are *functional* in that they help us prioritize our goals, signal the importance of events to relevant concerns, and/or prepare our mind and body for adaptive responses to relevant changes in the environment (e.g., Darwin, 1872; Ekman, 1992; Farb, Chapman, & Anderson, 2013; Frijda, 1986; Lazarus, 1991). Although these accounts differ in terms of the specific functions they ascribe to emotions, they share the assumption that (basic) emotions are evolved, biological adaptations that help the organism deal with issues that are crucial for survival, such as avoiding threats or noxious substances, approaching opportunities, and fighting off enemies. Emotions are systematically associated with physiological processes geared toward adequate (behavioral) responding to pertinent events. For instance, anger leads to enhanced distribution of blood to the hands, whereas fear involves a reduced blood flow to the periphery (Levenson, 1992). These processes have been suggested to facilitate adaptive fight and flight responses (Keltner, Haidt, & Shiota, 2006).

In addition, emotions have been proposed to contribute to the effective regulation of social interaction (Keltner & Haidt, 1999; Parkinson et al., 2005). Some argue, for instance, that emotions help to solve problems of commitment and cooperation, which are central to human ultrasociality (Frank, 1988, Keltner et al., 2006). For example, love and compassion signal psychological attachment and commitment to a relationship (Gonzaga, Keltner, Londahl, & Smith, 2001). Embarrassment and shame appease dominant individuals and signal submissiveness (Keltner & Buswell, 1997). Pride protects the social status of accomplished individuals (Tiedens, Ellsworth, & Mesquita, 2000). Anger motivates punishment of individuals who violate norms of reciprocity and cooperation (Lerner, Goldberg, & Tetlock, 1998). According to this perspective, emotions may have evolved because they help coordinate social life by solving problems of commitment and cooperation.

The theoretical framework and research discussed in this book highlight another – related – possibility, namely that emotions have evolved because of their role in facilitating communication and coordination and shaping processes of social influence. Individuals often lack information about others' internal states, which makes it difficult to predict their behavior and determine an appropriate course of action. It stands to reason that such lack of insight into other individuals' goals and intentions was even more pressing in preliterate times, when language as a communication device was not yet available. In the absence of language, observable nonverbal behaviors – including facial, vocal, and postural expressions of emotion – likely provided useful clues regarding other people's motives and intentions (Fridlund, 1992), making such expressions especially vital for adaptive responding, survival, and reproduction.

Humans' unique mastery of language later added an extra dimension to emotional expression (Oatley, 2003) and the regulation of social interaction (Keltner et al., 2006). It seems reasonable to assume that children who more effectively convey distress to their caregivers are more likely to be nurtured, and that parents who are better attuned to their children's suffering are more likely to intervene when needed, thereby increasing the chances of their offspring's survival. Similarly, individuals who display anger at appropriate times and in the appropriate manner are more likely to scare off dangerous enemies, just as attackers who are better attuned to signs of anger in their enemies are more likely to avoid deadly combat (cf. Fridlund, 1994). Finally, people who express happiness in the right circumstances probably develop better social networks, receive more social support, and lead more successful social lives (Lopes, Salovey, Côté, & Beers, 2005). In short, appropriate use of and responses to emotional expressions facilitate successful social adaptation, and these benefits derive in part from the capacity of emotional expressions to signal important information to others and thereby influence their behavior in ways that are beneficial for the self and/or for others.

Over the years several theorists have noted that emotional expressions may be used deliberately to influence others. Clark and colleagues (1996) reported anecdotal evidence that people strategically use displays of sadness to solicit help. This can be effective (especially in communal relationships), because observers may infer that the expresser is needy and dependent. Likewise, people may express anger to intimidate and influence others (Frank, 1988). For instance, managers have been reported to strategically feign anger in order to influence their subordinates (Fitness, 2000). Furthermore, people may purposefully express happiness to get others to like them (Clark et al., 1996). Finally, criminal interrogators and bill collectors report using emotional strategies to bring about compliance in their targets (Rafaeli & Sutton, 1991). The theory and research reviewed in this volume resonate with these arguments. Emotions are powerful agents of social influence (Côté & Hideg, 2011; Van Kleef, Van Doorn, Heerdink, & Koning, 2011), and this influence is driven in large part by the informational relevance of emotional displays.

The view of emotions as social information implies that emotional expressions should have a stronger impact on social behavior to the extent that other, more direct information about a person's social goals and intentions is unavailable (Van Kleef, De Dreu, & Manstead, 2010). If emotions serve to disambiguate social interaction, providing trustworthy information about another person's intentions might undermine the impact of that person's emotional expressions. Despite the intuitive plausibility of this idea, little direct evidence currently exists to support it. A rare exception is a study by Hareli and colleagues (2009), who examined how emotional expressions of customers influence service providers' inferences regarding the credibility of a complaint. They found that when the credibility of a complaint was uncertain, displays of anger by the customer bolstered perceptions of injustice and enhanced the perceived credibility of the complaint in the eyes of the service provider compared to displays of sadness. However, when the complaint was unambiguously justified, the customers' emotional expressions had no effect on perceptions of credibility because they provided no relevant additional information. Along similar lines, it is conceivable that emotional expressions have less impact when strong social norms are in place to guide behavior. Such norms might take over emotion's disambiguating function by making other people's behavior relatively easy to predict.

Another implication of the view of emotions as social information is that social interaction is shaped in important ways by individual differences in emotional expressivity and decoding accuracy (see Chapter 4). Some individuals are more emotionally expressive than others (Kring, Smith, & Neale, 1994), and it stands to reason that individuals who interact with emotionally expressive others are presented with more cues as to their interaction partner's inner states, goals, motives, and intentions. Observers, in turn, differ in the extent to which they are capable of accurately decoding others' emotional expressions, for instance as a result of variation in emotional intelligence (Salovey & Mayer, 1990) or clinical conditions such as Parkinson's disease (Jacobs, Shuren, Bowers, & Heilman, 1995) and certain types of autism spectrum disorder (Uljarevic & Hamilton, 2013), as discussed in Chapter 2. Individuals who are better at recognizing emotions in others should have more valuable information at their disposal to inform their behavior in interactions with other people. Evidence that people who are more emotionally expressive contribute to more comfortable interactions (Butler et al., 2003) and experience greater interpersonal closeness and social support (Srivastava, Tamir, McGonigal, John, & Gross, 2009) corroborates the notion that emotional expressions provide relevant information that is critical for social adaptation.

Bounded functionality: emotion regulation and emotional intelligence

It is important to stress that arguments for the social functionality of emotional expressions do not imply that every emotional expression is always functional (also see Fischer & Manstead, in press). Although it may be tempting to interpret many of the social consequences of emotional expressions reviewed here as functional, several effects can also be construed as dysfunctional, depending on the perspective one takes. Some interpersonal effects appear to be unequivocally beneficial, such as the tendency to provide consolation to distressed individuals. Other types of effects, however, can be positive or negative, depending on individuals' goals and situational requirements. For instance, even though contagion of positive emotions in groups may contribute to understanding and rapport among group members, the resulting affective homogeneity can constitute a liability insofar as it undermines critical evaluation of each other's ideas.

The functionality of emotional expressions also depends on characteristics of the social setting and on the goals and social motives of the parties that are involved. If we consider the functionality of emotional expressions in competitive settings such as negotiations, for instance, we run into a paradox. One could argue that expressions of anger are functional in that they may help a negotiator to extract concessions from his or her counterpart. However, from the perspective of the counterpart the functionality of such an effect is highly debatable, and in many cases the consequences of the anger will be perceived as unfavorable. One could argue that the anger is still functional at the system level (in this case the dyad) because it helps the two parties coordinate their offers and demands and thereby reach an agreement. However, there are also instances where (the expression of) anger and concomitant aggression unmistakably have unfavorable consequences at the system level, such as in intractable conflicts (Halperin & Gross, 2010).

One way of thinking about the functionality of emotional expressions is by considering issues they may help to address. Different emotions (or families of emotions) have been proposed to serve different social functions that may help to solve various types of problems that can emerge in social life (Keltner & Gross, 1999). Logically, then, the functionality of any emotional display depends on the degree to which it helps to remedy a relevant problem. For instance, expressions of anger may be functional to the extent that they sanction a transgression or call attention to a perceived injustice. However, when no injustice or transgression has been committed, displays of anger may exacerbate the quality of social relationships instead of improving them, partly because expressions of anger are more likely to be perceived as inappropriate in such circumstances. Clearly, then, the presumed functions of emotional expressions should be critically evaluated and weighed against the possibility of dysfunctional outcomes (Parrott, 2001).

Given the many complexities and contingencies surrounding the social effects of emotions, the functionality of any emotional display (from the perspective of the individual and/or the larger system) depends on the extent to which the expresser is able to *regulate* the emotional display in light of his or her goals and in light of the constraints and demands of the social context. This means that the social functionality of emotional displays hinges critically on expressers' emotional intelligence and associated emotion regulation abilities (Côté, 2005). Emotion regulation includes all efforts to increase, maintain, or decrease one or more components of an emotion, including its subjective experience and public display (Gross, 1998b). If emotional expressions can have favorable or unfavorable consequences depending on the degree to which they fit within the current social context, it follows that the ability (or lack thereof) to appropriately regulate one's emotional displays has repercussions for the quality of social exchange and, more broadly, for the functionality of emotional expressions. In keeping with this idea, research has documented links between emotion regulation ability and outcomes such as relationship quality (Lopes et al., 2005) and leadership effectiveness (Côté, Lopes, Salovey, & Miners, 2010; Kellett, Humphrey, & Sleeth, 2006). Other work has linked more general conceptions of emotional intelligence to customer service performance (Rozell, Pettijohn, & Parker, 2004) and negotiation success (Elfenbein, Foo, White, Tan, & Aik, 2007), although evidence for the latter relationship is mixed.

An implication of this argument is that the (dys)functionality of emotional displays can only be understood by considering the role of interacting partners' emotional intelligence, including not only the emotion perception skills and emotional understanding of the perceiving partner, but also the emotion regulation abilities of the expressing partner (see Figure 10.1).

Implications of the functional equivalence of expressive modalities

As noted earlier in this chapter, no studies have directly compared tests of EASI theory based on emotional expressions emitted via different channels. However, evidence from studies of basic responses to emotional expressions (which did involve direct comparisons of expressive modalities) supports the functional equivalence hypothesis. For instance, there is evidence that various discrete emotional expressions are well recognized (i.e., far above chance level) regardless of the expressive channel (Hawk, Van Kleef, Fischer, & Van der Schalk, 2009) and that emotions displayed via different expressive channels trigger comparable physiological responses in observers (Magnee, Stekelenburg, Kemner, & De Gelder, 2007). Moreover, as indicated above, a comparison of the social effects of emotional expressions emitted through various expressive channels *across* studies did not reveal differences in the direction of such effects. Even though the lack of such differences cannot be interpreted as conclusive evidence, these patterns are consistent with the assumption of functional equivalence.

If one accepts the possibility of such functional equivalence of expressive channels, several implications are worth considering. First, the notion of functional equivalence implies that the social-signaling function of emotions is served equally well by verbal, facial, and vocal expressions of emotion, provided that the emotional expression can be accurately registered. Thus, for instance, a distant cry of distress, a teary face at close range, and an e-mail stating one's distress may all be effective in eliciting social support by triggering affective reactions and/or inferential processes in an observer, even though the strength of the effects might differ across expressive modalities (Hawk et al., 2009).

Second, the notion of functional equivalence has implications for designing studies on the social effects of emotions. Some scholars appear to believe that nonverbal manipulations of emotional expression more accurately capture the essence of emotion than do verbal manipulations. The growing evidence for the functional equivalence of different manipulations of emotional expressions casts doubt on the tenability of this belief. In addition, now that communication increasingly occurs via social media that rely primarily on verbal communication, verbal expressions of emotion become ever more prevalent in social interaction. Disregarding them as unnatural does not do justice to the ways in which emotions are expressed in everyday life.

Third, on a more practical note, functional equivalence means that researchers interested in the social effects of emotions have a rich repertoire of manipulations at their disposal, none of which is inherently superior or inferior. This is not to say that the different procedures do not have different advantages and disadvantages. For instance, verbal expressions of emotion arguably afford the most tightly controlled manipulation, but they lack a certain degree of social richness. Face-to-face interaction involving verbal, facial, postural, and vocal emotional expressions provides the richest social context, but such a setting does not allow for rigid experimental control because the responses of the target may influence the behavior of the expresser. The choice of a particular procedure should therefore depend on the objective of the study (e.g., how much experimental control is desired) and on what is feasible and believable given the research setting.

Emotion specificity: the importance of studying discrete emotions

In the last decades, numerous scholars have argued and shown that there are robust and theoretically meaningful differences among the various discrete emotions that cannot be understood purely in terms of valence. Initial support for such emotion specificity came from studies on the distinct appraisal patterns (e.g., Frijda, Kuipers, & ter Schure, 1989; Roseman, 1984), physiological correlates (e.g., Levenson, 1992; Levenson, Ekman, & Friesen, 1990), and intrapersonal effects of emotional states on cognition and behavior (e.g., Bodenhausen, Sheppard, & Kramer, 1994; DeSteno, Petty, Wegener, & Rucker, 2000; Keltner, Ellsworth, & Edwards, 1993; Lerner & Keltner, 2001; Tiedens & Linton,

2001). The theoretical framework and the research reviewed here further add to this increasing awareness by emphasizing that the interpersonal effects of emotions are also emotion specific.

For instance, research on emotional expressions in close relationships has identified critical differences between the negative emotions of anger (which can have beneficial consequences for the quality of relationships) and contempt (which typically has negative consequences for relationships; e.g., Averill, 1982; Fischer & Roseman, 2007; Gottman, 1993). Research on the effects of emotional expressions on compliance with requests has found that expressing disappointment (which is deemed relatively appropriate in this context) is more effective than expressing anger (which is deemed quite inappropriate) in securing compliance with a request (Van Doorn et al., 2015b). This pattern may be explained by the fact that disappointment does not involve assigning blame to another person whereas anger does (Wubben, De Cremer, & Van Dijk, 2009a). Studies on the effects of emotional expressions in groups have shown that displays of anger versus sadness signal different levels of acceptance to targets (Heerdink, Van Kleef, Homan, & Fischer, 2015), which have differential consequences for conformity versus deviance in groups (Heerdink et al., 2013). Research on emotions in conflict and negotiation has documented opposite effects of expressions of anger versus guilt (Van Kleef et al., 2004a, 2006a). These patterns can be understood in terms of the "core relational themes" of anger and guilt, which are other-blame and self-blame, respectively (Smith, Haynes, Lazarus, & Pope, 1993). In the leadership realm, several researchers have reported differential effects of leaders' expressions of anger versus sadness, with expressions of anger by male leaders signaling greater status (Tiedens, 2001) and leadership effectiveness (K. Lewis, 2000) than expressions of sadness, but expressions of sadness eliciting greater liking (Madera & Smith, 2009). These patterns can be explained in terms of the greater action orientation that is implied by displays of anger rather than sadness (which suggests leadership capacities) in combination with the negative interpersonal signals that are radiated by expressions of anger (e.g., blame, aggression). These examples demonstrate that there is greater promise in conceptualizing emotions in terms of their unique appraisal patterns, action tendencies, and social signals than in terms of their valence. Even though crude distinctions in terms of valence may be sufficient for some research goals, measuring diffuse positive versus negative affect may inadvertently obfuscate theoretically meaningful differences among discrete emotional expressions.

Besides the limited conceptual and empirical precision involved in measuring diffuse positive versus negative affect instead of discrete emotional states and expressions, one may question what it *means* to

conceptualize emotions in terms of their valence. Even though this practice is widespread and viable alternative approaches have yet to be
proposed, several theorists have questioned the usefulness of referring
to emotions as "positive" or "negative." Some scholars have stressed that
both positive and negative emotions can have favorable as well as unfavorable consequences (Lindebaum & Jordan, 2014; Parrott, 2014),
depending on time, place, context, and culture (Lazarus, 2003; Nesse &
Ellsworth, 2009). Nesse (1990, p. 281) argued that "bad feelings exist for
good reasons." Focusing on one "bad feeling" in particular, others have
proposed that anger is an approach-related affect that is associated with
the appetitive motivational system (Carver & Harmon-Jones, 2009) and,
perhaps more controversially, that anger should be seen as a positive
rather than a negative emotion (Hess, 2014; Lerner & Tiedens, 2006).

The fundamental question is: What is positive and negative about
positive and negative emotions? Positive emotions may generally feel
more pleasant than negative emotions, but people also report experiencing particular instances of negative emotions such as anger or sadness as
pleasant in some way, and they voluntarily expose themselves to negative emotional stimuli such as sad movies, depressing music, or disturb-
ing art (Oliver, 1993; Schubert, 1996). Moreover, emotions that are
experienced as unpleasant may have quite beneficial social consequences
(e.g., displays of sadness may evoke social support and draw people
closer to one another; Clark et al., 1996), and emotions that are experienced as pleasant may have counterproductive social consequences (e.g.,
expressions of happiness may invite exploitation in negotiations; Van
Kleef et al, 2004a).

Adopting an evolutionary perspective, Nesse and Ellsworth (2009)
argued that emotions have been shaped by natural selection to regulate
responses to events that are relevant to an individual's ability to reach
personal goals. Accordingly, they stated that "in situations that decrease
fitness, negative emotions are useful and positive emotions are harmful"
(Nesse & Ellsworth, 2009, p. 129). In accordance with this presumed
flexibility, individuals have been observed to deliberately upregulate
their negative emotions to increase their chances of success in situations
that potentially "decrease fitness." For instance, people may strategically
upregulate anger to claim a larger share of the pie in a negotiation or
cultivate sadness so as to be more effective at soliciting help (Tamir, 2009).

Numerous studies discussed in this book further question the utility of
the positive-negative dimension. We have seen myriad examples of positive effects of expressions of negative emotions such as anger, sadness,
and disappointment on relationship quality (e.g., Fischer & Roseman,
2007; Graham, Huang, Clark, & Helgeson, 2008), various aspects of
group functioning (e.g., Heerdink et al., 2013; Klep, Wisse, & Van der

Flier, 2011), negotiation outcomes (e.g., Sinaceur & Tiedens, 2006; Van Kleef et al., 2004a), the quality of customer service (e.g., Hareli et al., 2009), and leadership effectiveness (e.g., Sy et al., 2005; Van Kleef, Homan, Beersma, & Van Knippenberg, 2010). We have also seen some instances of potentially counterproductive consequences of positive emotional expressions (typically of happiness), most notably in the context of group decision making (e.g., Heerdink et al., 2013; Klep et al., 2011; Tsai, Chi, Grandey, & Fung, 2012), conflict and negotiation (e.g., Steinel, Van Kleef, & Harinck, 2008; Van Kleef et al., 2004a), and leadership (e.g., Sy et al., 2005; Van Kleef et al., 2010).

All of this suggests that there is limited value in thinking about emotions primarily in terms of positivity versus negativity. In light of the growing body of evidence in support of emotion specificity at the interpersonal level of analysis, future research would do well to measure or manipulate discrete emotions rather than positive or negative affect. Clearly, the research context may constrain measurement options to some degree. It may be partly for this reason that many field studies on emotion have relied on measures of positive versus negative affect, especially in cases where consent and collaboration from organizations were needed to conduct the research. Such constraints notwithstanding, operationalizations of discrete emotions should be preferred to measures of general affect wherever possible.

Conclusion

The myriad studies that were reviewed in Part II of this book speak to the critical yet intricate ways in which emotional expressions regulate our social lives. EASI theory was developed in an attempt to account for the wide variety of social effects of emotional expressions that have been documented in the literature and to guide future research in this area. In this chapter I presented an integrative summary of the key tenets of the theory, which I critically reviewed in light of the available evidence. This review revealed that there is mounting support for the notion of (qualitative) functional equivalence of expressive modalities, for the mediating roles of affective reactions and inferential processes, and for the moderating influences of observers' information processing and the perceived appropriateness of emotional displays. The review also revealed that there are appreciable differences between the various literatures covered in Chapters 5 to 9 in terms of the emphasis they put on particular emotional processes and outcomes. As a result, several blind spots can be identified within each domain of research. When the five literatures are combined, however, considerable support for EASI's central propositions is observed.

An analysis of the various commonalities and differences between EASI theory and other theoretical approaches revealed that the EASI framework complements traditional perspectives in various ways. The most obvious difference with many other models concerns EASI's focus on the interpersonal rather than the intrapersonal effects of emotions. The theory further provides a way to integrate key elements of various approaches that are relevant to understanding the social effects of emotions. Specifically, it borrows insights from emotional contagion accounts and various appraisal models, and translates notions of information-processing motivation and ability from the dual-process tradition to the interpersonal level of analysis by considering how information processing shapes responses to other people's emotional expressions. I have addressed some of the implications of the EASI framework for theory and research, including theorizing about the evolution and social functionality of emotions, the role of emotion regulation and emotional intelligence, methodological implications of the assumption of functional equivalence of expressive modalities, and the importance of studying discrete emotions. In the final chapter I will discuss caveats in the current state of the art and present an agenda for future research.

CHAPTER 11

Caveats and future directions

Science never solves a problem without creating ten more.
George Bernard Shaw

In the preceding chapters of this book, I have offered a new integrative framework for understanding and investigating the interpersonal dynamics of emotions: Emotions as Social Information (EASI) theory. I have reviewed the empirical literature on the social effects of emotions across a wide range of domains, analyzed the current support for EASI theory, discussed some of its implications, and highlighted differences and commonalities between EASI theory and other theoretical approaches. In this final chapter I discuss boundaries and limitations of the theory that have remained somewhat implicit in the preceding chapters. In addition, I identify lacunae in our current understanding of the social effects of emotions more generally and provide an agenda for future research. Even though countless specific research questions pertaining to the social effects of emotions in each of the domains reviewed in Part II of this book await future research (several of which have been highlighted in the respective chapters), the focus here is on bigger-picture questions that cut across the various domains.

The elusive nature of evolutionary arguments

EASI theory is partly rooted in evolutionary accounts of the social functionality of emotion. The theory proposes that emotions have evolved at least in part because of their social-communicative functions (also see Fridlund, 1994). As is the case with more common arguments about the evolutionary benefits of the *intra*personal functions of emotions (e.g., fear preparing the organism to flee; Farb, Chapman, & Anderson, 2013; Frijda, 1986), this proposition cannot be directly tested or falsified. Empirically speaking, the usefulness of the proposition is therefore limited. Its primary value lies in the emphasis it puts on the social-communicative functions of emotions, which may serve the purpose of shifting attention toward the interpersonal effects of emotions and stimulating future theorizing and research in this direction.

Even though obtaining direct support for the idea that emotions have evolved because of their social-signaling functions is a scientific utopia, several arguments and observations provide suggestive evidence for this possibility. There is abundant evidence that emotional expressions play a pivotal role in regulating social behavior in non-human primates, as reviewed previously in this book. Although such data clearly do not constitute evidence that the social functionality of emotional expressions shaped the evolution of emotions, they are consistent with this possibility. Furthermore, we know that emotional expressions help coordinate human social behavior in the present day, and there are no apparent reasons to assume that they would not have had such potential in the evolutionary past, especially since many modern-day means of coordination (including language) were not available in those times. It would seem plausible that emotional displays played a role in coordinating social interaction in the era when our humanoid ancestors started living in groups, thus contributing to the development of human ultrasociality as we know it today (Buck, 1984; Fridlund, 1994; Keltner, Shiota, & Haidt, 2006).

Providing strong support for the role of emotional displays in shaping the evolutionary trajectory of human kind will require multi-disciplinary collaborations among biologists, evolutionary theorists, archaeologists, psychologists, philosophers, and anthropologists, among others. For instance, further research into the anatomy of the facial muscles of our various evolutionary ancestors, combined with data about solitary versus group living in the respective time periods, may reveal new cues as to when certain groups of muscles that are involved in creating emotional expressions evolved, and whether the emergence of such muscles coincided with a transition toward greater sociality. As a case in point, a study by Waller, Cray, and Burrows (2008) on the anatomy of contemporary faces revealed that some facial muscles are not present in all individuals and that individuals commonly exhibit considerable asymmetry in their facial musculature (i.e., muscles are larger on one side of the face than on the other, or entirely absent on one side). Interestingly, however, the facial muscles that are essential for producing the basic emotions of happiness, sadness, anger, surprise, fear, and disgust were always present and showed minimal asymmetry. The authors concluded that "specific facial muscle structures have likely been selected to allow individuals to produce universally recognizable signals" (p. 439). Arguments and data such as these combine to create a case for the important role of emotional displays throughout our evolutionary past, but clearly more research is needed.

Measurement and separability of affective versus inferential processes

EASI theory posits that affective and inferential processes have mutually influential yet conceptually distinct and empirically separable effects on observers' behavioral responses to others' emotional expressions. It further specifies two classes of moderating influences that jointly determine the relative influence of the two processes in shaping responses to emotional displays. Even though the incorporation of two distinct processes and two groups of moderators makes the theory flexible and therefore potentially capable of accounting for a wide range of interpersonal emotional phenomena, a number of conceptual and empirical issues merit attention.

EASI theory can be seen as part of a larger family of dual-process models that aim to describe the contributions of two distinct classes of processes to judgments and behavior. A problem of some of these models is the (often implicit) assumption of "process purity," the idea that only one process drives responses in a particular situation (Sherman, Krieglmeyer, & Calanchini, 2014). In reality, it is more likely that multiple processes simultaneously contribute to individuals' (behavioral) responses to stimuli. This is why EASI's propositions pertaining to mediating processes (i.e., affective reactions and inferential processes) and the moderating influences that govern them (i.e., observers' information processing and the perceived appropriateness of emotional displays) are stated in relative rather than absolute terms. That is, the theory posits that the relative influence of inferential processes (compared to affective reactions) in driving responses to emotional expressions increases to the degree that observers are more motivated and able to engage in thorough information processing and perceive the emotional expression as appropriate in light of the social context.

Even though EASI does not make the problematic assumption of process purity, several other issues pertaining to the interplay between affective reactions and inferential processes remain. One problem is that, in general, cognitive and affective processes are not always as neatly separable as one might like them to be. Even though affect and cognition are traditionally seen as distinct building blocks of human behavior (Zajonc, 1980), it is also well established that affect and cognition are mutually influential (LeDoux, 1998). Partly due to this potential for mutual influence, the boundaries between affect and cognition become blurry in some situations, and this is also true for EASI's distinction between affective reactions and inferential processes. For instance, where lies the boundary between inferences of threat and feelings of fear? Appraisal theories of emotion (e.g., Frijda, 1986;

Ortony, Clore, & Collins, 1988; Roseman, 1984; Scherer, Schorr, & Johnstone, 2001; Smith, Haynes, Lazarus, & Pope, 1993) stress that cognitive processes (e.g., inferences of threat) give rise to emotions (e.g., feelings of fear), which implies that sharp boundaries may not always exist.

The classic studies on social referencing (Klinnert, Campos, Sorce, Emde, & Svejda, 1983; Sorce, Emde, Campos, & Klinnert, 1985) that were discussed in Chapter 2 represent another case in point. Is social referencing predominantly affective or inferential in nature? Given that very young infants are already capable of using others' emotional displays to inform their own behavior, elaborate cognitive processing does not seem to be required for social referencing to occur. At the same time, there is also no compelling evidence that social referencing is mediated by affective processes. Social referencing most likely relies on well-learned associations between emotional displays and situational features that are easily accessed when relevant events occur. It is unclear exactly how and in which proportion affective and cognitive processes contribute to this phenomenon. Indeed, teasing apart the affective and cognitive constituents of social referencing is not an easy task. Self-report measures are obviously not an option in infant research, and physiological measurements also bring about significant challenges in such samples.

To illuminate the relative contribution of affective and inferential processes in shaping responses to emotional displays, investigations of the processes underlying the social effects of emotions should ideally include direct and unambiguous measures of both types of process. However, even though numerous studies have demonstrated mediating effects of affective reactions *or* inferential processes, to date only few investigations have simultaneously incorporated measures of affective reactions *and* inferential processes in the same study. This limits the conclusions that can currently be drawn regarding the underlying mechanisms of the social effects of emotions. For instance, if only affective reactions were measured in a study and mediation is properly established, one may conclude that affective reactions play a role in driving a particular effect, but it remains unclear how that role compares to the role of inferential processes, which were not measured. Researchers who are interested in the mechanisms underlying the social effects of emotions are therefore advised to incorporate measures of affective reactions as well as inferential processes where possible.

With regard to the measurement of underlying mechanisms, the somewhat heterogeneous nature of inferential processes also poses a challenge. Whereas affective reactions to the emotional expressions of others can be measured in fairly similar ways across different social settings (i.e., in terms of reciprocal and complementary emotions and sentiments), the inferences observers may draw from others' emotional expressions take on different forms depending on the context. Surely, there is considerable common ground at an abstract level. Based on the appraisals associated with discrete emotions, expressions of anger may be interpreted as a signal of goal blockage and other blame; expressions of happiness may be taken as a sign that good progress toward goal achievement is being made; expressions of sadness may be construed as evidence of irrevocable loss and lack of control over the situation; expressions of disappointment may be interpreted as an indication that the expresser had expected a more favorable outcome; and expressions of fear may be taken as a signal of a potential threat in the environment. It is doubtful, however, whether generic measures based on these global appraisal patterns (e.g., in terms of blame, goal progress, or irrevocable loss) are able to expose the inferential processes that drive responses to others' emotional displays in specific social settings.

Consider the case of anger. Even though anger typically arises from some form of goal blockage, the more detailed content of the inferences that may be drawn from displays of anger is likely to vary considerably as a function of the social setting. For instance, displays of anger by a romantic partner may point to a particular problem in the relationship that requires attention (Averill, 1982; Fischer & Roseman, 2007). Displays of anger in a group setting may spark inferences of deviance or failure to cooperate (Lerner, Goldberg, & Tetlock, 1998). Displays of anger in a negotiation may provide information regarding the expresser's limits and toughness (Sinaceur & Tiedens, 2006; Van Kleef, De Dreu, & Manstead, 2004a). Displays of anger by a customer may be taken as a sign of poor service (Mattila & Enz, 2002). And displays of anger on the part of a leader may be interpreted as a sign of subpar follower performance (Sy, Côté, & Saavedra, 2005; Van Kleef, Homan, Beersma, Van Knippenberg, Van Knippenberg, & Damen, 2009). In light of the situation-dependent nature of inferential processes, attempts to employ generic measures of inferences across different settings seem ill advised. Instead, researchers would do well to carefully think about the most relevant inferences that may be drawn from particular emotional expressions in a particular context, and to adapt their measures accordingly.

Besides making sure to measure inferential processes at the right level of specificity, researchers may consider complementing self-report measures with implicit and/or physiological measures. Questionnaire data rely on participants' access to and accurate reports of their inferential processes. Accordingly, poor introspection and self-report failures pose a threat to the validity of questionnaire data. Whereas self-report measures of affective processes can be complemented with physiological measures (e.g., heart rate, blood pressure, cardiac output, skin conductance) that help to circumvent problems of introspection and self-report (Kreibig, 2010; Mauss & Robinson, 2009), such measures are not suitable for assessing cognitive processes. However, in research designs that allow for the incorporation of implicit measures, situation-specific adaptations of procedures such as the lexical decision task (Meyer & Schvaneveldt, 1971), the implicit association test (Greenwald, McGhee, & Schwartz, 1998), and the affect misattribution paradigm (Payne, Cheng, Govorun, & Stewart, 2005) may provide additional insight into the contents of participants' inferential processes. In addition, some experimental designs allow for the measurement of neural activation in response to emotional expressions (e.g., using event-related fMRI), which provides yet another window on the cognitive processes that are involved in the processing of emotional expressions (Phan, Wager, Taylor, & Liberzon, 2002; Sato, Kochiyama, Yoshikawa, Naito, & Matsumura, 2004; Vuilleumier, 2005).

Another approach to separating the influences of affective reactions and inferential processes might be through multinomial modelling. This is a statistical technique that involves estimating hypothetical parameters to quantify the influence of multiple (unobservable) processes (Riefer & Batchelder, 1988). Multinomial modelling is frequently used in cognitive psychology to study the simultaneous influence of multiple processes, but it has so far not been applied to the study of emotions. It would seem worthwhile to examine the applicability of multinomial modelling as a way of simultaneously representing the contribution of affective reactions and inferential processes to observers' responses to emotional displays in mathematical terms.

Expanding the repertoire of emotional expressions

Even though research in recent decades has made considerable progress in enhancing insight into the interpersonal dynamics of emotion, current understanding is limited by a number of theoretical and methodological constraints that are evident in much of the extant literature on the social effects of emotions. Many of these constraints relate to the rather simplified ways in which emotional expressions tend to be conceptualized and operationalized. These caveats point to fruitful directions for future research.

The need to go (further) beyond valence

There still is a tendency in the literature to conceptualize emotions in terms of their positive or negative valence, although this practice differs somewhat between research domains (as discussed in Chapter 10). The theoretical framework and literature review presented in this book challenge the valence approach. We have seen, for instance, that dominance-related emotions such as anger and contempt, supplication emotions such as sadness and disappointment, and appeasement emotions such as guilt and embarrassment have qualitatively different interpersonal effects, even though all of these emotions share a negative valence. Together with a considerable body of research on the intrapersonal effects of emotions on judgment and behavior (e.g., Bodenhausen, Sheppard, & Kramer, 1994; DeSteno, Petty, Wegener, & Rucker, 2000; Keltner, Ellsworth, & Edwards, 1993; Lerner & Keltner, 2001; Tiedens & Linton, 2001), the conclusions that emerge from the interpersonal approach to emotion suggest that there is greater promise in conceptualizing emotions in terms of their unique appraisal patterns, action tendencies, and associated social signals than in terms of their valence. For instance, the "core relational themes" of anger and guilt are other-blame and self-blame, respectively (Smith et al., 1993), which helps to explain why they have opposite effects – displays of anger may help to enforce cooperation, whereas displays of guilt may invite exploitation (Van Kleef, De Dreu, & Manstead, 2010).

Even though emerging evidence points to the differential effects of discrete negative emotional expressions, the potential differential effects of positive emotional expressions remain a blind spot. Research on the social effects of positive emotions tends to be limited to happiness (Sauter, 2010). However, as is the case for negative emotions, positive emotions can be differentiated on the basis of their underlying appraisal patterns, their accompanying action tendencies, and their social signals (Leach, Spears, & Manstead, 2015). For instance, even though pride and gratitude are both positively valenced, the implied locus of responsibility for the positive state of affairs that triggered the emotion is different. As per appraisal theories of emotion (Frijda, 1986; Ortony et al., 1988; Roseman, 1984; Scherer et al., 2001; Smith et al., 1993), pride implies that responsibility for positive outcomes resides in the self, whereas gratitude implies that responsibility is located in another person. The question thus arises whether different positive emotions have different social effects, as is the case for negative emotions. For example, it is conceivable that positive emotions with an other-focus (e.g., gratitude, awe) elicit different types of responses than positive emotions with a self-focus (e.g., pride, self-content). Furthermore, positive emotions that are associated with different degrees of certainty (e.g., relief vs. hope) can be expected to trigger different kinds of inferences in observers and to evoke different reactions.

In light of these and other findings and considerations, future research would do well to measure or manipulate discrete emotions rather than more diffuse positive versus negative mood states whenever this is feasible. Failure to do so will result in an overly simplistic picture of the social effects of emotions. However, studying the differential effects of discrete emotional expressions is not an easy task. Although several emotions have clearly distinguishable facial expressions and bodily postures (e.g., anger, happiness, disgust, sadness, fear, pride, embarrassment, contempt, surprise), the nonverbal behavioral patterns of other emotions are less clear or at least not widely supported by systematic validation studies (e.g., guilt, regret, gratitude, disappointment, hope). This makes studying the interpersonal effects of such emotions a challenging enterprise.

One way around this problem is to use explicit verbal manipulations of emotional expressions, as has been done in several studies on the interpersonal effects of anger, happiness, guilt, sadness, disappointment, and contempt (e.g., Adam, Shirako, & Maddux, 2010; Clark & Taraban, 1991; Lelieveld, Van Dijk, Van Beest, & Van Kleef, 2013; Melwani & Barsade, 2011; Van Kleef, De Dreu, & Manstead, 2004a, 2006). However, as noted in the previous chapter, there are limits to this approach, especially in terms of lack of social richness. Another solution is to use correlational designs, in which the self-reported emotions of one person are used to predict the responses of another person (e.g., Anderson, Keltner, & John, 2003; Van Kleef et al., 2008). However, this method is limited by the fact that not all experienced emotions are expressed, and even if they are expressed they may not be recognized as such, especially if the profile of nonverbal displays of the emotion under study is unclear. A third option is to ask participants which emotions they perceived in another person and to record their (behavioral) responses (e.g., Grandey, Fisk, Mattila, Jansen, & Sideman, 2005; Pugh, 2001). Even though this approach can provide insight into how people may respond to the emotions they perceive in others, it does not speak to the question of whether the emotion that was perceived was actually experienced by the expresser.

Given the inherent limitations of each of these methods, robust conclusions regarding the differential effects of discrete emotional displays will require multimethod studies involving combinations of verbal and nonverbal expressions of emotions and subjective ratings of those emotions from the expresser as well as the perceiver. Furthermore, it will be important to invest in basic research aimed at pinpointing the configurations of nonverbal (facial) behavior associated with several discrete emotions whose expressive patterns are as yet unmapped.

The mystery of mixed and dynamic emotions

Almost without exception, studies on the social effects of emotions have examined the effects of "pure" expressions of a single emotion. Even though such investigations may capture a considerable portion of everyday emotional dynamics, there are at least three notable ways in which this research could be meaningfully extended by considering more intricate patterns of emotional expression. First, research on everyday emotional experiences has shown that individuals commonly experience blends of emotions in daily life (Scherer & Tannenbaum, 1986). These blends may even comprise emotions of different valence. For instance, individuals reported that they simultaneously experienced happiness and sadness on graduation day (Larsen, McGraw, & Cacioppo, 2001). Similarly, the emotional experience of nostalgia has been demonstrated to consist of a combination of positive and negative affective states (Sedikides, Wildschut, Arndt, & Routledge, 2008). To the degree that such mixed emotional experiences are expressed in perceptible ways, they may evoke social responses from others. However, the interpersonal effects of mixed emotional displays are uncharted territory.

Second, people may be confronted with different emotional expressions from two or more other individuals, be it simultaneously or in close succession. Early qualitative evidence suggests that the alternation or simultaneous expression of positive and negative emotions between two people (i.e., one person expressing positive emotions at a target and the other expressing negative emotions, as in a good-cop/bad-cop routine) may be an effective means of gaining compliance (Rafaeli & Sutton, 1991). The authors of this study proposed that the disparity between positive and negative emotional expressions creates a perceptual contrast in perceivers that enhances the perceived positivity and negativity of the respective expressions. Targets would then presumably comply with the expressers' requests either because they want to escape the interaction with the "bad cop" or to reciprocate the perceived kindness of the "good cop," or because they believe that doing so is in their own best interest. More research is needed to further substantiate these intriguing possibilities.

Third, individuals often display emotions that change over time. It is interesting to ponder how observers may respond to such dynamic emotional displays, especially in light of theoretical arguments that the signaling function of emotions derives from the fact that emotions change in response to relevant events (Frijda, 1986; Kuppens, Oravecz, & Tuerlinckx, 2010; Scherer, 2009). Although research is scarce, two negotiation studies suggest that changing emotions elicit different inferential processes, affective reactions, and behavioral responses from interaction partners than stable emotional expressions. Filipowicz, Barsade, and Melwani (2011) found that negotiators who first expressed happiness and then switched to anger during a negotiation elicited more favorable impressions and larger concessions from counterparts than negotiators who consistently expressed anger. The emotional transition from happiness to anger elicited more situational and less dispositional attributions, whereas steady-state anger elicited more dispositional and less situational attributions. In addition, there was evidence of emotional contagion, such that the initial happiness of the expresser was caught by observers and carried over as a positive emotional buffer for subsequent expressions of anger. In a related vein, Sinaceur, Adam, Van Kleef, and Galinsky (2013) found that negotiators who alternated several times between expressing anger and expressing happiness were able to claim more value in a negotiation than negotiators who consistently expressed anger or happiness. Such emotional inconsistency helped to extract concessions from counterparts because it made them feel less in control over the situation.

These studies can be seen as a proof of concept in that they indicate that changing emotional expressions can elicit markedly different responses from observers than stable emotional expressions, but they have merely begun to scratch the surface. The previous studies considered changes of emotions across valence (i.e., from positive to negative or vice versa), but changes across other dimensions than valence remain to be explored (e.g., changes in intensity and/or in appraisals related to blame, control, and uncertainty). For instance, what might observers infer when an interaction partner's emotional expressions change from sadness to anger, or from anger to fear? And how would they subsequently respond to such expressions? Clearly, future research is needed to shed more light on the effects of such intricate configurations of emotional expressions. Moreover, it remains to be investigated how such effects are modulated by factors such as the observer's information processing and the perceived appropriateness of the emotional displays.

The role of emotional intensity

Another aspect that has been largely overlooked so far concerns the intensity of emotional expressions. It seems intuitively plausible that emotional expressions have different effects depending on their intensity, but it is currently unknown exactly how intensity moderates the effects of emotional expressions. On the one hand, one could argue that more intense emotional expressions are interpreted by perceivers as signaling more urgent information, which would point to a linear relationship between emotion intensity and outcomes. On the other hand, EASI theory posits that emotional expressions that are perceived as overly intense are likely to elicit negative affective reactions in observers, which may counteract the effects of inferential processes. This suggests that there is an optimal level of intensity at which emotional expressions convey clear information without evoking negative reactions.

This idea resonates with Geddes and Callister's (2007) dual threshold model of anger (see Chapter 10), which postulates that anger can only have beneficial interpersonal effects when it is expressed in perceptible ways while the expression does not cross the "impropriety threshold." In keeping with this model, a field study across different organizations indicated that anger can have positive or negative consequences depending on the intensity with which it is displayed and the appropriateness of the display in light of organizational norms (Gibson, Schweitzer, Callister, & Gray, 2009). Similarly, a study on the effects of anger expressions of customer service representatives pointed to the interactive effects of anger intensity and cultural display rules in shaping the effects of anger expressions, which could be explained in terms of the perceived appropriateness of the expressions (Glikson, Rafaeli, & Wirtz, 2015). Thus, in the case of anger, it appears as though the likelihood of positive social consequences is best conceptualized as a curvilinear rather than a linear function of expression intensity.

Although the differential social effects of expressions of anger at different levels of intensity have thus begun to be addressed, the role of intensity in shaping the interpersonal effects of other emotions remains unclear. Preliminary findings from a customer service study suggest that mild expressions of happiness and sadness on the part of service employees have more favorable effects on customers than more intense expressions (Cheshin, Amit, & Van Kleef, 2015), suggesting that the effects of these emotions also follow a curvilinear pattern, but clearly more research is needed to substantiate this tentative conclusion. In addition, it would be interesting to examine whether the effects of emotional intensity depend on the perceiver's information-processing motivation and ability.

Integral versus incidental emotions

The studies reviewed in this book differ in the degree to which the cause of an emotion was clear to the observer of the emotional expression. In many studies, respondents were confronted with emotional displays of another person (e.g., a spouse, a fellow group member, a negotiation partner, a customer service representative, a leader) that were not explicitly connected to a particular antecedent event, whereas in other studies the emotional expression was explicitly related to a particular situation or an action. Interestingly, however, to date no studies have directly compared the interpersonal effects of emotions with a known versus an unknown cause. Yet there are theoretical reasons to assume that knowledge regarding the antecedent event that triggered an emotional expression makes a difference.

One way of approaching this problem is in terms of the distinction between integral and incidental emotions (Lerner, Small, & Loewenstein, 2004). Integral emotions arise during the particular social interaction of interest, whereas incidental emotions are spillovers from other situations. Classic research on the intrapersonal effects of emotions indicates that this difference matters. For instance, Schwarz and Clore's (1983) affect-as-information model describes how a person's judgments may be influenced by a positive or negative mood evoked by an unrelated and irrelevant event (i.e., an incidental mood state). According to this perspective, stronger affective influences occur when ambiguity regarding the source of one's mood leads one to *misattribute* the mood to the target of judgment, such as when a cheerful mood arising from beautiful weather is used to guide responses to questions about one's life satisfaction. Thus, stronger intrapersonal affective influences may be expected in the case of incidental as opposed to integral affect.

The distinction between incidental and integral emotions can be extended to the interpersonal level of analysis, where it might play out quite differently. Emotional expressions that are explicitly connected to an antecedent cause potentially contain more diagnostic information than emotional expressions whose history is unclear. In other words, integral emotional expressions provide more input for inferential processes than incidental emotional expressions. At the same time, both types of emotional expressions may trigger affective reactions. Logically, then, all else being equal, the relative influence of inferential processes compared to affective reactions can be expected to be stronger in the case of integral emotional expressions than in the case of incidental emotional expressions, which means that the two types of emotional expressions may have different downstream consequences. The possible differential processes and effects of integral versus incidental emotional displays represent a promising area for future research.

Temporal issues regarding the social effects of emotions

So far, studies on the social effects of emotions have focused almost exclusively on the immediate consequences of short-lasting episodes of emotional expressions. Even though this research has revealed a lot about the mechanisms and contingencies of the social effects of emotions, the bulk of the literature is limited by several temporal constraints. These limitations open up a number of interesting avenues for future research.

Long-term consequences of emotional expressions

One basic issue that is surprisingly poorly understood is how emotional expressions influence relationships, social interactions, and behavior over time. A few studies indicate that the effects of emotional expressions may extend beyond the immediacy of the current encounter. For instance, a negotiation study showed that the inferences that negotiators draw from their counterpart's emotions may continue to influence behavior in later interactions with the same person (Van Kleef & De Dreu, 2010). In a second encounter with an opponent who had previously expressed anger, participants conceded again because they believed that the opponent had ambitious limits, even when that person expressed no emotion during the second encounter. Another study found that the effects of expressions of anger in groups on conformity of deviant group members were still manifest three weeks after the anger expression (Heerdink, Van Kleef, Homan, & Fischer, 2013). Studies such as these indicate that emotional displays may have longer-term consequences that remained off the radar in most investigations. Clearly, however, more research is needed to clarify the boundary conditions of such longer-term effects and to establish whether they are limited to anger or generalize to other emotions.

Harker and Keltner (2001) took a different approach to the issue of longer-term effects by exploring in a longitudinal study whether the emotional displays of young women on their college yearbook photos predicted several aspects of the women's life trajectories. Their study (which is discussed in detail in Chapter 5) revealed that greater smile intensity predicted marital status and relationship satisfaction up to thirty years later. Although it is unclear to what extent these effects can be attributed to the interpersonal effects of smiling per se or to third variables associated with smiling behavior, the study highlights the intriguing possibility that individual differences in the propensity to smile can have a pervasive impact on important personal and social outcomes over the lifespan.

In light of these and other suggestive findings, it seems worthwhile to initiate more systematic research into the longer-term consequences of emotional expressions across domains of social interaction. For instance, it is interesting to consider the possibility that the emotional styles of group members contribute, over time, to the emergence, negotiation, and consolidation of stable group roles and processes (Keltner & Haidt, 1999). It is also possible that relationship partners' patterns of emotional expression shape recurring interpersonal processes in close relationships. Questions such as these await empirical examination. Furthermore, it would be interesting to investigate whether and how the longer-term effects of emotional expressions depend on the specific emotion in question, on its intensity, and on factors such as the observer's information processing and the perceived appropriateness of the emotional display. Addressing issues such as these will further enhance understanding of the interpersonal dynamics of emotions.

The frequency of emotional expressions

Another neglected temporal issue in the study of the social effects of emotions concerns the frequency with which emotions are expressed. In most studies conducted so far, respondents were confronted with one emotional expression or a few emotional expressions, upon which their responses were recorded. It is unclear whether and how the social consequences of emotions depend on the frequency with which they are expressed, yet there are reasons to assume that frequency of expression matters. It has long been established that organisms become progressively less responsive to stimuli that are repeated over time (Thompson & Spencer, 1966). It is conceivable that such habituation also occurs for responses to emotional displays. This would imply that one person's emotions come to exert weaker social effects on another person to the extent that they are expressed more often in the presence of that person.

A more fine-grained pattern is suggested by attribution theories (e.g., Weiner, 1986). The logic of such approaches suggests that behavior that is exhibited repeatedly by a particular person across different situations becomes more likely to be attributed to dispositions of that person than to characteristics of the situation. Extending this argument to the case of emotional expressions, it is conceivable that emotional expressions are perceived as more diagnostic about the expresser to the extent that they occur more frequently, whereas they would be perceived as more diagnostic about the situation to the degree that they occur less frequently. For instance, if a leader gets angry several times a week, followers may come to attribute the anger to the leader's personality, but if the leader only sporadically gets angry, followers may be more likely to connect the anger with a particular event or situation. Thus, individuals may distill qualitatively different kinds of information from others' emotional expressions depending on the frequency of the expressions. In addition, the frequency of emotional expressions may influence their perceived appropriateness, which would in turn shift the relative predictive strength of inferential processes and affective reactions on observers' behavioral responses, as per EASI theory. These and many other possibilities remain to be tested.

Feedback loops and reciprocal emotional influence

The extant literature on the social effects of emotions is also limited in the sense that research has focused almost exclusively on unidirectional effects, which were in most cases isolated from their temporal context. That is, the typical study would examine how one person's emotional displays influenced another person, without considering how the observer's response might subsequently influence the expresser. Clearly, however, in many real-life interactions one person's response to another's emotional expression is not the end point of the interaction but may set in motion further interpersonal processes (Hareli & Rafaeli, 2008; Walter & Bruch, 2008). Even though the potential importance of such feedback loops and processes of reciprocal emotional influence has been acknowledged in the literature, empirical research is lacking.

Two types of processes seem particularly relevant from the perspective of the interpersonal dynamics of emotion. First, an observer's behavioral response to another person's emotional expression may influence the original expresser's emotional display, which may in turn influence the observer (this process is visualized by the feedback arrow in Figure 10.1 in the previous chapter). For instance, someone who expresses anger at another person for failing to deliver on a promise may tone it down after the other promised to make up for the mistake, and the softened emotional expression may in turn encourage the other to act out his or her good intentions. Second, the original expresser's emotional display may evoke an emotional expression in the observer, which may in turn trigger affective and inferential processes and behavioral responses in the original expresser. Thus, two parallel instances of interpersonal emotional influence may emerge within the same interaction, in which both parties simultaneously act as expresser and as observer. All the variables that are depicted in Figure 10.1 would then factor into the affective reactions, inferential processes, and behavioral responses of both parties, and the resulting processes may further interact in ways that remain to be investigated. Although such investigations promise to be challenging, analytical approaches such as the Actor-Partner Interaction Model (Kenny, Kashy, & Cook, 2006) may help to separate the simultaneous reciprocal processes of emotional influence in dyads.

The social effects of anticipated emotions

A final temporal limitation of the extant body of research is that it has only addressed the effects of emotional expressions that already took place. Although at first blush it seems nonsensical to consider the interpersonal effects of nonexpressed emotions, a large literature on the intrapersonal effects of anticipated emotions suggests that there is value in entertaining the consequences of emotions that are not (yet) manifest (e.g., Mellers & McGraw, 2001; Perugini & Bagozzi, 2001; Zeelenberg, 1999). This literature has documented that human decision making is influenced by the anticipated emotions that are associated with the outcomes of choice alternatives (for a recent review, see Lerner, Li, Valdesolo, & Kassam, 2015). Furthermore, a recent study showed that the emotional expressions of other people in response to certain events may trigger anticipated emotions in observers, which in turn shape their behavior (Van der Schalk, Kuppens, Bruder, & Manstead, 2014). Participants in this study were exposed to a person who expressed pride or regret after having made a fair or unfair proposal in an economic game. Expressions of regret about acting fairly resulted in a lower likelihood of subsequent fair behavior on the part of participants compared to expressions of pride, whereas expressions of regret about acting unfairly resulted in a greater likelihood of subsequent fair behavior compared to expressions of pride. The effect of the other's emotional expressions on participants' behavior was mediated by participants' own anticipated pride and regret.

The logic of the intrapersonal effects of people's own anticipated emotions can be relatively straightforwardly extrapolated to the interpersonal level of analysis. People may learn through repeated interactions that certain behaviors tend to evoke anger in another person, and the expectation that anger will result if the behavior is shown may lead them to refrain from showing it in the first place. Conversely, people may deliberately decide to engage in behaviors that they know will make others whom they care about feel good. Thus, much as actual emotional expressions can serve as incentives or deterrents for behavior (Cacioppo & Gardner, 1999; Keltner & Haidt, 1999), so may anticipated emotional expressions.

Such interpersonal effects of anticipated emotions would appear to play a prominent role across domains of life, for instance in child-rearing, romantic relationships, and leader–follower interactions. A daughter who knows that her father will be proud of her when she eats her vegetables may be more inclined to finish her plate. Someone who goes out with colleagues after work may decide to have one less drink because she realizes that her partner will be sad if she comes home late for dinner. And an employee may work a little harder to make a deadline because he anticipates that his boss will get angry if he misses it. Future research could explore whether such interpersonal effects of anticipated emotions indeed occur, and whether and how they are modulated by factors such as the anticipator's information-processing motivation and ability.

Broadening the outlook on the social context

It is clear from the present review and analysis that the interpersonal dynamics of emotions are heavily shaped by the social context within which they occur. Emotional expressions take on different meanings depending on the situation and depending on characteristics of the expresser and the perceiver, and such differences have implications for the perceived appropriateness of the displays and for observers' subsequent responses. Scientific understanding of the social effects of emotions would benefit from more research into various aspects of the social context, of which I provide a few examples below.

Culture

The vast majority of studies on the social effects of emotions have been conducted within Western samples and contexts, even though there is a steadily growing body of research on the effects of emotional expressions in East Asian cultures. Very few researchers have examined the social effects of emotions in other areas of the world, such as South America, Africa, or the Middle East. One obvious direction for future research would thus be to examine the generalizability of emerging patterns in the social effects of emotions to these neglected regions of the world. Several findings indicate that such research is needed to develop a proper understanding of the interpersonal dynamics of emotion.

Although there are striking similarities in how emotions are expressed across cultures (Ekman, 1994), research has also documented cultural influences on several aspects of the emotion process, including experience, expression, regulation, and recognition (e.g., Elfenbein & Ambady, 2002b; Markus & Kitayama, 1991; Mesquita & Frijda, 1992). Partly related to the notion of emotional display rules (see Chapter 4), research has documented differences in the way individuals across cultures think about emotions. For instance, whereas Americans associate happiness with personal achievement, Japanese associate it with social harmony (Uchida & Kitayama, 2009). At the same time, this study suggested that Japanese are more aware than Americans of the potential negative side of happiness (e.g., social disruption, the envy of others) and the positive side of distress (e.g., the sympathy of others). Besides pointing to cross-cultural differences in the interpretation of emotions, these findings shed further doubt on the usefulness of conceptualizing emotions as positive versus negative (see Chapter 10).

With regard to social norms about the experience and expression of emotions, Matsumoto (1990) found that Japanese people tend to accept expressions of negative emotions toward lower-status individuals, because such expressions serve to uphold power distances that are valued in the Japanese culture. In comparison, Americans are less tolerant of negative emotions directed at lower-status individuals because such expressions highlight hierarchical differences that are at odds with the emphasis on equality in the American culture. Research by Eid and Diener (2001) further showed that pride and contentment are more desirable in individualistic cultures such as North America and Australia than in collectivistic cultures such as China and Taiwan, whereas no such differences emerged for joy and affection. Moreover, Americans and Australians appear to face stronger pressures than Chinese and Taiwanese to express pleasant emotions. Eid and Diener concluded that "deviation from this norm of happiness might have a substantial impact, and being unhappy might be regarded as a failure" (p. 880).

In light of the considerable literature on cross-cultural differences in display rules (Matsumoto et al., 2008) and emotion recognition (Elfenbein & Ambady, 2002b), it is surprising that only a few studies have begun to examine how culture shapes behavioral responses to others' emotional expressions. The rare exceptions reported by Kopelman and Rosette (2008) and Adam and colleagues (Adam et al., 2010; Adam & Shirako, 2013) were discussed in Chapter 7. These studies indicate that the social effects of emotional expressions in negotiations are moderated by the cultural backgrounds of both the expresser and the perceiver. Consistent with EASI theory, the moderating role of the perceiver's culture could be explained in terms of the perceived appropriateness of the emotional expressions, which differed systematically between cultures. These studies thus show that display rules play a theoretically meaningful role in shaping the behavioral consequences of emotional expressions across cultures, but clearly much more work needs to be done in this domain before solid conclusions can be drawn.

Another caveat is that much cross-cultural research operates on the basis of very broad conceptions of cultural differences (e.g., Easterners vs. Westerners), which do not do justice to the complexity of actual differences. It is also common to conceptualize cultural differences in terms of collectivism versus individualism, and this tendency goes at the expense of other relevant cultural differences that tend to remain off the radar. For instance, the aforementioned study by Matsumoto (1990) indicates that the cultural dimension of power distance is important for understanding cultural differences in social responses to emotional expressions. Moreover, effects of emotional expressions that are at odds with cultural norms of collectivism versus individualism or high versus low power distance may in turn be moderated by differences in tightness–looseness, yet another dimension of cultural differences. Tight cultures have many strong norms and a low tolerance of deviant behavior, whereas loose cultures have weak norms and a high tolerance of deviant behavior (Triandis, 1989). It seems plausible that emotional deviance from prevailing norms would have more adverse consequences in tight rather than loose cultures. Future studies should move beyond the individualism–collectivism dimension to paint a more complete picture of the ways in which culture shapes the interpersonal dynamics of emotion.

Finally, besides investigating cultural influences on affective and behavioral responses to emotional expressions, it would be worthwhile examining how cultural differences modulate the inferential processes that are triggered in observers by other people's emotional expressions. Given that people from different cultures have different associations with certain emotions (e.g., associating happiness with personal success vs. social harmony; Uchida & Kitayama, 2009), it seems plausible that observers of emotional expressions would also reach different conclusions about the appraisals of the expresser that gave rise to the emotion depending on their own cultural background. Future research is needed to uncover how culture shapes the content of the inferences individuals draw on the basis of others' emotional expressions.

The neglected option of "moving away"

Behavioral responses to the emotional expressions of others can be conceptualized in terms of Horney's (1945) classic distinction between "moving towards," "moving away," and "moving against" tendencies (Van Kleef, De Dreu, & Manstead, 2010). To date, research on the interpersonal effects of emotions has focused almost exclusively on behavioral responses that can be construed as instantiations of moving toward (e.g., providing support to one's partner, conforming to the majority position in a group, making concessions in a negotiation, spreading positive word of mouth about a store, exerting effort on behalf of a leader) or moving against (e.g., arguing with one's partner, deviating from the majority position in a group, making competitive demands in a negotiation, spreading negative word of mouth about a store, refusing to exert effort on behalf of a leader). Very little is known about when observers of emotional expressions may decide to avoid or end the interaction with the expresser, that is, when they choose to move away. The lion's share of research on the social effects of emotions is silent with regard to this question. This is due in large part to the fact that most (laboratory) studies do not afford participants an option to leave the situation. A notable exception is the literature on customer service (which is dominated by field studies rather than experiments), where customers' decisions to revisit a store or not make up a prominent dependent variable. Not revisiting a store can be seen as an instance of moving away.

The relative neglect of moving away tendencies poses a threat to the validity of studies on the social effects of emotions whose focus is on behavioral outcomes. In many real-life situations individuals have the option of ending the interaction or dissolving the interdependent relationship. Married couples may divorce, people may leave groups that they no longer enjoy being a part of, negotiators may seek a better deal with another partner, employees may find a job elsewhere, and followers may try to avoid their boss. By failing to incorporate such moving away responses in empirical studies, researchers may inadvertently force participants into certain behavioral tendencies, and this in turn may bias the conclusions we reach about the interpersonal effects of emotions. When the natural tendency to move away cannot be realized simply because that option is not made available, we may erroneously conclude that people freely show particular behaviors. The work by Heerdink and colleagues (2013) on conformity versus deviance in groups provides a case in point. Their studies indicated that expressions of anger on the part of fellow group members can, under particular circumstances, lead targets to conform to the majority's position. However, in a study in which the authors explicitly built in the option, in one condition, of leaving the group for another group, almost 60 percent of the participants who were confronted with expressions of anger chose that option. Future research on the social effects of emotional expressions would therefore do well to incorporate the option of moving away, especially if such an option is typically available in the types of situations that the study attempts to model.

Exploring the social effects of emotions in new domains

A final suggestion for future research is to expand our investigations of the social effects of emotions beyond the social settings that have been studied so far. The literature review presented in Part II of this book shows that many facets of the interpersonal dynamics of emotions have been examined across a wide range of settings, but many exciting new horizons remain to be explored. For instance, the view of emotions as social information is highly relevant to developmental psychology and clinical psychology. Indeed, although the amount of empirical research on the interpersonal effects of emotions in these disciplines is limited, several classic studies have been conducted in these areas (see Chapters 2 and 5). Furthermore, in the last decade, the interpersonal approach to emotions has begun to attract interest in the fields of political science (Richards, 2004), sports psychology (Friesen et al., 2013), and criminology (Leys, Licata, Marchal, & Bernard, 2012; Wrede, Ask, & Strömwall, 2015). Numerous interesting questions remain to be addressed in these various fields. For instance, can sports coaches boost the performance of their teams by expressing certain emotions? How do parents' emotional expressions influence their children's moral development? How should behavioral therapists regulate their emotions in order to create good rapport with their clients and also bring about the desired behavioral change? And how can political candidates best manage their emotions to garner support from the electorate? Exploring these and other questions will allow the study of the social effects of emotions to continue to blossom in the decades to come.

Coda

A thorough understanding of the intrinsically social nature of emotions requires a focus on their interpersonal dynamics. We do not just feel our emotions; we express them in the presence of others, and others in turn respond. Even though there are cultural dialects in emotion expression and cross-cultural variations in emotion perception, these differences are insignificant compared to the insurmountable incompatibility of most verbal languages. Wherever we travel, our emotional displays allow us to express our desires and intentions to others in a way that enables at least rudimentary communication. Emotions, then, constitute the only actual world language. In spite of the widely studied intrapersonal effects of emotions, their social-communicative functions may very well be emotions' primary raison d'être.

References

Adam, H., & Shirako, A. (2013). Not all anger is created equal: The impact of the expresser's culture on the social effects of anger in negotiations. *Journal of Applied Psychology*, 98, 785–798.

Adam, H., Shirako, A., & Maddux, W. W. (2010). Cultural variance in the interpersonal effects of anger in negotiations. *Psychological Science*, 21, 882–889.

Adelmann, P. K., & Zajonc, R. B. (1989). Facial efference and the experience of emotion. *Annual Review of Psychology*, 40, 249–280.

Adolphs, R., Tranel, D., Damasio, H., & Damasio, A. (1994). Impaired recognition of emotion in facial expressions following bilateral damage to the human amygdala. *Nature*, 372, 669–672.

Allred, K. G. (1999). Anger and retaliation: Toward an understanding of impassioned conflict in organizations. *Research on Negotiation in Organizations*, 7, 27–58.

Allred, K. G., Mallozzi, J. S., Matsui, F., & Raia, C. P. (1997). The influence of anger and compassion on negotiation performance. *Organizational Behavior and Human Decision Processes*, 70, 175–187.

Amabile, T. M., Barsade, S. G., Mueller, J. S., & Staw, B. M. (2005). Affect and creativity at work. *Administrative Science Quarterly*, 50, 367–403.

Ames, D. R., & Johar, G. V. (2009). I'll know what you're like when I see how you feel: How and when affective displays influence behavior-based impressions. *Psychological Science*, 20, 586–593.

Anderson, C., Keltner, D., & John, O. P. (2003). Emotional convergence between people over time. *Journal of Personality and Social Psychology*, 84, 1054–1068.

Anderson, C., & Kilduff, G. J. (2009). Why do dominant personalities attain influence in face-to-face groups? The competence-signaling effects of trait dominance. *Journal of Personality and Social Psychology*, 96, 491–503.

Anderson, P. A., & Guerrero, L. K. (1998). *The handbook of communication and emotion*. San Diego, CA: Academic Press.

Andrade, E. B., & Ho, T.-H. (2007). How is the boss's mood today? I want a raise. *Psychological Science*, 18, 668–671.

Andrade, E. B., & Ho, T.-H. (2009). Gaming emotions in social interactions. *Journal of Consumer Research*, 36, 539–551.

Andrew, R. J. (1963). The origin and evolution of the calls and facial expressions of the primates. *Behaviour*, 20, 1–109.

Andrew, R. J. (1965). The origins of facial expressions. *Scientific American*, 213, 88–94.

Argyle, M., Alkema, F., & Gilmour, R. (1972). The communication of friendly and hostile attitudes by verbal and non-verbal signals. *European Journal of Social Psychology*, 1, 385–402.

Aristotle, J. R. (350BCE/2004). *The Nicomachean studies* (J. A. K. Thompson, Trans.). New York: Oxford University Press.

Ashby, F. G., Isen, A. M., & Turken, A. U. (1999). A neuropsychological theory of positive affect and its influence on cognition. *Psychological Bulletin*, 106, 529–550.

Ashforth, B. E., & Humphrey, R. H. (1993). Emotional labor in service roles: The influence of identity. *Academy of Management Review*, 18, 88–115.

Ashkanasy, N. M., & Tse, B. (2000). Transformational leadership as management of emotion: A conceptual review. In N. M. Ashkanasy, C. E. Härtel, & W. J. Zerbe, (Eds.), *Emotions in the workplace: Research, theory, and practice* (pp. 221–235). Westport, CT: Quorum Books/Greenwood Publishing Group.

Averill, J. R. (1982). *Anger and aggression*. New York: Springer.

Aviezer, H., Trope, Y., & Todorov, A. (2012). Body cues, not facial expressions, discriminate between intense positive and negative emotions. *Science*, 338, 1225–1229.

Baccus, J. R., Baldwin, M. W., & Packer, D. J. (2004). Increasing implicit self-esteem through classical conditioning. *Psychological Science*, 15, 498–502.

Bachman, G. F., & Guerrero, L. K. (2006). Forgiveness, apology, and communicative responses to hurtful events. *Communication Reports*, 19, 45–56.

Barclay, L. J., Skarlicki, D. P., & Pugh, S. D. (2005). Exploring the role of emotions in injustice perceptions and retaliation. *Journal of Applied Psychology*, 90, 629–643.

Barger, P. B., & Grandey, A. A. (2006). Service with a smile and encounter satisfaction: Emotional contagion and appraisal mechanisms. *Academy of Management Journal*, 49, 1229–1238.

Barnett, M. A., Howard, J. A., Melton, E. M., & Dino, G. A. (1982). Effect of inducing sadness about self or other on helping behavior in high- and low-empathic children. *Child Development*, 53, 920–923.

Baron, R. A., Neuman, J. H., & Geddes, D. (1999). Social and personal determinants of workplace aggression: Evidence for the impact of perceived injustice and the type A behavior pattern. *Aggressive Behavior*, 25, 281–296.

Barry, B., & Oliver, R. L. (1996). Affect in dyadic negotiation: A model and propositions. *Organizational Behavior and Human Decision Processes*, 67, 127–143.

Barsade, S. G. (2002). The ripple effect: Emotional contagion and its influence on group behavior. *Administrative Science Quarterly*, 47, 644–675.

Barsade, S. G., & Gibson, D. E. (1998). Group emotion: A view from top and bottom. In D. Gruenfeld, E. Mannix, & M. Neale (Eds.), *Research on managing groups and teams* (pp. 81–102). Stamford, CT: JAI Press.

Barsade, S. G., Ward, A. J., Turner, J. D. F., & Sonnenfeld, J. A. (2000). To your heart's content: A model of affective diversity in top management teams. *Administrative Science Quarterly*, 45, 802–836.

Barsalou, L. W., Niedenthal, P. M., Barbey, A. K., & Ruppert, J. A. (2003). Social embodiment. In B. H. Ross (Ed.), *The psychology of learning and motivation, Vol. 43: Advances in research and theory* (pp. 43–92). New York: Academic Press.

Bartel, C. A., & Saavedra, R. (2000). The collective construction of work group moods. *Administrative Science Quarterly*, 45, 197–231.

Bartholow, B. D., Fabiani, M., Gratton, G., & Bettencourt, B. A. (2001). A psychophysiological examination of cognitive processing of and affective responses to social expectancy violations. *Psychological Science*, 12, 197–204.

Bass, B. M. (1985). *Leadership and performance beyond expectations*. New York: Free Press.

Bass, B. M., & Riggio, R. E. (2005). *Transformational leadership* (2nd ed.). Mahwah, NJ: Erlbaum.

Bateman, T. S., & Organ, D. W. (1983). Job satisfaction and the good soldier: The relationship between affect and employee "citizenship." *Academy of Management Journal*, 26, 587–595.

Batra, R., & Stayman, D. M. (1990). The role of mood in advertising effectiveness. *Journal of Consumer Research*, 17, 203–214.

Batson, C. D., Fultz, J., & Schoenrade, P. A. (1987). Distress and empathy: Two qualitatively distinct vicarious emotions with different motivational consequences. *Journal of Personality*, 55, 19–39.

Batson, C. D., O'Quin, K., Fultz, J., Vanderplas, M., & Isen, A. M. (1983). Influence of self-reported distress and empathy on egoistic versus altruistic motivation to help. *Journal of Personality and Social Psychology*, 45, 706–718.

Baumeister, R. F., & Leary, M. R. (1995). The need to belong: Desire for interpersonal attachments as a fundamental human motivation. *Psychological Bulletin*, 117, 497–529.

Baumeister, R. F., Stillwell, A. M., & Heatherton, T. F. (1994). Guilt: An interpersonal approach. *Psychological Bulletin*, 115, 243–267.

Bauminger, N., & Kasari, C. (2000). Loneliness and friendship in high-functioning children with autism. *Child Development*, 71, 447–456.

Bavelas, J. B., Black, A., Lemery, C. R., & Mullett, J. (1986). "I show how you feel": Motor mimicry as a communicative act. *Journal of Personality and Social Psychology*, 50, 322–329.

Bayliss, A. P., Frischen, A., Fenske, M. J., & Tipper, S. P. (2007). Affective evaluations of objects are influenced by observed gaze direction and emotional expression. *Cognition*, 104, 644–653.

Bazerman, M. H., Tenbrunsel, A. E., & Wade-Benzoni, K. A. (2008). When "sacred" issues are at stake. *Negotiation Journal*, 24, 113–117.

Beach, S. R. H., Smith, D. A., & Fincham, F. D. (1994). Marital interventions for depression: Empirical foundation and future prospects. *Applied and Preventive Psychology*, 3, 233–250.

Beal, D. J., Trougakos, J. P., Weiss, H. M., & Dalal, R. S. (2013). Affect spin and the emotion regulation process at work. *Journal of Applied Psychology*, 98, 593–605.

Bechtoldt, M. N., Rohrmann, S., De Pater, I. E., & Beersma, B. (2011). The primacy of perceiving: Emotion recognition buffers negative effects of emotional labor. *Journal of Applied Psychology*, 96, 1087–1094.

Bell, K. L., & Calkins, S. D. (2000). Relationships as inputs and outputs of emotion regulation. *Psychological Inquiry*, 11, 160–163.

Benjamin, L. S., & Wonderlich, S. A. (1994). Social perceptions and borderline personality disorder: The relation to mood disorders. *Journal of Abnormal Psychology*, 103, 610–624.

Berenbaum, H., & Oltmanns, T. F. (1992). Emotional experience and expression in schizophrenia and depression. *Journal of Abnormal Psychology*, 101, 37–44.

Berry, D. S., & Hansen, J. S. (1996). Positive affect, negative affect, and social interaction. *Journal of Personality and Social Psychology*, 71, 796–809.

Berry, D. S., & Willingham, J. K. (1997). Affective traits, responses to conflict, and satisfaction in romantic relationships. *Journal of Research in Personality*, 31, 564–576.

Berscheid, E., & Ammazzalorso, H. (2001). Emotional experience in close relationships. In G. J. O. Fletcher & M. S. Clark (Eds.), *Blackwell handbook of social psychology: Interpersonal processes* (pp. 308–330). London: Blackwell.

Blair, R. J. R. (2003). Facial expressions, their communicatory functions and neuro-cognitive substrates. *Philosophical Transactions of the Royal Society of London. Series B: Biological Sciences*, 358, 561–572.

Bodenhausen, G. V., Sheppard, L. A., & Kramer, G. P. (1994). Negative affect and social judgment: The differential impact of anger and sadness. *European Journal of Social Psychology*, 24, 45–62.

Bommer, W. H., Pesta, B. J., & Storrud-Barnes, S. F. (2011). Nonverbal emotion recognition and performance: Differences matter differently. *Journal of Managerial Psychology*, 26, 28–41.

Bonanno, G. A., Papa, A., Lalande, K., Westphal, M., & Coifman, K. (2004). The importance of being flexible: The ability to both enhance and suppress emotional expression predicts long-term adjustment. *Psychological Science*, 15, 482–487.

Bono, J. E., & Ilies, R. (2006). Charisma, positive emotions, and mood contagion. *The Leadership Quarterly*, 17, 317–334.

Boone, R. T., & Buck, R. (2003). Emotional expressivity and trustworthiness: The role of nonverbal behavior in the evolution of cooperation. *Journal of Nonverbal Behavior*, 27, 163–182.

Bower, G. H. (1981). Mood and memory. *American Psychologist*, 36, 129–148.

Boyum, L. A., & Parke, R. D. (1995). The role of family emotional expressiveness in the development of children's social competence. *Journal of Marriage and the Family*, 57, 593–608.

Brackett, M. A., Rivers, S., Shiffman, S., Lerner, N., & Salovey, P. (2006). Relating emotional abilities to social functioning: A comparison of self-report and performance measures of emotional intelligence. *Journal of Personality and Social Psychology*, 91, 780–795.

Bradley, G. W. (1978). Self-serving biases in the attribution process: A reexamination of the fact or fiction question. *Journal of Personality and Social Psychology*, 36, 56–71.

Bronstein, P., Fitzgerald, M., Briones, M., Pieniadz, J., & D'Ari, A. (1993). Family emotional expressiveness as a predictor of early adolescent social and psychological adjustment. *The Journal of Early Adolescence*, 13, 448–471.

Brown, C. S., & Sulzer-Azaroff, B. (1994). An assessment of the relationship between customer satisfaction and service friendliness. *Journal of Organizational Behavior Management*, 14, 55–76.

Brown, D. J., & Keeping, L. M. (2005). Elaborating the construct of transformational leadership: The role of affect. *The Leadership Quarterly*, 16, 245–272.

Bruder, M., Dosmukhambetova, D., Nerb, J., & Manstead, A. S. R. (2012). Emotional signals in nonverbal interaction: Dyadic facilitation and convergence in expressions, appraisals, and feelings. *Cognition & Emotion*, 26, 480–502.

Bruder, M., Fischer, A., & Manstead, A. S. R. (2014). Social appraisal as a cause of collective emotions. In C. von Scheve & M. Salmela (Eds.), *Collective emotions* (pp. 141–155). New York: Oxford University Press.

Buck, R. (1980). Nonverbal behavior and the theory of emotion: The facial feedback hypothesis. *Journal of Personality and Social Psychology*, 38, 811–824.

Buck, R. (1984). *The communication of emotion.* New York: Guilford Press.

Buck, R. (1985). Prime theory: An integrated view of motivation and emotion. *Psychological Review*, 92, 389–413.

Buck, R. (1994). Social and emotional functions in facial expression and communication: The readout hypothesis. *Biological Psychology*, 38, 95–115.

Buck, R., Losow, J. I., Murphy, M. M., & Costanzo, P. (1992). Social facilitation and inhibition of emotional expression and communication. *Journal of Personality and Social Psychology*, 63, 962–968.

Bucy, E. P. (2000). Emotional and evaluative consequences of inappropriate leader displays. *Communication Research*, 27, 194–226.

Bugental, D. (1974). Interpretations of naturally occurring discrepancies between words and intonation: Modes of inconsistency resolution. *Journal of Personality and Social Psychology*, 30, 125–133.

Buss, D. M. (1999). *Evolutionary psychology: The new science of the mind.* Boston, MA: Allyn & Bacon.

Butler, E. A. (2011). Temporal Interpersonal Emotion Systems: The "TIES" that form relationships. *Personality and Social Psychology Review*, 15, 367–393.

Butler, E. A., Egloff, B., Wilhelm, F. H., Smith, N. C., Erickson, E. A., & Gross, J. J. (2003). The social consequences of expressive suppression. *Emotion*, 3, 48–67.

Buttelmann, D., Call, J., & Tomasello, M. (2009). Do great apes use emotional expressions to infer desires? *Developmental Science*, 12, 688–698.

Byron, K. (2007). Male and female managers' ability to read emotions: Relationships with supervisor's performance ratings and subordinates' satisfaction ratings. *Journal of Occupational and Organizational Psychology*, 80, 713–733.

Byron, K. (2008). Carrying too heavy a load? The communication and miscommunication of emotion by email. *Academy of Management Review*, 33, 309–327.

Cacioppo, J. T., & Gardner, W. L. (1999). Emotion. *Annual Review of Psychology*, 50, 191–214.

Caporael, L. R. (1997). The evolution of truly social cognition: The core configurations model. *Personality and Social Psychology Review*, 1, 276–298.

Carlson, M., Charlin, V., & Miller, N. (1988). Positive mood and helping behavior: A test of six hypotheses. *Journal of Personality and Social Psychology, 55,* 211–229.

Carnevale, P. J., & Pruitt, D. G. (1992). Negotiation and mediation. *Annual Review of Psychology, 43,* 531–582.

Carstensen, L. L., Gottman, J. M., & Levenson, R. W. (1995). Emotional behavior in long-term marriage. *Psychology and Aging, 10,* 140–149.

Carver, C. S., & Harmon-Jones, E. (2009). Anger is an approach-related affect: evidence and implications. *Psychological Bulletin, 135,* 183–204.

Cassidy, J. (1994). Emotion regulation: Influences of attachment relationships. *Monographs of the Society for Research in Child Development, 59,* 228–249.

Castelfranchi, C., & Poggi, I. (1990). Blushing as discourse: Was Darwin wrong? In W. R. Crozier (Ed.), *Shyness and embarrassment: Perspectives from social psychology* (pp. 230–254). Cambridge: Cambridge University Press.

Chaiken, S. (1980). Heuristic versus systematic information-processing and the use of source versus message cues in persuasion. *Journal of Personality and Social Psychology, 39,* 752–766.

Chaiken, S., Liberman, A., & Eagly, A. H. (1989). Heuristic and systematic information processing within and beyond the persuasion context. In J. S. Uleman & J. A. Bargh (Eds.), *Unintended thought* (pp. 212–252). New York: Guilford.

Chaiken, S., & Trope, Y. (Eds.). (1999). *Dual-process theories in social psychology.* New York: Guilford Press.

Chalian, D. (2010, June 11). David Chalian Says "Farewell" to "Top Line." Available from http://abcnews.go.com/Politics/video/david-chalian-farewell-top-line-10888445

Chang, J. W., Sy, T., & Choi, J. N. (2012). Team emotional intelligence and performance: Interactive dynamics between leaders and members. *Small Group Research, 43,* 75–104.

Chapman, H. A., Kim, D. A., Susskind, J. M., & Anderson, A. K. (2009). In bad taste: Evidence for the oral origins of moral disgust. *Science, 323,* 1222–1226.

Chen, S., & Chaiken, S. (1999). The heuristic-systematic model in its broader context. In S. Chaiken & Y. Trope (Eds.), *Dual-process theories in social psychology* (pp. 73–96). New York: Guilford.

Cheshin, A., Amit, A., & Van Kleef, G. A. (2015). *The interpersonal effects of emotion intensity in customer service: How service providers' expressions of mild versus intense happiness and sadness shape customer trust and satisfaction.* Unpublished manuscript.

Cheshin, A., Glikson, E., Van Kleef, G. A., & Rafaeli, A. (2015). *Is the angry customer always right? How anger intensity of customers shapes service providers' responses.* Unpublished manuscript.

Cheshin, A., Israely, R., & Rafaeli, A. (2015). *Teammate's emotion as evaluative feedback: The effects of encountering anger and happiness of teammates and their influence on self-efficacy and performance.* Unpublished manuscript.

Cheshin, A. Rafaeli, A., & Bos, N. (2011). Anger and happiness in virtual teams: Emotional influences of text and behavior on others' affect in the absence of non-verbal cues. *Organizational Behavior and Human Decision Processes, 116,* 2–16.

Chi, N.-W., Chung, Y.-Y., & Tsai, W.-C. (2011). How do happy leaders enhance team success? The mediating roles of transformational leadership, group affective tone, and team process. *Journal of Applied Social Psychology, 41,* 1421–1454.

Chi, N.-W., & Ho, T.-R. (2014). Understanding when leader negative emotional expression enhances follower performance: The moderating roles of follower personality traits and perceived leader power. *Human Relations, 67,* 1051–1072.

Chovil, N. (1991). Social determinants of facial displays. *Journal of Nonverbal Behavior, 15,* 141–154.

Cialdini, R. B., & Goldstein, N. J. (2004). Social influence: Compliance and conformity. *Annual Review of Psychology, 55,* 591–621.

Cialdini, R. B, Reno, R. R., & Kallgren, C. A. (1990). A focus theory of normative conduct: Recycling the concept of norms to reduce littering in public places. *Journal of Personality and Social Psychology, 58,* 1015–1026.

Cialdini, R. B., Schaller, M., Houlihan, D., Arps, K., Fultz, J., & Beaman, A. L. (1987). Empathy-based helping: Is it selflessly or selfishly motivated? *Journal of Personality and Social Psychology, 52,* 749–758.

Clark, C. (1990). Emotions and the micropolitics in everyday life: Some patterns and paradoxes of "place." In T. D. Kemper (Ed.), *Research agendas in the sociology of emotions* (pp. 305–334). Albany: State University of New York Press.

Clark, M. S., Ouellette, R., Powell, M. C., & Milberg, S. (1987). Recipient's mood, relationship type, and helping. *Journal of Personality and Social Psychology, 53,* 94–103.

Clark, M. S., Pataki, S. P., & Carver, V. H. (1996). Some thoughts and findings on self-presentation of emotions in relationships. In G. J. O. Fletcher & J. Fitness (Eds.), *Knowledge structures in close relationships: A social psychological approach* (pp. 247–274). Mahwah, NJ: Erlbaum.

Clark, M. S., & Taraban, C. B. (1991). Reactions to and willingness to express emotion in two types of relationships. *Journal of Experimental Social Psychology, 27,* 324–336.

Cohn, J. F., & Tronick, E. Z. (1983). Three-month-old infants' reaction to simulated maternal depression. *Child Development, 54,* 185–193.

Collins, A. L., Lawrence, S. A., Troth, A. C., & Jordan, P. J. (2013). Group affective tone: A review and future research directions. *Journal of Organizational Behavior, 34,* S43–S62.

Collins, R. C. (1990). Stratification, emotional energy, and the transient emotions. In T. D. Kemper (Ed.), *Research agendas in the sociology of emotions* (pp. 27–57). Albany: State University of New York Press.

Condry, J., & Condry, S. (1976). Sex differences: A study of the eye of the beholder. *Child Development, 47,* 812–819.

Connelly, S., & Ruark, G. (2010). Leadership style and activating potential moderators of the relationships among leader emotional displays and outcomes. *The Leadership Quarterly, 21,* 745–764.

Conway, A. R., Cowan, N., Bunting, M. F., Therriault, D. J., & Minkoff, S. R. (2002). A latent variable analysis of working memory capacity, short-term memory capacity, processing speed, and general fluid intelligence. *Intelligence, 30,* 163–183.

Cornelius, R. R. (1984). A rule model of emotional expression. In C. Z. Malatesta & C. E. Izard (Eds.), *Emotion in adult development* (pp. 213–233). Beverly Hills, CA: Sage.

Cornelius, R. R., & Labott, S. M. (2001). The social psychological aspects of crying. In A. J. J. M. Vingerhoets & R. R. Cornelius (Eds.), *Adult crying: A biopsychosocial approach* (pp. 159–176). Hove: Brunner-Routledge.

Cornelius, R. R., & Lubliner, E. (2003, October). *The what and why of others' responses to our tears: Adult crying as an attachment behavior.* Paper presented at the third international conference on The (Non)Expression of Emotions in Health and Disease, Tilburg, The Netherlands.

Cornelius, R. R., Nussbaum, R., Warner, L., & Moeller, C. (2000, August). *An action full of meaning and of real service: The social and emotional messages of crying.* Paper presented at the XIth conference of the International Society for Research on Emotions, Quebec City, Canada.

Cosmides, L., & Tooby, J. (1992). Cognitive adaptations for social exchange. In J. H. Barkow, L. Cosmides, & J. Tooby (Eds.), *The adapted mind: Evolutionary psychology and the generation of culture* (pp. 163–228). New York: Oxford University Press.

Costa, P. T., Jr., & McCrae, R. R. (1988). Personality in adulthood: A six-year longitudinal study of self-reports and spouse ratings on the NEO Personality Inventory. *Journal of Personality and Social Psychology, 54,* 853–863.

Costa, P. T., Jr., & McCrae, R. R. (1992). *Revised NEO Personality Inventory.* Odessa, FL: Psychological Assessment Resources.

Côté, S. (2005). A social interaction model of the effects of emotion regulation on work strain. *Academy of Management Review, 30,* 509–530.

Côté, S. (2007). Group emotional intelligence and group performance. In E. A. Mannix, M. A. Neale, & C. P. Anderson (Eds.), *Research on managing groups and teams* (Vol. 10, pp. 309–336). Oxford: Elsevier.

Côté, S. (2010). Taking the "intelligence" in emotional intelligence seriously. *Industrial and Organizational Psychology, 3,* 127–130.

Côté, S., DeCelles, K., McCarthy, J., & Van Kleef, G. A., & Hideg, I. (2011). The Jekyll and Hyde of emotional intelligence: Emotion regulation knowledge facilitates prosocial and interpersonally deviant behavior. *Psychological Science, 22,* 1073–1080.

Côté, S., & Hideg, I. (2011). The ability to influence others via emotion displays: A new dimension of emotional intelligence. *Organizational Psychology Review, 1,* 53–71.

Côté, S., Hideg, I., & Van Kleef, G. A. (2013). The consequences of faking anger in negotiations. *Journal of Experimental Social Psychology, 49,* 453–463.

Côté, S., Lopes, P. N., Salovey, P., & Miners, C. T. (2010). Emotional intelligence and leadership emergence in small groups. *The Leadership Quarterly, 21,* 496–508.

Coyne, J. C. (1976). Depression and the response of others. *Journal of Abnormal Psychology, 85,* 186–193.

Dahling, J. J., & Perez, L. A. (2010). Older worker, different actor? Linking age and emotional labor strategies. *Personality and Individual Differences*, 48, 574–578.

Damasio, A. R. (1994). *Descartes' error: Emotion, reason, and the human brain*. New York: Putnam.

Damen, F., Van Knippenberg, B., & Van Knippenberg, D. (2008a). Affective match in leadership: Leader emotional display, follower positive affect, and follower performance. *Journal of Applied Social Psychology*, 38, 868–902.

Damen, F., Van Knippenberg, D., & Van Knippenberg, B. (2008b). Leader affective displays and attributions of charisma: The role of arousal. *Journal of Applied Social Psychology*, 38, 2594–2614.

Darby, B. W., & Schlenker, B. R. (1982). Children's reactions to apologies. *Journal of Personality and Social Psychology*, 43, 742–753.

Darwin, C. (1872). *The expression of the emotions in man and animals* (3rd ed.). London: HarperCollins.

Dasborough, M. T., & Ashkanasy, N. M. (2002). Emotion and attribution of intentionality of leader-member relationships. *The Leadership Quarterly*, 13, 615–634.

Davidson, R. J., Putnam, K. M., & Larson, C. L. (2000). Dysfunction in the neural circuitry of emotion regulation – a possible prelude to violence. *Science*, 289, 591–594.

De Dreu, C. K. W. (2003). Time pressure and closing of the mind in negotiation. *Organizational Behavior and Human Decision Processes*, 91, 280–295.

De Dreu, C. K. W. (2010). Social conflict: The emergence and consequences of struggle and negotiation. In S. T. Fiske, D. T. Gilbert, & L. Gardner (Eds.), *Handbook of social psychology* (5th ed., Vol. 2, pp. 983–1023). Hoboken, NJ: Wiley.

De Dreu, C. K. W., Baas, M., & Nijstad, B. A. (2008). Hedonic tone and activation level in the mood-creativity link: Towards a dual pathway to creativity model. *Journal of Personality and Social Psychology*, 94, 739–756.

De Dreu, C. K. W., Beersma, B., Steinel, W., & Van Kleef, G. A. (2007). The psychology of negotiation: Principles and basic processes. In A. W. Kruglanski & E. T. Higgins (Eds.), *Social psychology: Handbook of basic principles* (2nd ed., pp. 608–629). New York: Guilford.

De Dreu, C. K. W., & Carnevale, P. J. (2003). Motivational bases of information processing and strategy in conflict and negotiation. *Advances in Experimental Social Psychology*, 35, 235–291.

De Dreu, C. K. W., Carnevale, P. J., Emans, B. J. M., & Van De Vliert, E. (1994). Effects of gain-loss frames in negotiation: Loss aversion, mismatching, and frame adoption. *Organizational Behavior and Human Decision Processes*, 60, 90–107.

De Dreu, C. K. W., Nijstad, B. A., & Van Knippenberg, D. (2008). Motivated information processing in group judgment and decision making. *Personality and Social Psychology Review*, 12, 22–49.

De Dreu, C. K. W., & Van Kleef, G. A. (2004). The influence of power on the information search, impression formation, and demands in negotiation. *Journal of Experimental Social Psychology*, 40, 303–319.

De Houwer, J., Thomas, S., & Baeyens, F. (2001). Associative learning of likes and dislikes: A review of 25 years of research on human evaluative conditioning. *Psychological Bulletin, 127*, 853–869.

de Melo, C., Carnevale, P., & Gratch, J. (2011, July). Reverse appraisal: Inferring from emotion displays who is the cooperator and the competitor in a social dilemma. *Proceedings of the 33rd Annual Meeting of the Cognitive Science Society,* 396–401.

de Melo, C. M., Carnevale, P. J., Read, S. J., & Gratch, J. (2014). Reading people's minds from emotion expressions in interdependent decision making. *Journal of Personality and Social Psychology, 106*, 73–88.

de Waal, F. B. M. (1986). The integration of dominance and social bonding in primates. *Quarterly Review of Biology, 61*, 459–479.

de Waal, F. B. M. (1988). The reconciled hierarchy. In M. R. A. Chance (Ed.), *Social fabrics of the mind* (pp. 105–136). Hillsdale, NJ: Erlbaum.

de Waal, F. B. M. (1996). *Good natured.* Cambridge, MA: Harvard University Press.

de Waal, F. B. M. (2009). *The age of empathy: Nature's lessons for a kinder society.* New York: Harmony Books.

Dehghani, M., Carnevale, P. J., & Gratch, J. (2014). Interpersonal effects of expressed anger and sorrow in morally charged negotiation. *Judgment and Decision Making, 9*, 104–113.

Delcourt, C., Gremler, D. D., Van Riel, A. C., & Van Birgelen, M. (2013). Effects of perceived employee emotional competence on customer satisfaction and loyalty: The mediating role of rapport. *Journal of Service Management, 24*, 5–24.

Denham, S. A., Zoller, D., & Couchoud, E. A. (1994). Socialization of preschoolers' emotion understanding. *Developmental Psychology, 30*, 928–936.

DePaulo, B. M., Lindsay, J. L., Malone, B. E., Muhlenbruck, L., Charlton, K., & Cooper, H. (2003). Cues to deception. *Psychological Bulletin, 129*, 74–118.

DeSteno, D., Petty, R., Wegener, D. T., & Rucker, D. D. (2000). Beyond valence in the perception of likelihood: The role of emotion specificity. *Journal of Personality and Social Psychology, 78*, 397–416.

Deutsch, M. (1973). *The resolution of conflict: Constructive and destructive processes.* New Haven, CT: Yale University Press.

De Vos, B., Van Zomeren, M., Gordijn, E. H., & Postmes, T. (2013). The communication of "pure" group-based anger reduces tendencies toward intergroup conflict because it increases out-group empathy. *Personality and Social Psychology Bulletin, 39*, 1043–1052.

Dezecache, G., Conty, L., Chadwick, M., Philip, L., Soussignan, R., Sperber, D., & Grèzes, J. (2013). Evidence for unintentional emotional contagion beyond dyads. *PloS ONE, 8*, e67371.

Diefendorff, J. M., & Greguras, G. J. (2009). Contextualizing emotional display rules: Examining the roles of targets and discrete emotions in shaping display rule perceptions. *Journal of Management, 35*, 880–898.

Diefendorff, J., Morehart, J., & Gabriel, A. (2010). The influence of power and solidarity on emotional display rules at work. *Motivation and Emotion, 34*, 120–132.

Dimberg, U. (1988). Facial electromyography and the experience of emotion. *Journal of Psychophysiology*, 3, 277–282.

Dimberg, U., & Öhman, A. (1996). Behold the wrath: Psychophysiological responses to facial stimuli. *Motivation and Emotion*, 20, 149–182.

Dimberg, U., Thunberg, M., & Elmehed, K. (2000). Unconscious facial reactions to emotional facial expressions. *Psychological Science*, 11, 86–89.

Doosje, B., Branscombe, N. R., Spears, R., & Manstead, A. S. (1998). Guilty by association: When one's group has a negative history. *Journal of Personality and Social Psychology*, 75, 872–886.

Druckman, D., Broome, B. J., & Korper, S. H. (1988). Value differences and conflict resolution. *Journal of Conflict Resolution*, 32, 489–510.

Duarte, N. T., Goodson, J. R., & Klich, N. R. (1994). Effects of dyadic quality and duration on performance appraisal. *Academy of Management Journal*, 37, 499–521.

Duck, S. (1986). *Human relationships*. London: Sage.

Dunbar, R. I. M. (1992). Neocortex size as a constraint on group size in primates. *Journal of Human Evolution*, 20, 469–493.

Dunbar, R. I. M. (2004). *The human story: A new history of mankind's evolution*. London: Faber.

Dunbar, R. I. M. (2009). The social brain hypothesis and its implications for social evolution. *Annals of Human Biology*, 36, 562–572.

Dunham, Y. (2011). An angry = outgroup effect. *Journal of Experimental Social Psychology*, 47, 668–671.

Dunn, J. R., & Schweitzer, M. E. (2005). Feeling and believing: The influence of emotion on trust. *Journal of Personality and Social Psychology*, 88, 736–748.

Dunning, D., Heath, C., & Suls, J. (2004). Flawed self-assessment: Implications for health, education, and the workplace. *Psychological Science in the Public Interest*, 5, 69–106.

Eagly, A. H., & Chaiken, S. (1993). *The psychology of attitudes*. New York: Harcourt Brace Jovanovich.

Eagly, A. H., Karau, S. J., Makhijani, M. G. (1995). Gender and effectiveness of leaders: A meta-analysis. *Psychological Bulletin*, 117, 125–145.

Eberly, M. B., & Fong, C. T. (2013). Leading via the heart and mind: The roles of leader and follower emotions, attributions, and interdependence. *The Leadership Quarterly*, 24, 696–711.

Edell, J., & Burke, M. C. (1987). The power of feelings in understanding advertising effects. *Journal of Consumer Research*, 14, 421–433.

Eibl-Eibesfeldt, I. (1989). *Human ethology*. New York: Aldine de Gruyter.

Eid, M., & Diener, E. (2001). Norms for experiencing emotions in different cultures: Inter-and intranational differences. *Journal of Personality and Social Psychology*, 81, 869–885.

Eidelman, S., Silvia, P. J., & Biernat, M. (2006). Responding to deviance: Target exclusion and differential devaluation. *Personality and Social Psychology Bulletin*, 32, 1153–1164.

Eisenberg, N. (2000). Emotion, regulation, and moral development. *Annual Review of Psychology*, 51, 665–697.

Eisenberg, N., Cumberland, A., & Spinrad, T. L. (1998). Parental socialization of emotion. *Psychological Inquiry, 9,* 241–273.

Eisenberg, N., & Fabes, R. A. (1994). Mothers' reactions to children's negative emotions: Relations to children's temperament and anger behavior. *Merrill-Palmer Quarterly, 40,* 138–156.

Eisenberg, N., Fabes, R. A., Miller, P. A., Fultz, J., Mathy, R. M., Shell, R., et al. (1989). The relations of sympathy and personal distress to prosocial behavior: A multimethod study. *Journal of Personality and Social Psychology, 57,* 55–66.

Eisenberg, N., Gershoff, E. T., Fabes, R. A., Shepard, S. A., Cumberland, A. J., Losoya, S. H., Guthrie, I. K., & Murphy, B. C. (2001). Mother's emotional expressivity and children's behavior problems and social competence: Mediation through children's regulation. *Developmental Psychology, 37,* 475–490.

Eisenberg, N., & Miller, P. A. (1987). The relation of empathy to prosocial and related behaviors. *Psychological Bulletin, 101,* 91–119.

Ekman, P. (1972). Universals and cultural differences in facial expressions of emotion. In J. K. Cole (Ed.), *Nebraska Symposium on Motivation: Vol. 19* (pp. 207–283). Lincoln: University of Nebraska Press.

Ekman, P. (Ed.). (1982). *Emotion in the human face* (2nd ed.). Cambridge, UK: Cambridge University Press.

Ekman, P. (1992). An argument for basic emotions. *Cognition & Emotion, 6,* 169–200.

Ekman, P. (1993). Facial expression and emotion. *American Psychologist, 48,* 384–392.

Ekman, P. (1994). Strong evidence for universals in facial expressions: A reply to Russell's mistaken critique. *Psychological Bulletin, 115,* 268–287.

Ekman, P. (2001). *Telling lies: Clues to deceit in the marketplace, politics, and marriage.* New York: Norton.

Ekman, P. (2003). *Emotions revealed.* New York: Henry Holt.

Ekman, P., & Friesen, W. V. (1969). Nonverbal leakage and clues to deception. *Psychiatry: Journal for the Study of Interpersonal Processes, 32,* 88–106.

Ekman, P., & Friesen, W. V. (1975). *Unmasking the face.* Englewood Cliffs, NJ: Prentice-Hall.

Ekman, P., & Friesen, W. V. (1976). Measuring facial movement. *Environmental Psychology and Nonverbal Behavior, 1,* 56–75.

Ekman, P., & Friesen, W. V. (1978). *Facial Action Coding System: A technique for the measurement of facial movement. Palo Alto,* CA: Consulting Psychologists Press.

Ekman, P., Friesen, W. V., & O'Sullivan, M. (1988). Smiles when lying. *Journal of Personality and Social Psychology, 54,* 414–420.

Ekman, P., Friesen, W. V., O'Sullivan, M., Chan, A., Diacoyanni-Tarlatzis, I., Heider, K., et al. (1987). Universals and cultural differences in the judgements of facial expressions of emotion. *Journal of Personality and Social Psychology, 53,* 712–717.

Ekman, P., Hager, J. C., & Friesen, E. V. (1981). The symmetry of emotional and deliberate facial actions. *Psychophysiology, 18,* 101–106.

Ekman, P., & O'Sullivan, M. (1991). Who can catch a liar? *American Psychologist*, 46, 913–920.

Ekman, P., & Oster, H. (1979). Facial expressions of emotion. *Annual Review of Psychology*, 30, 527–554.

Elfenbein, H. A. (2005). Team emotional intelligence: What it can mean and how it can affect performance. In V. U. Druskat, F. Sala, & G. Mount (Eds.), *Linking emotional intelligence and performance at work* (pp. 165–184). Mahwah, NJ: Lawrence Erlbaum.

Elfenbein, H. A. (2007). Emotion in organizations: A review and theoretical integration. *Academy of Management Annals*, 1, 315–386.

Elfenbein, H. A. (2014). The many faces of emotional contagion: An affective process theory of affective linkage. *Organizational Psychology Review*, 4, 326–362.

Elfenbein, H. A., & Ambady, N. (2002a). Is there an in-group advantage in emotion? *Psychological Bulletin*, 128, 243–249.

Elfenbein, H. A., & Ambady, N. (2002b). On the universality and cultural specificity of emotion recognition: A meta-analysis. *Psychological Bulletin*, 128, 203–235.

Elfenbein, H. A., & Ambady, N. (2003). Universals and cultural differences in recognizing emotions. *Current Directions in Psychological Science*, 12, 159–164.

Elfenbein, H. A., Foo, M. D., White, J., Tan, H. H., & Aik, V. C. (2007). Reading your counterpart: The benefit of emotion recognition accuracy for effectiveness in negotiation. *Journal of Nonverbal Behavior*, 31, 205–223.

Ellis, B. J., & Malamuth, N. M. (2000). Love and anger in romantic relationships: A discrete systems model. *Journal of Personality*, 68, 525–556.

Engle, R. W. (2002). Working memory capacity as executive attention. *Current Directions in Psychological Science*, 11, 19–23.

Engle, R. W., Tuholski, S. W., Laughlin, J. E., & Conway, A. R. (1999). Working memory, short-term memory, and general fluid intelligence: A latent-variable approach. *Journal of Experimental Psychology: General*, 128, 309–331.

Erez, A., Misangyi, V. F., Johnson, D. E., LePine, M. A., & Halverson, K. C. (2008). Stirring the hearts of followers: Charismatic leadership as the transferal of affect. *Journal of Applied Psychology*, 93, 602–615.

Evans, J. St. B. T. (2008). Dual-processing accounts of reasoning, judgment, and social cognition. *Annual Review of Psychology*, 59, 255–278.

Evers, C., Fischer, A. H., Rodriguez Mosquera, P. M., & Manstead, A. S. R. (2005). Anger and social appraisal: A "spicy" sex difference? *Emotion*, 5, 258–266.

Farb, N. A., Chapman, H. A., & Anderson, A. K. (2013). Emotions: Form follows function. *Current Opinion in Neurobiology*, 23, 393–398.

Farchaus-Stein, K. (1996). Affect instability in adults with a borderline personality disorder. *Archives of Psychiatric Nursing*, 10, 32–40.

Fehr, B., Baldwin, M., Collins, L., Patterson, S., & Benditt, R. (1999). Anger in close relationships: An interpersonal script analysis. *Personality and Social Psychology Bulletin*, 25, 299–312.

Fehr, B., & Russell, J. A. (1984). Concept of emotion viewed from a prototype perspective. *Journal of Experimental Psychology: General*, 113, 464–486.

Fernández-Dols, J. M., & Ruiz-Belda, M. A. (1995). Are smiles a sign of happiness? Gold medal winners at the Olympic Games. *Journal of Personality and Social Psychology*, 69, 1113–1119.

Filipowicz, A., Barsade, S., & Melwani, S. (2011). Understanding emotional transitions: The interpersonal consequences of changing emotions in negotiations. *Journal of Personality and Social Psychology*, 101, 541–556.

Fischer, A. H. (2000). (Ed.) *Gender and emotion: Social psychological perspectives.* New York: Cambridge University Press.

Fischer, A. H., & Manstead, A. S. R. (in press). Social functions of emotion and emotion regulation. In M. Lewis, J. Haviland, & L. Feldman Barrett (Eds.), *Handbook of emotion* (4th ed.). New York: Guilford.

Fischer, A. H., Manstead, A. S. R., & Zaalberg, R. (2003). Social influences on the emotion process. *European Review of Social Psychology*, 14, 171–201.

Fischer, A. H., & Roseman, I. J. (2007). Beat them or ban them: The characteristics and social functions of anger and contempt. *Journal of Personality and Social Psychology*, 93, 103–115.

Fischer, A. H., Rotteveel, M., Evers, C., & Manstead, A. S. R. (2004). Emotional assimilation: How we are influenced by others' emotions. *Cahier de Psychologie Cognitive*, 22, 223–245.

Fisk, G. M., & Friesen, J. P. (2012). Perceptions of leader emotion regulation and LMX as predictors of followers' job satisfaction and organizational citizenship behaviors. *The Leadership Quarterly*, 23, 1–12.

Fiske, A. P. (1991). *Structures of social life: The four elementary forms of human relations: Communal sharing, authority ranking, equality matching, market pricing.* New York: Free Press.

Fiske, S. T. (1993). Controlling other people: The impact of power on stereotyping. *American Psychologist*, 48, 621–628.

Fiske, S. T., & Dépret, E. (1996). Control, interdependence, and power: Understanding social cognition in its social context. *European Review of Social Psychology*, 7, 31–61.

Fiske, S. T., & Taylor, S. E. (1991). *Social cognition* (2nd ed.). New York: McGraw-Hill.

Fitness, J. (2000). Anger in the workplace: An emotion script approach to anger episodes between workers and their superiors, co-workers and subordinates. *Journal of Organizational Behavior*, 21, 147–162.

Fitness, J., & Fletcher, G. J. (1993). Love, hate, anger, and jealousy in close relationships: A prototype and cognitive appraisal analysis. *Journal of Personality and Social Psychology*, 65, 942–958.

Flack, W. (2006). Peripheral feedback effects of facial expressions, bodily postures, and vocal expressions on emotional feelings. *Cognition & Emotion*, 20, 177–195.

Flynn, F. J. (2005). Having an open mind: The impact of openness to experience on interracial attitudes and impression formation. *Journal of Personality and Social Psychology*, 88, 816–826.

Foo, M. D., Elfenbein, H. A., Tan, H. H., & Aik, V. C. (2004). Emotional intelligence and negotiation: The tension between creating and claiming value. *International Journal of Conflict Management*, 15, 411–429.

Ford, T. E., & Kruglanski, A. W. (1995). Effects of epistemic motivations on the use of accessible constructs in social judgment. *Personality and Social Psychology Bulletin*, 21, 950–962.

Forgas, J. P. (1995). Mood and judgment: The affect infusion model (AIM). *Psychological Bulletin*, 117, 39–66.

Forgas, J. P. (1998). On feeling good and getting your way: Mood effects on negotiator cognition and behavior. *Journal of Personality and Social Psychology*, 74, 565–577.

Forgas, J. P. (2000). *Feeling and thinking: The role of affect in social cognition*. Cambridge: Cambridge University Press.

Forgas, J. P., & Bower, G. H. (1987). Mood effects on person perception judgements. *Journal of Personality and Social Psychology*, 53, 53–60.

Forgas, J. P., & George, J. M. (2001). Affective influences on judgments and behavior in organizations: An information processing perspective. *Organizational Behavior and Human Decision Processes*, 86, 3–34.

Francis, L. E. (1997). Ideology and interpersonal emotion management: Redefining identity in two support groups. *Social Psychology Quarterly*, 60, 153–171.

Francis, L. E., Monahan, K., & Berger, C. (1999). A laughing matter? The uses of humor in medical interactions. *Motivation and Emotion*, 23, 154–177.

Frank, R. H. (1988). *Passions within reason: The strategic role of the emotions*. New York: Norton.

Fredrickson, B. L. (1998). What good are positive emotions? *Review of General Psychology*, 2, 300–319.

Fredrickson, B. L. (2001). The role of positive emotions in positive psychology: The broaden-and-build theory of positive emotions. *American Psychologist*, 56, 218–226.

Fridlund, A. J. (1991a). Evolution and facial action in reflex, social motive, and paralanguage. *Biological Psychology* 32, 3–100.

Fridlund, A. J. (1991b). Sociality of solitary smiling: Potentiation by an implicit audience. *Journal of Personality and Social Psychology*, 60, 229–240.

Fridlund, A. J. (1992). The behavioral ecology and sociality of human faces. In M. S. Clark (Ed.), *Review of personality and social psychology* (Vol. 13, pp. 90–121). Thousand Oaks, CA: Sage.

Fridlund, A. J. (1994). *Human facial expression: An evolutionary view*. San Diego, CA: Academic Press.

Friedman, R., Anderson, C., Brett, J., Olekalns, M., Goates, N., & Lisco, C. C. (2004). The positive and negative effects of anger on dispute resolution: Evidence from electronically mediated disputes. *Journal of Applied Psychology*, 89, 369–376.

Friesen, A. P., Lane, A. M., Devonport, T. J., Sellars, C. N., Stanley, D. N., & Beedie, C. J. (2013). Emotion in sport: Considering interpersonal regulation strategies. *International Review of Sport and Exercise Psychology*, 6, 139–154.

Frijda, N. H. (1986). *The emotions*. Cambridge: Cambridge University Press.

Frijda, N. H. (1994). Varieties of affect: Emotions and episodes, moods, and sentiments. In P. Ekman & R. J. Davidson (Eds.), *The nature of emotion: Fundamental questions* (pp. 59–67). New York: Oxford University Press.

Frijda, N. H. (1995). Expression, emotion, neither, or both? *Cognition & Emotion, 9*, 617–635.

Frijda, N. H., Kuipers, P., & ter Schure, E. (1989). Relations among emotion, appraisal, and action readiness. *Journal of Personality and Social Psychology, 57*, 212–228.

Frijda, N. H., & Mesquita, B. (1994). The social roles and functions of emotions. In S. Kitayama & H. S. Markus (Eds.), *Emotion and culture: Empirical studies of mutual influence* (pp. 51–87). Washington, DC: American Psychological Association.

Frith, U. (2001). Mind blindness and the brain in autism. *Neuron, 32*, 969–979.

Gabriel, A. S., Cheshin, A., Moran, C. M., & Van Kleef, G. A. (in press). Enhancing emotional performance and customer service through human resources practices: A systems perspective. *Human Resource Management Review*.

Gaddis, B., Connelly, S., & Mumford, M. D. (2004). Failure feedback as an affective event: Influence of leader affect on subordinate attitudes and performance. *The Leadership Quarterly, 15*, 663–686.

Gaddis, J. (2005). *Strategies of containment: A critical appraisal of American national security policy during the Cold War*. New York: Oxford University Press.

Gardner, P. (1985). Mood states and consumer behavior: A critical review. *Journal of Consumer Research, 12*, 281–300.

Gardner, W. L., Fischer, D., & Hunt, J. G. J. (2009). Emotional labor and leadership: A threat to authenticity? *The Leadership Quarterly, 20*, 466–482.

Gardner, W. L., & Martinko, M. J. (1988). Impression management in organizations. *Journal of Management, 14*, 321–338.

Geddes, D., & Callister, R. R. (2007). Crossing the line(s): A dual threshold model of anger in organizations. *Academy of Management Review, 32*, 721–746.

George, J. M. (1990). Personality, affect, and behavior in groups. *Journal of Applied Psychology, 75*, 107–116.

George, J. M. (1995). Leader positive mood and group performance: The case of customer service. *Journal of Applied Social Psychology, 25*, 778–794.

George, J. M. (2000). Emotions and leadership: The role of emotional intelligence. *Human Relations, 53*, 1027–1055.

George, J. M., & Bettenhausen, K. (1990). Understanding prosocial behavior, sales performance, and turnover: A group-level analysis in a service context. *Journal of Applied Psychology, 75*, 698–709.

George, J. M., & Brief, A. P. (1992). Feeling good-doing good: A conceptual analysis of the mood at work-organizational spontaneity relationship. *Psychological Bulletin, 112*, 310–329.

George, J. M., & King, E. B. (2007). Potential pitfalls of affect convergence in teams: Functions and dysfunctions of group affective tone. In E. A. Mannix,

M. A. Neale, & C. P. Anderson (Eds.), *Research on managing groups and teams* (Vol. 10, pp. 97–123). New York: Elsevier.

Giardini, A., & Frese, M. (2008). Linking service employees' emotional competence to customer satisfaction: A multilevel approach. *Journal of Organizational Behavior*, 29, 155–170.

Gibson, C. B. (2003). The efficacy advantage: Factors related to the formation of group efficacy. *Journal of Applied Social Psychology*, 33, 2153–2186.

Gibson, D. E., Schweitzer, M., Callister, R. R., & Gray, B. (2009). The influence of anger expressions on outcomes in organizations. *Negotiation and Conflict Management Research*, 2, 236–262.

Gilbert, D. T., & Hixon, J. G. (1991). The trouble of thinking: Activation and application of stereotypic beliefs. *Journal of Personality and Social Psychology*, 60, 509–517.

Gilovich, T., & Medvec, V. H. (1995). The experience of regret: What, when, and why. *Psychological Review*, 102, 379–395.

Glasø, L., & Einarsen, S. (2008). Emotion regulation in leader-follower relationships. *European Journal of Work and Organizational Psychology*, 17, 482–500.

Glikson, E., Rafaeli, A, & Wirtz, J. (2015). *Does customer anger pay off? The role of anger intensity and the moderating effect of culture on the consequences of displayed anger*. Unpublished manuscript.

Glomb, T. M., & Hulin, C. L. (1997). Anger and gender effects in observed supervisor-subordinate dyadic interactions. *Organizational Behavior and Human Decision Processes*, 72, 281–307.

Godfrey, D. K., Jones, E. E., & Lord, C. G. (1986). Self-promotion is not ingratiating. *Journal of Personality and Social Psychology*, 50, 106–115.

Goffman, E. (1967). *Interaction ritual: Essays on face-to-face interaction*. Oxford: Aldine.

Gonzaga, G. C., Keltner, D., Londahl, E. A., & Smith, M. D. (2001). Love and the commitment problem in romantic relationships and friendship. *Journal of Personality and Social Psychology*, 81, 247–262.

Gotlib, I. H. (1992). Interpersonal and cognitive aspects of depression. *Current Directions in Psychological Science*, 1, 149–154.

Gottman, J. M. (1993). A theory of marital dissolution and stability. *Journal of Family Psychology*, 7, 57–75.

Gottman, J. M., Katz, L. F., & Hooven, C. (1996). Parental meta-emotion philosophy and the emotional life of families: Theoretical models and preliminary data. *Journal of Family Psychology*, 10, 243–268.

Gottman, J. M., & Levenson, R. W. (1988). The social psychophysiology of marriage. In P. Noller & M. A. Fitzpatrick (Eds.), *Perspectives on marital interaction* (pp. 182–200). Clevedon: Multilingual Matters.

Gottman, J. M., & Levenson, R. W. (1992). Marital processes predictive of later dissolution: Behavior, physiology, and health. *Journal of Personality and Social Psychology*, 63, 221–233.

Goussinsky, R. (2011). Does customer aggression more strongly affect happy employees? The moderating role of positive affectivity and extraversion. *Motivation and Emotion*, 35, 220–234.

Graham, S. M., Huang, J. Y., Clark, M. S., & Helgeson, V. S. (2008). The positives of negative emotions: Willingness to express negative emotions promotes relationships. *Personality and Social Psychology Bulletin*, 34, 394–406.

Grandey, A. (2003). When "the show must go on": Surface and deep acting as determinants of emotional exhaustion and peer-rated service delivery. *Academy of Management Journal*, 46, 86–96.

Grandey, A. A., Dickter, D. N., & Sin, H. P. (2004). The customer is not always right: Customer aggression and emotion regulation of service employees. *Journal of Organizational Behavior*, 25, 397–418.

Grandey, A. A., Diefendorff, J. M., & Rupp, D. E. (Eds.) (2013). *Emotional labor in the 21st century: Diverse perspectives on emotion regulation at work*. New York: Routledge.

Grandey, A. A., Fisk, G. M., Mattila, A. S., Jansen, K. J., & Sideman, L. A. (2005). Is "service with a smile" enough? Authenticity of positive displays during service encounters. *Organizational Behavior and Human Decision Processes*, 96, 38–55.

Grandey, A. A., Kern, J. H., & Frone, M. R. (2007). Verbal abuse from outsiders versus insiders: Comparing frequency, impact on emotional exhaustion, and the role of emotional labor. *Journal of Occupational Health Psychology*, 12, 63–79.

Grandey, A. A., Rafaeli, A., Ravid, S., Wirtz, J., & Steiner, D. D. (2010). Emotion display rules at work in the global service economy: The special case of the customer. *Journal of Service Management*, 21, 388–412.

Grawitch, M. J., Munz, D. C., & Kramer, T. J. (2003). Effects of member mood states on creative performance in temporary workgroups. *Group Dynamics: Theory, Research, and Practice*, 7, 41–54.

Graziano, W. G., Jensen-Campbell, L. A., & Hair, E. C. (1996). Perceiving interpersonal conflict and reacting to it: The case for agreeableness. *Journal of Personality and Social Psychology*, 70, 820–835.

Greenberg, J., Pyszczynski, T., Solomon, S., Rosenblatt, A. V. M., Kirkland, S., & Lyon, D. (1990). Evidence for terror management theory II: The effects of mortality salience on reactions to those who threaten or bolster the cultural worldview. *Journal of Personality and Social Psychology*, 58, 308–318.

Greenwald, A. G., McGhee, D. E., & Schwartz, J. L. (1998). Measuring individual differences in implicit cognition: The implicit association test. *Journal of Personality and Social Psychology*, 74, 1464–1480.

Gross, J. J. (1998a). Antecedent- and response-focused emotion regulation: Divergent consequences for experience, expression, and physiology. *Journal of Personality and Social Psychology*, 74, 224–237.

Gross, J. J. (1998b). The emerging field of emotion regulation: An integrative review. *Review of General Psychology*, 2, 271–299.

Gross, J. J., & John, O. P. (1997). Revealing feelings: Facets of emotional expressivity in self-reports, peer ratings, and behavior. *Journal of Personality and Social Psychology*, 72, 435–448.

Gross, J. J., & John, O. P. (2003). Individual differences in two emotion regulation processes: Implications for affect, relationships, and well-being. *Journal of Personality and Social Psychology*, 85, 348–362.

Groth, M., Hennig-Thurau, T., & Walsh, G. (2009). Customer reactions to emotional labor: The roles of employee acting strategies and customer detection accuracy. *Academy of Management Journal*, 52, 958–974.

Guerrero, L. K., La Valley, A. G., & Farinelli, L. (2008). The experience and expression of anger, guilt, and sadness in marriage: An equity theory explanation. *Journal of Social and Personal Relationships*, 25, 699–724.

Haddon, M. (2003). *The curious incident of the dog in the night time*. London: Jonathan Cape.

Hager, J. C., & Ekman, P. (1985). The asymmetry of facial actions is inconsistent with models of hemispheric specialization. *Psychophysiology*, 22, 307–318.

Halperin, E., & Gross, J. J. (2010). Intergroup anger in intractable conflict: Long-term sentiments predict anger responses during the Gaza war. *Group Processes & Intergroup Relations*, 14, 477–488.

Hamilton, D. L., & Sherman, S. J. (1996). Perceiving persons and groups. *Psychological Review*, 103, 336–355.

Hammer, M. (1986). The role of social networks in schizophrenia. In G. D. Burrow, T. R. Norman & G. Rubinstein (Eds.), *Handbook of studies on schizophrenia, Part 2* (pp. 115–128). New York: Elsevier.

Hareli, S. (2014). Making sense of the social world and influencing it by using a naïve attribution theory of emotions. *Emotion Review*, 6, 336–343.

Hareli, S., Harush, R., Suleiman, R., Cossette, M., Bergeron, S., Lavoie, V., Dugay, G., & Hess, U. (2009). When scowling may be a good thing: The influence of anger expressions on credibility. *European Journal of Social Psychology*, 39, 631–638.

Hareli, S., & Hess, U. (2010). What emotional reactions can tell us about the nature of others: An appraisal perspective on person perception. *Cognition & Emotion*, 24, 128–140.

Hareli, S., Moran-Amir, O., David, S., & Hess, U. (2013). Emotions as signals of normative conduct. *Cognition & Emotion*, 27, 1395–1404.

Hareli, S., & Rafaeli, A. (2008). Emotion cycles: On the social influence of emotion in organizations. *Research in Organizational Behavior*, 28, 35–59.

Hareli, S., Shomrat, N., & Hess, U. (2009). Emotional versus neutral expressions and perceptions of social dominance and submissiveness. *Emotion*, 9, 378–384.

Hargreaves, W., Starkweather, J., & Blacker, K. (1965). Voice quality in depression. *Journal of Abnormal Psychology*, 70, 218–229.

Harinck, F., De Dreu, C. K. W., & Van Vianen, A. E. M (2000). The impact of conflict issue on fixed-pie perceptions, problem solving, and integrative outcomes in negotiation. *Organizational Behaviour and Human Decision Processes*, 81, 329–358.

Harinck, F., & Van Kleef, G. A. (2012). Be hard on the interests and soft on the values: Conflict issue moderates the effects of anger in negotiations. *British Journal of Social Psychology*, 51, 741–752.

Harker, L. A., & Keltner, D. (2001). Expressions of positive emotion in women's college yearbook pictures and their relationship to personality and life outcomes across adulthood. *Journal of Personality and Social Psychology*, 80, 112–124.

Hatfield, E., Cacioppo, J. T., & Rapson, R. L. (1992). Primitive emotional contagion. *Review of Personality and Social Psychology*, 14, 151–177.

Hatfield, E., Cacioppo, J. T., & Rapson, R. L. (1994). *Emotional contagion*. New York: Cambridge University Press.

Havas, D. A., Glenberg, A. M., Gutowski, K. A., Lucarelli, M. J., & Davidson, R. J. (2010). Cosmetic use of botulinum toxin-A affects processing of emotional language. *Psychological Science*, 21, 895–900.

Hawk, S. T., Fischer, A. H., & Van Kleef, G. A. (2011). Taking your place or matching your face: Two routes to empathic embarrassment. *Emotion*, 11, 502–513.

Hawk, S. T., Fischer, A. H., & Van Kleef, G. A. (2012). Face the noise: Embodied responses to nonverbal vocalizations of discrete emotions. *Journal of Personality and Social Psychology*, 102, 796–814.

Hawk, S. T., Van Kleef, G. A., Fischer, A. H., & Van der Schalk, J. (2009). Worth a thousand words: Absolute and relative decodability of nonlinguistic affect vocalizations. *Emotion*, 9, 293–305.

Hazan, C., & Shaver, P. R. (1987). Romantic love conceptualized as an attachment process. *Journal of Personality and Social Psychology*, 52, 511–524.

Heerdink, M. W., Van Kleef, G. A., Homan, A. C., & Fischer, A. H. (2013). On the social influence of emotions in groups: Interpersonal effects of anger and happiness on conformity versus deviance. *Journal of Personality and Social Psychology*, 105, 262–284.

Heerdink, M. W., Van Kleef, G. A., Homan, A. C., & Fischer, A. H. (2015). Emotional expressions as cues of rejection and acceptance: Evidence from the affect misattribution paradigm. *Journal of Experimental Social Psychology*, 56, 60–68.

Heise, D. R., & O'Brien, J. (1993). Emotion expression in groups. In M. Lewis & J. M. Haviland (Eds.), *Handbook of emotions* (pp. 489–498). New York: Guilford Press.

Hendriks, M. C., & Vingerhoets, A. J. (2006). Social messages of crying faces: Their influence on anticipated person perception, emotions and behavioural responses. *Cognition & Emotion*, 20, 878–886.

Hendriks, M. C. P., Croon, M. A., & Vingerhoets, A. J. J. M. (2008). Social reactions to adult crying: The help-soliciting function of tears. *Journal of Social Psychology*, 148, 22–41.

Hennig-Thurau, T., Groth, M., Paul, M., & Gremler, D. D. (2006). Are all smiles created equal? How emotional contagion and emotional labor affect service relationships. *Journal of Marketing*, 70, 58–73.

Hess, U. (2014). Anger is a positive emotion. In W. G. Parrott (Ed.), *The positive side of negative emotions* (pp. 55–75). New York: Guilford Press.

Hess, U., Banse, R., & Kappas, A. (1995). The intensity of facial expression is determined by underlying affective state and social situation. *Journal of Personality and Social Psychology*, 69, 280–288.

Hess, U., Beaupré, M. G., & Cheung, N. (2002). Who, to whom, and why: Cultural differences and similarities in the function of smiles. In M. H. Abel (Ed.), *An empirical reflection on the smile* (pp. 187–216). Lewiston, NY: Edwin Mellen Press.

Hess, U., & Blairy, S. (2001). Facial mimicry and emotional contagion to dynamic emotional facial expressions and their influence on decoding accuracy. *International Journal of Psychophysiology*, 40, 129–141.

Hess, U., Blairy, S., & Kleck, R. E. (2000). The influence of facial emotion displays, gender, and ethnicity on judgments of dominance and affiliation. *Journal of Nonverbal Behavior*, 24, 265–283.

Hess, U., & Fischer, A. (2013). Emotional mimicry as social regulation. *Personality and Social Psychology Review*, 17, 142–157.

Hewstone, M., Rubin, M., & Willis, H. (2002). Intergroup bias. *Annual Review of Psychology*, 53, 575–604.

Hietanen, J. K., Surakka, V., & Linnankoski, I. (1998). Facial electromyographic responses to vocal affect expressions. *Psychophysiology*, 35, 530–536.

Higgins, E. T. (1997). Beyond pleasure and pain. *American Psychologist*, 52, 1280–1300.

Higgins, E. T. (1998). Promotion and prevention: Regulatory focus as a motivational principle. *Advances in Experimental Social Psychology*, 30, 1–46.

Hochschild, A. R. (1983). *The managed heart*. Berkeley, CA: University of California Press.

Hoffman, D. (1992). A conceptual framework of the influence of positive mood state on service exchange relationships. In C. Allen et al. (Eds.), *Marketing theory and practice* (pp. 144–150). Chicago, IL: American Marketing Association.

Hogg, M. A. (2001). A social identity theory of leadership. *Personality and Social Psychology Review*, 5, 184–200.

Holbrooke, R. (1999). *To end a war*. New York: Modern Library.

Homan, A. C., Hollenbeck, J. R., Humphrey, S. E., van Knippenberg, D., Ilgen, D. R., & Van Kleef, G. A. (2008). Facing differences with an open mind: Openness to experience, salience of intra-group differences, and performance of diverse work groups. *Academy of Management Journal*, 51, 1204–1222.

Homan, A. C., & Jehn, K. A. (2010). How leaders can make diverse groups less difficult: The role of attitudes and perceptions of diversity. In S. Schuman (Ed.), *Handbook for working with difficult groups* (pp. 311–322). Hoboken, NJ: Jossey-Bass.

Homan, A. C., Van Kleef, G. A., Côté, S., & Bogo, A. (2014, May). *The importance of leader emotion management in dealing with team diversity*. Paper presented at the annual conference of the Society for Industrial and Organizational Psychology, Honolulu, HI, USA.

Homan, A. C., Van Kleef, G. A., & Sanchez-Burks, J. (2016). Team members' emotional displays as indicators of team functioning. *Cognition & Emotion*, 30, 134–149.

Hooley, J. M., Richters, J. E., Weintraub, S., & Neale, J. M. (1987). Psychopathology and marital distress: The positive side of positive symptoms. *Journal of Abnormal Psychology*, 96, 27–33.

Horney, K. (1945). *Our inner conflicts*. New York: Norton.

Horstmann, G. (2003). What do facial expressions convey: Feeling states, behavioral intentions, or actions requests? *Emotion*, 3, 150–166.

Howard, D. J., & Gengler, C. (2001). Emotional contagion effects on product attitudes. *Journal of Consumer Research*, 28, 189–201.

Howell, J. M., & Shamir, B. (2005). The role of followers in the charismatic leadership process: Relationships and their consequences. *Academy of Management Review*, 30, 96–112.

Hsee, C. K., Hatfield, E., & Chemtob, C. (1992). Assessments of the emotional states of others: Conscious judgments versus emotional contagion. *Journal of Social and Clinical Psychology*, 11, 119–128.

Hülsheger, U. R., & Schewe, A. F. (2011). On the costs and benefits of emotional labor: A meta-analysis of three decades of research. *Journal of Occupational Health Psychology*, 16, 361–389.

Humphrey, R. H., Pollack, J. M., & Hawver, T. (2008). Leading with emotional labor. *Journal of Managerial Psychology*, 23, 151–168.

Ilies, R., Wagner, D. T., & Morgeson, F. P. (2007). Explaining affective linkages in teams: Individual differences in susceptibility to contagion and individualism–collectivism. *Journal of Applied Psychology*, 92, 1140–1148.

Isen A. M. (2004). Some perspectives on positive feelings and emotions: Positive affect facilitates thinking and problem solving. In A. S. R. Manstead, N. H. Frijda, & A. H. Fisher (Eds.), *Feelings and emotions: The Amsterdam symposium* (pp. 263–281). Cambridge: Cambridge University Press.

Isen, A. M. (1987). Positive affect, cognitive processes, and social behavior. *Advances in Experimental Social Psychology*, 20, 203–253.

Isen, A. M., Shalker, T. E., Clark, M., & Karp, L. (1978). Affect, accessibility of material in memory, and behavior: A cognitive loop? *Journal of Personality and Social Psychology*, 36, 1–12.

Iyer, A., & Leach, C. W. (2008). Emotion in inter-group relations. *European Review of Social Psychology*, 19, 86–125.

Izard, C. E. (1971). *The face of emotion*. New York: Appleton-Century-Crofts.

Izard, C. E. (1977). *Human emotions*. New York: Plenum.

Jackall, R. (1988). *Moral mazes: The world of corporate managers*. Oxford: Oxford University Press.

Jacobs, D. H., Shuren, J., Bowers, D., & Heilman, K. M. (1995). Emotional facial imagery, perception, and expression in Parkinson's disease. *Neurology*, 45, 1696–1702.

Jakobs, E., Manstead, A. S. R., & Fischer, A. H. (1999a). Social motives and subjective feelings as determinants of facial displays: The case of smiling. *Personality and Social Psychology Bulletin*, 25, 424–435.

Jakobs, E., Manstead, A. S. R., & Fischer, A. H. (1999b). Social motives, emotional feelings, and smiling. *Cognition & Emotion*, 13, 321–345.

Jakobs, E., Manstead, A. S. R., & Fischer, A. H. (2001). Social context effects on facial activity in a negative emotional setting. *Emotion*, 1, 51–69.

James, N. (1989). Emotional labour: Skill and work in the social regulation of feelings. *Sociological Review*, 37, 15–42.

James, W. (1884). What is an emotion? *Mind*, 9, 188–205.

Janis, I. L. (1972). *Victims of groupthink: A psychological study of foreign-policy decisions and fiascoes*. Oxford: Houghton Mifflin.

Jehn, K. A., Northcraft, G. B., & Neale, M. A. (1999). Why differences make a difference: A field study of diversity, conflict, and performance in workgroups. *Administrative Science Quarterly, 44*, 741–764.

Jobe, L. E., & Williams White, S. (2007). Loneliness, social relationships, and a broader autism phenotype in college students. *Personality and Individual Differences, 42*, 1479–1489.

Johnson, G., & Connelly, S. (2014). Negative emotions in informal feedback: The benefits of disappointment and drawbacks of anger. *Human Relations, 67*, 1265–1290.

Johnson, H.-A. M., & Spector, P. E. (2007). Service with a smile: Do emotional intelligence, gender, and autonomy moderate the emotional labor process? *Journal of Occupational Health Psychology, 12*, 319–333.

Johnson, S. K. (2008). I second that emotion: Effects of emotional contagion and affect at work on leader and follower outcomes. *The Leadership Quarterly, 19*, 1–19.

Johnson, S. K. (2009). Do you feel what I feel? Mood contagion and leadership outcomes. *The Leadership Quarterly, 20*, 814–827.

Johnston, L., Miles, L., & Macrae, C. N. (2010). Why are you smiling at me? Social functions of enjoyment and non-enjoyment smiles. *British Journal of Social Psychology, 49*, 107–127.

Joiner, T. E., Alfano, M. S., & Metalsky, G. I. (1992). When depression breeds contempt: Reassurance seeking, self-esteem, and rejection of depressed college students by their roommates. *Journal of Abnormal Psychology, 101*, 165–173.

Joiner, T. E. (1994). Contagious depression: Existence, specificity to depressed symptoms, and the role of reassurance seeking. *Journal of Personality and Social Psychology, 67*, 287–296.

Jones, S. S., Collins, K., & Hong, H. W. (1991). An audience effect on smile production in 10-month-old infants. *Psychological Science, 2*, 45–49.

Jones, S. S., & Raag, T. (1989). Smile production in older infants: The importance of a social recipient for the facial signal. *Child Development, 60*, 811–818.

Jordan, P. J., Ashkanasy, N. M., Härtel, C. E. J., & Hooper, G. S. (2002). Workgroup emotional intelligence: Scale development and relationship to team process effectiveness and goal focus. *Human Resource Management Review, 12*, 195–214.

Jordan, P. J., Lawrence, S. A., & Troth, A. C. (2006). The impact of negative mood on team performance. *Journal of Management & Organization, 12*, 131–145.

Jordan, P. J., & Troth, A. C. (2002). Emotional intelligence and conflict resolution: Implications for human resource development. *Advances in Developing Human Resources, 4*, 62–79.

Jordan, P. J., & Troth, A. C. (2004). Managing emotions during team problem solving: Emotional intelligence and conflict resolution. *Human Performance, 17*, 195–218.

Kaiser, R. B., Hogan, R., & Craig, S. B. (2008). Leadership and the fate of organizations. *American Psychologist, 63*, 96–110.

Kaiser, S., & Wehrle, T. (2001). Facial expressions as indicators of appraisal processes. In K. R. Scherer, A. Schorr, & T. Johnstone, *Appraisal processes in emotion: Theory, methods, research* (pp. 285–300). Oxford University Press.

Kantor, J. (2008, January 9). A show of emotion that reverberated beyond the campaign. Retrieved from www.nytimes.com/2008/01/09/us/politics/09moment.html?pagewanted=print

Karatepe, O. M., Yorganci, I., & Haktanir, M. (2009). Outcomes of customer verbal aggression among hotel employees. *International Journal of Contemporary Hospitality Management, 21,* 713–733.

Kellett, J. B., Humphrey, R. H., & Sleeth, R. G. (2002). Empathy and complex task performance: Two routes to leadership. *The Leadership Quarterly, 13,* 523–544.

Kellett, J. B., Humphrey, R. H., & Sleeth, R. G. (2006). Empathy and the emergence of task and relation leaders. *The Leadership Quarterly, 17,* 146–162.

Kelley, H. H., & Thibaut, J. (1978). *Interpersonal relations: A theory of interdependence.* New York: Wiley.

Kelley, H. H., Holmes, J. G., Kerr, N. L., Reis, H. T., Rusbult, C. E., & Van Lange, P. A. M. (2003). *An atlas of interpersonal situations.* New York: Cambridge University Press.

Kelly, J. R., & Barsade, S. G. (2001). Mood and emotions in small groups and work teams. *Organizational Behavior and Human Decision Processes, 86,* 99–130.

Keltner, D. (1995). Signs of appeasement: Evidence for the distinct displays of embarrassment, amusement, and shame. *Journal of Personality and Social Psychology, 68,* 441–454.

Keltner, D. (1996). Evidence for the distinctness of embarrassment, shame, and guilt: A study of recalled antecedents and facial expressions of emotion. *Cognition & Emotion, 10,* 155–172.

Keltner, D., & Anderson, C. (2000). Saving face for Darwin: The functions and uses of embarrassment. *Current Directions in Psychological Science, 9,* 187–192.

Keltner, D., & Buswell, B. N. (1997). Embarrassment: Its distinct form and appeasement functions. *Psychological Bulletin, 122,* 250–270.

Keltner, D., Ellsworth, P. C., & Edwards, K. (1993). Beyond simple pessimism: Effects of sadness and anger on social perception. *Journal of Personality and Social Psychology, 64,* 740–752.

Keltner, D., & Gross, J. J. (1999). Functional accounts of emotions. *Cognition & Emotion, 13,* 467–480.

Keltner, D., & Haidt, J. (1999). Social functions of emotions at four levels of analysis. *Cognition & Emotion, 13,* 505–521.

Keltner, D., Haidt, J., & Shiota, M. N. (2006). Social functionalism and the evolution of emotions. In M. Schaller, J. A. Simpson & D. T. Kenrick (Eds.), *Evolution and social psychology* (pp. 115–142). Madison, CT: Psychosocial Press.

Keltner, D., & Kring, A. M. (1998). Emotion, social function, and psychopathology. *Review of General Psychology, 2,* 320–342.

Keltner, D., Van Kleef, G. A., Chen, S., & Kraus, M. W. (2008). A reciprocal influence model of social power: Emerging principles and lines of inquiry. *Advances in Experimental Social Psychology, 40,* 151–192.

Keltner, D., Young, R. C., & Buswell, B. N. (1997). Appeasement in human emotion, social practice, and personality. *Aggressive Behavior, 23,* 359–374.

Keltner, D., Young, R. C., Heerey, E. A., Oemig, C., & Monarch, N. D. (1998). Teasing in hierarchical and intimate relations. *Journal of Personality and Social Psychology*, 75, 1231–1247.

Kennedy-Moore, E., & Watson, J. C. (2001). How and when does emotional expression help? *Review of General Psychology*, 5, 187–212.

Kenny, D. A., Kashy, D. A., & Cook, W. L. (2006). *Dyadic data analysis*. New York: Guilford.

Kerr, R., Garvin, J., Heaton, N., & Boyle, E. (2006). Emotional intelligence and leadership effectiveness. *Leadership & Organization Development Journal*, 27, 265–279.

Ketelaar, T., & Au, W. T. (2003). The effects of feelings of guilt on the behaviour of uncooperative individuals in repeated social bargaining games: An affect-as-information interpretation of the role of emotion in social interaction. *Cognition & Emotion*, 17, 429–453.

Kilduff, M., Chiaburu, D. S., & Menges, J. I. (2010). Strategic use of emotional intelligence in organizational settings: Exploring the dark side. *Research in Organizational Behavior*, 30, 129–152.

Kim, K., Cundiff, N. L., & Choi, S. B. (2014). The influence of emotional intelligence on negotiation outcomes and the mediating effect of rapport: A structural equation modeling approach. *Negotiation Journal*, 30, 49–68.

Kim, T. T., Yoo, J. J. E., Lee, G., & Kim, J. (2012). Emotional intelligence and emotional labor acting strategies among frontline hotel employees. *International Journal of Contemporary Hospitality Management*, 24, 1029–1046.

Kimball, J. (2004). *The Vietnam War files: Uncovering the secret history of Nixon-era strategy*. Lawrence, KS: University Press of Kansas.

Kitayama, S., Mesquita, B., & Karasawa, M. (2006). Cultural affordances and emotional experience: Socially engaging and disengaging emotions in Japan and the United States. *Journal of Personality and Social Psychology*, 91, 890–903.

Klapwijk, E. T., Peters, S., Vermeiren, R. R. J. M., & Lelieveld, G.-J. (2013). Emotional reactions of peers influence decisions about fairness in adolescence. *Frontiers in Human Neuroscience*, 7, 745.

Klep, A., Wisse, B., & Van der Flier, H. (2011). Interactive affective sharing versus non-interactive affective sharing in work groups: Comparative effects of group affect on work group performance and dynamics. *European Journal of Social Psychology*, 41, 312–323.

Klinnert, M., Campos, J., Sorce, J., Emde, R., & Svejda, M. (1983). Emotions as behavior regulators: Social referencing in infants. In R. Plutchik, & H. Kellerman (Eds.), *Emotion theory, research, and experience: Vol 2. Emotions in early development* (pp. 57–68). New York: Academic Press.

Knapp, A., & Clark, M. (1991). Some detrimental effects of negative mood on individuals' ability to solve resource dilemmas. *Personality and Social Psychology Bulletin*, 17, 678–688.

Knutson, B. (1996). Facial expressions of emotion influence interpersonal trait inferences. *Journal of Nonverbal Behavior*, 20, 165–182.

Komorita, S. S., & Parks, C. D. (1995). Interpersonal relations: Mixed-motive interaction. *Annual Review of Psychology*, 46, 183–207.

Koning, L. F., & Van Kleef, G. A. (2015). How leaders' emotional displays shape followers' organizational citizenship behavior. *The Leadership Quarterly*, 26, 489–501.

Kooij-de Bode, H. J., Van Knippenberg, D., & Van Ginkel, W. P. (2010). Good effects of bad feelings: Negative affectivity and group decision-making. *British Journal of Management*, 21, 375–392.

Kopelman, S., & Rosette, A. S. (2008). Cultural variation in response to strategic emotions in negotiations. *Group Decision and Negotiation*, 17, 65–77.

Kopelman, S., Rosette, A. S., & Thompson, L. (2006). The three faces of eve: An examination of the strategic display of positive, negative, and neutral emotions in negotiations. *Organizational Behavior and Human Decision Processes*, 99, 81–101.

Kraut, R. E., & Johnston, R. E. (1979). Social and emotional messages of smiling: An ethological approach. *Journal of Personality and Social Psychology*, 37, 1539–1553.

Kreibig, S. D. (2010). Autonomic nervous system activity in emotion: A review. *Biological Psychology*, 84, 394–421.

Kring, A. M. (2000). Gender and anger. In A. H. Fischer (Ed.), *Gender and emotion: Social psychological perspectives* (pp. 211–231). New York: Cambridge University Press.

Kring, A. M., Smith, D. A., & Neale, J. M. (1994). Individual differences in dispositional expressiveness: Development and validation of the emotional expressivity scale. *Journal of Personality and Social Psychology*, 66, 934–949.

Kruglanski, A. W. (1989). *Lay epistemics and human knowledge: Cognitive and motivational bases*. New York: Plenum.

Kruglanski, A. W., & Thompson, E. P. (1999). Persuasion by a single route: A view from the unimodel. *Psychological Inquiry*, 10, 83–109.

Kruglanski, A. W., & Webster, D. M. (1991). Group members' reactions to opinion deviates and conformists at varying degrees of proximity to decision deadline and of environmental noise. *Journal of Personality and Social Psychology*, 61, 212–225.

Kruglanski, A. W., & Webster, D. M. (1996). Motivated closing of the mind: "Seizing" and "freezing." *Psychological Review*, 103, 263–283.

Krumhuber, E., & Manstead, A. S. (2009). Are you joking? The moderating role of smiles in the perception of verbal statements. *Cognition & Emotion*, 23, 1504–1515.

Krumhuber, E., Manstead, A. S. R., Cosker, D., Marshall, D., & Rosin, P. L. (2009). Effects of dynamic attributes of smiles in human and synthetic faces: A simulated job interview setting. *Journal of Nonverbal Behavior*, 33, 1–15.

Krumhuber, E., Manstead, A. S. R., Cosker, D., Marshall, D., Rosin, P. L., & Kappas, A. (2007). Facial dynamics as indicators of trustworthiness and cooperative behavior. *Emotion*, 7, 730–735.

Kubany, E. S., Bauer, G. B., Muraoka, M. Y., Richard, D. C., & Read, P. (1995). Impact of labeled anger and blame in intimate relationships. *Journal of Social and Clinical Psychology*, 14, 53–60.

Kuppens, P., Oravecz, Z., & Tuerlinckx, F. (2010). Feelings change: Accounting for individual differences in the temporal dynamics of affect. *Journal of Personality and Social Psychology*, 99, 1042–1060.

Kuppens, P., Van Mechelen, I., & Meulders, M. (2004). Every cloud has a silver lining: Interpersonal and individual differences determinants of anger-related behaviors. *Personality and Social Psychology Bulletin*, 30, 1550–1564.

Kuppens, P., Van Mechelen, I., Smits, D. J., & De Boeck, P. (2003). The appraisal basis of anger: Specificity, necessity, and sufficiency of components. *Emotion*, 3(3), 254–269.

Labott, S. M., Martin, R. B., Eason, P. S., & Berkey, E. Y. (1991). Social reactions to the expression of emotion. *Cognition & Emotion*, 5, 397–417.

Lanzetta, J. T., & Englis, B. G. (1989). Expectations of cooperation and competition and their effects on observers' vicarious emotional responses. *Journal of Personality and Social Psychology*, 56, 543–554.

Lara, M. E., Leader, J., & Klein, D. N. (1997). The association between social support and course of depression: Is it confounded with personality? *Journal of Abnormal Psychology*, 106, 478–482.

Larsen, J. T., McGraw, A. P., & Cacioppo, J. (2001). Can people feel happy and sad at the same time? *Journal of Personality and Social Psychology*, 81, 684–696.

Lavie, N. (2010). Attention, distraction, and cognitive control under load. *Current Directions in Psychological Science*, 19, 143–148.

Lavie, N., Hirst, A., De Fockert, J. W., & Viding, E. (2004). Load theory of selective attention and cognitive control. *Journal of Experimental Psychology: General*, 133, 339–354.

Lazarus, R. S. (1991). *Emotion and adaptation*. New York: Oxford University Press.

Lazarus, R. S. (2003). Does the positive psychology movement have legs? *Psychological Inquiry*, 14, 93–109.

Leach, C. W., Spears, R., & Manstead, A. S. R. (2015). Parsing (malicious) pleasures: Schadenfreude and gloating at others' adversity. *Frontiers in Psychology*, 6, 201.

Le Bon, G. (1895). *The crowd: A study of the popular mind*. London: Ernest Benn.

Leary, K., Pillemer, J., & Wheeler, M. (2013). Negotiating with emotion. *Harvard Business Review*, 91, 96–103.

Leary, M. R., Britt, T. W., Cutlip, W. D., & Templeton, J. L. (1992). Social blushing. *Psychological Bulletin*, 112, 446–460.

LeDoux, J. E. (1998). *The emotional brain: The mysterious underpinnings of emotional life*. New York: Touchstone.

Leith, K. P., & Baumeister, R. F. (1998). Empathy, shame, guilt, and narratives of interpersonal conflicts: Guilt-prone people are better at perspective taking. *Journal of Personality and Social Psychology*, 66, 1–37.

Lelieveld, G.-J., Van Dijk, E., Van Beest, I., & Van Kleef, G. A. (2012). Why anger and disappointment affect bargaining behavior differently: The moderating role of power and the mediating role of reciprocal and complementary emotions. *Personality and Social Psychology Bulletin*, 38, 1209–1221.

Lelieveld, G.-J., Van Dijk, E., Van Beest, I., & Van Kleef, G. A. (2013). Does communicating disappointment in negotiations help or hurt? Solving an apparent inconsistency in the social-functional approach to emotions. *Journal of Personality and Social Psychology*, 105, 605–620.

Lelieveld, G.-J., Van Dijk, E., Van Beest, I., Steinel, W., & Van Kleef, G. A. (2011). Disappointed in you, angry about your offer: Distinct negative emotions induce concessions via different mechanisms. *Journal of Experimental Social Psychology*, 47, 635–641.

Lerner, J. S., Goldberg, J. H., & Tetlock, P. E. (1998). Sober second thoughts: The effects of accountability, anger, and authoritarianism on attributions of responsibility. *Personality and Social Psychology Bulletin*, 24, 563–574.

Lerner, J. S., & Keltner, D. (2001). Fear, anger, and risk. *Journal of Personality and Social Psychology*, 81, 146–159.

Lerner, J. S., Li, Y., Valdesolo, P., & Kassam, K. S. (2015). Emotion and decision making. *Annual Review of Psychology*, 66, 799–823.

Lerner, J. S., Small, D. A., & Loewenstein, G. (2004). Heart strings and purse strings: Carryover effects of emotions on economic decisions. *Psychological Science*, 15, 337–341.

Lerner, J. S., & Tiedens, L. Z. (2006). Portrait of the angry decision maker: How appraisal tendencies shape anger's influence on cognition. *Journal of Behavioral Decision Making*, 19, 115–137.

Leslie, A. M. (1987). Pretense and representation: The origins of "theory of mind." *Psychological Review*, 94, 412–426.

Levenson, R. W. (1992). Autonomic nervous system differences among emotions. *Psychological Science*, 3, 23–27.

Levenson, R. W., Ekman, P., & Friesen, W. V. (1990). Voluntary facial action generates emotion-specific autonomic nervous system activity. *Psychophysiology*, 27, 363–384.

Levenson, R. W., & Gottman, J. M. (1985). Physiological and affective predictors of change in relationship satisfaction. *Journal of Personality and Social Psychology*, 49, 85–94.

Levine, J. M., & Moreland, R. L. (1990). Progress in small group research. *Annual Review of Psychology*, 41, 585–634.

Lewis, K. M. (2000). When leaders display emotion: How followers respond to negative emotional expression of male and female leaders. *Journal of Organizational Behavior*, 21, 221–234.

Lewis, M. (2000). Self-conscious emotions: Embarrassment, pride, shame, and guilt. In M. Lewis & J. M. Haviland-Jones (Eds.), *Handbook of emotions* (2nd ed., pp. 623–636). New York: Guilford Press.

Leys, C., Licata, L., Marchal, C., & Bernard, P. (2012). The influence of defendants' feelings of guilt on their penalties: The mediating role of attribution processes. *Revue Internationale de Psychologie Sociale*, 4, 45–58.

Lindebaum, D., & Fielden, S. L. (2011). "It's good to be angry": Enacting anger in construction project management to achieve perceived leader effectiveness. *Human Relations*, 64, 437–458.

Lindebaum, D., & Jordan, P. J. (2014). When it can be good to feel bad and bad to feel good: Exploring asymmetries in workplace emotional outcomes. *Human Relations*, 67, 1037–1050.

Linnankoski, I., Laasko, M. L., & Leinonen, L. (1994). Recognition of emotions in macaque vocalizations by children and adults. *Language and Communication*, 14, 183–192.

Little, L. M., Kluemper, D., Nelson, D. L., & Gooty, J. (2012). Development and validation of the Interpersonal Emotion Management Scale. *Journal of Occupational and Organizational Psychology*, 85, 407–420.

Little, L. M., Kluemper, D., Nelson, D. L., & Ward, A. (2013). More than happy to help? Customer-focused emotion management strategies. *Personnel Psychology*, 66, 261–286.

Lively, K. (2000). Reciprocal emotion management: Working together to maintain stratification in private law firms. *Work and Occupations*, 27, 32–63.

Loades, D. (2006). *Elizabeth I: A life*. London: Hambledon Press.

Locke, K. (1996). A funny thing happened! The management of consumer emotions in service encounters. *Organization Science*, 7, 4–59.

Locke, K. D., & Horowitz, L. M. (1990). Satisfaction in interpersonal interactions as a function of similarity in level of dysphoria. *Journal of Personality and Social Psychology*, 58, 823–831.

Lopes, P. N., Brackett, M. A., Nezlek, J. B., Schütz, A., Sellin, I., & Salovey, P. (2004). Emotional intelligence and social interaction. *Personality and Social Psychology Bulletin*, 30, 1018–1034.

Lopes, P. N., Salovey, P., Côté, S., & Beers, M. (2005). Emotion regulation abilities and the quality of social interaction. *Emotion*, 5, 113–118.

Lopes, P. N., Salovey, P., & Straus, R. (2003). Emotional intelligence, personality, and the perceived quality of social relationships. *Personality and individual Differences*, 35, 641–658.

Lord, R. G., De Vader, C. L., & Alliger, G. M. (1986). A meta-analysis of the relation between personality traits and leadership perceptions: An application of validity generalization procedures. *Journal of Applied Psychology*, 71, 402–410.

Lumsden, E. A. (1993). Borderline personality disorder: A consequence of experiencing affect within a truncated time frame? *Journal of Personality Disorders*, 7, 265–274.

Lundquist, L.-O., & Dimberg, U. (1995). Facial expressions are contagious. *Journal of Psychophysiology*, 9, 203–211.

Lutz, C., & White, G. M. (1986). The anthropology of emotions. *Annual Review of Anthropology*, 15, 405–436.

Lyubomirsky, S., King, L., & Diener, E. (2005). The benefits of frequent positive affect: Does happiness lead to success? *Psychological Bulletin*, 131, 803–855.

Mackie, D. M., Devos, T., & Smith, E. R. (2000). Intergroup emotions: Explaining offensive action tendencies in an intergroup context. *Journal of Personality and Social Psychology*, 79, 602–616.

MacLean, Paul D. (1990). *The triune brain in evolution: Role in paleocerebral functions*. New York: Plenum Press.

Madera, J., & Smith, D. B. (2009). The effects of leader negative emotions on evaluations of leadership in a crisis situation: The role of anger and sadness. *The Leadership Quarterly, 20,* 103–114.

Magee, J. C., & Smith, P. K. (2013). The social distance theory of power. *Personality and Social Psychology Review, 17,* 158–186.

Magee, J. C., & Tiedens, L. Z. (2006). Emotional ties that bind: The roles of valence and consistency of group emotion in inferences of cohesiveness and common fate. *Personality and Social Psychology Bulletin, 32,* 1703–1715.

Magnée, M. J. C. M., Stekelenburg, J. J., Kemner, C., & De Gelder, B. (2007). Similar facial electromyographic responses to faces, voices, and body expressions. NeuroReport, 18, 369–372.

Malouff, J. M., Schutte, N. S., & Thorsteinsson, E. B. (2014). Trait emotional intelligence and romantic relationship satisfaction: A meta-analysis. *The American Journal of Family Therapy, 42,* 53–66.

Mannetti, L., Levine, J. M., Pierro, A., & Kruglanski, A. W. (2010). Group reaction to defection: The impact of shared reality. *Social Cognition, 28,* 447–464.

Manstead, A. S. R. (1991). Expressiveness as an individual difference. In R. S. Feldman & B. Rimé (Eds.), *Fundamentals of nonverbal behavior* (pp. 285–328). Cambridge: Cambridge University Press.

Manstead, A. S. R., & Fischer, A. H. (2001). Social appraisal: The social world as object of and influence on appraisal processes. In K. R. Scherer, A. Schorr, & T. Johnstone (Eds.), *Appraisal processes in emotion: Theory, research, application* (pp. 221–232). New York: Oxford University Press.

Manstead, A. S. R., Fischer, A. H., & Jakobs, E. (1999). The social and emotional functions of facial displays. In P. Philippot, R. S. Feldman, and E. J. Coats (Eds.), *The social context of nonverbal behavior* (pp. 287–313). New York: Cambridge University Press.

Manstead, A. S. R., & Tetlock, P. E. (1989). Cognitive appraisals and emotional experience: Further evidence. *Cognition & Emotion, 3,* 225–239.

Manstead, A. S. R., Wagner, H. L., & MacDonald, C. J. (1984). Face, body, and speech as channels of communication in the detection of deception. *Basic and Applied Social Psychology, 5,* 317–332.

Markus, H. R., & Kitayama, S. (1991). Culture and the self: Implications for cognition, emotion, and motivation. *Psychological Review, 98,* 224–253.

Marques, J., Abrams, D., Paez, D., & Martinez-Taboada, C. (1998). The role of categorization and in-group norms in judgments of groups and their members. *Journal of Personality and Social Psychology, 75,* 976–988.

Martin, L. L., Ward, D. W., Achee, J. W., & Wyer, R. S. (1993). Mood as input: People have to interpret the motivational implications of their moods. *Journal of Personality and Social Psychology, 64,* 317–326.

Mason, C. M., & Griffin, M. A. (2003). Group absenteeism and positive affective tone: A longitudinal study. *Journal of Organizational Behavior, 24,* 667–687.

Matsumoto, D. (1990). Cultural similarities and differences in display rules. *Motivation and Emotion, 14,* 195–214.

Matsumoto, D., Yoo, S. H., Nakagawa, S., & 37 Members of the Multinational Study of Cultural Display Rules (2008). Culture, emotion regulation, and adjustment. *Journal of Personality and Social Psychology*, 94, 925–937.

Mattila, A. S., & Enz, C. A. (2002). The role of emotions in service encounters. *Journal of Service Research*, 4, 268–277.

Mauss, I. B., & Robinson, M. D. (2009). Measures of emotion: A review. *Cognition & Emotion*, 23, 209–237.

Mauss, I. B., Shallcross, A. J., Troy, A. S., John, O. P., Ferrer, E., Wilhelm, F. H., & Gross, J. J. (2011). Don't hide your happiness! Positive emotion dissociation, social connectedness, and psychological functioning. *Journal of Personality and Social Psychology*, 100, 738–748.

Mayer, J. D., Caruso, D. R., & Salovey, P. (1999). Emotional intelligence meets traditional standards for an intelligence. *Intelligence*, 27, 267–298.

Mayer, J. D., DiPaolo, M., & Salovey, P. (1990). Perceiving affective content in ambiguous visual stimuli: A component of emotional intelligence. *Journal of Personality Assessment*, 54, 772–781.

Mayer, J. D., & Salovey, P. (1997). What is emotional intelligence? In P. Salovey & D. Sluyter (Eds.), *Emotional development and emotional intelligence: Educational implications* (pp. 3–31). New York: Basic Books.

Mayer, J. D., Salovey, J., & Caruso, D. R. (2004). Emotional intelligence: Theory, findings, and implications. *Psychological Inquiry*, 15, 197–215.

McCrae, R. R, & Costa, P. T., Jr. (1987). Validation of the five-factor model of personality across instruments and observers. *Journal of Personality and Social Psychology*, 52, 81–90.

McCrone, J. (1991). *The ape that spoke: Language and the evolution of the human mind*. New York: Avon Books.

McDougall, W. (1923). *Outline of psychology*. New York: Scribner.

Mehrabian, A., & Ferris, S. R. (1967). Inference of attitudes from nonverbal communication in two channels. *Journal of Consulting Psychology*, 31, 248–252.

Mellers, B. A., & McGraw, A. P. (2001). Anticipated emotions as guides to choice. *Current Directions in Psychological Science*, 10, 210–214.

Melwani, S., & Barsade, S. G. (2011). Held in contempt: The psychological, interpersonal, and performance consequences of contempt in a work context. *Journal of Personality and Social Psychology*, 101, 503–520.

Menon, K., & Dubé, L. (2000). Ensuring greater satisfaction by engineering salesperson response to customer emotions. *Journal of Retailing*, 76, 285–307.

Mesquita, B., & Frijda, N. H. (1992). Cultural variations in emotions: A review. *Psychological Bulletin*, 112, 179–204.

Mesquita, B., Frijda, N. H., & Scherer, K. R. (1997). Culture and emotion. In J. W. Berry, P. R. Dasen, & T. S. Saraswathi (Eds.), *Handbook of cross-cultural psychology: Vol. 2: Basic processes and human development* (2nd ed., pp. 255–297). Boston: Allyn & Bacon.

Meyer, D. E., & Schvaneveldt, R. W. (1971). Facilitation in recognizing pairs of words: evidence of a dependence between retrieval operations. *Journal of Experimental Psychology*, 90, 227–234.

Miller, D. T, & Ross, M. (1975). Self-serving biases in attribution of causality: Fact or fiction? *Psychological Bulletin*, 82, 213–225.

Miller, R. E., Murphy, J. V., & Mirsky, I. A. (1959). Non-verbal communication of affect. *Journal of Clinical Psychology*, 15, 155–158.

Miller, R. S. (2004). Emotion as adaptive interpersonal communication: The case of embarrassment. In L. Z. Tiedens & C. W. Leach (Eds.), *The social life of emotions* (pp. 87–105). Cambridge: Cambridge University Press.

Miller, R. S., & Leary, M. R. (1992). Social sources and interactive functions of embarrassment. In M. Clark (Ed.), *Emotion and social behavior* (pp. 322–339). New York: Russell Sage Foundation.

Miron-Spektor, E., Efrat-Treister, D., Rafaeli, A., & Schwarz-Cohen, O. (2011). Others' anger makes people work harder not smarter: The effect of observing anger and sarcasm on creative and analytic thinking. *Journal of Applied Psychology*, 96, 1065–1075.

Miron-Spektor, E., & Rafaeli, A. (2009). The effects of anger in the workplace: When, where, and why observing anger enhances or hinders performance. *Research in Personnel and Human Resources Management*, 28, 153–178.

Mirsky, I. A., Miller, R. E., & Murphy, J. V. (1958). The communication of affect in rhesus monkeys: I. *An experimental method. Journal of the American Psychoanalytic Association*, 6, 433–441.

Modestin, J., & Villiger, C. (1989). Follow-up study on borderline versus non-borderline personality disorders. *Comprehensive Psychiatry*, 30, 236–244.

Moody, E. J., McIntosh, D. N., Mann, L. J., & Weisser, K. R. (2007). More than mere mimicry? The influence of emotion on rapid facial reactions to faces. *Emotion*, 7, 447–457.

Morris, M. W., & Keltner, D. (2000). How emotions work: An analysis of the social functions of emotional expression in negotiations. *Research in Organizational Behavior*, 22, 1–50.

Mueller, J. S., & Curhan, J. R. (2006). Emotional intelligence and counterpart mood induction in a negotiation. *International Journal of Conflict Management*, 17, 110–128.

Mueser, K. T., Bellack, A. S., Morrison, R. L., & Wixted, J. T. (1990). Social competence in schizophrenia: Premorbid adjustment, social skill, and domains of functioning. *Journal of Psychiatric Research*, 24, 51–63.

Mullen, B., Futrell, D., Stairs, D., Tice, D. M., Baumeister, R. F., Dawson, K. E., Riordan, C. A., Radloff, C. E., Goethals, G. R., Kennedy, J. G., & Rosenfeld, P. (1986). Newscaster's facial expressions and voting behavior of viewers: Can a smile elect a president? *Journal of Personality and Social Psychology*, 51, 291–295.

Mumenthaler, C., & Sander, D. (2012). Social appraisal influences recognition of emotions. *Journal of Personality and Social Psychology*, 102, 1118–1135.

Murphy, S. T., & Zajonc, R. B. (1993). Affect, cognition, and awareness: Affective priming with optimal and suboptimal stimulus exposures. *Journal of Personality and Social Psychology*, 64, 723–739.

Nelson, C. A. (1987). The recognition of facial expressions in the 1st 2 years of life: Mechanisms of development. *Child Development*, 58, 889–909.

Nelson, J. K. (2005). *Seeing through tears: Crying and attachment.* New York: Brunner-Routledge.

Nesse, R. M. (1990). Evolutionary explanations of emotions. *Human Nature, 1,* 261–289.

Nesse, R. M., & Ellsworth, P. C. (2009). Evolution, emotions, and emotional disorders. *American Psychologist, 64,* 129–139.

Neuberg, S. L., & Newsom, J. T. (1993). Personal need for structure: Individual differences in the desire for simpler structure. *Journal of Personality and Social Psychology, 65,* 113–131.

Neumann, R., & Strack, F. (2000). "Mood contagion": The automatic transfer of mood between persons. *Journal of Personality and Social Psychology, 79,* 211–223.

Newcombe, M. J., & Ashkanasy, N. M. (2002). The role of affect and affective congruence in perceptions of leaders: An experimental study. *The Leadership Quarterly, 13,* 601–614.

Nezlak, J. B., Imbrie, M., & Shean, G. D. (1994). Depression and everyday social interaction. *Journal of Personality and Social Psychology, 67,* 1101–1111.

Niedenthal, P. M. (2007). Embodying emotion. *Science, 316,* 1002–1005.

Niedenthal, P. M., & Brauer, M. (2012). Social functionality of human emotion. *Annual Review of Psychology, 63,* 259–285.

Niedenthal, P. M., Winkielman, P. Mondillon, L., & Vermeulen, N. (2009). Embodiment of emotional concepts. *Journal of Personality and Social Psychology, 96,* 1120–1136.

Nisbett, R. E., & Wilson, T. D. (1977). The halo effect: Evidence for unconscious alteration of judgments. *Journal of Personality and Social Psychology, 35,* 250–256.

Niven, K., Totterdell, P., & Holman, D. (2009). A classification of controlled interpersonal affect regulation strategies. *Emotion, 9,* 498–509.

Niven, K., Totterdell, P., Holman, D., & Headley, T. (2012). Does regulating others' feelings influence people's own affective well-being? *The Journal of Social Psychology, 152,* 246–260.

Nordgren, L. F., Banas, K., & MacDonald, G. (2011). Empathy gaps for social pain: Why people underestimate the pain of social suffering. *Journal of Personality and Social Psychology, 100,* 120–128.

Oatley, K. (2003). Creative expression and communication of emotions in the visual and narrative arts. In R. J. Davidson, K. R. Scherer, & H. H. Goldsmith (Eds.), *Handbook of affective sciences* (pp. 481–502). New York: Oxford University Press.

Oatley, K. (2004). *Emotions: A brief history.* Malden, MA: Blackwell.

Oatley, K., & Jenkins, J. M. (1992). Human emotions: Function and dysfunction. *Annual Review of Psychology, 43,* 55–85.

Oatley, K., & Johnson-Laird, P. N. (1987). Towards a cognitive theory of emotions. *Cognition & Emotion, 1,* 29–50.

Oberman, L. M., Winkielman, P., & Ramachandran, V. S. (2007). Face to face: Blocking facial mimicry can selectively impair recognition of emotional expressions. *Social Neuroscience, 2,* 167–178.

Ochsner, K. N., Knierim, K., Ludlow, D. H., Hanelin, J., Ramachandran, T., Glover, G., & Mackey, S. C. (2004). Reflecting upon feelings: An fMRI study of neural systems supporting the attribution of emotion to self and other. *Journal of cognitive neuroscience*, 16, 1746–1772.

Ohbuchi, K., Kameda, M., & Agarie, N. (1989). Apology as aggression control: Its role in mediating appraisal of and response to harm. *Journal of Personality and Social Psychology*, 56, 219–227.

Öhman, A. (1986). Face the beast and fear the face: Animal and social fears as prototypes for evolutionary analysis of emotion. *Psychophysiology*, 23, 123–145.

Oliver, M. B. (1993). Exploring the paradox of the enjoyment of sad films. *Human Communication Research*, 19, 315–342.

Olson, J. M., Roese, N. J., & Zanna, M. P. (1996). Expectancies. In E. T. Higgins & A. W. Kruglanski (Eds.), *Social psychology: Handbook of basic principles* (pp. 211–238). New York: Guilford Press.

Ortony, A., Clore, G. L., & Collins, A. (1988). *The cognitive structure of emotion.* Cambridge: Cambridge University Press.

Overbeck, J. R., Neale, M. A., & Govan, C. L. (2010). I feel, therefore you act: Intrapersonal and interpersonal effects of emotion on negotiation as a function of social power. *Organizational Behavior and Human Decision Processes*, 112, 126–139.

Pareene, A. (2010, June 2). Why won't Obama just get even madder about this oil spill? Salon.com. Retrieved from www.salon.com/2010/06/02/obama_anger_pundits/singleton/

Parkinson, B. (1996). Emotions are social. *British Journal of Psychology*, 87, 663–683.

Parkinson, B. (2001). Putting appraisal in context. In K. R. Scherer, A. Schorr, & T. Johnstone (Eds.), *Appraisal processes in emotion: Theory, method, research* (pp. 173–186). New York: Oxford University Press.

Parkinson, B. (2005). Do facial movements express emotions or communicate motives? *Personality and Social Psychology Review*, 9, 278–311.

Parkinson, B., Fischer, A. H., & Manstead, A. S. R. (2005). *Emotion in social relations: Cultural, group, and interpersonal processes.* New York: Psychology Press.

Parkinson, B., Phiri, N., & Simons, G. (2012). Bursting with anxiety: Adult social referencing in an interpersonal Balloon Analogue Risk Task (BART). *Emotion*, 12, 817–826.

Parkinson, B., & Simons, G. (2009). Affecting others: Social appraisal and emotion contagion in everyday decision making. *Personality and Social Psychology Bulletin*, 35, 1071–1084.

Parkinson, B., & Totterdell, P. (1999). Classifying affect-regulation strategies. *Cognition & Emotion*, 13, 277–303.

Parr, L. A., Hopkins, W. D., & de Waal, F. B. M. (1998). The perception of facial expressions in chimpanzees, *Pan Troglodytes. Evolution of Communication*, 2, 1–23.

Parr, L. A., Waller, B. M., & Fugate, J. (2005). Emotional communication in primates: Implications for neurobiology. *Current Opinion in Neurobiology*, 15, 716–720.

Parr, L. A., Waller, B. M., Vick, S. J., & Bard, K. A. (2007). Classifying chimpanzee facial expressions by muscle action. *Emotion, 7*, 172–181.

Parrott, W. G. (2001). Implications of dysfunctional emotions for understanding how emotions function. *Review of General Psychology, 5*, 180–186.

Parrott, W. G. (Ed.). (2014). *The positive side of negative emotions.* New York: Guilford Press.

Payne, B. K., Cheng, C. M., Govorun, O., & Stewart, B. D. (2005). An inkblot for attitudes: Affect misattribution as implicit measurement. *Journal of Personality and Social Psychology, 89*, 277–293.

Perugini, M., & Bagozzi, R. P. (2001). The role of desires and anticipated emotions in goal-directed behaviours: Broadening and deepening the theory of planned behaviour. *British Journal of Social Psychology, 40*, 79–98.

Pescosolido, A. T. (2002). Emergent leaders as managers of group emotion. *The Leadership Quarterly, 13*, 583–599.

Pessoa, L., McKenna, M., Gutierrez, E., & Ungerleider, L. G. (2002). Neural processing of emotional faces requires attention. *Proceedings of the National Academy of Sciences of the United States of America, 99*, 11458–11463.

Petty, R. E., & Cacioppo, J. T. (1986). The elaboration likelihood model of persuasion. *Advances in Experimental Social Psychology, 19*, 123–205.

Phan, K. L., Wager, T., Taylor, S. F., & Liberzon, I. (2002). Functional neuroanatomy of emotion: A meta-analysis of emotion activation studies in PET and fMRI. *Neuroimage, 16*, 331–348.

Pietroni, D., Van Kleef, G. A., De Dreu, C. K. W., & Pagliaro, S. (2008). Emotions as strategic information: Effects of other's emotions on fixed-pie perception, demands and integrative behavior in negotiation. *Journal of Experimental Social Psychology, 44*, 1444–1454.

Pillutla, M. M., & Murnighan, J. K. (1996). Unfairness, anger, and spite: Emotional rejections of ultimatum offers. *Organizational Behavior and Human Decision Processes, 68*, 208–224.

Planalp, S. (1999). *Communicating emotion: Social, moral, and cultural processes.* Cambridge: Cambridge University Press.

Plant, E. A., Hyde, J. S., Keltner, D., & Devine, P. G. (2000). The gender stereotyping of emotions. *Psychology of Women Quarterly, 24*, 81–92.

Porges, S. W. (1999). Emotion: An evolutionary by-product of the neural regulation of the autonomic nervous system. In C. S. Carter, I. I. Lederhendler, & B. Kirkpatrick (Eds.), *The integrative neurobiology of affiliation* (pp. 65–80). Cambridge, MA: MIT Press.

Premack, D., & Woodruff, G. (1978). Does the chimpanzee have a theory of mind? *Behavioral and Brain Sciences, 1*, 515–526.

Prentice, C., & King, B. E. (2013). Emotional intelligence and adaptability – Service encounters between casino hosts and premium players. *International Journal of Hospitality Management, 32*, 287–294.

Preston, S. D., & de Waal, F. B. M. (2002). Empathy: Its ultimate and proximate bases. *Behavioral and Brain Sciences, 25*, 1–20.

Pruitt, D. G., & Carnevale, P. J. (1993). *Negotiation in social conflict.* Buckingham: Open University Press.

Pugh, S. D. (2001). Service with a smile: Emotional contagion in the service encounter. *Academy of Management Journal*, 44, 1018–1027.

Quigley, B. M., & Tedeschi, J. T. (1996). Mediating effects of blame attributions on feelings of anger. *Personality and Social Psychology Bulletin*, 22, 1280–1288.

Rafaeli, A., Erez, A., Ravid, S., Derfler-Rozin, R., Treister, D. E., & Scheyer, R. (2012). When customers exhibit verbal aggression, employees pay cognitive costs. *Journal of Applied Psychology*, 97, 931–950.

Rafaeli, A., & Sutton, R. I. (1987). Expression of emotion as part of the work role. *Academy of Management Review*, 12, 23–37.

Rafaeli, A., & Sutton, R. I. (1989). The expression of emotion in organizational life. *Research in Organizational Behavior*, 11, 1–42.

Rafaeli, A., & Sutton, R. I. (1991). Emotional contrast strategies as means of social influence: Lessons from criminal interrogators and bill collectors. *Academy of Management Journal*, 34, 749–775.

Raiffa, H. (1982). *The art and science of negotiation*. Cambridge, MA: Harvard University Press.

Reddy, W. M. (2001). *The navigation of feeling: A framework for the history of emotions*. Cambridge: Cambridge University Press.

Redican, W. K. (1982). An evolutionary perspective on human facial displays. In P. Ekman (Ed.), *Emotion in the human face* (2nd ed., pp. 212–280). Elmsford, NY: Pergamon Press.

Reis, H. T., McDougal Wilson, I., Monestere, C., Bernstein, S., Clark, K., Seidl, E., Franco, M., Giososo, E., Freeman, L., & Radoane, K. (1990). What is smiling is beautiful and good. *European Journal of Social Psychology*, 20, 259–267.

Repacholi, B. M. (1998). Infants' use of attentional cues to identify the referent of another person's emotional expression. *Developmental Psychology*, 34, 1017–1025.

Repacholi, B. M., & Gopnik, A. (1997). Early reasoning about desires: Evidence from 14- and 18-month-olds. *Developmental Psychology*, 33, 12–21.

Richards, B. (2004). The emotional deficit in political communication. *Political Communication*, 21, 339–352.

Riefer, D. M., & Batchelder, W. H. (1988). Multinomial modeling and the measurement of cognitive processes. *Psychological Review*, 95, 318–339.

Rimé, B., Finkenauer, C., Luminet, O., Zech, E., & Philippot, P. (1998). Social sharing of emotion: New evidence and new questions. *European Review of Social Psychology*, 9, 145–189.

Rimé, B., Philippot, P., Boca, S., & Mesquita, B. (1992). Long-lasting cognitive and social consequences of emotion: Social sharing and rumination. *European Review of Social Psychology*, 3, 225–258.

Roberts, B. W., & Robins, R. W. (2000). Broad dispositions, broad aspirations: The intersection of personality traits and major life goals. *Personality and Social Psychology Bulletin*, 26, 1284–1296.

Roberts, W. L., & Strayer, J. (1987). Parents' responses to the emotional distress of their children: Relations with children's competence. *Developmental Psychology*, 23, 415–422.

Roccas, S., Sagiv, L., Schwartz, S. H., & Knafo, A. (2002). The big five personality factors and personal values. *Personality and Social Psychology Bulletin, 28,* 789–801.

Roseman, I. J. (1984). Cognitive determinants of emotion: A structural theory. In P. Shaver (Ed.), *Review of personality and social psychology* (Vol. 5, pp. 11–36). Beverly Hills, CA: Sage.

Roseman, I. J., Wiest, C., & Swartz, T. S. (1994). Phenomenology, behaviors, and goals differentiate discrete emotions. *Journal of Personality and Social Psychology, 67,* 206–221.

Rosenfeld, H. M. (1966). Approval-seeking and approval-inducing functions of verbal and nonverbal responses in the dyad. *Journal of Personality and Social Psychology, 6,* 597–605.

Rosete, D., & Ciarrochi, J. (2005). Emotional intelligence and its relationship to workplace performance outcomes of leadership effectiveness. *Leadership & Organization Development Journal, 26,* 388–399.

Rozell, E. J., Pettijohn, C. E., & Parker, R. S. (2004). Customer-oriented selling: Exploring the roles of emotional intelligence and organizational commitment. *Psychology & Marketing, 21,* 405–424.

Rubin, J. Z., Pruitt, D. G., & Kim, S. H. (1994). *Social conflict; escalation, stalemate, and settlement.* New York: McGraw-Hill.

Rubin, R. S., Munz, D. C., & Bommer, W. H. (2005). Leading from within: The effects of emotion recognition and personality on transformational leadership behavior. *Academy of Management Journal, 48,* 845–858.

Rupp, D. E., & Spencer, S. (2006). When customers lash out: The effects of customer interactional injustice on emotional labor and the mediating role of discrete emotions. *Journal of Applied Psychology, 91,* 971–978.

Rusbult, C. E., & Van Lange, P. A. (2003). Interdependence, interaction, and relationships. *Annual Review of Psychology, 54,* 351–375.

Russell, B. (1951). *New hopes for a changing world.* London: George Allen and Unwin.

Russell, J. A. (1994). Is there universal recognition of emotion from facial expression? A review of the cross-cultural studies. *Psychological Bulletin, 115,* 102–141.

Saarni, C. (1999). *The development of emotional competence.* New York: Guilford Press.

Salovey, P., & Grewal, D. (2005). The science of emotional intelligence. *Current Directions in Psychological Science, 14,* 281–285.

Salovey, P., & Mayer, J. D. (1990). Emotional intelligence. *Imagination, Cognition, and Personality, 9,* 185–211.

Salzman, C. D., & Fusi, S. (2010). Emotion, cognition, and mental state representation in amygdala and prefrontal cortex. *Annual Review of Neuroscience, 33,* 173–202.

Sanchez-Burks, J., Bartel, C. A., Rees, L., & Huy, Q. (2016). Assessing collective affect recognition via the EAM (Emotional Aperture Measure). *Cognition & Emotion, 30,* 117–133.

Sanchez-Burks, J., & Huy, Q. N. (2009). Emotional aperture and strategic change: The accurate recognition of collective emotions. *Organization Science, 20,* 22–34.

Sato, W., Kochiyama, T., Yoshikawa, S., Naito, E., & Matsumura, M. (2004). Enhanced neural activity in response to dynamic facial expressions of emotion: An fMRI study. *Cognitive Brain Research, 20,* 81–91.

Sauter, D. (2010). More than happy: The need for disentangling positive emotions. *Current Directions in Psychological Science, 19,* 36–40.

Sauter, D. A., Eisner, F., Ekman, P., & Scott, S. K. (2010). Cross-cultural recognition of basic emotions through nonverbal emotional vocalizations. *Proceedings of the National Academy of Sciences of the United States of America, 107,* 2408–2412.

Schachter, S. (1959). *The psychology of affiliation.* Stanford, CA: Stanford University Press.

Schaller, M., & Cialdini, R. B. (1988). The economics of empathic helping: Support for a mood management motive. *Journal of Experimental Social Psychology, 24,* 163–181.

Schelling, T. C. (1960). *The strategy of conflict.* Cambridge, MA: Harvard University Press.

Scherer, K. R. (1986). Vocal affect expression: A review and model for future research. *Psychological Bulletin, 99,* 143–165.

Scherer, K. R. (2009). The dynamic architecture of emotion: Evidence for the component process model. *Cognition & Emotion, 23,* 1307–1351.

Scherer, K. R., Banse, R., & Wallbott, H. G. (2001). Emotion inferences from vocal expression correlate across languages and cultures. *Journal of Cross-Cultural Psychology, 32,* 76–92.

Scherer, K. R., Feldstein, S., Bond, R. N., & Rosenthal, R. (1985). Vocal cues to deception: A comparative channel approach. *Journal of Psycholinguistic Research, 14,* 409–425.

Scherer, K., & Grandjean, D. (2008). Facial expressions allow inference of both emotions and their components. *Cognition & Emotion, 22,* 789–801.

Scherer, K. R., Schorr, A., & Johnstone, T. (2001) (Eds.). *Appraisal processes in emotion: Theory, methods, research.* New York: Oxford University Press.

Scherer, K. R., & Tannenbaum, P. H. (1986). Emotional experiences in everyday life: A survey approach. *Motivation and Emotion, 10,* 295–314.

Scherer, K. R., & Wallbott, H. G. (1994). Evidence for universality and cultural variation of differential emotion response patterning. *Journal of Personality and social psychology, 66,* 310–328.

Scherer, K. R., Wallbott, H. G., & Summerfield, A. B. (1986). *Experiencing emotion: A cross-cultural study.* New York: Cambridge University Press.

Schneider, B. (1987). The people make the place. *Personnel Psychology, 40,* 437–454.

Schubert, E. (1996). Enjoyment of negative emotions in music: An associative network explanation. *Psychology of Music, 24,* 18–28.

Schutte, N. S., Malouff, J. M., Bobik, C., Coston, T. D., Greeson, C., Jedlicka, C., Rhodes, E., & Wendorf, G. (2001). Emotional intelligence and interpersonal relations. *The Journal of Social Psychology, 141,* 523–536.

Schwarz, N., & Bless, H. (1991). Happy and mindless, but sad and smart? The impact of affective states on analytic reasoning. In J. P. Forgas (Ed.), *Emotion and social judgment* (pp. 55–71). Oxford: Pergamon.

Schwarz, N., Bless, H., & Bohner, G. (1991). Mood and persuasion: Affective states influence the processing of persuasive communications. *Advances in Experimental Social Psychology*, 24, 161–195.

Schwarz, N., & Clore, G. L. (1983). Mood, misattribution, and judgments of well-being: Informative and directive functions of affective states. *Journal of Personality and Social Psychology*, 45, 513–523.

Schwarz, N., & Clore, G. L. (1988). How do I feel about it? The informative function of affective states. In K. Fiedler & J. P. Forgas (Eds.), *Affect, cognition, and social behavior* (pp. 44–62). Toronto, ON: Hogrefe.

Sedikides, C., Wildschut, T., Arndt, J., & Routledge, C. (2008). Nostalgia: Past, present, and future. *Current Directions in Psychological Science*, 17, 304–307.

Semin, G. R., & Manstead, A. S. R. (1982). The social implications of embarrassment displays and restitution behaviour. *European Journal of Social Psychology*, 12, 367–377.

Shariff, A. F., & Tracy, J. L. (2011). What are emotion expressions for? *Current Directions in Psychological Science*, 20, 395–399.

Shariff, A. F., Tracy, J. L., & Markusoff, J. L. (2012). (Implicitly) judging a book by its cover: The power of pride and shame expressions in shaping judgments of social status. *Personality and Social Psychology Bulletin*, 38, 1178–1193.

Shaver, P. R., Morgan, H. J., & Wu, S. (1996). Is love a "basic" emotion? *Personal Relationships*, 3, 81–96.

Shaver, P., Schwartz, J., Kirson, D., & O'Connor, C. (1987). Emotion knowledge: Further exploration of a prototype approach. *Journal of Personality and Social Psychology*, 52, 1061–1086.

Sherman, J. W., Krieglmeyer, R., & Calanchini, J. (2014). Process models require process measures. In J. W. Sherman, B. Gawronski, & Y. Trope (Eds.), *Dual process theories of the social mind* (pp. 121–138). New York: Guilford Press.

Shields, S. A. (2005). The politics of emotion in everyday life: "Appropriate" emotion and claims on identity. *Review of General Psychology*, 9, 3–15.

Sinaceur, M., Adam, H., Van Kleef, G. A., & Galinsky, A. D. (2013). The advantages of being unpredictable: How emotional inconsistency extracts concessions in negotiation. *Journal of Experimental Social Psychology*, 49, 498–508.

Sinaceur, M., Kopelman, S., Vasiljevic, D., & Haag, C. (2015). Weep and get more: When and why sadness expression is effective in negotiations. *Journal of Applied Psychology*, 100, 1847–1871.

Sinaceur, M., & Tiedens, L. Z. (2006). Get mad and get more than even: When and why anger expression is effective in negotiations. *Journal of Experimental Social Psychology*, 42, 314–322.

Sinaceur, M., Van Kleef, G. A., Neale, M. A., Adam, H., & Haag, C. (2011). Hot or cold: Is communicating anger or threats more effective in negotiation? *Journal of Applied Psychology*, 96, 1018–1032.

Singer, J. A., & Salovey, P. (1988). Mood and memory: Evaluating the network theory of affect. *Clinical Psychology Review*, 8, 211–251.

Skarlicki, D. P., & Folger, R. (1997). Retaliation in the workplace: The roles of distributive, procedural, and interactional justice. *Journal of Applied Psychology*, 82, 434–443.

Skinner, M., & Mullen, B. (1991). Facial asymmetry in emotional expression: A meta-analysis of research. *British Journal of Social Psychology*, 30, 113–124.

Small, D. A., & Verrochi, N. M. (2009). The face of need: Facial emotion expression on charity advertisements. *Journal of Marketing Research*, 46, 777–787.

Smith, C. A., Haynes, K. N., Lazarus, R. S., & Pope, L. K. (1993). In search of the "hot" cognitions: Attributions, appraisals, and their relation to emotion. *Journal of Personality and Social Psychology*, 65, 916–929.

Smith, C. A., Organ, D. W., & Near, J. P. (1983). Organizational citizenship behavior: Its nature and antecedents. *Journal of Applied Psychology*, 68, 653–663.

Smith, C. A., & Scott, H. S. (1997). A componential approach to the meaning of facial expressions. In: J. A. Russell & J. M. Fernández-Dols (red.). *The Psychology of Facial Expression* (pp. 229–254). New York: Cambridge University Press.

Smith, E. R., & DeCoster, J. (2000). Dual-process models in social and cognitive psychology: Conceptual integration and links to underlying memory systems. *Personality and Social Psychology Review*, 4, 108–131.

Smith, E. R., Seger, C. R., & Mackie, D. M. (2007). Can emotions be truly group level? Evidence regarding four conceptual criteria. *Journal of Personality and Social Psychology*, 93, 431–446.

Smith, M. C., Smith, M. K., & Ellgring, H. (1996). Spontaneous and posed facial expression in Parkinson's disease. *Journal of the International Neuropsychological Society*, 2, 383–391.

Soloff, P. H., & Ulrich, R. F. (1981). Diagnostic interview for borderline patients: A replication study. *Archives of General Psychiatry*, 38, 686–692.

Sommers, S. (1984). Reported emotions and conventions of emotionality among college students. *Journal of Personality and Social Psychology*, 46, 207–215.

Sorce, J. F., Emde, R. N., Campos, J., & Klinnert, M. D. (1985). Maternal emotional signaling: Its effect on the visual cliff behavior of 1 year olds. *Developmental Psychology*, 21, 195–200.

Spoor, J. R., & Kelly, J. R. (2004). The evolutionary significance of affect in groups: Communication and group bonding. *Group Processes & Intergroup Relations*, 7, 398–412.

Srivastava, S., Tamir, M., McGonigal, K. M., John, O. P., & Gross, J. J. (2009). The social costs of emotional suppression: A prospective study of the transition to college. *Journal of Personality and Social Psychology*, 96, 883–897.

Stasser, G., & Titus, W. (1985). Pooling of unshared information in group decision making: Biased information sampling during discussion. *Journal of Personality and Social Psychology*, 48, 1467–1478.

Staw, B. M., Sutton, R. I., & Pelled, L. H. (1994). Employee positive emotion and favorable outcomes at the workplace. *Organization Science*, 5, 51–71.

Steinel, W., Van Kleef, G. A., & Harinck, F. (2008). Are you talking to me?! Separating the people from the problem when expressing emotions in negotiation. *Journal of Experimental Social Psychology*, 44, 362–369.

Steiner, C. (2000). Apology: The transactional analysis of a fundamental exchange. *Transactional Analysis Journal*, 30, 145–149.

Steiner, I. D. (1974). Whatever happened to the group in social psychology? *Journal of Experimental Social Psychology*, 10, 94–108.

Stern, L. D., Marrs, S., Millar, M. G., & Cole, E. (1984). Processing time and the recall of inconsistent and consistent behaviors of individuals and groups. *Journal of Personality and Social Psychology*, 47, 253–262.

Stouten, J., & De Cremer, D. (2010). "Seeing is believing": The effects of facial expressions of emotion and verbal communication in social dilemmas. *Journal of Behavioral Decision Making*, 23, 271–287.

Suls, J., Martin, R., & David, J. P. (1998). Person-environment fit and its limits: Agreeableness, neuroticism, and emotional reactivity to interpersonal conflict. *Personality and Social Psychology Bulletin*, 24, 88–98.

Sutton, R. I. (1991). Maintaining norms about expressed emotions: The case of bill collectors. *Administrative Science Quarterly*, 36, 245–268.

Sy, T., Côté, S., & Saavedra, R. (2005). The contagious leader: Impact of the leader's mood on the mood of group members, group affective tone, and group processes. *Journal of Applied Psychology*, 90, 295–305.

Tamir, M. (2009). What do people want to feel and why? Pleasure and utility in emotion regulation. *Current Directions in Psychological Science*, 18, 101–105.

Tamir, M., Mitchell, C., & Gross, J. J. (2008). Hedonic and instrumental motives in anger regulation. *Psychological Science*, 19, 324–328.

Tanghe, J., Wisse, B., & Van der Flier, H. (2010). The formation of group affect and team effectiveness: The moderating role of identification. *British Journal of Management*, 21, 340–358.

Tangney, J. P., Miller, R. S., Flicker, L., & Barlow, D. H. (1996). Are shame, guilt, and embarrassment distinct emotions? *Journal of Personality and Social Psychology*, 70, 1256–1264.

Tavris, C. (1984). On the wisdom of counting to ten: Personal and social dangers of anger expression. *Review of Personality & Social Psychology*, 5, 170–191.

Tavuchis, N. (1991). *Mea culpa: A sociology of apology and reconciliation*. Stanford, CA: Stanford University Press.

Tee, E, Y. J., Ashkanasy, N. M., & Paulsen, N. (2013). The influence of follower mood on leader mood and task performance: An affective, follower-centric perspective of leadership. *The Leadership Quarterly*, 24, 496–515.

Tetlock, P. E. (1992). The impact of accountability on judgment and choice: Toward a social contingency model. *Advances in Experimental Social Psychology*, 25, 331–376.

Thompson, L. (2001). *The mind and heart of the negotiator* (2nd ed., pp. 18–19). Upper Saddle River, NJ: Prentice Hall.

Thompson, L., Medvec, V. H., Seiden, V., & Kopelman, S. (2001). Poker face, smiley face, and rant 'n' rave: Myths and realities about emotion in negotiation. In M. A. Hogg & R. S. Tindale (Eds.), *Blackwell handbook of social psychology: Group processes* (pp. 139–163). Malden, MA: Blackwell.

Thompson, L., Valley, K. L., & Kramer, R. M. (1995). The bittersweet feeling of success: An examination of social perception in negotiation. *Journal of Experimental Social Psychology*, 31, 467–492.

Thompson, R. F., & Spencer, W. A. (1966). Habituation: A model phenomenon for the study of neuronal substrates of behavior. *Psychological Review*, 73, 16–43.

Tidd, K. L., & Lockard, J. S. (1978). Monetary significance of the affiliative smile: A case for reciprocal altruism. *Bulletin of the Psychonomic Society*, 11, 344–346.

Tiedens, L. Z. (2001). Anger and advancement versus sadness and subjugation: The effect of negative emotion expressions on social status conferral. *Journal of Personality and Social Psychology*, 80, 86–94.

Tiedens, L. Z., Ellsworth, P. C., & Mesquita, B. (2000). Sentimental stereotypes: Emotional expectations for high- and low-status group members. *Personality and Social Psychology Bulletin*, 26, 560–575.

Tiedens, L. Z., & Fragale, A. R. (2003). Power moves: Complementarity in dominant and submissive nonverbal behavior. *Journal of Personality and Social Psychology*, 84, 558–568.

Tiedens, L. Z., & Leach, C. W. (Eds.). (2004). *The social life of emotions*. Cambridge University Press.

Tiedens, L. Z., & Linton, S. (2001). Judgment under emotional certainty and uncertainty: The effects of specific emotions on information processing. *Journal of Personality and Social Psychology*, 81, 973–988.

Tiedens, L. Z., Sutton, R. I., & Fong, C. T. (2004). Emotional variation in workgroups: Causes and performance consequences. In L. Z. Tiedens & C. W. Leach (Eds.), *The social life of emotions* (pp. 164–186). New York: Cambridge University Press.

Timmers, M., Fischer, A. H., & Manstead, A. S. R. (1998). Gender differences in motives for regulating emotions. *Personality and Social Psychology Bulletin*, 24, 974–985.

Tomkins, S. (1962). *Affect, imagery, and consciousness: The positive affects. Vol. 1.* New York: Springer.

Tomkins, S. (1963). *Affect, imagery, and consciousness: The negative affects. Vol. 2.* New York: Springer.

Tooby, J., & Cosmides, L. (1990). The past explains the present: Emotional adaptations and the structure of ancestral environments. *Ethology and Sociobiology*, 11, 375–424.

Totterdell, P. (2000). Catching moods and hitting runs: Mood linkage and subjective performance in professional sport teams. *Journal of Applied Psychology*, 85, 848–859.

Totterdell, P., Kellett, S., Teuchmann, K., & Briner, B. (1998). Evidence of mood linkage in work groups. *Journal of Personality and Social Psychology*, 74, 1504–1515.

Triandis, H. C. (1989). The self and social behavior in differing cultural contexts. *Psychological Review*, 96, 506–520.

Trivers, R. L. (1971). The evolution of reciprocal altruism. *Quarterly Review of Biology*, 46, 35–57.

Tronick, E. Z. (1989). Emotions and emotional communication in infants. *American Psychologist*, 44, 112–119.

Tsai, W. C. (2001). Determinants and consequences of employee displayed positive emotions. *Journal of Management*, 27, 497–512.

Tsai, W., & Huang, Y. (2002). Mechanisms linking employee affective delivery and customer behavioral intentions. *Journal of Applied Psychology*, 87, 1001–1008.

Tsai, W.-C., Chi, N.-W., Grandey, A. A., & Fung, S.-C. (2012). Positive group affective tone and team creativity: Negative group affective tone and team trust as boundary conditions. *Journal of Organizational Behavior*, 33, 638–656.

Tsui, A. S., & Barry, B. (1986). Interpersonal affect and rating errors. *Academy of Management Journal*, 29, 586–599.

Tuncel, E., & Doucet, L. (2005). *Mixed feelings: Impact of mood diversity on confirmation bias and decision accuracy in groups.* Unpublished manuscript.

Tversky, A., & Kahneman, D. (1974). Judgment under uncertainty: Heuristics and biases. *Science*, 185, 1124–1131.

Uchida, Y., & Kitayama, S. (2009). Happiness and unhappiness in east and west: Themes and variations. *Emotion*, 9, 441–456.

Uljarevic, M., & Hamilton, A. (2013). Recognition of emotions in autism: A formal meta-analysis. *Journal of Autism and Developmental Disorders*, 43, 1517–1526.

Van Beest, I., Van Kleef, G. A., & Van Dijk, E. (2008). Get angry, get out: The interpersonal effects of anger communication in multiparty negotiation. *Journal of Experimental Social Psychology*, 44, 993–1002.

Van der Schalk, J., Fischer, A., Doosje, B., Wigboldus, D., Hawk, S., Rotteveel, M., & Hess, U. (2011). Convergent and divergent responses to emotional displays of ingroup and outgroup. *Emotion*, 11, 286–298.

Van der Schalk, J., Kuppens, T., Bruder, M., & Manstead, A. S. R. (2014). The social power of regret: The effect of social appraisal and anticipated emotions on fair and unfair allocations in resource dilemmas. *Journal of Experimental Psychology: General*, 144, 151–157.

Van Dijk, E., Van Kleef, G. A., Steinel, W., & Van Beest (2008). A social functional approach to emotions in bargaining: When communicating anger pays and when it backfires. *Journal of Personality and Social Psychology*, 94, 600–614.

Van Doorn, E. A., Heerdink, M. W., & Van Kleef, G. A. (2012). Emotion and the construal of social situations: Inferences of cooperation versus competition from expressions of anger, happiness, and disappointment. *Cognition & Emotion*, 12, 442–461.

Van Doorn, E. A., Van Kleef, G. A., & Van der Pligt, J. (2014). How instructors' emotional expressions shape students' learning performance: The roles of anger, happiness, and regulatory focus. *Journal of Experimental Psychology: General*, 143, 980–984.

Van Doorn, E. A., Van Kleef, G. A., & Van der Pligt, J. (2015a). Deriving meaning from others' emotions: Attribution, appraisal, and the use of emotions as social information. *Frontiers in Psychology*, 6, 1077.

Van Doorn, E. A., Van Kleef, G. A., & Van der Pligt, J. (2015b). How emotional expressions shape prosocial behavior: Interpersonal effects of anger and disappointment on compliance with requests. *Motivation and Emotion, 39,* 128–141.

van Hooff, J. A. R. A. M. (1972). A comparative approach to the phylogeny of laughter and smiling. In R. A. Hinde (Ed.), *Non-verbal communication* (pp. 209–240). Cambridge: Cambridge University Press.

Van Kleef, G. A. (2009). How emotions regulate social life: The emotions as social information (EASI) model. *Current Directions in Psychological Science, 18,* 184–188.

Van Kleef, G. A. (2010). The emerging view of emotion as social information. *Social and Personality Psychology Compass, 4/5,* 331–343.

Van Kleef, G. A., Anastasopoulou, C., & Nijstad, B. A. (2010). Can expressions of anger enhance creativity? A test of the emotions as social information (EASI) model. *Journal of Experimental Social Psychology, 46,* 1042–1048.

Van Kleef, G. A., & Côté, S. (2007). Expressing anger in conflict: When it helps and when it hurts. *Journal of Applied Psychology, 92,* 1557–1569.

Van Kleef, G. A., & De Dreu, C. K. W. (2002). Social value orientation and impression formation: A test of two competing hypotheses about information search in negotiation. *International Journal of Conflict Management, 13,* 59–77.

Van Kleef, G. A., & De Dreu, C. K. W. (2010). Longer-term consequences of anger expression in negotiation: Retaliation or spill-over? *Journal of Experimental Social Psychology, 46,* 753–760.

Van Kleef, G. A., De Dreu, C. K. W., & Manstead, A. S. R. (2004a). The interpersonal effects of anger and happiness in negotiations. *Journal of Personality and Social Psychology, 86,* 57–76.

Van Kleef, G. A., De Dreu, C. K. W., & Manstead, A. S. R. (2004b). The interpersonal effects of emotions in negotiations: A motivated information processing approach. *Journal of Personality and Social Psychology, 87,* 510–528.

Van Kleef, G. A., De Dreu, C. K. W., & Manstead, A. S. R. (2006). Supplication and appeasement in conflict and negotiation: The interpersonal effects of disappointment, worry, guilt, and regret. *Journal of Personality and Social Psychology, 91,* 124–142.

Van Kleef, G. A., De Dreu, C. K. W., & Manstead, A. S. R. (2010). An interpersonal approach to emotion in social decision making: The emotions as social information model. *Advances in Experimental Social Psychology, 42,* 45–96.

Van Kleef, G. A., De Dreu, C. K. W., Pietroni, D., & Manstead, A. S. R. (2006). Power and emotion in negotiations: Power moderates the interpersonal effects of anger and happiness on concession making. *European Journal of Social Psychology, 36,* 557–581.

Van Kleef, G. A., & Fischer, A. H. (2016). Emotional collectives: How groups shape emotions and emotions shape groups. *Cognition & Emotion, 30,* 3–19.

Van Kleef, G. A., Homan, A. C., Beersma, B., & Van Knippenberg, D. (2010). On angry leaders and agreeable followers: How leaders' emotions and followers' personalities shape motivation and team performance. *Psychological Science*, 21, 1827–1834.

Van Kleef, G. A., Homan, A. C., Beersma, B., Van Knippenberg, D., Van Knippenberg, B., & Damen, F. (2009). Searing sentiment or cold calculation? The effects of leader emotional displays on team performance depend on follower epistemic motivation. *Academy of Management Journal*, 52, 562–580.

Van Kleef, G. A., Homan, A. C., & Cheshin, A. (2012). Emotional influence at work: Take it EASI. *Organizational Psychology Review*, 2, 311–339.

Van Kleef, G. A., Oveis, C., Van der Löwe, I., LuoKogan, A., Goetz, J., & Keltner, D. (2008). Power, distress, and compassion: Turning a blind eye to the suffering of others. *Psychological Science*, 19, 1315–1322.

Van Kleef, G. A., & Sinaceur, M. (2013). The demise of the "rational" negotiator: Emotional forces in conflict and negotiation. In M. Olekalns & W. L. Adair (Eds.), *Handbook of research on negotiation* (pp. 103–130). Cheltenham: Edward Elgar.

Van Kleef, G. A., Stamkou, E., & Larsen, M. (2014, May). *Music teachers' emotional expressions and pupils' musical performance: A test of emotions as social information (EASI) theory*. Paper presented at the annual conference of the Society for Industrial and Organizational Psychology, Honolulu, HI.

Van Kleef, G. A., Steinel, W., & Homan, A. C. (2013). On being peripheral and paying attention: Social information processing in intergroup conflict. *Journal of Applied Psychology*, 98, 63–79.

Van Kleef, G. A., Van den Berg, H., & Heerdink, M. W. (2015). The persuasive power of emotions: Effects of emotional expressions on attitude formation and change. *Journal of Applied Psychology*, 100, 1124–1142.

Van Kleef, G. A., Van Doorn, E. A., Heerdink, M. W., & Koning, L. F. (2011). Emotion is for influence. *European Review of Social Psychology*, 22, 114–163.

Van Kleef, G. A., & Van Lange, P. A. M. (2008). What other's disappointment may do to selfish people: Emotion and social value orientation in a negotiation context. *Personality and Social Psychology Bulletin*, 34, 1084–1095.

Van Knippenberg, D., De Dreu, C. K. W., & Homan, A. C. (2004). Work group diversity and group performance: An integrative model and research agenda. *Journal of Applied Psychology*, 89, 1008–1022.

Van Knippenberg, D., & Hogg, M. A. (2003). A social identity model of leadership effectiveness in organizations. *Research in Organizational Behavior*, 25, 243–295.

Van Knippenberg, D., Kooij-de Bode, H. J. M., & Van Ginkel, W. P. (2010). The interactive effects of mood and trait negative affect in group decision making. *Organization Science*, 21, 731–744.

Van Rooy, D. L., Alonso, A., & Viswesvaran, C. (2005). Group differences in emotional intelligence scores: Theoretical and practical implications. *Personality and Individual Differences*, 38, 689–700.

Van Zomeren, M., Spears, R., Fischer, A. H., & Leach, C. W. (2004). Put your money where your mouth is! Explaining collective action tendencies through group-based anger and group efficacy. *Journal of Personality and Social Psychology*, 87, 649–664.

Vernon, P. A. (1983). Speed of information processing and general intelligence. *Intelligence, 7,* 53–70.

Vingerhoets, A. J. J. M., Cornelius, R. R., Van Heck, G. L., & Becht, M. C. (2000). Adult crying: A model and review of the literature. *Review of General Psychology, 4,* 354–377.

Visser, V. A., Van Knippenberg, D., Van Kleef, G. A., & Wisse, B. (2013). How leader displays of happiness and sadness influence follower performance: Emotional contagion and creative versus analytical performance. *The Leadership Quarterly, 24,* 172–188.

Volkmar, F., Chawarska, K., & Klin, A. (2005). Autism in infancy and early childhood. *Annual Review of Psychology, 56,* 315–336.

Vuilleumier, P. (2005). How brains beware: Neural mechanisms of emotional attention. *Trends in Cognitive Sciences, 9,* 585–594.

Wade-Benzoni, K. A., Hoffman, A. J., Thompson, L. L., Moore, D. A., Gillespie, J. J., & Bazerman, M. H. (2002). Barriers to resolution in ideologically based negotiations: The role of values and institutions. *Academy of Management Review, 27,* 41–57.

Wallbott, H. G. (1998). Bodily expression of emotion. *European Journal of Social Psychology, 28,* 879–896.

Waller, B. M., Cray Jr, J. J., & Burrows, A. M. (2008). Selection for universal facial emotion. *Emotion, 8,* 435–439.

Walter, F., & Bruch, H. (2008). The positive group affect spiral: A dynamic model of the emergence of positive affective similarity in work groups. *Journal of Organizational Behavior, 29,* 239–261.

Walter, F., Cole, M. S., & Humphrey, R. H. (2011). Emotional intelligence: Sine qua non of leadership or folderol? *Academy of Management Perspectives, 25,* 45–59.

Walter, F., Cole, M. S., Van der Vegt, G. S., Rubin, R. S., & Bommer, W. H. (2012). Emotion recognition and emergent leadership: Unraveling mediating mechanisms and boundary conditions. *The Leadership Quarterly, 23,* 977–991.

Wang, L., Northcraft, G., & Van Kleef, G. A. (2012). Beyond negotiated outcomes: The hidden costs of anger expression in dyadic negotiation. *Organizational Behavior and Human Decision Processes, 119,* 54–63.

Wang, M., Liao, H., Zhan, Y., & Shi, J. (2011). Daily customer mistreatment and employee sabotage against customers: Examining emotion and resource perspectives. *Academy of Management Journal, 54,* 312–334.

Waples, E. P., & Connelly, S. (2008). Leader emotions and vision implementation: Effects of activation potential and valence. In R. H. Humphrey (Ed.), *Affect and emotions: New directions in management theory and research* (pp. 67–96). Charlotte, NC: Information Age Publishing.

Watson, D. (1988). Intraindividual and interindividual analyses of positive and negative affect: Their relation to health complaints, perceived stress, and daily activities. *Journal of Personality and Social Psychology, 54,* 1020–1030.

Watson, D., Clark, L. A., & Carey, G. (1988). Positive and negative affectivity and their relation to anxiety and depressive disorders. *Journal of Abnormal Psychology, 97,* 346–353.

Watson, D., Clark, L. A., & Tellegen, A. (1988). Development and validation of brief measures of positive and negative affect: The PANAS scales. *Journal of Personality and Social Psychology, 54*, 1063–1070.

Waxer, P. H. (1974). Nonverbal cues for depression. *Journal of Abnormal Psychology, 83*, 319–322.

Weber, J. M., Kopelman, S., & Messick, D. M. (2004). A conceptual review of decision making in social dilemmas: Applying a logic of appropriateness. *Personality and Social Psychology Review, 8*, 281–307.

Webster, D. M., & Kruglanski, A. W. (1994). Individual differences in need for cognitive closure. *Journal of Personality and Social Psychology, 67*, 1049–1062.

Webster, D. M., Richter, L., & Kruglanski, A. W. (1996). On leaping to conclusions when feeling tired: Mental fatigue effects on impressional primacy. *Journal of Experimental Social Psychology, 32*, 181–195.

Wegener, D. T., & Petty, R. E. (1994). Mood management across affective states: The hedonic contingency hypothesis. *Journal of Personality and Social Psychology, 66*, 1034–1048.

Weiner, B. (1986). *An attributional theory of motivation and emotion.* New York: Springer.

Weisbuch, M., & Adams, R. B., Jr. (2012). The functional forecast model of emotion expression processing. *Social and Personality Psychology Compass, 6/7*, 499–514.

Weisbuch, M., & Ambady, N. (2008). Affective divergence: Automatic responses to others' emotions depend on group membership. *Journal of Personality and Social Psychology, 95*, 1063–1079.

Weiss, H. M., & Cropanzano, R. (1996). Affective events theory: A theoretical discussion of the structure, causes, and consequences of affective experiences at work. *Research in Organizational Behavior, 18*, 1–74.

Weng, H. C. (2008). Does the physician's emotional intelligence matter? Impacts of the physician's emotional intelligence on the trust, patient-physician relationship, and satisfaction. *Health Care Management Review, 33*, 280–288.

Wierzbicka, A. (1994). Emotion, language, and cultural scripts. In S. Kitayama & H. R. Markus (Eds.), *Emotion and culture: Empirical studies of mutual influence.* Washington, DC: American Psychological Association.

Wild, B., Erb, M., & Bartels, M. (2001). Are emotions contagious? Evoked emotions while viewing emotionally expressive faces: Quality, quantity, time course, and gender differences. *Psychiatry Research, 102*, 109–124.

Williams, K. D. (2007). Ostracism. *Annual Review of Psychology, 58*, 425–452.

Williams, M. (2007). Building genuine trust through interpersonal emotion management: A threat regulation model of trust and collaboration across boundaries. *Academy of Management Review, 32*, 595–621.

Winkielman, P., Zajonc, R. B., & Schwarz, N. (1997). Subliminal affective priming resists attributional interventions. *Cognition & Emotion, 11*, 433–465.

Wolff, S. B., Pescosolido, A. T., & Druskat, V. U. (2002). Emotional intelligence as the basis of leadership emergence in self-managing teams. *The Leadership Quarterly, 13*, 505–522.

Wrede, O., Ask, K., & Strömwall, L. A. (2015). Sad and exposed, angry and resilient? Effects of crime victims' emotional expressions on perceived need for support. *Social Psychology*, 46, 55–64.

Wubben, M. J., De Cremer, D., & Van Dijk, E. (2009a). How emotion communication guides reciprocity: Establishing cooperation through disappointment and anger. *Journal of Experimental Social Psychology*, 45, 987–990.

Wubben, M. J., De Cremer, D., & Van Dijk, E. (2009b). When and how communicated guilt affects contributions in public good dilemmas. *Journal of Experimental Social Psychology*, 45, 15–23.

Yee, J. L., & Greenberg, M. S. (1998). Reactions to crime victims: Effects of victims' emotional state and type of relationship. *Journal of Social and Clinical Psychology*, 17, 209–226.

Yoo, S. H., Clark, M. S., Lemay, E. P., Salovey, P., & Monin, J. K. (2011). Responding to partners' expression of anger: The role of communal motivation. *Personality and Social Psychology Bulletin*, 37(2), 229–241.

Yukl, G. A. (2010). *Leadership in organizations* (7th ed). Upper Saddle River, NJ: Pearson.

Zajonc, R. B. (1980). Feeling and thinking: Preferences need no inferences. *American Psychologist*, 35, 151–175.

Zapf, D., & Holz, M. (2006). On the positive and negative effects of emotion work in organizations. *European Journal of Work and Organizational Psychology*, 15, 1–28.

Zeelenberg, M. (1999). Anticipated regret, expected feedback and behavioral decision making. *Journal of Behavioral Decision Making*, 12, 93–106.

Zeelenberg, M., van der Pligt, J., & Manstead, A. S. R. (1998). Undoing regret on Dutch television: Apologizing for interpersonal regrets involving actions and inactions. *Personality and Social Psychology Bulletin*, 24, 1113–1119.

Zeman, J., & Shipman, K. (1996). Children's expression of negative affect: Reasons and methods. *Developmental Psychology*, 32, 842–849.

Author Index

Subject Index

absenteeism by service providers,
    customer aggression linked to,
    155–158
acceptance, motivation in groups for,
    117–118
action readiness, emotions and, 4
affect
    cognition and, 225–228
    defined, 4
    Emotions as Social Information (EASI)
        theory and, 7
    infusion of, 206–208
affect-as-information model, 43–45,
    206–208, 233–234
"affect infusion," 43–45
affective convergence
    group emotions and, 104–108
    of groups, 116–117
    in negotiations, 125–127
    team performance and, 116–117
affective delivery
    authenticity of emotional displays by
        service providers and, 150–153
    inauthentic emotional expression and,
        69–71
    by service providers, impact on custo-
        mers of, 149–150
affective divergence and diversity, group
    behavior and, 109–112
affective diversity, group behavior and,
    109–112
affective events theory (AET), 211–212
affective reactions
    appropriateness of leaders' emotional
        displays and, 184–190
    behavioral consequences of, 125
    complementary reactions, 42–43
    customers' displays of, 155–158,
        168–169
    downstream consequences of, 43–45

emotional expressions as trigger for,
    38–45
in Emotions as Social Information (EASI)
    theory, 198–201
of followers, leaders' expressions of
    anger and, 180
group functioning and, 104
immediacy of, 61–62
impacting factors in, 60–61
inferential processes and, 52–55
ingroup vs. outgroup members, 109–112
leadership quality and, 172–177
measurement and separability of, 225–228
mediating role of, 203–204
moderating role information processing
    and perceived appropriateness,
    204–206
during negotiation, 125–127, 134–135,
    138–142
perceived appropriateness and, 64–67
reciprocal reactions, anger and happi-
    ness and, 125–127
service providers' behavior and,
    159–160, 168–169
smiling by service providers, impact on
    customers of, 149–150
social effects of, 98–100
affect misattribution paradigm, 225–228
    group emotions, inferences from fellow
        members' emotional displays and,
        113–115
affect-priming models, 43–45
afferent feedback, primitive emotional
    contagion and, 38–42
affiliation emotions
    happiness and social bonding, 87–90
    social effects of, 27–30, 98–100
aggression
    crying as buffer against, 92–93
    by customers, 155–158

295

Studies in Emotion and Social Interaction

CPSIA information can be obtained
at www.ICGtesting.com
Printed in the USA
FSHW021906130921
84736FS